TRANS CHILDREN IN TODAY'S SCHOOLS

ADVANCE PRAISE FOR *TRANS CHILDREN IN TODAY'S SCHOOLS*

"Aidan Key has written about the trans experience with profound compassion, not only for trans kids, but also for the families and schools that struggle to accept and support them. Detractors have often accused the movement for trans rights of being somehow immoral, but this book is written with such generosity of spirit and such irrefutable logic that it would be hard to take against it even if you were uncomfortable with or outraged about trans kids. And if you were already sympathetic to their experiences, this book would show you how to turn that sympathy into authentic support. Key's invaluable words should calm down the hysteria around a phenomenon that he reveals as a beautiful, rich component of human diversity."

—Andrew Solomon, Professor of Clinical Psychology, Columbia University and author, *Far from the Tree*

"*Trans Children in Today's Schools* is an urgently necessary guidebook to the ins and outs of teaching, parenting, understanding, and supporting trans kids, as well as their classmates, families, communities, and schools. Thankfully, in contrast to that urgency, Aidan Key writes with his trademark balance of knowledge, experience, confidence, and calm. This book serves as an introduction and a guide but mostly as an even keel. Via lived and witnessed experience, hundreds of stories from a wide range of families, professional expertise, well-documented research, and the unwavering assurance that trans children—and by extension all children—can thrive, *Trans Children in Today's Schools* is practical and informative on its way to reassuring, inspiring, and empowering."

—Laurie Frankel, New York Times bestselling author of *This Is How It Always Is*

"In *Trans Children in Today's Schools*, Aidan Key brilliantly does what many think is impossible—he breaks down the ever-changing and politically charged world of gender and children in a manner that is simultaneously accessible and profound. In easy-to-understand prose, this book explains how to forge through difficult conversations regarding gender diversity to ensure that all children, not just trans kids, feel at home in our classrooms. Whether you are a parent, teacher, principal, or none of the above, Aidan Key provides the answers to those questions you've always wondered about, but never knew whom to ask."

—**Dr. Kristina Olson, Professor of Psychology,**
Princeton University

"This book is a priceless and long overdue resource for any educator looking to better understand the experience of transgender and gender diverse youth in schools. Key's clarity, depth of knowledge, and attuned insight make this text comprehensive in scope and accessible in practice—a must read for all!"

—**Benjamin Davis, ATR-BC, LCAT, Director, Full Spectrum Creative Arts**
Therapy, co-author of *Gender: What Everyone Needs to Know*

"Every student needs a safe, affirming learning space to fully experience the transformational power of education. Achieving this space requires us to recognize the needs of trans students and commit to their inclusion. As we consider our educational future, we can greatly benefit from Aidan Key's compassionate approach and resolute commitment to trans and nonbinary student inclusion. His words show us how to achieve this future—a future where each and every student feels seen, heard, and affirmed. This is needed now more than ever. *Trans Children in Today's Schools* is a must-read for those committed to the catalyzing change needed to achieve authentically inclusive learning spaces."

—**Dr. Michelle C Reid, AASA National Superintendent of the Year 2021**

TRANS CHILDREN
IN TODAY'S SCHOOLS

Aidan Key

OXFORD
UNIVERSITY PRESS

OXFORD
UNIVERSITY PRESS

Oxford University Press is a department of the University of Oxford. It furthers
the University's objective of excellence in research, scholarship, and education
by publishing worldwide. Oxford is a registered trade mark of Oxford University
Press in the UK and certain other countries.

Published in the United States of America by Oxford University Press
198 Madison Avenue, New York, NY 10016, United States of America.

CIP data is on file at the Library of Congress

ISBN 978–0–19–088654–7

DOI: 10.1093/oso/9780190886547.001.0001

Printed by Marquis Book Printing, Canada

This book is dedicated to Kristin, showing up in my universe
with all her brilliance at just the right time.

CONTENTS

CONTENTS

FOREWORD BY AARON DEVOR

Many American schools in the twenty-first century have become embattled over the changing meaning of gender. Both parents and educators have become anxious about what young people should be taught concerning the relationship between physical bodies and the everyday enactment of gender. Even as we see unprecedented numbers of youth stepping away from the expectations of their parents' generations that their genitals should define them, we see our schools continue to be almost entirely organized on binary sex/gender assumptions. Nonetheless, trans, nonbinary, and other gender-diverse (Trans+) children are in schools everywhere, and they deserve to be respected for who they are.

In schools today, who has the right to be a boy, a girl, neither, or both has become a matter of much debate, and no small amount of acrimony. Aidan Key, in *Trans Children in Today's Schools*, brings years of experience and a calm common sense to this morass. He understands what it is that Trans+ kids need to thrive. He understands the fears, hopes, and dreams of parents of these children, and of parents of all the other young people who go to school with Trans+ youth. He knows well that all parents want what is best for their children, and that when it comes to Trans+ children, few parents understand what that is, or how to get there from here. He also knows that our educational professionals have dedicated themselves to ensuring that all the children in their care have the best possible experiences in their schools. At the same time, it is clear that Key has important insights into the challenges that educators face in trying to navigate the conflicting demands of legislation, school board policies, parent expectations, and the needs of the full range of the young people who populate schools today.

Having spent years working with parents, kids, families, and school professionals from all across the United States, Key understands. He has seen and heard about the pain and the triumphs. He empathizes with Trans+ kids, and those who care for them, as he walks readers through the complexities of the issues that keep people awake at night. He is a skilled guide who cuts through the hype and hysteria with clarity and compassion. He doesn't simplify tough questions, nor does he discount the very real concerns of all concerned. He makes it all very real by amply illustrating the knotty challenges using the words of real people as they have talked with him about their anguish and growth in confronting their conflicting thoughts and feelings. What he does is to carefully, and in plain language, provide the information that people need to move beyond unfounded fears and us-versus-them thinking. He helps people to step into approaches that are respectful and safe for children of all genders. He offers practical strategies and techniques to understand and deal with common questions.

Key is, above all, sensible, compassionate, and kind throughout. He never condescends. He never patronizes. Nor does he slide into dogmatism. He looks squarely at the realities of the many stress points between schools that have been built on a strict sex-at-birth–based system and Trans+ children who require something different to thrive. He gently and respectfully acknowledges that change is not easy, and points to different ways that have the potential to be respectful and nurturing to all.

Trans Children in Today's Schools is a book that should be in the hands of every parent and every educator. Don't wait until your own child says that they are Trans+. Most never will—but they will have Trans+ friends and schoolmates; they will have Trans+ family members; they will have Trans+ teachers. Don't wait until you have a gender-diverse student in your school. You need to know this information now. You need to be ready to do the right thing when a vulnerable child looks to you for leadership, guidance, and protection. You will find good, solid, sensible, easy-to-grasp information and advice in this book, and you can come back to it over and over again.

If we all followed Aidan Key's approach, our schools would be better places for all of our kids, not just the Trans+ kids because, in the final analysis, all kids need the room to explore gender free from the straitjacket of rigid stereotypes. Ultimately, giving Trans+ kids room to grow and thrive creates room for all kids to confidently and safely find, and become, their true selves. Isn't that what every parent and educator wants for the youth in their care?

Aaron Devor, PhD, FSSSS, FSTLHE, https://onlineacademiccommunity.uvic.ca/ahdevor/

Founder and Inaugural Chair in Transgender Studies, https://www.uvic.ca/research/transchair/

Founder and Subject Matter Expert, The Transgender Archives, https://www.uvic.ca/transgenderarchives/

Founder and Host, Moving Trans History Forward conferences, https://www.uvic.ca/mthf2023/

Professor, Sociology Department

University of Victoria, BC, Canada

ACKNOWLEDGMENTS

Over the five plus years it took to complete this book, it has been difficult to describe to others how challenging it was to put these conversations and experiences—and the lives of the humans associated with them—onto the page. I mentioned to one person that extracting the content of this book from my head felt, at times, like stripping the insides of every cell within my body. I sometimes questioned whether the writing was a wise, survivable choice. People assured me that it was, and they were right—the wisdom of it is something that will be revealed in time. We often see the "this book would not be possible without" exaltations of authors, and now I know why!

My wife, Kristin Wilson-Key, bore the lion's share of ensuring that this book was clear and straightforward. As the person who read the earliest of drafts, she often said, "I know what you are trying to say, Aidan, but you are not quite doing it." My sister, Brenda Bowers, put on her English tutor hat and supported many of the structural edits. Kristin and Brenda shouldered the emotional support—the most crucial job, from my perspective. Jennie Goode was exceedingly instrumental in getting this book off the ground early on. My only regret is that life demands prevented her from crossing the finish line with me. Speaking of finish lines, Jennifer Nace became the superhero in the eleventh hour. Who in the world geeks out on citations, appendices, line edits, and abstracts? Jennifer does that and so much more. Much gratitude to Scott Peacock—school district superintendent extraordinaire—who advised on every chapter.

I have benefited from the generosity and mentoring of Caitlin Ryan and her remarkable work at the Family Acceptance Project and author Cory Silverberg's vision of the future. My gratitude goes out to both Dana Bliss and Stefano Imbert at Oxford University Press. Dana, I know you went to bat for me over and over again. I like to think you won't regret it. Stefano, thank you for crawling inside my head to extract your beautifully crafted illustrations peppered throughout this book. Thank you to the board, staff, and volunteers at TransFamilies.org who especially encouraged me in the final stretch. Not enough gratitude can ever be expressed to the families of gender-diverse youth who are now part of my family—this book wouldn't exist without you. Additional thanks must go to Kristina Olson, Aaron Devor, Laurie Frankel, Andrew Solomon, Asaf Orr, Kory Martin-Damon, Bryan Dunncan, Eve Carr, Shari Dworkin, Vlada Knowlton, Arthur Padilla, Eli Green, Sharon Reed, Jimmy Jo Allen, Marlo Mack, Jen Hastings, Kevin Hatfield, Laura Erickson-Schroth, Eleanor Jones, Shannon Panszi, the indomitable Kate Bornstein, and the external reviewers that took precious time to offer input, support, and encouragement. Already offering my *mea culpa* to those I've overlooked on the page but not in my heart.

Introduction

*True belonging doesn't require you to change who you are; it requires you to be
who you are.*

Brené Brown

BECOMING A GENDER EDUCATOR

In the early 2000s, I began work in the field of gender diversity education, with
a focus on the health care and employment industries, as others sought to better
serve their gender-diverse constituents. I also founded and directed an international gender conference that provides educational workshops and a place for
much-needed peer discussions. Originally, the Gender Odyssey conference
served trans adults and helped strengthen a community where very little had

previously existed. It gradually grew to include and address the needs of families with gender-diverse children.

The needs of these families were significant and urgent. Not only did they need guidance on how best to support their children at home but questions about their child's inclusion at school often found their way to the top of their list. I was deeply moved as I witnessed the way they tentatively but courageously stepped into their fears. The love they had for their child propelled them when they could find little else to grasp. To me, their children were the living, breathing embodiment of a future I had not previously been able to imagine—a future with support, love, and inclusion beginning at the youngest of ages. I turned my full attention—and organization—to them.

By 2007, I had received my first invitation to lead a training for school staff. The impetus for this request was the presence of just one trans child in the third grade. The educators and I knew this was a new conversation—there were no established resources to tap anywhere—and the learning journey for all of us began. None of the educators had ever met a trans person before— child or adult. Their curiosity was high, and their questions were plentiful. It didn't take long before their questions extended beyond what societal etiquette might usually dictate, including questions about genitalia, sexual practices, and transition-related medical intervention. Their adult curiosities about adult lives were understandable given their lack of exposure, but I pointed out that children were not at all likely to ask the same questions. It was truly an "aha" moment for these teachers.

We then shifted into considering what questions children might actually raise. We identified simple, straightforward questions the kids were likely to ask and readily found our way to straightforward responses. The school staff were pleasantly surprised to see how easy it could be to navigate these conversations with children.

What I learned on that first day, and in the years since, was that we as adults have a more complex path to travel to return to the uncomplicated, powerful place that children intuitively understand. *Trans Children in Today's Schools* is my effort to address that complexity—and simplicity—simultaneously.

A few months after my engagement with that first school, I began a support group for parents and caregivers of trans and nonbinary youth. Over the span of more than a dozen years, that group rapidly grew from the handful of families who met monthly at our local children's hospital to hundreds accessing twelve groups within a one-hundred-mile radius. Today, there are thousands of caregivers who meet regularly through our most recent iteration of support—TransFamilies.org. TransFamilies—building on the foundation of the original conference programming and support groups—is a virtual support program that has an expanding, international reach.

When asked how I came to this career path, I will frankly share that it came to me. I chose to respond to the apprehensive educators, the scared but brave families, and so many others when they had nowhere else to turn. Today, after leading hundreds of school staff trainings across the United States and supporting thousands of families around the world, my learning continues and my desire to share that learning is paramount.

AUDIENCE FOR *TRANS CHILDREN IN TODAY'S SCHOOLS*

Each parent who wonders how to best support their unique child often will, in the very next breath, express their fears as to how their child will be received at school. I wrote this book with parents in mind. I want them to have a clear picture of what they may encounter within the educational system. Yet, these parents are not the only audience I want to reach.

The second equally—if not more important—group of people I want to read this book are teachers, administrators, other educators, and school staff who touch the lives of students on a daily basis. I hope this book finds its way into the hands of university professors and students going into fields of education. I believe there will be many others with personal and/or professional interest in the lives of trans children who will also find this book valuable. What I've shared in this book speaks to a particular moment in time when trans and nonbinary children are becoming more and more visible in schools everywhere. It speaks to a time where the roadmap for how and why to strive for greater inclusion is still being crafted.

Whether the reader is a superintendent or coach, parent or grandparent, or college student pursuing a degree in teaching, psychology, law, health care, or social work, my strong hope is that *each person will read each chapter* regardless of its seeming relevance to them personally or professionally. Here's why. Chapter 6, for example, gives an overview of what is involved when a child considers a gender transition. It is a lengthy chapter but is important in laying a foundation of understanding that is general and not specific to any single child. Does the head of the cafeteria staff need to know all the potential steps a transitioning child may take? No. But will that staff member ask questions about transition-related steps during a staff training? Unequivocally, yes. Will a school nurse ask about a child's genital configuration? Unfortunately, yes, they will. Do they need to know? No, otherwise they would ask this of all children. Is it right for them to ask those questions? No. It is important to recognize that a student's right to privacy supersedes the needs of adults to have their curiosities satisfied. But their questions do mirror those of a society experiencing a significant learning curve. If that cafeteria staffer or school nurse has a resource available from which they can get their questions—or curiosities—addressed, then they can head to school each day with a deeper perspective and an increased understanding of how to honor every child.

If a caregiver is arranging a meeting with a principal to discuss their child's immediate needs with respect to pronouns, names, and bathroom access, I would like that caregiver to have this resource at their fingertips. Chapters 9 and 10, while primarily addressing educators, highlight some of the challenges that could, and often do, occur at schools, especially those schools for whom the discussion of gender inclusion is new. A parent will benefit from this perspective as they engage with school personnel.

I strongly hope a principal or superintendent will read Chapter 4 where some of the challenges and heartaches that parents of trans youth face are better understood. Chapter 2 could provide the administrator with much needed insight as to why there is volatility and resistance in these early days of gender inclusion. A more informed administrator can more compassionately recognize the complex path of these families and their children.

If every reader takes in the book as a whole, my hope is that they will come away having gained multiple perspectives regarding the complex relationship between parents and schools as well as an understanding of unprecedented moment in history in which we find ourselves. Change is underway—significant change is imminent—and it is being driven by the crucial needs of these gender-diverse children. I've shared many of these children's stories throughout and I encourage the reader to engage with an open heart and mind.

MORE ABOUT THIS MOMENT IN TIME

We are in the midst of a volatile, messy time when it comes to the "debate" about inclusion of gender-diverse students in schools. Polarizing political debates abound and legal challenges to gender-affirming health care are at an all-time high. Parental support of gender-diverse children is, in some places, viewed as child abuse. Without question, this volatility is painful to watch and is harmful to children. Even as this occurs, I can't help but contrast it with what I witness day-in and day-out in school districts everywhere. After more than fifteen years of engaging with school districts in conservative *and* liberal communities through-out the United States, I see consistent progress and burgeoning understanding. This is the lens through which I've written this book. It is what provides me with confident optimism that we can continue this progression and look after these students in the ways they need.

Many readers may be tempted to look ahead to chapters addressing present-day controversies: bathrooms and sports, for example, that come later in the book. If you do skip ahead, I strongly encourage you to circle back to the earlier chapters. I've led many trainings where these contested topics are mentioned early on. I always make sure to address these questions, but I've found that it is very effective to have a foundation first.

What educators and parents often have in common is a wish for a checklist—something that tells them what to do and when to do it. This wish is understand-able yet not entirely realistic. It is important that we figure out what to do in the immediate future and that we commit to this learning. We need to implement some of the long range, systemic changes that will allow us to move out of a time of controversy and volatility. I can share that both educator and parent each desire guidance from the other in the hopes of easing a child's path and of easing a community's journey.

The stories in this book are from real families. They have allowed me to use their experiences and photos and they understand the power inherent in doing so. It moves all of us from an abstract, speculative discussion to concrete reality. Anecdotes from educators within schools are included and present real situa-tions and actual conversations. Many weren't able to be part of this book, but I honor and acknowledge them as being integral to this text.

As is often the case with authors on any subject, I didn't cover all topics with the depth they deserve. Each chapter could have been its own book. Nor did

I cover every perspective for the most obvious reason that I don't have every perspective. This learning I've gained is exclusive to United States public and private schools, as are the stories of the included families. That said, I believe the content of this book can be helpful to people everywhere as it speaks to the humanity in all of us, especially as we navigate times of change.

As the saying goes, write about what you know. *Trans Children in Today's Schools* is my effort to share some of the knowledge imparted to me by so many courageous people who have the gift of being part of a gender-diverse child's life. All the stories included here were gathered over the course of my twenty-plus years as a gender diversity educator—I have done my utmost to recount accurately the pain, struggles, and joys these families have shared with me as I met them on their journey. I've worked with countless families and educators, and I am indebted to each and every one for trusting me with their stories and inviting me into their worlds.

1

So Many Trans Kids—What's Going On?

That is what learning is. You suddenly understand something you've understood all your life, but in a new way.

Doris Lessing

As I stood outside a K–8 parochial school in Oakland, California, I worked on calming my nerves. On that beautiful fall day in 2007, I was still pretty green as a gender diversity educator. I was soon to engage over 150 children in multiple classroom discussions so that they could better understand the upcoming gender transition of one of their schoolmates, a third-grade transgender girl.

The training with staff had gone well, as had the conversation with parents the following day.

Today was about the children. Wrangling large groups of boisterous children may be second nature to teachers, but not to me. I knew my content, but I could tell that some of it was intimidating to the teachers. None of us wanted the school to make the nightly news, awash with images of scared children and angry parents. Nevertheless, we found the courage to dive in together. We stuck to our respective skill sets—I led the conversation about gender and each classroom teacher took care of the child-wrangling.

As I described the concept of gender identity to the first class, a child raised her hand and said, "That's me!" Okay, I thought, *this* must be the trans child (whom I had not met in advance). Afterward, the wide-eyed teacher whispered, "That's *not* the child we've been talking about!" Okay, so another child is expressing a gender difference. I reassured her that if they could support one child, they would just as easily be able to support two. Off to the next classroom. The same thing happened. As I moved through the day, classroom by classroom, another student or two would raise their hand in the air with statements like: "Everyone sees me as a girl on the outside, but I am a boy on the inside."

By the end of the day, the principal had heard updates from these teachers. She knew that the conversations had gone well and that, while they knew they had one trans student, the reality might be much greater. "Aidan, could we really have that many trans children? What is going on?!" We discussed this for a bit, and to be reassuring, I added, "Just as you are willing to step into unfamiliar territory to support one known transgender student, so too will these steps serve to support *any* student coming through your doors for years to come." She smiled, nodded, and replied: "When we say we are committed to social justice and diversity, we do not pick and choose who fits into that category because of what is easiest—or most familiar—gender diversity *is* our next frontier."

It is natural for us to speculate about any new phenomenon, even to resist or deny its validity.[1] The increased visibility of transgender children in schools and the complexity this presents are no exception. We have learned, to some extent, that transgender individuals have existed and sometimes thrived in other times, cultures, and places, but now we see and hear stories of transgender people everywhere. Part of this can be attributed to what is known as *frequency illusion*.[2] A parent of a trans boy explained it this way, "It's like when you buy a red truck. You never notice red trucks and then they are just everywhere!"

Nowhere is this more evident than with transgender children in today's schools. And not just one or two—there seem to be so many! Administrators and teachers alike may feel broadsided when face-to-face with these gender-diverse children. Over and over they ask, "What is going on? Why are there so many? The terms they use—nonbinary, transgender, agender—what do these mean and how do we know if this is real when they are so young?"

Frequency illusion is not enough to explain what is really going on. It is important to consider the possibility that we are not witnessing an actual increase in the number of transgender children, but an increase in the visibility and openness of these children and their families. The reality is that trans and other gender-diverse youth are finding their voice. We need to listen. They are insistent upon their need to be seen. We need to pay attention. "In other words, children as a whole have not become more likely to be transgender; rather, transgender children are no longer suffering in silence."[3]

WE CAN DO THIS; WE'VE DONE IT BEFORE

Acknowledging and including trans and other gender-diverse children in schools can feel like a daunting task. How do we accomplish this? Do we have models or other examples to follow? If we don't have the answers to these questions, is that a good enough reason to steer away from making inclusive efforts? No, I don't think it is.

We can change our society to include those who've been excluded, targeted, or hidden—we've done it before. In the United States, the latter half of the twentieth century saw progressive social justice movements gathering strength. The civil rights movement sought to racially desegregate schools. The disability rights movement insisted that children with disabilities should not be hidden away and instead have a right to be included, contributing members of society. Title IX is a law that seeks to increase opportunities for girls by prohibiting sex-based discrimination in educational settings. These movements have not always seen linear progress in how they have changed policy, language, and the very lives they impact. There is always more work to be done. While these movements surely faced obstacles that felt insurmountable at the outset, we now recognize their historical precedent and a present-day need for a sustained commitment to their goals.

Similar to the crucial role of parental advocacy within the disability rights movement, parents today can provide powerful advocacy for the acceptance and inclusion of gender-diverse children. Medical and mental health providers, social and life scientists, and other childhood specialists are serving as vital advocates, by mutually sharing a growing body of research and supplying their observations and experiences.

Teachers and educational leaders also have a pivotal role in this movement toward gender inclusion. They are tasked with creating a supportive environment within schools. Fortunately, the work has begun. If we draw parallels to social justice movements, any adult advocate—parent, teacher, doctor, and others—can better recognize the tools that are available to them and make a positive impact on the lives of all children.

GENDER DIVERSITY IS NOT NEW

Before we examine the present-day visibility of trans children, it will be helpful to take a glance back in time for perspective. Native American cultures during pre-colonial times recognized more than just two gender roles and that these roles were not based on anatomical delineations dependent on genitalia. Often referred to as Two-Spirit, it is estimated that over 150 tribes embraced more expansive gender language, roles, relationships, responsibilities, and presentations.[4]

Early colonial writings originating from authors such as Spanish conquistador Cabeza de Vaca, fur trader Edwin Thompson Denig of Danish descent, and French artist and member of Jean Ribault's expedition to the New World, Jacques Le Moyne de Morgues, provide us with observations of these Native American tribes and their acceptance and inclusion of people of differing genders. While individuals who assumed different genders were accepted in most of the Native American societies in which they have been known to exist, the reactions of the Europeans who encountered them ranged from curious astonishment to violent repulsion.[5]

While three or more gender identity roles existed and were embraced within Native American cultures at one time, the devastation to these people, their culture, and their homeland has all but erased this understanding of a more gender-inclusive world. In their book, *Gender: What Everyone Needs to Know*, coauthors Erickson-Schroth and Davis write, "Colonization brought an abrupt and violent halt to many freedoms Two-Spirit people had lived with for centuries. Historical accounts present the confusion early colonizers had upon meeting them. Missionaries were often cruel and are reported to have fed Two-Spirit people to the dogs, forced them into the clothing and hairstyles of a cis-normative and eurocentric standard, separated them from family, and altogether erased their histories."[6]

Since antiquity, around the globe, there are accounts of gender-diverse people.[7] How often do we hear these stories, learn their histories, or see them represented in historical records? As the lives of trans and other gender-diverse people are amplified today, our conceptual understanding of what it means to be transgender serves an important purpose—one where we do not need to vilify, erase, or destroy the lives of other humans to ease the misapprehension of the uninitiated. Instead, we can deepen our understanding of gender-diverse lives and consequently deepen our understanding of what it means to be human.

TODAY'S INCREASED VISIBILITY

Perhaps the most significant factor in today's visibility of trans children is the world at our fingertips—the internet.[8] With the advent of the world wide web, largely inaccessible just twenty-five years ago, we can more immediately access knowledge that may have existed only in larger city libraries or institutions of higher education.

If a gender-diverse person wanted to search for information regarding gender identity differences, they would need specialized access, an idea of *how* to begin their solo search, and the courage to do so. One colleague of mine, attempting to find her way to gender-affirming resources and providers, shared this story with me:

> I was in Europe in the early 70s and knew no one who could help. Occasionally, you might hear a whispered story of the gender transition of someone who was the cousin of a neighbor's friend, but these people were so difficult to track down. Over time, as some of us were finally able to make a few connections, we set up a postal box where others could write to us. Then we created business cards with that address and strategically left them in the card catalog drawers of libraries under content sections where we thought others might look. *That* is how we found each other!

Over the latter half of the twentieth century, the need for connection led to other resources, such as print newsletters and magazines that served to build a fledgling community. Yet, most would not have access to these resources unless they were in larger cities that might have a gay and lesbian bookstore or community center. The majority of gay and lesbian people did not live open and accepting lives until they reached maturity and could make these integral decisions for themselves. That meant that *any* resource a person might find was likely to be an adult-focused resource. If a gay or lesbian person's membership in their community is foundationally defined by their sexual orientation, it reinforces the impression that any community resource that might be available would contain "mature content."

These communities had not yet begun to embrace the distinction between gender identity and sexual orientation, a crucial distinction that further hindered trans adults who might have had access to these early resources. Adolescents and older teens—whether gay, lesbian, bi, or trans—had to get by on their own, most without familial or emotional support, until they were old enough to access any resources that might exist. During this nascent movement toward gender diversity, younger gender-diverse children were simply invisible and unacknowledged.[9]

MEDIA AND THE INTERNET

Mainstream media stories about the lives of trans children only started to appear in the mid-2000s. One such story found its way into American homes when, in 2007, veteran journalist Barbara Walters profiled the stories of three transgender children on the television newsmagazine show *20/20*.[10] Since then, the lives of trans children and their families have become an increasingly regular occurrence in magazines, talk shows, documentaries, and even small-town newspapers.

It should not be hard to imagine then the impact personal computers had as these stories showed up in homes, libraries, and schools. The relative safety, anonymity, and access the internet can afford to an individual or parent is an obvious benefit to those seeking support, information, and validation. Social media giants like YouTube, Facebook, and Instagram provide platforms for the real-time journeys of these families. These stories, which were literally at our fingertips, put real faces to an issue that had, up to that point, been largely ignored, feared, or misunderstood.

Only a decade ago, many of us had never heard the word transgender. Some people may still have the misconception that they have never met a transgender person.[11] However, today many people find they have only a degree or two of separation from a transgender person or a family with a transgender child. Your neighbor has a transgender granddaughter. A person at your office recently transitioned. Your child comes home from school and says a boy she knows is now a girl. With this closer proximity and ever-increasing media coverage of this topic, it's the rare person who has not read an article or heard a radio interview about a transgender child, teen, or adult.

TV programs now increasingly include transgender characters—thankfully, not as a freakish sideshow or as disturbed individuals, but simply as another crucial character in a storyline.[12] We see stories in the media representing the diversity of transgender people from all walks of life—musicians, politicians, filmmakers, military elite, clergy, athletes, police officers, and, of course, K–12 students.

As a result of increasing online access, trans children and their parents can more readily find information that addresses their gender identity and experience. The willingness of an increasing number of individuals and families to publicly share their journeys helps others feel less isolated and alone. Their stories provide a name—*transgender*—to a legitimate and meaningful life experience.

HISTORICAL TREATMENT OF TRANSGENDER INDIVIDUALS

While diverse conceptions of gender may have always existed, there is a minimal historical context for this within a Euro-American mindset. Many trans adults have shared with me that, as children, they had an innate sense that their gender identity did not match their bodies, but with no language with which to describe their identity, it remained nebulous and unspoken.

Of course, some children could (and would) articulate, "I'm not a boy, I'm a girl!" However, those children would likely have experienced immediate pushback. A parent might tell their child that they were confused and seek out gender corrective therapy from a psychologist. The child may face begrudging tolerance at best or active resistance and physical punishment at worst. Many trans children have reported experiences of direct rejection and persecution from others. While a fortunate few had some level of familial support, they were often subject to harsh experiences outside the home, at school, on the neighborhood playground, with extended family, or within their church communities.[13]

What we know is that most transgender adults did not receive support or encouragement as children from their family, peers, school, or society for their gender-atypical identities or expressions. These experiences taught them early on to hide their innate, gendered selves as much as possible. These situations were often further compounded when others, unable to intervene because of a lack of understanding, stood by helplessly, either unwilling or unable to offer much-needed support.[14]

Research shows that today's adult transgender population, at some point in their lives, including childhood, has experienced physical harm and sexual assault at rates far higher than the national average. These attacks are often delivered with the message that victims deserve "punishment" for not conforming to mainstream norms in the ways they express their gender, for having bodies that aren't masculine or feminine enough, or for simply stating their core gender identification. Finding a trans-identified adult who has *not* experienced physical/sexual violence, emotional or sexual abuse, and societal or familial ostracism is a rarity. It is crucial to note that trans women of color are most significantly and disproportionately the victims of violence, sexual assault, and murder.[15]

Adding to this injustice, those fortunate enough to survive these assaults may find themselves blamed for the attacks, watching as their perpetrators go unpunished, and even find themselves incarcerated for acting in self-defense.

The resulting damage to a trans person's self-esteem, mental health, and even their ability to function optimally in society does take its toll. This toll, however, is often cited as "proof" that trans people are innately deficient *because* of their identity rather than suffering from a number of adverse impacts from a hostile society. Pervasive, life-long gender denigration creates a self-fulfilling prophecy that handicaps self-esteem, life-functioning, and personal resiliency, further perpetuating the misclassification of gender identity differences as mental illness. Suicide, violence, familial ostracism, job loss, addiction, and homelessness are the dark shadows that accompany many transgender people throughout their lives.[16]

HISTORICAL PATHWAYS TO TRANSITIONING

Until recent years, health care providers imposed strict gender transition requirements, which assumed that patients wanted a post-transition, heterosexually aligned relationship and would do everything they could to fully present, or "pass," as the gender with which they identified. The messaging was along the lines of, *If you insist on being a woman, you need to do everything possible to behave and present as a woman—and be a woman that wants to be with a man.*

Requirements like these came from the small handful of psychologists and medical providers who were among the first of those "willing" to care for trans people. Their own biases—some implicit, some overt—informed the parameters of what providers decided would work best to achieve assimilation into cis-heteronormative society. The *appearance* of heteronormativity was the agreed-upon objective. These expectations fit the needs and experiences of very few trans people, but they served to inform decades of inaccurate trans-related requirements, data, and outcomes.[17]

Another historical notion regarding gender transition was that a trans person should hide one's gender history, which often involved reinventing one's childhood. For example, the expectation for a transgender man would include modifying his experience of Girl Scout participation into that of the Boy Scouts (with requisite homework on the distinctions between the two programs!). If his sexual orientation was toward men, he would likely have been denied the professional validation required to transition because of the post-transition expectation of providers to end up "straight" (i.e., attracted to women) upon "completion." Or, he may have felt he had to lie about his orientation to access transition-related care. The expectations for a trans person required creating fiction more akin to a witness protection program—relocation; erasure of history; and even permanent separation from family, friends, and one's children.[18]

In addition, those with limited financial means would certainly be prevented from pursuing transition-related health care, as exclusions were rampant throughout the health insurance industry (if one were fortunate enough to be insured at all). All gender-related care was funded "out-of-pocket," often to the tune of thousands or tens of thousands of dollars—certainly out of reach for most individuals.[19] One early website I found offering advice to transgender people suggested that the ideal way to begin a gender transition was to simply "retire early," a ridiculous and impossible option for most people.

This life of enforced secrecy, coupled with other disparities, all but ensured that gender-diverse people would remain invisible to the larger society. Restrictive, unrealistic transition protocols ensured that the only visible transgender people were those who were *highly* visible because they either couldn't or wouldn't hide. Still, others, when contemplating the "price tag" of gender transition—including the associated stigma; loss of employment, family, friends, community; and other increased dangers—felt forced to deny themselves a gender-authentic life. Gender transition, in short, was dangerous, isolating, and largely unattainable for all but a small percentage of people.

GENDER CONFORMITY VS. HEALTHY SELF-EXPRESSION

Trans adults have spent a lifetime attempting to make sense of their own gender experiences within a world that denies the very possibility of distinct gender identity. As adults, they eventually found the language and courage to express themselves and move forward with their lives. If transgender adults had these and many other obstacles preventing them from being visible members of society, the possibility of visibility for transgender children was not even a consideration. Childhood was viewed as a crucial window of time whereby desperate parents might successfully eliminate any expressed gender differences in their children.[20]

Collective concern for a gender-diverse child's well-being and a desire to prevent future hardship was expressed simply and directly: discourage the behavior and expression to eliminate it. This school of thought was grounded in the assumption that a child's gender identity was malleable. Professional guidance suggested to parents that the best way to treat a gender-diverse child was to change *them*—make *them* fit into societal norms.

There are very few parents who are immediately ecstatic upon realizing that their child is transgender. The most common reaction to this news is usually fear, confusion, and even anger.[21] For that matter, any adult in a child's life—including neighbors, teachers, extended family, and other community members—may also experience these reactions.

Teasing and bullying a child for atypical gender expression is still a rampant and relatively common phenomenon, and, for the most part, still considered *normal* childhood behavior. This gender-based discrimination continues into adulthood. Transgender adults experience very high rates of unemployment, housing discrimination, suicidal ideation, and many other risk factors. When coupled with the burden of silence that transgender individuals face, these statistics paint a vicious cycle of revictimization and discrimination.[22]

Whether one is bullied on the playground or assaulted on the street, society is still strongly inclined to place the blame on the transgender person for these traumatic experiences. *If they would only dress differently, not behave that way, and just be "normal," then they wouldn't be bullied, they might get that job, or they might still be alive.* What parent, grandparent, teacher, or health care provider wants a child to experience this kind of hardship if it can be avoided?

Conformity, the majority of professionals agreed, would allow a child to experience more opportunities in life, have a greater chance of experiencing societal acceptance, and—the hope was—be *safer in the world*. While originally well-intentioned, this approach—what is now referred to as reparative or conversion therapy—has been shown to result in significant harm.[23] Denial of their true selves and conformity to others' expectations of who they should be or become costs a child their healthy self-esteem, authentic expression, and an overall sense of belonging and acceptance in the world.[24]

We are only beginning to recognize and understand that efforts to stifle or change a child's innate gender identification can be harmful. The significance of this is great. If we stop asking the child to change to better fit into society, we find ourselves tasked with asking society to change to embrace and include them.

SO, IF WE DON'T EXPECT A CHILD TO CHANGE THEIR GENDER, WHAT DO WE DO INSTEAD?

Current research has identified best practices for the treatment of gender identity differences expressed by children. Familial support, validation, and—in many cases—earlier medical intervention are now viewed as necessary and appropriate components to ensuring the well-being and healthy development of a trans child.[25]

Yet, if providing support is increasingly recognized as the appropriate path to take, why does this approach so often cause distress in families and others close to the child? Why does it inspire resistance from society as a whole? Again, accepting trans children for who they are requires a shift in the cultural/societal norms surrounding children. This is a tall order.

THE STRUGGLE TO UNDERSTAND

Even though increased visibility has made the term *transgender* a household word, our society's overall understanding of gender is still very limited.[26] And, while understanding is at a low, emotions are at an all-time high. With strong feelings at play, it's difficult to sort through the noise. Factual information can be slow to disseminate. This has resulted in an abundance of strong, unsubstantiated *opinions* about what influences have contributed to the growing presence of transgender people, especially children. Many will offer up what they see as contributing factors. These factors are often based on misinformation, such as speculation of possible environmental toxins, overly permissive parenting, or antiquated parenting theories.[27] One parent wondered if her child was transgender because during pregnancy she had *wished* so hard for a boy that her child decided to become one.

Poorly conceived ideas about what might precipitate a child's transition include peer pressure, teen fads, or even the notion of some kind of gender "confusion" arising from a hyper-sexualized culture. Other pseudo-theories try to connect it to childhood sexual abuse. During one school district training, an administrator offered his opinion that teens' easy access to internet porn was probably an influence. One thing is certain, the array of vastly different explanations just illustrates the significant void of factual information.

If single-parent households, certain parenting styles, absent parents, fads, porn, or wishful thinking were indeed contributing factors to a child's transgender identification, it could be argued that an even greater number of children might be trans. The reality is, however, that transgender people—children or otherwise—are just a small percentage of the overall population.[28]

The crucial questions we need to ask ourselves are these: How we can best support this increasingly visible presence of gender-diverse children? Have transgender people always existed? Have there always been so many? How can children be transgender? Aren't they too young to know? If they have always existed, why haven't we seen them all along? Why now?

WHAT DO WE KNOW ABOUT GENDER IDENTITY?

While current research points to neurobiological and genetic origins, we still have some way to go before we fully understand the factors that inform any individual's gender identity. In the book, *Gender: What Everyone Needs to Know*, authors Erickson-Schroth and Davis state, "Because many children seem to have a sense of their gender identity very early on, it is likely that gender identity is biologically influenced, although biology does not appear to be the sole determinant of gender identity. There is growing evidence connecting gender identity to prenatal hormone exposure, although there is much debate about where, why, and how gender identity is formed."[29]

A significant omission in prior gender research is that it did not acknowledge that a transgender person's sense of their gender, like anyone else's, is inherently rooted in gender identity—not behavior or sexuality as is commonly assumed—and that this is a core element of identity that applies to all people. A majority of people have a solid understanding of their gender from the earliest age of recollection.[30] That solidity is not questioned. Yet, when it comes to trans and other gender-diverse children, there is the misconception that their understanding of their own gender is amorphous, malleable, and/or mired in confusion. This has led to a misguided approach by doctors, psychologists, and other providers to "fix" what they perceived as a psychological disorder through reparative therapy methods.

Professionals working in the field of gender identity now understand that reparative therapy was unsuccessful in its efforts to rid a child of their core gender identification.[31] Reparative therapy has proven to be a practice that is damaging and harmful. It is no longer considered to be in the category of "best practice" and is illegal in a growing number of states. Recent studies quite clearly validate that gender cognition of transgender children is the same as that of any non-transgender child—that kids are who they say they are—dispelling the myths that the gender identity of these children originates from sources like parental permissiveness, a child's exaggerated or fantastical thinking, or a child's confusion or misunderstanding concerning the concept of gender.[32]

As a society, we are developing an ever-increasing understanding of what it means to be transgender. More and more people have a transgender family member, co-worker, classmate, or friend. When someone has a direct, personal connection with a trans person, it often results in increased compassion and empathy that might not otherwise occur if that same person had little to no connection at all. Transgender people of all ages have greater confidence to share their true selves with other family members and friends. These connections increase the overall visibility of trans people, bringing a more accurate, *more diverse* range of gender identities and experiences to the world as a whole. The resulting visibility shines a beacon of hope for those who may have once felt hidden, silenced, and isolated in their experience.

When previously invisible populations start to become more visible, often as part of larger social justice movements (people with disabilities, people of color, people who are gay/lesbian), they are met with skepticism, derision, and resistance to change. But then we *do* change. We integrate, accommodate, and adapt—and we are all the better for it. This pattern plays out again and again, in different ways each time. As a general rule, it is how society progresses.

Trans children are now visible members of society within this new social context. In short, a combination of factors—information access, increased understanding, higher visibility, and a shift in therapeutic care—have led us to this moment where *transgender* has become a household word and a new social justice movement to embrace.

EFFORTS TO CHANGE GENDER DIFFERENCES IN CHILDREN

Throughout time, culture, and place there have been children who have *expressed* their gender in ways that were considered atypical—for instance, a boy who behaved in a way we considered too feminine (e.g., a sissy) or a girl whose gender expression was viewed as too masculine (e.g., a tomboy). Likewise, there have always been children who have stated that they had a *gender identification* that did not match their sex assigned at birth—for instance, a child says, "I am not a girl, I'm a boy!" Assuming confusion or a playful imagination on the child's part, a parent may indulge in the "play." But if it persists, they may simply "correct" the child and discuss the anatomical evidence that "disproves" this child's gender identification statement.

However, when teachers, parents, or even other children consistently refute, correct, or shut down a child's articulation of who they are or the things they like, a child receives a clear message: *Who I am and what I like is bad and wrong. I won't be loved if I share my true self with others.* Children may then attempt to suppress or hide who they are simply to please others or to evade punishment. In my experience, this does not change their core identity—only their ability to express it openly.

Out of love and concern for the child, adults may make efforts to change this expression and/or identification because they want what is best for the child. They are concerned that the child will be bullied and rejected and that their communities will be disparaging toward not only the child but the family as well. If they are successful in "changing" the child's gender identification and/or expression, the problem is solved, right? In such a situation, the motivations are good, but the initial premise is flawed. This premise is the belief that a child's innate gender identification *can* shift or change as a result of external influences.[33] Their encouragements, expectations, or even punishments of these children often *do* accomplish a shift, just not in the way they intend.

SHIFTING FROM REJECTION TO SUPPORT

Suppose we made the choice to change society's attitudes, norms, and policies as to what is acceptable and "normal" in relation to gender. What if parents accepted their child's innate gender identity—or presentation of that gender—as normal? What would happen to these children if schools were to create an inclusive environment where gender differences fell into the same category as other distinct qualities in a child's life—skin color, ability, ethnicity, faith, and diverse family structure—and we collectively sought acceptance, even celebration, for all our diverse experiences and qualities?

What if we understood that pink is just a color, a doll is just a toy, clothes are just clothes, and short and long hair are options available to all kids? What if the medical and therapeutic community were to suggest that love and nurturance are the best things to provide to a transgender child? What if our society were to recognize that attempts to change a child's innate self are destructive and harmful to that child?

Implementing this vision is a tall order, but the reality is that a significant evolution *is* needed. Ironically, many of the changes needed are sometimes very small. Once adults manage their oftentimes intense internal struggles, they realize they still have the same beautiful child—thriving and happy as a result of the love and support they received.

This positive shift is a constant refrain for the families of these children. Resolving their internal conflicts encompass the lion's share of the work. Once parents, teachers, and communities navigate these conflicts, sometimes the only remaining challenge might be consistently using a new name or pronoun, which boils down to "practice makes perfect." Other children, given the opportunity, more readily understand the experience of a trans child, accomplishing tasks like name and pronoun changes with greater ease. And, contrary to what administrators and educators initially think, implementing needed school changes often proves to be far easier than expected, and they even discover that *these changes end up being beneficial to all children in the school,* not just the trans child. The locker room or bathroom a trans child uses, for example, has been a volatile issue for schools, with privacy being the key issue. The reality is that the privacy needs of all children are deserving of a thoughtful examination.

Societal attitudes and understanding are changing rapidly, and this vision of a more supportive world is becoming a reality in many places. Schools and communities are readily recognizing the presence of trans youth and working hard to find ways to be inclusive.

Ultimately, when a family or school has a transgender child in its midst, the search for definitive answers is still a process, especially when much-needed policies and practices have yet to be put in place. Our understanding will continue as time progresses—years, perhaps decades from now. What is relevant, and highly so, is that these children *are* present within families and classrooms and we need to know how best to respond and support them. Supporting a child's natural exploration—accepting them for who they are, at the time they need it most, is the best way to establish and grow a child's self-esteem.[34] This support is what will provide them with the foundation needed for a strong, fulfilled, and happy life.

HOW DO WE MANIFEST THE INCLUSION AND ACCEPTANCE OF TRANSGENDER CHILDREN?

"How do we create a gender-inclusive environment for children?" is a common question from educators. One way to begin answering this question is by first asking ourselves what response we would have wanted as children, from our parents, teachers, or friends, when we authentically expressed ourselves and our interests? How did we feel as we experienced happiness and excitement about new toys; new clothes; or an interest in music, sports, art, or any other activity, only to have the wind knocked out of our sails when someone was disparaging that object or interest? When we recognized that our family structure, our faith community, our skin color, or even the food we ate was different from our peers, how long did it take for those distinctions to be ridiculed by our peers at school? Or were those distinctions considered odd when contrasted to the mainstream culture's idea of "normal"? Any of us can share times when we did *not* have positive experiences and were excluded, invalidated, or bullied. We may have felt sadness, anger, frustration, and even fear or distress.

What response would we have liked instead? It's not hard to answer that question. We easily recognize that what we wanted was *acceptance, support, excitement, kindness, understanding, empathy,* and *compassion.* Educators already have the tools they need to support transgender children, but they haven't realized how to employ them in this new, unfamiliar terrain. What are these tools? In addition to showing understanding and compassion, teachers have tools of intervention to use when students behave inappropriately. While they work to model acceptance and support, they also need to use their skills in adapting to the needs of different students while maintaining a cohesive classroom. They know the value of expressing encouragement as they engage students in classroom discussions. They know how to consistently communicate expectations and timelines. Ideally, teachers have been trained to handle unpredictable situations and have peer and leadership support to turn to when needed.

After leading hundreds of trainings in schools and in many types of communities, I've learned that positive outcomes transcend, and are not derailed by, people's different viewpoints related to politics, culture, faith, and place. Why is this? Because the majority of members of any community consistently embrace the core values of tolerance, acceptance, and inclusivity. They already know how to show up for their kids. Also, based on my experience with schools, these positive outcomes do not "just happen." Imagine, for example, the difference between taking the time to read this book or putting it under your pillow hoping the words will seep in overnight.

Schools that make the commitment of time and the investment in learning are the ones with greater success stories. Contrary to the popular opinion that "liberal" schools will do better than "conservative" schools, my experience does not support that opinion. Everyone feels confused and challenged. We must acknowledge that these feelings are necessary. Dedicating time to deepen the learning for everyone is the key.

You might expect that the main inquiry I receive from school personnel would be along the lines of, "Aidan, how do we include trans children in our school?" To a degree, it is. However, I would like to expand this view to give you a more accurate representation of what is *really* being asked. "We've never done this before, we've never seen it done, we don't know how to get started or even if we *should*, as some of my staff already are saying: *no way!* Surely, we can't talk to young children about this, right? Even if we could, there is no way their parents are going to sign on. So, Aidan, really, how do we include trans children in our school?"

It will take more than a paragraph or two, even more than this book, perhaps, to fully answer this question. It will take exploration, time, action, and courage. As with any journey, let's consider a good first step. Instead of wondering how to create a gender-inclusive environment for trans kids, let's expand this thought to: "How do we create a gender-inclusive environment for *every* child?" With this reframing, we can shift our thinking from the uncertainty of a brand-new endeavor to one that is at least partially familiar. Any educator, during their studies to become a teacher, principal, school nurse, or counselor, will have at least cursorily addressed gender differences and gender equity—if only within a binary context—within their academic courses and texts. We have a foundation upon which we can build.

We have a long history of misinformation about gender identity. To address the difficult climate created by this misinformation, we need to shift our ideas about and responses to trans children. Needed steps include the following:

1. We need to understand more clearly what it means to be transgender *and* what it *doesn't* mean.
2. We need to recognize that we are moving from a long history of transgender invisibility to a rapidly growing visible presence.
3. We need to change the misalignment, stigmatization, and negative portrayals of transgender people that have resulted in a great deal of fear for others.
4. We need to start with listening to each child, then offering them validation and support for their journey toward gender authenticity.

I hope that as you delve further into this book, you will realize that the goal of achieving inclusion for trans children is indeed attainable.

NOTES

1. The use of the word *phenomenon* is purposeful here in that this book is not intended to debate the relative newness of transgender embodiment, but rather to acknowledge the tensions in (and attentions to) current transgender paradigms.
2. "Frequency Illusion," n.d., https://en.wikipedia.org/wiki/Frequency_illusion.
3. Sally Hines, *Is Gender Fluid? A Primer for the 21st Century*, The Big Idea Series (London; New York: Thames & Hudson, 2018), 103.
4. Several scholars have given this subject the treatment it deserves, albeit with varying perspectives: Will Roscoe, *Changing Ones: Third and Fourth Genders in Native North America*, 1st ed. (New York: St. Martin's Press, 1998); Leslie Feinberg, *Transgender Warriors: Making History from Joan of Arc to RuPaul* (Boston: Beacon Press, 1996); Sue-Ellen Jacobs, Wesley Thomas, and Sabine Lang, eds., *Two-Spirit People: Native American Gender Identity, Sexuality, and Spirituality* (Urbana: University of Illinois Press, 1997).
5. Will Roscoe, *Changing Ones: Third and Fourth Genders in Native North America*, 1st ed. (New York: St. Martin's Press, 1998), 4. For further discussion of the reaction of European colonizers to gender variance in Native American culture, see Laura Erickson-Schroth, ed., *Trans Bodies, Trans Selves: A Resource for the Transgender Community* (Oxford; New York: Oxford University Press, 2014), 501–503.
6. Laura Erickson-Schroth and Benjamin Davis, *Gender: What Everyone Needs to Know* (New York: Oxford University Press, 2021), 40.

7. For an overview of gender diversity throughout history and across cultures, see Aaron H. Devor and Ardel Haefele-Thomas, *Transgender: A Reference Handbook*, Contemporary World Issues (Santa Barbara: ABC-CLIO, 2019), 3–42. For a playful analysis that is also easily accessible, see Sally Hines, *Is Gender Fluid? A Primer for the 21st Century*, The Big Idea Series (London; New York: Thames & Hudson, 2018), 79–93.

8. The transformative effect of the internet and social media networking on visibility is remarked upon in several texts regarding transgender individuals. See Melinda M. Mangin, *Transgender Students in Elementary School: Creating an Affirming and Inclusive School Culture*, Youth Development and Education (Cambridge, MA: Harvard Education Press, 2020), 24; Ann Travers, *The Trans Generation: How Trans Kids (and Their Parents) Are Creating a Gender Revolution* (New York: New York University Press, 2018), 5.

9. The concept of visibility is important here, especially when we consider the psychic toll of concealment, hiding, or "non-apparency" as put forth by Mark Hellen, "Transgender Children in Schools," *Liminalis: Journal for Sex/Gender Emancipation and Resistance* 3 (2009): 81–99.

10. "My Secret Self: A Story of Transgender Children," Barbara Walters interview with Jazz Jennings, *20/20*, aired April 27, 2007, on ABC, https://www.imdb.com/title/tt1928346/.

11. Laura Erickson-Schroth and Laura A. Jacobs, *"You're in the Wrong Bathroom!": And 20 Other Myths and Misconceptions about Transgender and Gender-Nonconforming People* (Boston: Beacon Press, 2017), 3–7.

12. Jamie C. Capuzza and Leland G. Spencer, "Regressing, Progressing, or Transgressing on the Small Screen? Transgender Characters on U.S. Scripted Television Series," *Communication Quarterly* 65, no. 2 (2017): 214–230.

13. Peter Goldblum, ed., *Youth Suicide and Bullying: Challenges and Strategies for Prevention and Intervention* (Oxford; New York: Oxford University Press, 2015), 122.

14. Elizabeth J. Meyer, "Gendered Harassment in Secondary Schools: Understanding Teachers' (Non) Interventions," *Gender and Education* 20, no. 6 (November 2008): 555, http://dx.doi.org/10.1080/09540250802213115.

15. Dean Fox and Barbara Sims, "The Victimization of Transgender Individuals: Addressing the Needs of a Hidden Population," in *Invisible Victims and the Pursuit of Justice: Analyzing Frequently Victimized Yet Rarely Discussed Populations*, ed. Raleigh Blasdell, Laura Krieger-Sample, and Michelle Kilburn (Hershey, PA: IGI Global, 2021), 327–352.

16. For an interpretation of data surrounding the victimization of transgender individuals and how this manifests in a burden of silence and revictimization, see Cindy L. Griffin, *Beyond Gender Binaries: An Intersectional Orientation to Communication and Identities* (Oakland: University of California Press, 2020), 148–150. See also Rebecca L. Stotzer, "Violence against Transgender People: A Review of United States Data," *Aggression and Violent Behavior* 14, no. 3 (May 2009): 170–179, https://doi.org/10.1016/j.avb.2009.01.006.

17. Beans Velocci, "Standards of Care," *TSQ: Transgender Studies Quarterly* 8, no. 4 (November 1, 2021): 462–480, https://doi.org/10.1215/23289252-9311060.

18. For a discussion regarding transgender transition narratives, see J. E. Sumerau and Lain A. B. Mathers, *America through Transgender Eyes* (Lanham: Rowman & Littlefield, 2019), 113–132.

19. This tiny book takes a scathing look at trans care and the costs and relative privilege of transition in the context of medical gatekeeping: Hil Malatino, *Trans Care*, Forerunners: Ideas First Series (Minneapolis; London: University of Minnesota Press, 2020), 61–72.

20. For a discussion of the "plastic body" of children and how this was racialized in a clinical setting, see Jules Gill-Peterson, *Histories of the Transgender Child* (Minneapolis: University of Minnesota Press, 2018), 131.

21. Em Matsuno et al., "'I Am Fortunate to Have a Transgender Child': An Investigation into the Barriers and Facilitators to Support among Parents of Trans and Nonbinary Youth," *LGBTQ+ Family: An Interdisciplinary Journal* (October 20, 2021): 1–19, https://doi.org/10.1080/1550428X.2021.1991541.

22. Cindy L. Griffin, *Beyond Gender Binaries: An Intersectional Orientation to Communication and Identities* (Oakland: University of California Press, 2020), 148–150.

23. "Recommendations for Promoting the Health and Well-Being of Lesbian, Gay, Bisexual, and Transgender Adolescents: A Position Paper of the Society for Adolescent Health and Medicine," *Journal of Adolescent Health* 52, no. 4 (April 1, 2013): 506–510, https://doi.org/10.1016/j.jadohealth.2013.01.015.

24. Elizabeth P. Rahilly, *Trans-Affirmative Parenting: Raising Kids across the Gender Spectrum* (New York: New York University Press, 2020), 24.

25. Lisa Simons et al., "Parental Support and Mental Health among Transgender Adolescents," Journal of Adolescent Health 53, no. 6 (December 2013): 791–793, https://doi.org/10.1016/j.jadohealth.2013.07.019.

26. As difficult as it is to pinpoint when exactly cultural shifts happen, Halberstam identifies 2015 as the defining moment for transgender becoming a household word: Judith Halberstam, Trans*: A Quick and Quirky Account of Gender Variability (Oakland: University of California Press, 2018), 46.

27. While misinformation regarding transgender individuals is rooted in race, class, and other societal constructs, this work seeks to address ways of remedying this prejudice: Melissa R. Michelson and Brian F. Harrison, *Transforming Prejudice: Identity, Fear, and Transgender Rights* (New York: Oxford University Press, 2020), 147–162.

28. Jody L. Herman et al., *Age of Individuals Who Identify as Transgender in the United States* (Los Angeles: The Williams Institute, 2017).

29. Laura Erickson-Schroth and Benjamin Davis, *Gender: What Everyone Needs to Know* (New York: Oxford University Press, 2021), 4.

30. Carol Lynn Martin and Diane N. Ruble, "Patterns of Gender Development," *Annual Review of Psychology* 61, no. 1 (2010): 353–381, https://doi.org/10.1146/annurev.psych.093008.100511.

31. Caitlin Ryan et al., "Parent-Initiated Sexual Orientation Change Efforts with LGBT Adolescents: Implications for Young Adult Mental Health and Adjustment," *Journal of Homosexuality* 67, no. 2 (2020): 159–173, https://doi.org/10.1080/00918369.2018.1538407.

32. Kristina R. Olson, Aidan C. Key, and Nicholas R. Eaton, "Gender Cognition in Transgender Children," *Psychological Science* 26, no. 4 (2015): 467–474.

33. For a discussion of the gaps in research on gender development in children and where this field of research may be headed, see Christy L. Olezeski et al., "Assessing Gender in Young Children: Constructs and Considerations," *Psychology of Sexual Orientation and Gender Diversity* 7, no. 3 (September 2020): 293–303, http://dx.doi.org/10.1037/sgd0000381.

34. Steven Meanley et al., "The Interplay of Familial Warmth and LGBTQ+ Specific Family Rejection on LGBTQ+ Adolescents' Self-Esteem," *Journal of Adolescence* 93 (December 1, 2021): 40–52, https://doi.org/10.1016/j.adolescence.2021.10.002.

2

Supporting Trans Children

This is your time and it feels normal to you, but really, there is no normal. There's only change and resistance to it and then more change.

Meryl Streep

As part of a dominant culture or Western mindset, people commonly experience a great degree of hesitancy, or even overt resistance, to accepting the notion that a child might be transgender.[1] The urge to dismiss this notion is strong, yet it feels difficult to land on exactly why this is so. How can we move past this resistance and consider a proactive approach to supporting a child's gender identification? It may appear to some to be a rash, even ludicrous path. Health care providers, also, may feel at a loss, often defaulting to an overly cautious approach where they take no gender-supportive steps at all. Their hope is that by delaying this support, it will somehow result in the "phasing out" of the child's gender identification. Why is this resistance so powerful?

In this chapter, we will look at some of the historical sources of this collective resistance, which can delay, prolong, or prevent much-needed support for a transgender child. This resistance stems from a lack of visibility and awareness; outdated, inaccurate research; misrepresentations and vilification of trans people in literature, television, and film; religious doctrines that have influenced cultural mores; and a wide generational divide.

These combined factors result in a sociocultural void—trans children, we feel, do not, or should not, exist.

First, it is important to acknowledge that discussions exploring gender-diverse identities in humans *are* unfamiliar for many. Transgender people have been largely invisible within society until more recently, with only an occasional media story of a high-profile person's gender transition. Even with a gradual increase in visibility, there are still too few opportunities to deepen one's knowledge of gender diversity through educational pathways, the workplace, or social environments. Some people have never had the opportunity to meet a trans person or child. Others may be unaware of the trans people they *have* encountered.[2] This lack of personal context makes it difficult to incorporate new information into our established understanding of gender.

Couple this lack of familiarity with society's belief in an immutable, binary framework for understanding gender as strictly male or female, and we're left with no middle ground, no fluidity, and no room to incorporate the great variety of experiences that do exist.[3] Despite understanding that gender diversity is pervasive throughout the natural world—within both animal and plant kingdoms—there has been a degree of unwillingness to explore or acknowledge that this gender diversity extends to humans as well.

Unfamiliarity and gender rigidity are the tip of the iceberg when it comes to factors that contribute to this resistance. There are many fear-based misrepresentations of adult transgender individuals as sick or deviant, and next to no representations of children at all. The negativity toward adults and the invisibility of trans children contribute to making this a dangerous, unstable time for gender-diverse people. The societal stigma and vilification placed on adult trans lives are, by default, extended to the lives of trans children.[4] It is within this environment that trans children struggle to exist, often unable or afraid to voice their experiences. It is a crushing burden that trans children shoulder and one which any supportive adult caregiver struggles to navigate.

Without enough positive ways of identifying with others, children are unable to establish context for their internal experiences. If others refute, challenge, or invalidate that experience, this results in feelings of isolation, shame, and loneliness. If unchecked, continued negative impacts include lower cognitive functioning, higher levels of stress, and other long-term detrimental effects on their adult health.[5]

GUT REACTIONS

Within a fraction of a second of laying eyes on a stranger, we make some immediate observations, which may include a person's approximate age, skin color, height, and weight. As another second ticks by, we're likely to make other subconscious determinations, accurate or otherwise, about that person's sexuality, ethnicity, native language, education level, economic status, and level of physical ability. We may even guess their political affiliation. Of course, one of the first determinations we make is about a person's gender.

One second is a short amount of time to ascertain important information about a person. We do this subconsciously. There may be a degree of accuracy with some initial observations, but others may be wildly off. These immediate observations are part of human nature. The brain stem, sometimes referred to as the reptilian brain, comes into play when we encounter someone or something new. Like any other creature in the animal kingdom, we are determining possible friends (known) or potential foes (unknown). The brain stem dictates instinctual responses to any particular situation.

However, what makes humans distinct from the majority of the animal kingdom is the section of the brain known as the neocortex. Part of the functioning of the neocortex includes things like spatial reasoning, cognition, and language, which allow a person the opportunity to *assess their reaction* to an unknown situation or encounter—like meeting a trans person—and adjust accordingly. When we can delineate between an uncomfortable situation and one that is dangerous, we incorporate that understanding from then onward. But for people to make these cognitive adjustments, we must have access to accurate and authentic information, in this case, accurate and authentic representations of gender-diverse people.

Cognitive adjustments are hard to make, especially if people believe that they have never met a gender-diverse person; in fact, more Americans claim to have seen a ghost than the number of people who believe they have met a trans person.[6] They are even more likely to assume they have never met a trans child. As recently as thirty years ago, there was a belief that trans children did *not even exist*.[7] So, why wouldn't we be suspicious of today's visible presence of trans children, perhaps chalking it up to a temporary, trendy social phenomenon?

It's important to acknowledge that this invisibility or perceived non-existence was less a matter of actual visibility and more about *the inability to name, describe, or appropriately address what we were seeing*. In more recent years, language has emerged to describe gender differences—gender-diverse, transgender, gender-expansive, and nonbinary, among many others. Having this newer language helps us recognize that when we meet a transgender person, presumably "for the first time," it may *not* actually be our first exposure to gender-diverse people. If meeting a transgender person was simply a matter of the newness of an unfamiliar experience, we might merely puzzle at the novelty of it. Instead, there are more complicated factors that play into our initial reaction. We experience an uneasiness but may not recognize or understand why. These complicated layers come from influences such as societal biases, faulty research conclusions, and misinformation continually recycled online. Keeping in mind historical misinformation and the lack of adequate language to describe gender differences, I believe it is important to understand that we are not having an *instinctual* response. We are more likely reacting to the historical societal biases that *predispose* us toward negative reactions. These influences of the past continue to inform our societal contextualization—and dehumanization—of gender-diverse people today. What many people experience is an adverse emotional response that appears to validate that dehumanization. This dehumanization can result in alarming situations that can be very dangerous for gender-diverse people.

Violence and murder against trans people are rampant.[8] The continuation of violence sometimes occurs for the victim and/or victim's friends and family when the perpetrator employs a legal strategy sometimes referred to as the "trans panic defense."[9] This is a legal strategy in which a defendant explains or justifies their violent behavior and argues that they experienced an understandable, temporary loss of control upon learning of the victim's gender identity:

> In the documentary, *The Most Dangerous Year*, a middle-aged white man testified at a school board meeting. The board had invited a discussion regarding the adoption of a gender-inclusive policy. Shortly after Véondre, a twelve-year-old trans girl spoke to the board about what the policy would mean to her, the older man had this to say, "A transsexual's very presence as an 'anatomical opposite' constitutes an *assault* in and of itself."[10]

By recognizing the influence of biased perspectives—just as we do when encountering an individual, situation, or experience that is different than our own—we then learn to discern between what is *threatening* and what is simply *unfamiliar*.

MYTHS, STEREOTYPES, AND MISCHARACTERIZATIONS IN POPULAR CULTURE

Just because a person doesn't believe they have met a trans person before doesn't mean they lack a frame of reference for that experience. Most people have had some level of exposure to the topic through cultural references, including books, movies, and talk shows. These experiences are powerful influencers—whether we realize it or not—in shaping our individual and societal perceptions.

As a person who grew up in the 1970s, I encountered particular movies and TV shows that shaped my perceptions of trans people. One of the first was the iconic Alfred Hitchcock movie, *Psycho*, released in 1960, about a violent killer. While there is no mention of the main character's gender identity or expression, nor any mention of the word transgender or similar terminology, the audience readily connects the male killer's inclination to wear feminine attire and speak with a feminine voice with his violent, brutal acts.[11]

In a similar vein, the film *Silence of the Lambs* presents a deeply disturbed serial killer who is trying to "become" a woman in the most grotesque manner. There is a tepid effort to clarify that the killer is not a "true transsexual," but the source of this information, an equally grotesque killer, is unreliable and the qualifier is all but lost on most viewers. Both films portray transgender individuals as dangerous, deeply disturbed, and homicidal.[12]

The Crying Game, which garnered accolades in 1992, contained a shocking plot twist in which the main character discovers, in a moment of intimacy, that his love interest is actually a trans woman. His reaction is immediate as he races to the bathroom to vomit.[13]

Ace Ventura: Pet Detective, a comedy that came out two years after *The Crying Game*, took the disclosure theme to a new level. The main character in the film discovers he has *kissed* a trans woman—a discovery that leads to a lengthy, caricatured vomiting episode, as he curls up in the shower, sobs, and sets his clothes on fire.[14] The underlying themes in these two films include the perpetration of deception by the trans characters and revulsion and disgust on the part of those who are intimate with them.

Even movies with lasting popularity can reinforce negative portrayals of trans people. Consider the campy musical comedy *The Rocky Horror Picture Show*, a cult classic from the mid-1970s. The gender-bending lead character, Frank N. Furter, and his fellow alien cronies engage in sexual mayhem, murder, deception, cannibalism, and incest, all the while enticing/corrupting the unsuspecting Brad and Janet, an innocent young couple with the misfortune of experiencing car trouble.[15]

Saturday Night Live presented a popular sketch of a skeevy character named Pat, which spawned the film, *It's Pat: The Movie*. Pat's androgynous presentation left those around Pat unable to determine Pat's gender—and desperate to find out. Pat's simpering manner coupled with the gender-ambiguous presentation created significant discomfort in others, especially when conversations about sex and dating arose. Here, the transgender character was presented as deceitful, hypersexual, immoral, disgusting, and worthy of ridicule.[16]

In addition to the few above-mentioned films, numerous tabloid publications and television/radio talk shows over the decades have presented transgender people to the mainstream public as curious enigmas at best, and despicable, dangerous freaks at worst. These stories routinely focus on genital surgery—literally, what is in their pants—in an effort to satisfy titillated audiences.[17] Often, trans people are misrepresented as mentally incompetent or selfish, the latter quality seemingly validated by what is viewed by many as a trans person's narcissistic gender pursuit at all costs and at the expense of the feelings of family, friends, spouses, and children.

Interestingly, there are substantially fewer media portrayals that include trans male/masculine characters on talk shows, in films, or in television offerings portraying the lives of trans men or other gender diverse people (initially assigned the designation of female at birth). These portrayals came much later, such as the appearance of Dr. Jason Cromwell on the *Geraldo Rivera Show* (1988) and the film *Boys Don't Cry* (1999) with actors Hilary Swank and Chloë Sevigny.[18] These representations, however, still perpetuated the theme of duplicitousness (the implication being that these people are *really* female, and just pretending to be male) and, in the case of Dr. Cromwell, Geraldo's voyeuristic interest in discussing genitalia and genital surgery.

It is no wonder that with so much negative media representation, many people feel uncomfortable about transgender people. If the only visible portrayals of trans people have perpetuated themes of sexual deviancy, criminal insanity, duplicitousness, disgust, and revulsion, or a source of comedic ridicule, how can the average person possibly have an accurate or positive viewpoint?

IMPACT OF MISREPRESENTATION AND MYTHS

Until recently, it has been nearly impossible to find any positive portrayal of a trans *adult* in media or textbooks, or as having a valued leadership role in society. Many trans individuals, fully aware of the stigma associated with their experience, simply chose, if they were able, to live their lives in a low-profile or hidden way. Trans children have been even less visible. This is largely due to nonexistent pathways for affirming their gender identities. Nonexistent because, as minor dependents, these children have no autonomy to move forward without adult support or because society has only recently acknowledged that such pathways could or should exist for them. This lack of visibility fosters the assumption that trans children do not exist and, therefore, the question of supporting them becomes irrelevant and easily deniable.

Horrible media portrayals of trans people make the support of a trans child's identity appear to be an unconscionable act. The intensity of these stereotypes results in collective resistance to providing support for trans children. Even when presented with studies that show the positive outcomes of support, such as those published by the Family Acceptance Project (FAP) and the Trans Youth Project, parents and caregivers are still hesitant to provide this much-needed support.

Resistance is exacerbated by increasingly hostile nationwide legislative efforts that seek to criminalize the gender-affirming health care offered by medical providers and the affirming parenting practices of caregivers. These actions place the lives and futures of trans children in significant jeopardy.

PAST MISREPRESENTATIONS CANNOT BE APPLIED TO CHILDREN

If transgender identification is something we *only* associate with adults, it is easier to cling to our associations with deviant sexual practices, deceptive behaviors, or other immoral acts. Because society still associates trans identity with these undesirable traits and behaviors, it is understandable, albeit unfortunate, that we would be loath to affirm a *child's* gender identity as trans.[19]

Because of our mutual belief in the *innocence* of children, acceptance of a trans child's gender identity can seem paradoxical. Parents—when faced with their own child who emphatically, cautiously, or even fearfully declares their gender identification—feel this paradox, yet often have no idea how to resolve it.

We can start with an assumption that those who seem unsupportive of a trans child may not necessarily be unsupportive at all. As a result of pervasive misrepresentations, they may simply not know what constitutes best supportive practices. When we only have, as our framework, notions of trans people as mentally ill, perpetrators of deception, objects of disgust, people to ridicule, and sexual deviants, we might latch onto options promising to eliminate or convert a child's gender identity. This can lead many to seek a "cure," which has included some severe and damaging "therapies," including electroshock therapy, institutionalization, and conversion therapy.[20]

When provided with an opportunity to learn more, the majority of people, in my experience, recognize the impact of society's mischaracterizations of trans people and how it inhibits supportive paths for children. The validity of these mischaracterizations softens when we consider the existence of a trans child.

Their innocence provides us with a chance to reboot what we thought we knew. Not only can we provide gender-diverse children the support they need but we are better able to extend that acceptance to trans adults. After all, these adults were once trans children who had the misfortune to be born before society was ready to embrace them.

A DEARTH OF INFORMATION FOR FAMILIES

Not surprisingly, many parents today turn to the internet for information. While the information on the internet is more of a blessing today, it was certainly a curse for parents seeking resources just two decades ago. A web search for gender identity differences in children would have garnered very few results, most of which were contradictory, inaccurate, and ultimately not helpful.

In 2004, a parent of a trans teenage boy attended my conference, Gender Odyssey, an annual conference that, at the time, provided a range of supports and resources focused on the needs of trans and gender diverse *adults*. The family had traveled across two state lines desperate in their search for help. This father approached me and said, "Aidan, what do I do with my kid?" He was scared, confused, and did not know where to turn. While his internet search had led him to this conference, it had otherwise proved unfruitful. It was as close as he could get to finding resources.

It was not surprising, as the resources available at that time for transitioning adults were scarce and discussion of youth support had hardly begun. Any parent, like this father, inclined to turn to the internet for guidance was likely to be even more dismayed as an initial search like—a *boy who says he's a girl*—would have only garnered results from sites discussing abnormal psychological or sexual conditions, as well as a plethora of porn sites. Definitely nothing of relevance that could provide a parent a degree of comfort, much less positive guidance!

Today, a parent or educator's web search will be more fruitful. While there are a variety of articles, anecdotes, and research to be found at one's fingertips, it is important to recognize that some of the available information is still contradictory, outdated, and controversial. This contributes to a great deal of confusion for parents, educators, and other professionals as they seek information they can trust.

GENDER: NATURE VERSUS NURTURE?

Another source of misinformation that may contribute to a parent or provider's hesitancy is the belief that gender is malleable, or that it can be coaxed into a more fixed position, one that is aligned with society's cisgender, heteronormative expectations. Past research encouraged us to focus on the first several years of a gender-diverse child's life as the pivotal time in which a child's "confused" gender identification could be redirected. It was believed that a transgender child could be, with behavior-modifying efforts, directed toward the roles and behaviors associated with their designated biological sex. A convenient fiction, often cited as the source of many other societal ills, was the likelihood that a passive/ absent father and/or a domineering mother was the cause of a child's gender confusion. *Toss the football around, Dad. Mom, stop smothering him and don't let him play with dolls.* The implication at the time was that any child whose gender identity does not match their body is simply "confused" and the parent(s) are responsible.

The theory that gender is *nurture-based* (malleable by external influences) was tested in the mid-1960s on a young infant (not transgender) whose penis was severely damaged during circumcision. At the advice of Johns Hopkins psychologist, John Money, the family of this child raised him as a girl. Money, eager to validate his theory of gender malleability, deceptively reported the success of converting this child from a boy to a girl, despite the child's deep unhappiness and multiple suicide attempts by the time he had reached his teenage years. When, as a young man, he was finally told the truth about his childhood, he immediately stepped into his male identity. The tragic story, documented in the book *As Nature Made Him: The Boy Who Was Raised as a Girl*, by John Colapinto, details this child's lived experience.[21] Meanwhile, Money's "experiment" and self-touted success is misinforming the general public today, as well as those within the medical and mental health professions.[22]

Another school of thought is that gender is not malleable at all *and* that it is undeniably determined by genitalia and/or chromosomes alone. The theory that gender is *nature-based*, biologically determined by the presence of specific genitalia and chromosomes, is one that claims to provide concrete evidence by which one is designated as male or female. It is a theory to which many ascribe, but few realize the factual reality that the human genitalia, chromosomes, and endocrine systems are far more diverse than the binary pairings of penis/XY and vulva/XX so commonly taught in schools.

Either school of thought—nurture or nature—presumes that a person's gender identity will be male or female. But can we truly influence a child's nature from one gender to the other as if a switch were flipped from "on" to "off"? What if we did not exert enough influence? Would that gender identification get "stuck" in the middle? If gender is binary, and solely about chromosomes and genitalia, what about intersex differences like Androgen Insensitivity Syndrome (AIS)? What do we do about the child with AIS who is perceived by all, medical and laypeople alike, to be a girl who is later discovered to have XY chromosomes? Do we insist that she lives as a male because of what we can see only under a microscope? Both gender origin theories—nature and nurture—have aspects that are of value and worth consideration. Our environment does shape much of our identity and experience. Our physical body, genetics, and hormonal influences cannot be dismissed or discounted. We would do ourselves a greater service to consider a much broader picture including all the complexities of experience and natural diversity within the human species. Our impatient reliance on a binary framing of *anything*—a social issue, a human body, a personal experience—rarely gets us close to the brilliant complexity that is innately present. We can embrace a more expansive view that allows us to include children who experience their identity outside of the male/female binary—the nonbinary youth of today who are raising their voices with more and more frequency. Nature or nurture? It's simply not the right question.

PAST GENDER ASSESSMENT CRITERIA: USING BLUNT TOOLS TO UNDERSTAND A COMPLEX SUBJECT

A difficulty for someone conducting a web search today is that they are likely to find outdated information that offers simplistic "assessment criteria" for determining a child's gender identity. These older assessment versions—providing a checklist of sorts—often take the same misleading approach of relying on gender expression (hair, clothing, toy preferences, etc.) for discerning an identity determination. For example, a parent may encounter "diagnostic" questions like these:

- Does your child prefer clothing of the opposite gender?
- Does your child engage in activities of the opposite gender?
- Does your child adopt behaviors specific to the opposite gender?

Does a greater degree of masculinity/femininity mean a child is gay? A parent may read that a child's atypical *gender expression* is considered to be an indicator of their *sexual orientation* and that their feminine-expressing boy will grow up to be a gay man. Or they may read that a greater degree of feminine expression means that their child is transgender. So, is a boy who likes dolls and dresses really a transgender girl or a soon-to-be gay man? Neither?

This dated assessment approach does not distinguish between a child whose gender expression is what we consider to be feminine and a child who is clearly stating that their *gender identity is that of a girl*. Gender expression is simply how gender is expressed—toys, clothes, activities, interests—but is often mistakenly used as a shorthand indicator of either a child's gender identity or their sexual orientation when ultimately it is not a definitive indicator of either. The only thing we can say for sure about a boy who likes dolls is that *he is a child who likes dolls.*

That child may or may not grow up to be gay or trans but how the child expresses, identifies, or orients is not the point. If a child is experiencing bullying or other hardships because of their gender expression or identity, their needs should be immediately addressed regardless of *perceived* sexual orientation. In Chapter 3, we will look at the inaccuracy of framing a child's gender expression as an indicator of sexuality. This conflation of sexuality and identity all but ensure the likelihood that a child's need for protection will be delayed, minimized, or prevented altogether.

Without clarity and understanding, a parent (provider, teacher, or princi-pal) may feel as if *inaction and the withholding of support* are the best or only choices. "Let's wait and see if the child 'outgrows' this" is a common refrain. One decades-old study that parents may still encounter shows a high desistance rate for children with a transgender identification. Eighty percent of these children, the study says, will desist—or "outgrow"—this temporary cross-gender iden-tification.[23] Many parents, however, are unaware that this study (in addition to conflating the above-mentioned concepts of sexuality, identity, and gender interests) fails to mention that one of the reasons for this high desistance rate is a lack of reporting. Almost one-half of the participants *never completed the study*. The families dropped out. The outcomes for those participants were reported as "desisting" in their identification. The real story is simply not known because no one followed up with these families.

Nor did this study consider the impact of having little to no contextual understanding by which their families, peers, teachers, or society-at-large could provide support. It would have been very difficult for a child to persistently state their gender identity under those circumstances. If everyone and everything surrounding that child is explicitly or implicitly stating that the child's sense of their gender is an impossibility, it can easily erode a child's confidence. Gaining the acceptance and approval of those most crucial in a child's life means that a child may deny or repress their earlier stated gender identification if that acceptance and understanding are absent. Any number of the children might have then resorted to "denial" simply because they felt their survival depended upon it.

Again, we can't rely on a child's interests, behaviors, and preferences to be anything other than that. Sports were once considered the domain of boys. Housework was women's work. Pink was once a boy's color . . . until that too changed. What is normal? At what point is a child's expression deemed not "normal"? How does a provider take into consideration any racial and/or cultural distinctions when considering "normal"? One community's acceptance of what is considered an acceptable "masculine" expression for a girl could inspire a high degree of distress for a family within another community whose daughter has identical interests. How does any research study or gender assessment criteria account for the greater tolerance for "masculine" expression in girls and adjust for the much deeper intolerance of "feminine" expression in boys?

What counts as feminine or masculine and who decides? Do we have a way to concretely define a criterion for all societal variations and norms? Of course not. These variations in societal norms are many and change over time—geography, culture, faith, place, and age are only a few of the conditions that drive this diversity. Many understand the hand-holding practice of Arab men to be a show of affection and friendship while the same public gesture elsewhere would be interpreted as an indicator of homosexuality and could result in name-calling, assault, or even death.

It bears repeating that the only thing we can definitively state about gender expression is that it is an amorphous, evolving, distinctly individual way of expressing preferences or interests. And, that it is unreliable as a predictor of gender identity.

Like many in our society today, the authors of older studies conflated sexual orientation, gender identity, and gender expression in their research methods.

These studies did not consider what we more clearly understand today to be distinct variables (expression, identity, and orientation) that need both independent *and* interconnected consideration. If we do not consider the independence and interconnection of these aspects, it can prevent parents, teachers, or providers from having clarity on any specific child's needs.

REPARATIVE THERAPY

Reparative therapy, sometimes called conversion therapy, is a discredited therapeutic approach that presumed an ability to change a person's sexual orientation and/or gender identity. Reparative or conversion therapy was carried out primarily by religious leaders, licensed counselors, and even peer support groups in the attempt to change a person's sexual orientation or gender identity. These interventions, most often based on religious dogma, are considered dangerous and harmful and all major medical associations have denounced these practices.[24] An increasing number of states and municipalities have regulated against the use of these practices on minors. These laws, when challenged, have been upheld by higher courts in the United States and other parts of the world. Professional entities like the American Psychiatric Association, American Psychological Association, American Academy of Pediatrics, American College of Physicians, American Medical Association, American Association for Marriage and Family Therapy, National Association of Social Workers, and the American School Counselors and School Health Associations oppose conversion therapy and advocate for the support and validation of a student's gender identity.

The challenge for a parent comes when an internet search generates results of reparative therapeutic modalities promising to "cure" or permanently repress a child's gender identification. These modalities, when offered by religious groups, consider sexual orientation and gender identities outside of the cultural norm to be a pathological state and/or psychological illness. The person in question is considered to be "trapped in the lifestyle" and the hope is that God would cure or transform them.

Small ministries began to crop up during the mid-1970s to address sickness, sin, or even crimes against God, believing that the hand of the Lord could pull the person out of the darkness.[25] These institutional approaches were predicated on the idea that a child must have been traumatized, abused, or neglected; for example, a boy may have been abused by his father, and that broken relationship with the father caused the identity problem. Political advocacy groups cropped up as an outgrowth of these religious mandates, and some practicing psychologists partnered with religious organizations.

Today, many parents, recognizing that the life experience of a transgender person can be difficult, even dangerous, will still clutch at the promises of reparative therapy, hoping for an elusive but "positive" outcome. Unfortunately, conversion therapy still exists, primarily in religious organizations which continue to try to influence political legislation.

It is no wonder that these religious, political, and psychological influences of the past still strongly impact a parent who clings to hope that "this will all go away." They may not necessarily be steeped in anti-trans bias; rather, they are simply a terrified parent that wants what is best for their child.[26] In over fifteen years of leading support programs for thousands of parents of trans and gender diverse children, I've met only two families who, at the outset, were excited to realize their child was trans. The rest struggled. The thing that these two families had in common was that they both felt they were dangerously close to losing their children to suicide. Understanding that their child's distress was originating from an unexpressed gender difference meant they had something tangible to address. A trans child was a far better parental challenge to navigate than losing their child entirely. Only one additional family expressed a positive reaction when learning their child was transgender—he disclosed this when he had finally completed his chemotherapy treatments. When faced with the prospect of their child's death, managing a gender identity journey seemed pretty reasonable.

BRIDGING A GENERATIONAL DIVIDE

Generational differences can play a role in a person's initial ability to understand the concept of gender identity. Teachers and administrators from earlier generations may struggle to distinguish between gender identity and sexual orientation because gender was firmly believed to be a result of biological determinism. The rarely visible transgender person was considered to be suffering from a mental illness that *seemed* to be somehow linked to sexuality. The younger colleagues of these educators are often better able to grasp the distinctions between a person's gender expression, anatomy, identity, and orientation simply because those concepts, and their delineation of them, are more understood today. They have also had the benefit of pursuing their education during a time of greater scientific, psychological, and sociological advances in the study of gender.

While adults—parents, teachers, administrators, and staff—try to understand the sources of collective distress with the goal of addressing it in a respectful, compassionate manner, we should also recognize that children today are not growing up with the same false representations and misinformation that we faced. Consequently, many young people lack the negative preconceptions that we are burdened with. Younger generations give validity to the notion of gender identity. Many of the cultural portrayals described earlier in this chapter are decades old, and today's teens have access to more positive representations of trans characters in a variety of media. Filmmakers are adding depth and integrity to trans characters, talk shows and documentaries are moving beyond the more prurient questions when featuring trans lives, and youth-centric TV shows are incorporating trans characters in a much more positive light. The reality television series, *I Am Jazz*, premiering in 2015, features a trans teenage girl as she navigates her day-to-day life. This acclaimed series is providing our nation's youth with a much different first impression of trans individuals than that of older generations and has inspired educators to focus on it in K–12 units and lesson plans.[27] While there is still a long way to go, the effect of these improved and more realistic representations is evident in the lives of younger generations.

This resulting demystification of trans lives for younger generations was underscored for me during a high school staff training. The principal shared with the teaching staff that, while they as staff had had many in-depth conversations about gender, he had had a much different experience with one particular student. As the principal was sharing some of the staff discussion with the student, he shrugged and said, "Why are you all *still* talking about this? What is the big deal?"

When we reflect on the disparaging representations of trans people that came out of popular culture, it's important to have compassion for ourselves, for others, and especially for the trans children we encounter along the way.

We may be stymied by the complexities we encounter. We have difficulty relating to a child's experience of a gender disconnect, of mind and body not aligned. Because *we* may struggle to personally relate to a gender identity difference, we tend to presume that our sense of gender *congruence* serves as validation that the child's experience *must not be real*. If we are unable to find a pathway to increase our understanding, we may simply deny the validity of a child's experience before any real inquiry has begun.

Honoring a child's pursuit of gender self-determination and allowing time for that exploration is all we need to do. We must recognize the immensity of the human experience, even if it makes us feel unsettled.

DON'T GIVE UP—ACCURATE INFORMATION IS OUT THERE

Historical factors, such as media mischaracterizations of trans people and the visceral reactions they inspire, the invisibility of trans lives, the troublesome conflation of gender identity with sexual orientation, minimal resources, and harmful reparative therapy efforts, have shaped—or misshaped—societal perceptions. But society has progressed, nonetheless. We have new, more accurate research, greater visibility of trans lives, and both parents and providers recognize the importance of supporting a child's gender identity rather than suppressing or denying it. This means our society is at a crossroads. Moving from the past, assessing the present, and stepping into a future we are just beginning to imagine.

This paradigm shift means that, for some, the notion of moving forward in an accepting and expansive manner is reasonable and necessary. Gender identity is viewed as a self-determined, normal part of our human lives. For others, this shift feels threatening and dangerous. The prospect of moving forward feels reckless and uninformed. We must examine this paradigm shift for exactly what it is and especially *when* it is occurring, that is, right now! If we recognize we are in a crucial moment in history, we will more clearly recognize our top priority—supporting these trans and nonbinary children. While trans adults have been making strides, those strides don't particularly "trickle down" to inform the paths of children. The gender-diverse children of today *are* creating the pathways for future trans children. They desperately need adults to step in so they do not bear the brunt of the inevitable upheaval that is always associated with significant societal change.

Is there current and accurate information to be found on the internet? Absolutely! Is it sometimes difficult to find? Yes! Competing articles and divergent perspectives are rampant. How does one discern the chaff from the wheat? My recommendation to parents, teachers, and providers is multifold. Read books from authors like Dr. Diane Ehrensaft and Dr. Michele Angello, two psychologists with extensive experience on the subject of gender diversity in children.[28] Find current research that not only discusses gender identification in children, but that also emphasizes the impact and importance of family support throughout the journey. Two such sources for this research are the Trans Youth Project at Princeton University and the Williams Institute, a public policy research institute that focuses on gender identities.

Find other families willing to share their stories—they will have both shared experiences and ways in which their stories are uniquely different. Parents and caregivers should seek out or create support groups to decrease their sense of isolation. This will help a family gain a broader, more accurate perspective. National organizations like TransFamilies.org offer direct support to families of gender-diverse children and can also point to additional resources. GenderDiversity.org provides training and professional development for K–12 educators and other youth-serving agencies and organizations. Work to create a supportive home and school environment and then observe the impact on the child. While easier said than done, do not fear the unknown.

If we look at gender through the present-day lens—the lens that better serves the needs of our gender-diverse children—we will see our way to a deeper understanding of them and, frankly, a deeper understanding of ourselves.

NOTES

1. For a discussion of the dominant culture world view and how it impacts transgender children, see sj Miller, *Teaching, Affirming, and Recognizing Trans* and Gender Creative Youth: A Queer Literacy Framework*, Queer Studies and Education (New York: Palgrave Macmillan, 2019), 64.

2. Laura Erickson-Schroth and Laura A. Jacobs, *"You're in the Wrong Bathroom!": And 20 Other Myths and Misconceptions about Transgender and Gender-Nonconforming People* (Boston: Beacon Press, 2017), 3–7.

3. Sally Hines, *Is Gender Fluid? A Primer for the 21st Century*, The Big Idea (London; New York: Thames & Hudson, 2018), 85.

4. "Negative Trans Media Depictions Harm the Community's Mental Health." *them* (November 25, 2020), https://www.them.us/story/negative-media-depictions-trans-peo ple-harms-communitys-mental-health.

5. Jae A. Puckett et al., "Coping with Discrimination: The Insidious Effects of Gender Minority Stigma on Depression and Anxiety in Transgender Individuals," *Journal of Clinical Psychology* 76, no. 1 (January 2020): 176–194, https://doi.org/10.1002/jclp.22865.

6. Marissa Higgins, "More Americans Claim to Have Seen a Ghost Than Met a Trans Person & It's the Most Depressingly Perfect Metaphor for Trans Invisibility," *Bustle* (December 21, 2015), https://www.bustle.com/articles/131279-more-americans-claim-to-have-seen-a-ghost-than-met-a-trans-person-its-the.

7. For a discussion of the emergence of the trans child as a social category, see Tey Meadow, *Trans Kids: Being Gendered in the Twenty-First Century* (Oakland: University of California Press, 2018), 73.

8. "Transgender People over Four Times More Likely than Cisgender People to Be Victims of Violent Crime," Williams Institute, https://williamsinstitute.law.ucla.edu/press/ncvs-trans-press-release/.

9. "Banning the Use of Gay and Trans Panic Defenses," Williams Institute, https://williamsin stitute.law.ucla.edu/publications/model-leg-gay-trans-panic/.

10. Vlada Knowlton, *The Most Dangerous Year* (Marymoor Productions, 2019), 1.21.

11. Alfred Hitchcock, *Psycho* (Shamley Productions, 1960).

12. Jonathan Demme, *The Silence of the Lambs* (Strong Heart/Demme Production, Orion Pictures, 1991).

13. Neil Jordan, *The Crying Game* (Palace Pictures, Channel Four Films, Eurotrustees, 1993).

14. Tom Shadyac, *Ace Ventura: Pet Detective* (Morgan Creek Entertainment, 1994).

15. Jim Sharman, *The Rocky Horror Picture Show* (Twentieth Century Fox, Michael White Productions, 1975).

16. Adam Bernstein, *It's Pat: The Movie* (Touchstone Pictures, 1994).

17. For a discussion of the inappropriate attention paid to transgender bodies, see Laura Erickson-Schroth and Laura A. Jacobs, *"You're in the Wrong Bathroom!": And 20 Other Myths and Misconceptions about Transgender and Gender-Nonconforming People* (Boston: Beacon Press, 2017), 45–48.

18. See "Transsexuals and Their Families," *Geraldo Rivera* (1988), http://www.visual-icon.com; Kimberly Peirce, *Boys Don't Cry* (Fox Searchlight Pictures, The Independent Film Channel Productions, Killer Films, 2000).

19. The intricacies of children and childhood in relation to race, gender, and sexuality are well laid out in the following texts: Kathryn Bond Stockton, *The Queer Child, or Growing Sideways in the Twentieth Century*, Series Q (Durham: Duke University Press, 2009); Jules Gill-Peterson, *Histories of the Transgender Child* (Minneapolis: University of Minnesota Press, 2018).

20. Amy E. Green et al., "Self-Reported Conversion Efforts and Suicidality Among US LGBTQ Youths and Young Adults, 2018," *American Journal of Public Health* 110, no. 8 (August 2020): 1221–1227, https://doi.org/10.2105/AJPH.2020.305701.

21. John Colapinto, *As Nature Made Him: The Boy Who Was Raised as a Girl*, 2nd ed. (New York; London; Toronto; Sydney: Harper Perennial, 2006).

22. Jules Gill-Peterson, *Histories of the Transgender Child* (Minneapolis: University of Minnesota Press, 2018), 129–162.

23. For a comprehensive examination of some of these early studies and the desistance/persistence narrative going forward in time, see Tey Meadow, *Trans Kids: Being Gendered in the Twenty-First Century* (Oakland: University of California Press, 2018), 73–81.

24. Jessica N. Fish and Stephen T. Russell, "Sexual Orientation and Gender Identity Change Efforts Are Unethical and Harmful," *American Journal of Public Health* 110, no. 8 (August 2020): 1113–1114, https://doi.org/10.2105/AJPH.2020.305765.

25. Kristine Stolakis, *Pray Away* (Artemis Rising Foundation, Blumhouse Productions, Chicken and Egg Pictures, 2021), https://www.imdb.com/title/tt11224358/.

26. Today, parents can turn to resources that provide specific guidance: Owl Fisher and Fox Fisher, *Trans Teen Survival Guide* (London; Philadelphia: Jessica Kingsley Publishers, 2019).

27. Ashley Lauren Sullivan, "Kindergartners Studying Trans* Issues Through *I Am Jazz*," in *Teaching, Affirming, and Recognizing Trans* and Gender Creative Youth: A Queer Literacy Framework*, ed. sj Miller (New York: Palgrave Macmillan, 2019), 63–80.

28. See Diane Ehrensaft, *The Gender Creative Child: Pathways for Nurturing and Supporting Children Who Live Outside Gender Boxes* (New York: Experiment, 2016); Michele Angello and Alisa Bowman, *Raising the Transgender Child: A Complete Guide for Parents, Families & Caregivers* (Berkeley: Seal Press, A Hachette Book Group Company, 2016).

Teaching Gender

The AEIOU Framework

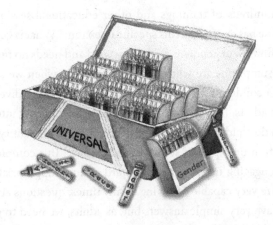

Rather than discard the way we have viewed gender, we can embrace an expanded framework—one that gives attention, clarity, and distinction to what we already know.

Aidan Key

As a gender diversity educator, I hope to serve as a guide through the hidden terrain of *gender identity*, which, until more recent times, has been unfamiliar to many people. Concrete stories that highlight the experiences of transgender children are illuminating and helpful, but if we are to truly understand concepts like gender identity and gender expression or what it feels like for a child to have a sense of gender that is different from their physical bodies, we'll need to dig in a little further.

How do these terms apply to *any* individual and then, more specifically, to gender-diverse children? We need to understand the realities of these different worlds—the experience of the trans or nonbinary child and that of the typically gendered parent, teacher, or ally who has had little opportunity to consider gender outside the fixed notions of female and male. We need to build bridges between these experiences so that parents, teachers, doctors, therapists, and other influential adults can be part of the collective that enables a trans child the opportunity to thrive.

WHAT DO WE MEAN WHEN WE SAY THE WORD *GENDER*?

Throughout hundreds of trainings and other educational sessions I've led or attended, no one has ever asked this specific question: "What is gender?" People believe the definition of gender is straightforward and needs no further explanation. These assumptions are what get us into trouble when we approach conversations with children that explore the concepts of gender diversity. In some respect, we, as adults, incorporate a much greater complexity into the concept of gender than do children. We include separate aspects of identity; for example, sexual orientation or expected societal gender roles. This complexity can prevent us from engaging in the straightforward and age-appropriate discussions that children are very capable of having. Many times, questions about transgender children have very simple answers but, as adults, we need to get out of our own way to understand these concepts.

If we have a common framework for understanding and delineating the conceptual layers that we bring into discussions of gender, we will better be able to reason and intuit our way through these layers. Acquiring this shared framework is beneficial to all educators, students, and their families independent of any political, cultural, and faith-based differences.

WHAT ADULTS HAVE TO SAY ABOUT GENDER

If I were to ask any adult audience how they might truly determine someone's gender, the majority would likely comment on biological distinctions: specifically, genitalia. Some might bring up chromosomal differences. The collective agreement?

Girls/women have vaginas and XX chromosomes.

Boys/men have penises and XY chromosomes.

Simple, end of the story, right?

Let's start there . . .

Anatomy

It is important to recognize the distinction between a person's gender and the biological indicators of that person's anatomical sex. These two factors might be congruent for some, but not for others. Most people consider gender to be fairly straightforward—a person is either female or male, with corresponding genitalia and anatomy. Yet, with an examination of the anatomical complexity of humans, we soon discover a different reality. We tend to think of anatomy in terms of body parts, but it includes our cellular makeup as well.

For most of us, our lived experience has reinforced this simplistic portrayal of these biological differences between men and women. Even those who have advanced beyond health class or high school biology may have only minimally delved into the complex diversity of the human body, including internal and external genitalia differences and chromosomal variations.

Yet, anatomical sex is not a simple matter. Various "intersex" differences, such as Turner's Syndrome, Klinefelter's Syndrome, and others, result in chromosomal variations beyond XX and XY, such as XXY, XYY, XO, a single X, and even a combined XX, XY.[1] Biological variations are not exclusive to chromosomes, but they also extend to gonadal differences and atypical genitalia that don't fall neatly into the categories of penis and vagina.

The average adult hasn't had the necessity or opportunity to learn about intersex differences. These are sometimes referred to as Disorders of Sex Development, or DSDs for short, and this language has evolved over time to *Differences* in Sex Development.[2] Even if one is somewhat familiar with intersex differences, the belief may be that it is an extremely rare biological fluke that should be corrected with surgery at the earliest opportunity.

I regularly poll my professional audiences as to whether they've ever heard the term "intersex." Sometimes there won't be a single hand raised. Other times, at least half of the hands go up. This is not a case of ignorance, but simply a lack of exposure to the topic.

Intersex differences are surprisingly common, with more than thirty different intersex differences of varying frequencies documented.[3] Some are minor in the way they manifest, while others may require medical intervention. In fact, a person may not even be aware that they have an intersex difference. Estimates of the frequency of intersex differences vary depending on how they are classified. But, regardless of which estimates you examine, all differences present at a much higher frequency than the average person might expect. One study estimates that "the frequency of deviation from the ideal [sic] male or female" may be as high as two percent of live births![4] To put this in context, identical twins occur in approximately one in one thousand births. Most people have met a set of identical twins, so it's reasonable to assume that it is *significantly more likely* that someone has met a person with an intersex difference.

Assuming that a person *is* aware that they have an intersex difference, the misperceptions and stigmatization surrounding this, and the lack of societal awareness, may cause them to cautiously disclose this information only to those closest to them.[5] Medical professionals have historically advised patients with intersex differences to not disclose this information.

A colleague of mine shared her story with me:

As a young teenager, many of my girlfriends were starting their periods. I waited for it, but nothing happened. So, I went to ask my mother about this and she said, "Honey, all the women in our family are late-bloomers. One, don't worry, it's coming, and two, enjoy the time off while you have it!" Time marched on. I'm sixteen, seventeen, eighteen, and still not menstruating. I graduated from high school and got married. Nothing. At age twenty-two, I needed to understand what was or, in my case, wasn't happening and why. So, I went to the doctor. He ran tests. I returned to hear the results. When I entered the doctor's office, he said, "Sit down." Not what I wanted to hear!

"You have AIS," he said. "That stands for Androgen Insensitivity Syndrome. What that means is that, in utero, you were male. You have XY chromosomes. But your body is not able to respond to androgens, and therefore you developed as a female. I'm sorry, but you won't be able to have children. It's best that you don't talk about it and just go on with your life."

Stunned and devastated, I went home to my husband. It took me a long time, between sobs and tears, to tell him. I was sure he would want a divorce.

He paused for a few seconds and then said, "Okay, honey, but what's for dinner?" I've been married for decades since.

The hardest part was the shame I felt at my "secret." I held that in, at my doctor's advice, for many years. Finally, I said, "No more!" I began to share my story—without apology or shame. I found so many others who had AIS like I did and those with other intersex differences as well. We had many different stories, but what we all had in common was that we had struggled with the shame and stigma placed on us by an uninformed society. Now, I offer support to others and it makes all the difference in the world, to them, and to me!

Androgen Insensitivity Syndrome is just one example of an intersex/DSD difference that is not immediately identifiable at birth. If one were to rely solely on chromosomes to determine gender, the woman in the story above would be classified as male. If the gender determination were based on external genitalia, she would be classified as female. Other intersex differences can result in a single person having different chromosomal variations, known as mosaicism, in different locations of their own body.[6] The diverse ways in which humans develop can include genetic predisposition, in utero environs, and potentially other factors that make it difficult for many to ever fully know the "reason" for having one of these differences.

ARE YOU SAYING THAT HAVING AN INTERSEX DIFFERENCE IS
THE SAME AS BEING TRANSGENDER?
DSDs or "differences of sex development" (once referred to as *disorders* of sex development) are defined by congenital conditions in which the development of chromosomal, gonadal, or anatomic sex is atypical. By definition, then, being transgender is not an intersex difference.[7] However, there are a growing number of studies that suggest a biological origin for those whose gender identity differs from the sex they were assigned at birth (i.e., transgender). The conclusions point to neuroanatomical differences in transgender people that provide a biological basis for atypical gender identity.[8] Thus, some medical researchers are beginning to view cross-gender identification as a possible intersex difference.

I've found that it's helpful for adults—parents, teachers, and others—to hear about these biological and chromosomal distinctions, and the frequency within which they occur, to (1) gain an understanding of the complexity of the human physical experience, and (2) let go of an inaccurate measure (genitalia) for the designation of a person's gender.

Whether a person has any familiarity with intersex differences is not really the point; neither is the presence of XX, XY, XO, XXY, or XYY chromosomes, especially as the vast majority of people never have chromosomal testing. *The existence of chromosomal and gonadal variation is relevant because people make gender determinations every day based on an assumed presence of specific genitalia and chromosomes, not actual fact.* Examining these scientific truths of the physiological human experience provides a way to examine gender in greater detail, beyond a nonexistent, yet entrenched, genitalia/chromosomal "truth."

AM I SUPPOSED TO EXPLAIN ALL OF THIS TO CHILDREN?

While the discussion of biological diversity can help adults better understand physical realities, it isn't necessary to have these conversations with young children. This is not because I underestimate the intelligence of children, but rather because, in my experience, children make gender determinations based on what they *actually see*, not on assumptions about what they don't.

Children will sometimes bring up questions about "private parts" in relation to a transgender student, and a teacher may feel unsure of how to respond. In this case, a simple comparison test can help a teacher readily identify the best course of action. Ask yourself, "Would I talk about a child's genitals with another student for any other reason?" The answer, we know, is definitely not! Such discussions are not appropriate. A simple response to children is that private parts are called "private" for a very good reason and that that child would not want their private parts discussed with others.

If another parent were to make an inquiry about a trans student's body (yes, they sometimes do), the response would be similar. It is not appropriate for school personnel to discuss personal information regarding a student with any other person. A reminder of a student's federally mandated right to privacy is usually all that is needed to quell any further inappropriate questions.

Gender Expression

The canine species has a norm of sniffing what we consider pretty intimate areas. Dogs are literally sniffing out important information about the other—its gender, emotional state, diet, and more.[9] While this might work for dogs, we as humans are (thankfully!) less direct.

We do not have a cultural norm of *visibly* presenting our genitalia upon meeting to express our gender. Because no skirt-lifting or pants-dropping is expected, we rely instead on *assumptions* about the presence of certain genitalia in deciding about another person's gender. Neither do we expect lab results documenting androgen levels or chromosome test results to communicate our gender to each other. *Adults make gender determinations about people in the same way children do—based only on what we observe.*

WHAT CHILDREN HAVE TO SAY ABOUT GENDER

When children are asked about the differences between girls and boys, they mention any number of variables, such as hair length, the sound of a voice, wearing certain clothing, the presence of jewelry, body shape, and so on. The qualities we observe are referred to as a person's *gender expression.*

Yet children, like adults, also recognize that there are variations and exceptions to these characteristics. Both men and women may have either long or short hair. Women and men have wide vocal ranges. Bodies come in all shapes and sizes. Clothing, makeup, jewelry, and other accessories vary significantly, especially when one considers societal norms and other influential variables like geographical location or historical shifts.

That said, within a fraction of a second of meeting a stranger, we can and do make a gender determination for that person. Interestingly, we don't often make a mistake; however, the visual cues we observe, coupled with assumptions of specific genitalia, are just that—observations and assumptions. The reason we are so often accurate in our day-to-day gender determinations is simply that these observations and assumptions will work for a *majority* of people, just not all.

We rely on societal norms to determine gender, but these norms do not work for everyone. These cues are not absolute, nor are they consistent over time. They never have been and never will be unchanging because humans are amazingly complex and diverse. The limitations of gender expression that are arbitrarily imposed by society don't only impact transgender children. These rigid norms limit the natural gender expression of just about anyone at some point in their life.

HOW CHILDREN THINK ABOUT GENDER

Children learn the gender norms of our society early—if not before, then certainly by the time they are of school age.[10] Their understanding of gender is informed by their families, peers, media, consumer messaging, and their day-to-day experiences within the communities to which they belong. A child's sense of self within these environments and experiences is also an integral component.

It's important to understand that the way these younger children engage in gender conversations is quite different than those of adults. They approach the topic of gender with the same simplicity that we, as adults, once did. Kindergartners rely almost exclusively on a person's outward appearance, again, their *gender expression* (which will be discussed further in this chapter), to describe how they make a gender determination for any person they may encounter.[11]

For example, when asked about gender—"How do you know if someone is a boy or a girl?"—the answers that children supply are quite different from the genital- or chromosome-centric answers provided by adults. There are two things that are important to recognize about this child-versus-adult perspective. One, while adults identify genitalia/chromosomal differences as the primary way to distinguish between genders, no one, adult or otherwise, is *observing, or expecting to observe, a person's genitalia or chromosomes* before making that gender determination for that individual. Nor are they expecting physiological confirmation any time *after* that initial determination either. Secondly, adults, like children, rely on an individual's gender expression to know whether that person is female or male (getting it right much of the time) but they also understand that they don't *always* get it right.

How do preschoolers and kindergartners step into gender discussions? What do they actually say? The discussions I've had in classrooms typically start like this: "Hey kids, I wonder if anyone can tell me, how do you know if someone is a boy or a girl?"

They answer easily, with responses that fall within categories like these:

- Hair: "Girls have long hair, boys don't."
- Clothing: "Girls wear dresses, boys don't."
- Accessories: "Boys don't paint their fingernails."
- Toy choices: "Girls play with dolls, boys play with trucks."
- Sports and other activities: "Boys play football, girls don't."
- Colors: "Pink is a girls' color, blue is for boys"
- Height: "Boys are tall, girls are short."

As is clear in these examples of gender expression, children learn narrow gender norms early in life. As adults, we too will have clear, early childhood memories that are related to our gender expression. It is often easiest to recall situations where we were told we *couldn't* do something because of our gender:

- Get a hold of yourself—boys don't cry!
- Girls shouldn't get dirty.
- No, you can't have a doll!
- Yes, you have to wear a dress.

Girls shouldn't climb trees; boys can't wear fancy shoes—the list goes on and on. Depending on the vehemence in which these particular messages are delivered, and by whom, children can feel a range of emotions: disappointment, embarrassment, shame, anger, confusion, or a sense of injustice.

Of course, not all gender messages are negative, but they are still there, ever present. Parents might say to a boy, "You were so brave after you scraped your knee, you didn't even cry," or to a girl, "You look so pretty in that beautiful dress, and you kept it so clean all day!" Praise, yes, but with a subtler, stereotypical gender subtext.

All children are affected and molded by these constant messages about gender expression, not just transgender children. Children learn quickly to stifle some aspects of their expression so that they aren't singled out for punishment or ridicule. The child with a gender expression that is different, unique, or unexpected stands out. There is almost an urgency on the part of adults to ensure children conform, especially as they mature. It is this early enforcement of inflexible gender norms—consciously or subconsciously—that can adversely affect a child with a unique gender expression. Because children naturally want to be accepted and to belong, the pressure to conform to these norms weighs heavily and they often acquiesce to their own detriment. So how might this change for the better? How do we support a child's authentic gender expression?

DISCUSSING GENDER EXPRESSION WITH CHILDREN IN THE CLASSROOM

Any teacher can lead positive, age-appropriate conversations about gender expression with their students. It is not necessary to have any understanding of a transgender experience to do this! I've yet to encounter a teacher who didn't feel like they could lead this kind of discussion when they were provided some sample conversation prompts, such as "How do you know if someone is a boy or girl?" or "What are some things that only girls can do or only boys can do?"

Why talk about gender expression with children at all? What will that accomplish? The reasons are simple and straightforward: all children, not just trans children, have distinct ways of expressing their gender. Some expressions of gender might remain consistent throughout a child's growing up, but it is more likely that it will change over time. A child's favorite activity in kindergarten is not likely to be the same activity they enjoy in the fifth grade. An interest in drawing may fade as a student encounters a theater program, while an avid kickball player in elementary school later develops an interest in high school track and field. Leading conversations about gender expression can create a rich environment filled with acceptance, exploration, and flexibility. It can give a child greater freedom to find themselves and pursue their interests independent of the confines of gender stereotypes.

It can really be straightforward. Here are some simple concepts easily understood by young children:

- Toys are toys
- Colors are just colors
- Our friends are our friends, and they can be boys and girls.
- Games, sports, and activities are just things we like to do.
- We're similar in some ways and unique in others. Let's celebrate our uniqueness!

As simple as these examples are, don't be afraid to bring in some complexity for these children. Don't underestimate them—they can handle it! Older students will be excited to explore the intersections of identity such as racial or class differences and explore how this may shift and influence gender expression. For example, a classroom teacher could pose questions like the following:

What are some of the inconsistencies we encounter—with respect to gender expression—that we may not notice? What do we choose to overlook? What do we simply accept without acknowledging it? For example, we consider pink to be a "girl's" color yet a number of glam rockers wear pink, right? Why is that? Did you also know that pink was considered to be a "boy's" color until the mid-1900s? Why do you think it changes? We don't expect men to wear skirts, yet some do. Depending on the type of skirt, we feel some situations are acceptable (ex. the Scottish kilt) and some are not. Yet, we have some double standards too—think about RuPaul, Elton John, and just about any "glam" rocker or "hair-metal band" that ever existed. Why do we accept some situations and mock others?[12]

Younger students can engage in this conversation, too. Instead of posing a question, a teacher might present images from magazines or the internet showing mass marketing of pink toys and clothing to girls juxtaposed with images of men wearing pink. The teacher could then ask the students to comment as to why these seemingly contradictory images exist. Students of any age would likely enjoy the YouTube rant of young Riley as she expresses her frustration at the gendered marketing of toys at a particular toy company.[13]

ENCOURAGE CHILDREN TO DIG DEEPER

Exploring societal inconsistencies of gender expression, or shifts that occur over time, can be very eye-opening for students and teachers alike. These conversations will deepen as other factors are considered in relation to gender expression:

- Shifts over time and the reasons for those shifts;
- Cultural norms including the influence of language differences and immigrant status;
- Distinctions and expectations based on race and ethnicity;
- Geographic differences when considering rural, urban, suburban environments;
- The influence of any particular individual's status and power; and
- Class distinctions that inform what, when, and for whom certain expressions are acceptable.

Children of all ages are able to engage in these conversations when these factors are discussed using age-appropriate language. The influence of power and status, for example, could be addressed in this way for children in the earlier elementary grades:

Someone tells you that you shouldn't wear the clothes you want to wear. How do you feel about this and what do you do if . . . ?

1. ... that person is a kid in your class?
2. ... that person is your younger sibling?
3. ... that person is the principal?
4. ... that person is your parent?

Making note of the varied responses that occur in these different scenarios will then make room for introducing the concepts of power and authority and how they influence our feelings and choices. When starting a conversational activity such as engaging children with the questions listed above, it can be helpful for teachers to think back to when they were young children and consider whether they were prevented from engaging in an interest or activity because of their gender. They might remember how they felt at the time—the frustration, disappointment, shame, anger, or embarrassment. Remembering these experiences and accompanying feelings can help teachers and other adults comprehend how children today might feel in similar situations.

While at the outset some teachers may feel a little nervous to lead conversations about gender expression, they usually experience a sense of relief and excitement once they've done so. The relief comes about because of the simplicity or "face value" with which kids engage the topic. Teachers soon realize that they already have the skills needed to engage in these discussions. After all, these discussions are not so different from discussions of gender equality, for example, that have been going on for generations.

One teacher said this about her experience:

I wasn't sure what to expect when the students all circled up. One thing I discovered for sure is that I worried way too much! The students were very excited to talk about gender in this way *and* they took it all at face value. I realized that *I* was the one complicating things in my own mind, not them. What a relief!

Another teacher had this to say:

It sure was an eye-opener to hear what the kids had to say. As we talked about things like dolls, trucks, football, and dresses, all the kids agreed. *Toys are just toys. Clothes are just clothes and colors are just colors. We should all be able to play the games we want, wear the clothes we like best, and do the things we want to do.* I sure was surprised when one of the boys said—and several other boys agreed—how unfair it was that girls get to wear skirts, pants, dresses, and shorts while the boys only got to wear pants and shorts. *It was also unfair, he said, that girls get to wear ALL the colors while we only get blue, black, and brown.* I was afraid this boy might get laughed at, but the others boys just nodded their heads, sharing in his disappointment.

Is it really that simple? Ultimately, yes. The discussion about gender expression can be very simple and straightforward. We do not need to worry about the conversations extending beyond their understanding if we allow the students to provide examples from their own experiences and observations. Additionally, it provides a way for students to gain broader perspectives from their peers and deeper empathy for challenges faced by all.

Gender Identity

Gender identity, simply defined, is a person's innate sense of their own gender. That said, when was the last, or first, time someone asked you to share your gender identity? Most people would say they've never been asked! If I were to ask any person I encounter on a daily basis to share how they describe their gender identity, I would likely get quizzical looks at best and surely some stronger reactions as well. The reasons for this are complicated. For example, if someone is obviously and intentionally masculine in their gender expression, to inquire whether they actually *identify* as a man might imply that they were unsuccessful in achieving their personal and/or societally desired level of masculinity. That person may feel insulted.

Many people assume that the term "gender identity" is relevant only to transgender people. But *every person* has a gender identity because everyone has an internal sense of their own gender. People whose gender aligns with the sex assigned to them at birth may never ponder their own gender identity. And they may never ask another person, "What is your gender identity?" The problem arises when we assume that the *majority* experience is the *only* experience.

A person's gender identity—how they feel about themselves—may differ from the gender they were raised as. And a person's gender identity may differ from a person's gender expression—how they look, dress, or act. Because of our society's unfamiliarity with the term "gender identity," we may be unaware that someone who *appears* female because of her body type, looks, and dress may actually *identify* as male. What complicates this understanding even further is that the number of people whose gender identity is incongruent with their physical anatomy is a small, and therefore less visible, percentage of the population.[14]

DISCUSSING GENDER IDENTITY WITH STUDENTS

In my experience, gender identity is one of the simplest concepts to discuss with children, even at very young ages. Children can readily relate to the notion of "who I am on the inside." As one seven-year-old explained to his parent, "When are you going to understand, I may have the body of a girl, but I have the heart and mind of a boy." We as adults can also understand this concept as it is defined—a person's innate sense of their own gender. Our challenge as adults, however, is that we haven't necessarily had the opportunity to consider and discuss the concept of gender identity throughout our lives.

It is not uncommon to find a child of any age who will, when asked about their internal sense of their own gender, say, "I'm both" or, sometimes, "Neither gender works for me," or "I'm mostly a girl, but a little bit boy." Children can incorporate an understanding of gender identity as an integral aspect of self and add as much complexity as they feel suits them. One kindergartner simply said, "I'm a boy that likes girl things," while another third-grader said, "I'm two-thirds girl and one-third gender-queer."

While this can be challenging for parents and teachers alike, the reality is that adult acceptance of a child's autonomous framing of their gender identity provides that child with a tremendous sense of support at the very core of their being.[15] This support is not about the outcome—these children may or may not go through a gender transition—but it serves to strengthen a child's core sense of self throughout the process of discovery.

As our society deepens its understanding of gender identity through research and discourse, we can better understand the experience of transgender children and take the simple steps needed to include them in our schools and in society as a whole.

While the concept of *gender identity* is new and unfamiliar to many, there is a long global history revealing that diverse gender identities and expressions have existed for centuries.[16] Many within Native American tribes use the term *Two-Spirit* to collectively describe a number of gender experiences and expressions which most certainly predates today's western European-centric notion of a "transgender" experience. The Two-Spirit person embodies both the feminine and the masculine spirits and their presence is considered a spiritual gift to their community.[17] Samoan culture recognizes the fa'afafine as a third gender. The Mahu embody a female and male spirit in Hawai'ian culture, and South Asia recognizes the Hijra as being neither male nor female. The Supreme Court in India has ruled that the Hijra are a legally recognized third gender. There are many other examples, such as the indigenous *sisterboys* and *brothergirls* of Australia, the Chuckshi of Siberia, the Ashtime in southern Ethiopia, the Mashoga in Kenya, and the Burrnesha of Albania. These cultures may or may not identify with or embrace the term *transgender*.[18]

The visibility of transgender and gender-diverse people is increasing with each passing year. The existence of transgender children is more and more evident in schools across the nation. With this increased visibility comes an increased desire to understand the notion of gender more fully as a component of identity that is distinct and independent.

People often confuse and conflate biological sex, gender expression, and sexual orientation, inevitably complicating their understanding of the transgender child. It is worthwhile to further this examination.

Sexual Orientation

Sexual orientation is about who you're attracted to. This can include romantic, emotional, and/or sexual attraction. Teachers sometimes get nervous when considering how to have conversations with young children about gender because they *assume it must involve talking about sexual orientation*. Sexual orientation describes our romantic, intimate, and/or sexual attractions to another person. Our gender, *and* the gender of the person who catches our eye, are needed to label this orientation as heterosexual, homosexual, bisexual, and so on. While some teachers feel confident having a conversation about sexual orientation in an age-appropriate way, they still recognize that families within the school community may not agree to or approve of having that discussion with their children. One family may feel that discussions about bodies, relationships, and sex within the school setting are very reasonable, while another may feel quite differently. Cultural norms, faith beliefs, and family traditions are just a few factors influencing these perspectives. In some instances, state law mandates what the school health education curriculum will be. Whether or not to include topics addressing sexual activity, abstinence, birth control, sexually transmitted diseases, and sexual assault awareness can be fiercely debated and politicized. It's not surprising that many of the administrators and educators I encounter are hesitant to add discussions about transgender children into the mix—it feels like adding fuel to the fire.

There is good news! There is no need to discuss sexuality or sexual orientation with young, elementary-age children when discussing the topics of *gender expression* and *gender identity*. While historically linked in our society (and especially from an adult mindset), gender identity and sexual orientation are distinct concepts. How do we parse them? We can start by understanding why they are linked in the first place. There are many reasons but let's start with an obvious one—the LGBTQ acronym.

LGBTQ—A WELL-MEANING, INCREASINGLY COMPLEX—SOMETIMES PROBLEMATIC—ACRONYM

Let's take a moment to consider the widely known acronym "LGBT." Most of my audiences know what this acronym refers to . . . up to a point. People are familiar with the terms that make up the acronym: Lesbian, Gay, Bisexual, and Transgender. The LGBT community, or queer community as it is sometimes called, is comprised of people who have identities other than straight, or heterosexual, right? But what do we really know about these identities? Let's look at the first three letters of the acronym: L, G, and B. Lesbian, Gay, and Bisexual all refer to *sexual orientation*. But what about the T . . . Transgender? We learned that this is not about sexual orientation, *this is about gender identity*. Let's pause for a moment. Sexual orientation is about *who we are attracted to*. Gender identity is about *who a person is*, and their innate sense of their own gender. So, we can see that the T, although outside of the heteronormative paradigm, is not congruent with the acronym's original intent of grouping sexually diverse communities.

Let's continue. Many of us also know the current acronym does not stop at LGBT. It has further expanded in ways like this: LGBTQIA+. When I ask educators if they know what any additional letters stand for in the acronym, many know "Q" stands for the word *queer* and, occasionally, they know "I" is for *intersex*.

When discussing the LGBTQIA+ acronym during trainings, I present them with a more expansive acronym incorporating *some* of the identity labels encountered in my work: LGBTQQIAAAPGG2(S)EDD+.

Simply seeing these letters on a presentation slide invariably elicits laughter. I believe the laughter comes from feelings of surprise, nervousness, and being overwhelmed. Most teachers are relieved when I tell them I don't expect them to know what all the letters stand for and that I'm not going to delve into deep definitions of them either.[19] With the pressure off, people are much more willing to express their curiosity so I will list off the terms represented by these letters: Lesbian, Gay, Bisexual, Transgender, Queer, Questioning, Intersex, Ally, Agender, Asexual, Pansexual, Genderfluid, Genderqueer, Two-Spirit or 2(S), Exploring, Demigender, Demisexual, and the "plus" symbol intended to convey that this list is dynamic and far from exhaustive. The most important understanding I would like the audience to gain is that each letter represented *fits into one of the four primary gender components* we've discussed—anatomy, expression, identity, and orientation. Understanding these distinct components is crucial to achieving clarity on the identity descriptors found in that ever-increasing LGBTQ+ acronym.

Whether you use a longer or shorter version of this acronym to reference a collection of diverse communities, it presents a problem that can get in the way of further understanding the experiences of gender-diverse children. If we examine the descriptors, we do see that some of the terms reference *sexual orientation* (gay, lesbian, asexual, etc.) while some describe *gender identity* (transgender, agender, genderfluid, etc.).

At least one other term—the letter I, for intersex—actually represents a number of physical differences that affect a person's body (*anatomy*). The majority of people with intersex differences will likely not use that term as an identity label but rather as a descriptive term of bodily differences. For example, "I am a man with an intersex difference," rather than "I am an intersex person."

When people see the acronym LGBTQ+ and note, either consciously or unconsciously that three of the terms (LGB) describe sexual orientation, it is then natural to take the least familiar of the terms, transgender (the T), and assume that it, too, is a type of sexual orientation. This assumption is one of the primary barriers that adults experience when considering how to have constructive, age-appropriate conversations with children. A transgender child is simply a child whose core recognition of their internal gender differs from their sex assigned at birth.

THE AEIOUS OF GENDER—A BETTER FRAMEWORK

I would like to present a simple alternative framework for understanding gender that relies on a familiar acronym that most of us learned in elementary school when learning the alphabet: the vowels are AEIOU. We can adopt these letters as a playbook to understand much of the new vernacular of gender:

- **A for ANATOMY.** We all come into the world with the bodies that we have. Many things about our bodies are fixed and immutable (our chromosomes, eye color, our heartbeat, and the fact that everyone ages, for example); other things we can change (examples include modifying the shape of our bodies through diet or exercise, changing our hair color, and so on).

- **E for EXPRESSION.** Our gender expression is arbitrary and mutable. Children, teens, and adults can readily understand this. The gendered expectations in relation to clothing, toys, behaviors, and activities in which any person engages can change over time, change at different ages, and vary by geography or culture, and family norms. How any individual expresses their gender can be viewed as a *lifelong negotiation* between self (authenticity) and society (expectations). This negotiation can be one of ease or one of controversy (or anywhere in between) *depending on whether one's self-expression is congruent with societal expectations.*

- **I for IDENTITY.** Gender identity is such a simple concept, yet we have only recently begun to assert its importance in the dialogue of gender. Gender identity is a person's innate sense of their own gender. Children readily understand this concept. The best way to communicate this concept in a classroom conversation is to use the language the children themselves use. *You may see me as a girl, but in my heart and my mind, I am a boy.*

- **O for ORIENTATION.** Sexual orientation is the term used to describe romantic and/or sexual attraction. The word *transgender* does NOT describe a sexual orientation. Being transgender is NOT a label describing one's sexuality. This distinction is not clear for many people is primarily why many in our society struggle with understanding the experience of a transgender child. We need to clearly recognize that discussions about sexual orientation are completely unnecessary when considering ways to lead young children in conversations about gender.

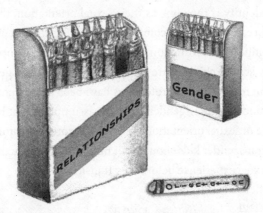

- **U for UNIVERSAL.** Each of the four terms listed above is relevant to *all* people. We are born with a certain body, a way of expressing our gender, an innate sense of our own gender identity, and, as we mature, a recognition of our physical and romantic attractions (or lack thereof) to others.

I can hear a number of readers asking about the "Y." After all, we likely learned that Y is sometimes a vowel as well. There is room for a Y too. YOU! All of us wish to be our full selves and to have that self-authenticity recognized and respected. We strive to teach this to our children at even the youngest ages. What child wouldn't want to hear, "YOU are amazing, special, and beautiful for exactly who you are!"

The conflation of sexual orientation and gender identity and gender expression is one of the single most significant barriers to providing support and understanding for transgender children. When a person inaccurately believes that a child's gender identity is the same as their sexual orientation, that person may feel conflicted because they're uncomfortable thinking about a child's sexuality. This is a very important distinction. This is why so many people will assume that elementary school children are too young to know their gender. It is also why medical and mental health professions have been so reticent to validate an affirming care model for transgender kids. The assumption that being transgender is some type of sexual orientation is also at the core of a common argument stating that all transgender kids should wait until they go through puberty and/or have some sexual experience before they transition.

What Happens When Kindergarten Teachers Say…
"Oh, I have at least one kid like that in my class every year. I just assume they're going to be gay so I don't know what to say or do when other children make comments."

That child is the sweet, sensitive boy who isn't quite boy enough, or the girl who is indiscernible from all the other little fellas in baseball caps. At many of the Gender Diversity school staff trainings that I lead, quite often a kindergarten teacher will make the above statement, while the remaining staff members nod in agreement. This comment may seem harmless enough, but what I share with the staff is that it is well worth our while to examine the consequences of this passive observation.

What these teachers are observing—clothing, interests, temperament, color preferences, and so on—are actually attributes of that child's gender expression. These attributes are very frequently—and mistakenly—assumed to be an indicator of that child's potential sexual orientation.

The child is not gay. At least, we don't know that yet. We are talking about a five-year-old. As children mature into adolescence, they will have romantic attractions. Ultimately, they will claim a sexual orientation, and of course, they may identify as gay, straight, or a number of other possibilities.

But for now, that child is just that—a child. The child is self-expressing, not trying to attract a sexual or romantic partner. Every child has their own interests, their own friends, and their own way of engaging in the world. A teacher who observes a child's interests, friendships, and specific ways of engaging, and incorrectly assumes that a child is gay because of them, is making a significant conflation of the concepts of gender identity, gender expression, and sexual orientation. Confusing these distinct notions can foster an environment of teasing and bullying and one that any particular teacher may feel helpless to address.

It is not just teachers who are observant. Children, too, readily perceive differences in gender expression. Consider this scenario where a child says, "Why does Jackson always wear girl's clothes? His hair is too long."

The teacher, not quite recognizing the distinction between gender expression and sexual orientation, becomes uncomfortable or nervous. She doesn't want to address a child's sexual orientation, feeling—and knowing many others will agree—that discussions of sexuality are not appropriate at this age. So, avoiding eye contact, the teacher brusquely responds, "Never mind about Jackson. Focus on your schoolwork!"

The teacher hurriedly changes the subject and seems flustered. This unease can lead that student to believe that something is wrong with Jackson, simply for being himself. By avoiding a child's simple expression of curiosity, the kindergarten teacher has inadvertently drawn potentially negative attention to Jackson.

Additionally, Jackson—who may be aware that he is different from most other boys—may internalize this difference as being wrong or somehow shameful because the teacher did not intervene appropriately.

A number of unintended consequences can arise:

- A teacher's inaction conveys implicit approval for other children's behavior to escalate into teasing, isolating, harassment, or even violence. By the time recess rolls around, Jackson may be directly confronted, but now the questions can easily move to the realm of bullying.
- A teacher's discomfort or inaction sends a message to a child that they are unworthy of support and inherently wrong or bad. Jackson may internalize these messages from his teacher and peers, ultimately crushing his authentic and innocent nature.
- Prematurely labeling a child as gay or lesbian, whether passively, as in this scenario, or actively by a peer or teacher, creates the unintended consequence of sexualizing that child's experience, precisely the result we all hope to avoid. Stigmatizing a child in this way can lay the groundwork for further vulnerability, low self-esteem, and even targeting by sexual predators who seek out isolated or vulnerable children.

If commenting on a child's perceived sexual orientation were normal, reasonable, and age-appropriate, we theoretically could make similar observations in other situations, such as, "Cecelia is such a delightful heterosexual girl, isn't she?" If you can't imagine the raised eyebrow or disapproving look you might get, just make that comment out loud the next time you are at a playground or church picnic.

When educators frame the gender expression of an elementary-school child in the context of sexual orientation (in this case, gay), they miss a huge opportunity to create greater inclusivity and acceptance for a significant percentage of students—one could argue all students—who don't fit our society's restrictive gender expectations. With this new perspective, a teacher who once felt stymied or silenced can now address, respect, and celebrate the concept of gender expression in the early schooling years and in age-appropriate ways.

That is why a trip back to the basics is helpful, especially for adults. We have a strong tendency to forget the simplicity of gender that we knew as children. Yes, we understood that gender had to do with our bodies (anatomy) but that our understanding was primarily centered on what clothing we were told we could wear, what toys we could or couldn't play with, who we are allowed to spend time with, and how we were expected to behave (expression). Even as children, we could recognize the arbitrary nature and contradictions of these expectations. The most common refrain was that it simply *wasn't fair*. Today's children are no exception.

Should the LGBTQ+ Acronym Be Eliminated?

I'm not advocating for the abandonment of this acronym. There is great value to having this acronym: the benefit of having a shorthand way of referring to a collection of communities is that it helps those within these communities find resources, services, community, and friendships. It allows people to search the internet for more knowledgeable providers, organizations that offer community events, and a chance to find or grow the community. We must understand the historical importance of making communities visible and identifiable. Without a community name, the result is a lack of historical context, invisibility of experience, and a lack of place and protection within society. The progression of added letters (and the communities they represent) of the LGBTQ+ acronym also represents a walk down a society's historical timeline to more accurately provide visibility and acknowledgment to people who have always been a present and active part of that society.

Within the more narrowly defined gay/lesbian community of years past, there was room for inclusion for those with gender-diverse expressions. The acceptance of trans people and others who pushed gender boundaries to a greater degree was far from perfect, yet this acceptance more often provided at least some haven. The gay and lesbian communities aligned together based on the common foundation of same-sex relationships. But gender expression often extended beyond what was considered the norm within the heterosexual communities. Therefore, a transgender person might not have the common, core foundation of a "same-sex" relationship but they had a closer affiliation than they could find within a heterosexual community that failed to make or understand the distinctions between sexuality and gender identity and/or expression.

Equally important to consider is the complexity that comes when considering the racial, ethnic, and cultural differences within communities and around the world and how this can set those (who may not even use identifiers like gay, lesbian, bisexual *or trans*) outside of the white dominant culture framework of LGBTQ+ communities altogether. This highlights the challenge of any person with intersectional identities, as they seek a place to belong where their whole self is met with acceptance.

Does the LGBTQ+ acronym serve a purpose? Yes. Does it cover all? Far from it. A good place to start, however, is to correct misperceptions and inaccurate understandings that have resulted from the conflation of identifiers that the acronym inadvertently inspires.

Are You Saying We Should Ignore the Experiences of People Who Identify as Gay, Lesbian, or Bisexual?

Absolutely not. While the youngest of children are not typically describing themselves with sexual orientation labels, they often do so when reaching adolescence. An older child, for example, may share a descriptor of their orientation *and* their gender identity (e.g., pansexual and nonbinary) with a friend or caregiver. The journey of child-rearing includes addressing the changing bodies during adolescence and the intimate and physical relationships that are part of their maturation. To best address this journey as it relates to all children then means we should not use heterosexuality as the assumptive default.

Many children, too, have parents who are lesbian or gay—descriptors that address the sexual orientation of those parents. Those families may have friends and community that have shared experiences based on that identity just as a child who has heterosexual parents too may have friends of the family and a greater community where many are heterosexual. It is important to acknowledge and embrace the diversity of identity and experience within any child's family and/or community. The point I wish to make is that we can easily do this without discussing the specific sexual practices of any adult in a young child's life. We *can* discuss the range of sexuality when we deem that to be age appropriate. We already do; we just don't always include the diverse experiences that are reflective of the society in which we live.

Lastly, we can embrace this *relational* diversity within families—mom/dad, two dads, two moms, and other blended families—knowing that it serves to better include all children from diverse families and provide them a crucial sense of *belonging*. If we consider our life experiences within the context of the AEIOU framework, then we will have a much clearer idea of what we are discussing when it is age-appropriate to do so, and in a way that does not perpetuate the notion of normalcy with what is most common and, by default, abnormal, with what is simply less common.

Understanding and incorporating the AEIOUs of gender is the key to easy, productive conversations with students of all ages. These discussions can vary in length, terminology, helpful books and/or other classroom activities based on the age of the children. Of course, conversations with teens *can* incorporate issues of attraction and relationships that may be deemed not yet appropriate for younger children. We'll discuss this in greater depth in Chapter 8.

I believe we owe it to ourselves to step away from a binary way of viewing gender. The rigidity of this dualistic approach forces children, teens, and adults to compromise their truth and authenticity. It only appears to have validity because we've been collectively willing to ignore the evidence all around us. The complexity that resides in our bodies, the myriad ways we have of expressing ourselves, and the beautiful dance we do with others simply mirrors the diversity we see all around us and across the globe.[20] It's something worthy of celebration.

NOTES

1. Elizabeth Reis, *Bodies in Doubt: An American History of Intersex*, 2nd ed. (Baltimore: Johns Hopkins University Press, 2021), 170–190.

2. Selma Feldman Witchel, "Disorders of Sex Development," *Best Practice & Research Clinical Obstetrics & Gynaecology* 48 (April 2018): 90–102, https://doi.org/10.1016/j.bpobgyn.2017.11.005.

3. "How Common Is Intersex? | Intersex Society of North America," https://isna.org/faq/frequency/.

4. Melanie Blackless et al., "How Sexually Dimorphic Are We? Review and Synthesis," *American Journal of Human Biology: The Official Journal of the Human Biology Council* 12, no. 2 (March 2000): 151–166, https://doi.org/10.1002/(SICI)1520-6300(200003/04)12:2<151::AID-AJHB1>3.0.CO;2-F.

5. Georgiann Davis, *Contesting Intersex: The Dubious Diagnosis* (New York: New York University Press, 2015), 87.

6. "Mosaicism Involving Sex Chromosomes | Intersex Society of North America," https://isna.org/faq/conditions/mosaicism/.

7. There is considerable contention in the transgender community regarding the evolution of medical categories regarding sex and gender and the impact these classifications have had on hearts, bodies, and minds. See Kathryn Bond Stockton, *Gender(s)*, The MIT Press Essential Knowledge Series (Cambridge, MA; London, UK: The MIT Press, 2021),

190–191; Georgiann Davis, *Contesting Intersex: The Dubious Diagnosis* (New York: New York University Press, 2015), 87–115.

8. Aruna Saraswat, Jamie D. Weinand, and Joshua D. Safer, "Evidence Supporting the Biologic Nature of Gender Identity," *Endocrine Practice* 21, no. 2 (February 2015): 199–204.

9. "Here's The Icky Reason Dogs Sniff Each Other's Butts," *HuffPost* (July 28, 2014), https://www.huffpost.com/entry/why-do-dogs-sniff-each-others-butts-video_n_5627304.

10. Christia Spears Brown, Sharla D. Biefeld, and Michelle J. Tam, *Gender in Childhood*, Cambridge Elements (Cambridge, MA: Cambridge University Press, 2020), 25.

11. Carol Lynn Martin and Diane Ruble, "Children's Search for Gender Cues: Cognitive Perspectives on Gender Development," *Current Directions in Psychological Science* 13, no. 2 (April 1, 2004): 67–70, https://doi.org/10.1111/j.0963-7214.2004.00276.x.

12. Jeanne Maglaty, "When Did Girls Start Wearing Pink?," *Smithsonian Magazine* (April 7, 2011), https://www.smithsonianmag.com/arts-culture/when-did-girls-start-wearing-pink-1370097/.

13. dbarry1917, *Riley on Marketing* (2011), https://www.youtube.com/watch?v=-CU0 40Hqbas.

14. "How Many Adults Identify as Transgender in the United States?" Williams Institute, https://williamsinstitute.law.ucla.edu/publications/trans-adults-united-states/.

15. Kristina R. Olson et al., "Mental Health of Transgender Children Who Are Supported in Their Identities," *Pediatrics* 137, no. 3 (March 2016): e20153223, https://doi.org/10.1542/peds.2015-3223.

16. This timeline of diverse gender history is beautiful and accessible: Aaron H. Devor and Ardel Haefele-Thomas, *Transgender: A Reference Handbook*, Contemporary World Issues (Santa Barbara: ABC-CLIO, 2019), 327–340.

17. Walter L. Williams, "The 'Two-Spirit' People of Indigenous North Americans," *The Guardian* (October 11, 2010), https://www.theguardian.com/music/2010/oct/11/two-spirit-peo ple-north-america.

18. Sally Hines, *Is Gender Fluid? A Primer for the 21st Century*, The Big Idea Series (London; New York: Thames & Hudson, 2018).

19. It is nearly impossible to develop a complete catalog of the lexicon surrounding gender and sexuality, which is part of its charm: Michele Angello and Alisa Bowman, *Raising the Transgender Child: A Complete Guide for Parents, Families & Caregivers* (Berkeley: Seal Press, A Hachette Book Group Company, 2016), 27–45; Owl Fisher and Fox Fisher, *Trans Teen Survival Guide* (London; Philadelphia: Jessica Kingsley Publishers, 2019), 218.

20. For a nuanced but concise discussion of gender diversity, see Aaron H. Devor, "Gender Diversity: Trans, Transgender, Transsexual, and Genderqueer People," in *The Blackwell Encyclopedia of Sociology* (John Wiley & Sons, Ltd, 2016), 1–6, https://doi.org/10.1002/9781405165518.wbeos0748.

4

The Journey of Parents

Never. We never lose our loved ones. They accompany us; they don't disappear from our lives. We are merely in different rooms.

Paulo Coelho

By the time school personnel first become aware that a child is transgender or exploring a trans identity, parents are already actively dealing with their own discomfort, fear, confusion, and lack of information. They find themselves trying to explain something they don't yet understand to everyone around them—immediate and extended family members, friends and neighbors, coworkers, faith communities, health providers, teachers, and other school personnel. This process can be daunting, leading to conflict, exhaustion, and pain.

When a teacher or administrator encounters a parent in turmoil, having a broader perspective on the caregiver's experience increases the likelihood that the school, parent, and student will move forward together, rather than at odds with each other.

This chapter describes what parents go through as they struggle to understand and accept their child's gender identity. Parents have significant challenges: they must manage their own confusion and preconceived notions and figure out the best ways to support their child while also shouldering the experiences of everyone around them. Experiencing discomfort, confusion, and fear is not the exclusive domain of a gender-diverse child's parent. Teachers and other parents may also be confused and apprehensive, regardless of whether they have a close connection to the child or not. All the more reason why it is helpful to recognize the need for compassionate understanding.

It's important for school personnel to have perspective on the parent's journey to better recognize their own responsibility. While some parents may already be in a gender-supportive mindset, others may not yet have reached that stage. Either way, schools must not solely rely on parents (or children, for that matter) to drive the process of creating an inclusive environment for trans kids.[1]

CULTURAL *AND* COGNITIVE DISSONANCE: *MY* KID CAN'T BE *THAT!*

While there are plenty of positive representations of trans individuals in society today, it is understandable that many people can't fathom a *positive* life outcome for a trans child. Few of us have had the opportunity to actually meet a trans person in day-to-day life. Without an awareness that trans children *do* exist and can even *thrive* in society, how can a parent reconcile the inner conflict they feel when their child says, "I am not a boy, I'm a girl"? A statement like this deeply contradicts the fixed-gender norms of almost any parent in our mainstream society and may trigger a deep sense of *cultural dissonance*. Cultural dissonance is an uncomfortable sense of confusion and conflict that people experience when they encounter unexpected or confusing changes within a specific cultural environment. We may have prior experience with cultural dissonance: shifts in language, politics, traditions, and racial or ethnic demographics. Our conception of gender is no different. The intersection of these diverse identities and experiences places some families at an even further disadvantage:

> During one support group, the parent of a teenage trans girl, who had recently disclosed her gender identity to her parents, shared what happened shortly thereafter. The teen decided to disclose her gender identity to her

grandmother, a first-generation Italian immigrant to the United States, who also lived with the family. The grandmother immediately flew into a rage, beating her grandchild while screaming, "No grandchild of mine is going to be a streetwalker!" The only frame of reference for transgender people that this grandparent had encountered was the disparaged prostitutes in her Italian homeland.

We are in the midst of significant changes in many countries and cultures across the world, including the United States, as we seek to understand, acknowledge, and include an increasingly visible number of trans and gender-diverse children. In the United States, cultural dissonance manifests in the form of fear-stoking legislative efforts; lawsuits against school districts with respect to trans student usage of bath/locker rooms; attacks on gender-affirming care providers; and community initiatives to deny, prevent, or rescind gender protections.[2] One mixed-race parent of a teenage trans girl told other support group parents the following:

I understand, *now*, that I have to fight *against* this state initiative effort to repeal gender protections for trans people. But, I have to say, before I understood this issue, and before I realized my own child was transgender, I know I would have joined this fight and fought *for* this initiative. I am like many people in my community who have felt uncomfortable and unsafe in the presence of trans people.

Similarly, when a parent of a trans child—or parents of other children within the same school community—has specific beliefs, attitudes, or personal experiences that seem to preclude an accepting approach to the trans child, it can inspire a level of *cognitive dissonance* as well. Cognitive dissonance is the mental discomfort or stress that occurs when a person engages in an action or is confronted with new information that appears to contradict their values or beliefs.

Many families have never met a trans person, never heard of any positive portrayal of a trans person, nor considered that a *child* could be transgender. Some have never even heard the word *transgender* before. Twentieth-century gender theory framed gender cognition in children as one-dimensional and postulated that this awareness solidifies in all children between the ages of three and seven.[3] It's no exaggeration that most parents of trans children will immediately and definitively dismiss the idea that their child is transgender. For them, it borders on a cognitive impossibility.

Dissonance is sometimes more pronounced within black and Latino families. Gender norms can be more strictly enforced within communities, such as the Latino/a/x community, that experienced greater racial discrimination, and bias from the dominant culture. As elements of racism, transphobia, xenophobia, and classism intersect, it is understandable that a parent might be all the more hesitant to support a child's gender identity/expression. This intersection results in a further exacerbation of hardship for both child and family. While this is not always the case, it is important to recognize that dissonance can occur with greater severity within these families.

During a parent support group meeting, a tearful Latina mother of a five-year-old trans girl had this to say:

> I feel so ashamed. In my culture, this is not okay and my husband has been
> quite upset. I felt I could not support my child's wish to wear dresses and,

when he would state that he was really a girl, I didn't know what to do. So, I just tried to beat it out of him.

EMOTIONAL TURMOIL

As parents grapple with this perceived *impossibility* of having a transgender child despite their child's insistence about their gender, they can experience significant psychological turmoil.

They can feel deep frustration and anger at their child and expect the child to "prove" their gender and/or "deal with" the repercussions of their gender nonconformity. Because of such internal conflict, parents can find themselves challenged to reconcile fears for their child's safety within a society/culture/community ill-prepared for their inclusion. Sadly, this time of internal contradiction can cloud parents' judgment, and they can inadvertently place a child at risk. The impact of cognitive dissonance can range from concerning to outright dangerous:

> During one parent support group, a white, heterosexual stepfather struggled with his transgender teenage stepson's male identity. The stepson was about to take a summer job on a commercial fishing vessel. The stepfather was a large-statured man who was a supervising manager of the Alaska fish processing fleet. He resisted acknowledging that his stepson, only 5' 1" tall, might be vulnerable in a predominantly male, live-in work environment, especially as it would likely be known that he was transgender. Since the youth was early in his transition, his ambiguous gender presentation would have drawn attention and certainly increased his vulnerability to physical and/or sexual assault during the months-long, live-aboard work environment. The

stepfather had difficulty recognizing that he was in a position to make positive change in the largely male-dominated work environment by instituting training and setting expectations for his employees. He could not recognize his stepson's vulnerability and said, "If he wants to be a man, he has to learn how to be a man!"

Certainly, one of the hardest stories I've heard involved the parents of a fifteen-year-old trans boy. The father and mother were first-generation Chinese. By the time they found some support, they were at the end of their options:

> "Our child first told us she was a lesbian," one parent said. "I don't know this word, lesbian. There are no lesbians in China. Now she is saying she is a boy. We don't know what to do. We feel we have no choice but to kill our child and then to kill ourselves."

While this may seem extreme to someone raised in the United States, where individual self-expression and choice are valued, in traditional Chinese culture, the importance of obedience to parents, adherence to strict gender roles, and not bringing shame to the family is of much greater significance.

The dangers that trans children face as they seek to express their authentic gender identity cannot be overestimated. Fortunately, all the children in the above-mentioned examples now have the full support of their families. These are just a few examples of a family member's experience with both cognitive and cultural dissonance that resulted in a parent's visceral fight/flight response. Without any positive societal/cultural representation of that child's identity, the immediate response was one of actual or strongly considered physical assault. If this is the response of loving family members, imagine the dangers associated with disclosure to others that a child might face on any given day.

One caveat: It is also important to recognize that not all families experience this dissonance. As mentioned earlier, many cultures acknowledge—in both language and role—other gender presentations. As a result, the cultural and/or cognitive dissonance can be greatly lessened or even non-existent. Pathways to resolve or eliminate this dissonance with respect to trans youth are possible. Seeing positive representations of trans children and adults, as we are beginning to see today, is one way to replace inaccurate, inflammatory portrayals that exist. Increased understanding, support for families, and accessible resources can make all the difference.

COMING TO TERMS WITH A CHILD'S GENDER IDENTITY

Rarely is a parent ready for a child's pronouncement about their gender. They may be deeply surprised if a doctor or therapist suggests their child has a gender identity issue that needs attention. Nearly all families I encounter through my work tell me they knew next to nothing about gender identity differences and were in no way prepared for this information.

Having listened to the experiences of thousands of families over the years, I can say that no two families' stories are the same. Still, there are shared core aspects of the process many families go through, which very much resemble Elizabeth Kubler-Ross' five stages of grief: denial/isolation, anger, bargaining, depression/anxiety, and acceptance.[4]

Stage One: Denial and Isolation

Whether they live in a large metropolitan area or a small rural environment, most parents of a trans child are unlikely to know of any other families with trans children within their immediate community. Reaching out to friends or other family members may seem impossible because parents fear no one will understand. Trans children who are both visible and receiving affirming support within their families and/or schools are still rare. Friends and family may be unable to provide compassion and understanding, not because they are heartless but because they simply lack knowledge and familiarity with trans issues.

Rahmija, the parent of a trans child, is a Muslim woman who lives in a culturally diverse American city and is in close proximity to her extended Pakistani family. When her oldest child, then eight years old, stated she was not a boy, but actually a girl, Rahmija had nowhere to turn. "Between our culture and our faith, there is no place for being transgender. I could see the suffering of my child but felt so torn. It seemed like I had a terrible choice between listening to my child and feeling like I would *lose everyone else*."

Even when parents search for connections with others, they may find that there are no family support groups in their area. The nearest family with shared experience could be hundreds or thousands of miles away. At the time when parents most desperately need someone who understands what they're going through, there is often no one to be found. The resulting isolation can immobilize a parent during a crucial time for their child and the family as a whole.

Parents' understanding of what it means to be transgender can, like anyone else's, be negatively informed by stereotypes of trans people. How do parents reconcile their beloved child's stated gender identity with society's stereotypes of trans people as deviant, perverse, deceptive, and the target of ridicule and revulsion? For many, this cognitive dissonance ultimately leads to denial.

One lesbian mom shared how she felt when her child told her he was trans:

My child can't be transgender. She's just a tomboy. I'm a lesbian and I felt the same way when I was a child. Boys got to do all the cool things so, of course, I wished I was a boy. There is no way I am going to call her by a different name and pronoun, that's ridiculous. I know a transsexual, and she's got some serious mental problems. That's not my kid!

Another mother struggled for many, many months. She dubbed herself the "Kleenex Lady" because of her constant tears as she sought to understand her teenage trans daughter"

"He can't be a girl!" she said. "He's on the soccer team and is a leader in the Boy Scouts."

For a year, the Kleenex Lady struggled to make the distinction between her child's *gender expression*—the interest in sports and other group activities—and her child's *gender identity*. It wasn't until her child began presenting as a girl in everyday life that it finally seemed to click that her child might indeed have a female identity.

Significant loss of family, friends, and community members is something many parents speak of. The pain hits every family member:

By the time our child was five, our families and church members were beginning to make negative comments about our trans son. Some families were not allowing their child to play with ours. He was already suffering and had barely started kindergarten! One day, when my husband came home from work, I said, "That's it! You've got to get us out of here. They are going to crush him! Everyone who is important to our family is working against us."

This family of five uprooted their lives and moved out of state to better help their youngest. They had no guarantees that they would find what they needed. It was a choice that meant leaving everyone and everything they had ever known. They chose his well-being, feeling as if his survival depended on it. Yet, for several years afterward, the whole family felt the pain of isolation and rejection from their now distant extended family, faith community, and friends as they rebuilt their lives far away. They feared the pain might never go away.

Stage Two: Anger

Some parents feel angry at their child for making what *seem* to be very selfish demands, such as asking to be referred to by a different name and pronoun; insisting that a parent tell no one else, including another parent; or deciding to disclose to everyone on social media with no advance notice. Often, they are simultaneously fearful about their child's depression or self-harming behavior. The feelings of anger are disturbing, conflicting, and very difficult for parents to move through. A trans child may disclose during a deeply inopportune time when other family issues are present. One parent shared her experience with me. She had recently learned that her husband, the primary provider for their family of five, had a terminal illness and was not expected to live more than a few months:

> I don't know what my kid was thinking! He decides to tell me he is transgender over the Christmas holiday, most likely our last Christmas together as a whole family. It's not that I don't want to support him, I do. I just *can't* right now. I'm going to be a single parent soon. I have to help my husband *die*. I love my kid but why did he pick this time, of all times, to drop this bomb?!

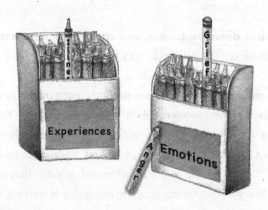

Parents can be confused about how, or even if, to provide supportive care, and their confusion can lead to resentment at having to address the issue at all. They may even direct their anger at their child. This mother's love and acceptance were something I could clearly hear during our conversation, but her anguish and anger were there, too.

Anger can also be directed at a spouse or partner, especially if the parents are struggling, separated, or divorced. Because parental responses to a child's gender journey may vary, a parent may blame the other for coddling juvenile behavior or indulging a harmful fantasy. Differing parental perspectives about a child's gender identity, and how to respond to it, can surely deepen the conflict, leading to increased anguish for the child (and any siblings) and potentially endangering the parents' relationship. Many families, unfortunately, have found their way into courtrooms, each passionately certain they know what's best for their child, while attorneys, judges, and other involved but often uninformed professionals struggle to sort it all out.

Shame, embarrassment, and resentment can accompany feelings of anger. Many parents in our support groups have shared how they've experienced this complex mix of emotions. "I love my child, of course," one parent stated, "but I'm embarrassed to say that I wonder what people will think about *me* in all this." Another parent shared similar feelings of discomfort and embarrassment:

My child is upset because everyone at the family reunion was uncomfortable around them. I have to say that, seeing my teenager through their eyes, I was embarrassed and—this is hard to say—ashamed too. I'm uncomfortable with my child's skirt, leggings, makeup, *and* facial hair! I can't even get the pronouns right, much less explain it to others. I just wanted it to all be over, but of course, it's not. My kid is a mess and I want to scream, "Well, what did you expect?!!"

Anger, often exacerbated by other emotions, may not arrive on a predictable timeline. This emotional complexity can distort a parent's thinking and, subsequently, their actions and reactions. Parents might believe their child is rebelling or finding ways to escape responsibility. They may have feelings of inadequacy causing them to inappropriately turn to their child for emotional support. A parent's feelings of shame, and the impact on their self-perception, can coexist with feelings of embarrassment as a parent grapples with any real or anticipated negative perceptions from others. The complexity of these intertwined emotions, paired with fear for their child's (or their own) safety, can create a volatile flashpoint that could inadvertently lead to actions that result in physical and emotional harm to the child.[5]

Stage Three: Bargaining and Resistance

The greatest conflict for many parents is reconciling the desire to love and support their child with the fear that this love and support will send their child down a path—either real or perceived—of hardship, ostracism, and danger. As it is likely that the average parent is unable to *fully* comprehend the internal distress a trans child may feel (because the vast majority don't have a gender identity issue of their own upon which to draw), it can seem a much better choice to *not* immediately support a child's gender identification in the hopes of protecting the child from a terrifying world of unknown dangers. This is a time when parents can find themselves bargaining, delaying support, or negotiating options other than seeking gender-related medical care for their child or supporting their child's transition steps.

These are normal reactions by which a parent hopes to regain some normalcy and control in life rather than continue to feel vulnerable and helpless in the face of some unknown pathway. Yet, while a parent's resistance is typical, it is important to note that a child may interpret any delay or resistance as an unsupportive response.

Many families with strong religious values may be deeply conflicted. If a parent feels that their child's gender identification is in conflict with God and/or with their faith community's teachings, they may find themselves diminishing the suffering of their child to the level of childish impetuousness and disobedience. Even if a parent recognizes the depth of their child's distress, it may not be enough to counter what they view as the directive of the divine:

A mother and father of an adult trans son attended a parent support group and assumed they were the only fundamentalist Christians in attendance. "I hope we are welcome here," said one. As the other parents shared stories of struggle, faith, and acceptance, the mother said, "It's difficult to be here listening to all of you. We've prayed and prayed that God would help our child understand that he's going against God's teachings. When I listen to those of you supporting your child, I can't help but wonder if I'm hearing the voice of Satan sitting on my shoulder." Another parent replied, "Lack of parental support is directly linked to suicide. Would you rather have a dead son or one who is alive?" The mother, with a pained expression on her face, said, "Dead. Because then at least his eternal soul might be redeemed."

One family discussed their commitment to a healthy lifestyle, including things like regular exercise, minimal screen time, healthy foods, no sugar, and no medications. When they realized their ten-year-old child might be transgender, the child was already beginning to show signs of puberty. They understood enough to know that this was a crucial time for puberty delay intervention if their child indeed was transgender. They felt both immobilized and torn. One parent shared:

If we've taught our child things like "You are what you eat" and "The body is a temple," how can we say yes to something huge and scary like hormones? We didn't circumcise our child and now I have to think about someday taking the whole thing off?! We don't even use aspirin!

Other parents find themselves using transition steps as a bargaining chip with their children. In one case, a Latino father of a fourteen-year-old trans girl said:

I support her gender identity but she has a lot of growing up to do. We have expectations in our house. You get good grades, take care of your chores, respect your parents, and be kind to your siblings. She does none of those things consistently. When she shows us that she is a responsible person and her behavioral outbursts are under control, then we'll take the step of starting her on estrogen.

Another parent in the support group responded:

Well, I understand where you are coming from, but I wonder how it might work out if every teen had to be on top of these things before we *allowed* them to go through puberty? It might be preferable, but it ain't gonna happen!

Unfortunately, in situations of separation or divorce, the parents' ability to get on the same page can be compromised, and the child's gender needs become a variable that turns a challenging time of negotiation into a bitter war. One mother recounted:

I've reasoned with my ex, I've begged, I've argued, used diplomacy—nothing works. My trans son is starting puberty and my ex won't allow him to start puberty blockers. My son puts on a good face for his dad while at his house but crumbles into depression and despair when he is home with me. It's getting worse. I can't believe that our child's puberty has become the central factor in our divorce. Courts move slow and my child's body is changing every day! I'm scared. I don't know if he'll make it!

Some parents are more reluctant than others to offer validation and support for their child's gender identity:

One parent of a child adopted from Russia was slow in coming to terms with her nine-year-old's identity as a boy. She bargained with him, suggesting that he could have a short haircut as long as he promised to wear earrings. Considering puberty delay intervention for her child was especially hard. Over the period of a few parent support meetings, she told group members that, if he was indeed transgender, she would support him by allowing him to start hormones when he was nineteen.

Meanwhile, during the first few visits to our children's play group, her child was reserved and angry throughout. The first time he smiled was when he was asked if he wanted to have a different name on his name tag. He chose a typically masculine name. On their long drive home, his mother later reported, he was more animated than he had been for a long time.

While this parent's fear initially delayed her supportive actions, seeing his happiness—which had been absent for so long—was the motivator she needed to realize she could take affirming steps like pronoun and name changes. It wasn't long before she understood the importance of puberty delay intervention, and that age-appropriate hormone care could be considered much sooner for her teen rather than her arbitrary, rigid, ten-year timeline.

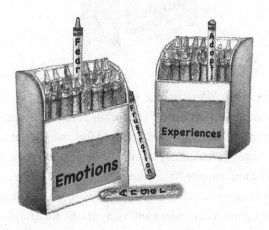

Sometimes parents find themselves in a predicament because their child's gender identity is *not* definitive. A child may say they are neither gender—or both. This is more common than many caregivers realize. Some children are adopting newer terms to describe a more fluid sense of gender: genderqueer, genderfluid, agender, nonbinary, and many other words that are often unfamiliar to parents. When a child's gender identification is not definitively boy or girl, sometimes a parent actually exerts pressure on their child to "make a decision, already." This, too, is a bargaining step meant to ease a *parent's* struggle with cognitive dissonance rather than supporting a child's more expansive identity and/ or exploration. A parent of a nonbinary fifteen-year-old shared this with his support group:

All of you with transgender kids are lucky, you know. My kid says he's binary [sic], or something, and isn't male *or* female. What am I supposed to do with that? I'm sorry, but I'm not going to use the name he picked out or change pronouns until he can make up his mind. It's not that I'm not supportive but why should I bother if he doesn't even know what he is? I just wish he'd get on with it!

While some might relate to this parent's frustration, the fifteen-year-old likely won't. What they will hear is a lack of support for the tentative first steps of their own discovery process. The child could feel a significant amount of pressure to make decisions prematurely or even make decisions that are not right for them. It would be unfortunate if the youth felt pressured to begin hormones, for example, solely because the child's father wanted them to "get on with it." It is important to recognize that gender identity decisions are complex. A nonbinary identity, for many, is a legitimate *destination*, not just a step from one gender to another.

Stage Four: Depression, Fatigue, and Guilt

For many caregivers, the pathway to acceptance and support is a long one. Even parents who roll their sleeves up to "power through this" soon realize there are many layers to a child's transition process and being "done" with transition is a somewhat elusive goal. A parent might identify transition-related steps and try to tackle them like a "checklist." This "checklist" can typically include items like a name and pronoun change, disclosing to family and others, hair and wardrobe changes, addressing transition at school, a legal name change, and any medical intervention.

Conspicuously missing from this checklist is a parent's own transition process. How do parents address their own anxiety, grief, and conflicting feelings while simultaneously serving as the point person for navigating a trajectory that they didn't ask for, don't want (at least initially), and for which they have no accompanying "how-to" manual?

Parents who are trying to be supportive are rarely ready for the emotional storm that comes with a child's gender journey. Caregivers are immediately faced with confronting—and sometimes having to protect their child from— the reactions of others, be they family, friends, neighbors, other children, health providers, teachers, coworkers, and even strangers. Any bullying, ridiculing, or other negative situation faced by their child only serves to exacerbate the parent's personal feelings of helplessness, grief, and isolation. This burden can be exhausting and ongoing.[6]

Whether parents are moving forward, hoping to ride out what they feel could be a phase, or actively resisting any supportive steps, they are on what is undoubtedly a long, bumpy road. As with any stressful situation in life, facing a child's gender identity issues can take a physical and psychological toll. Depression, fatigue, grief, guilt, and anxiety can all be a common part of this pathway. One mother, after attending a support group for over a year, said:

> "I've hesitated to say this because it doesn't seem like anyone else experiences this. Don't get me wrong, I definitely support my trans son. I know this is the right thing to do. I'm just really grieving my *daughter*. I guess I'm the only one struggling with this." So many others immediately nodded in agreement or raised their hand that everyone burst into laughter.

Another parent was particularly passionate about supporting her sixteen-year-old child through the early process of transition. Over the eighteen months, since her child had disclosed their gender status, this parent had become a strong advocate, educating anyone who would listen. At one particular meeting where the group's discussion covered many complex, emotional topics, she took a huge, deep breath and sighed. Sweeping her hand across the room, she said, "I'm wiped out! I can't wait until my child is eighteen and has all this behind him!" She had been treating her child's gender journey more like a sprint that she could power through rather than pacing herself for the long haul.

It is common for parents to move through an array of emotions as they struggle to understand their child's experience. For instance, after they have accepted their child's gender transition and they see the positive benefit on their child or teen, many parents express guilt at not "having seen it sooner." This is most common with parents who have older children, either teens or young adults, especially when they realize the body dysphoria their child might have experienced during puberty and the physical changes resulting from that puberty that might have been avoided. Sometimes parents of younger children experience this guilt, too. One mom of a five-year-old said this:

> My daughter has been telling me she was a girl since the age of three. I didn't believe her. She was so sad that I didn't understand. It took her father and me one year to learn that she might be transgender and that we should support her. I sometimes wonder where my little boy went. It was as if he were just a dream I had and, at the same time, I can't tell you how much guilt I feel for not stepping up sooner.

Stage Five: Acceptance and Celebration

Most parents say that their child's transition was a transition for them as well. They report finding courage they didn't know they had and strength beyond what they ever thought they would need. Many share stories of unexpected epiphanies and life changes. One father, who is white, middle class, and heterosexual, spoke of his own growth:

> I'm learning a lot about the privilege I experience now that I have a trans daughter. I've had to educate myself and deal with my own discomfort with that recognition. I understood very little, yet soon found myself testifying publicly before legislators just so my nine-year-old can use the bathroom safely! I would never have imagined that I'd be in this fight. I'm passionate about making change for her and others but sometimes feel as if the ground beneath me has disappeared. That said, my daughter's strength is amazing and I'll move heaven and earth for her!

This soft-spoken mother shared some unexpected news with other support group parents:

> We've come a long way since our child first told us he was a boy in his heart and mind. He is fully accepted by his peers and excels in sports. He was accepted to a private school that has one of the most competitive soccer teams in the nation. We've easily dealt with the issue of locker rooms—he showers at home and can blame that on us, his parents, for being cleanliness freaks. His drive and ambition are such a far cry from where he was just a few years ago. His courage inspires me every day. As a matter of fact, I've never really liked my first name. As a child, I had a nickname that I loved—Poppy—so the other day, I just changed my name! My son gives me so much courage to be myself.

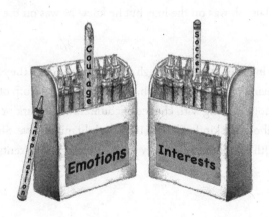

Sometimes accepting and loving a trans child unconditionally comes at a price. Many families have left their home and community to seek a more supportive environment. Parents may struggle to come to an agreement when it comes to their child's gender identity. Even if they eventually both get to a place of acceptance, the timelines may vary so significantly that their relationship has been stressed beyond repair. Or, especially with older trans children, the time it takes a parent to learn and understand enough to get to a place of acceptance may place a wedge between parent and child that may take months or years to repair:

> Another parent, a former police officer, initially refused to accept that his teenage son could possibly be his daughter. His wife also struggled but made earlier efforts to be supportive, even though it was something she couldn't fathom either. She felt forced to "pick a side" between her child and her spouse. Their marriage seemed destined for destruction even though they both were hurting. Life dealt the family more challenges as the daughter attempted to run away from home, the father was diagnosed with terminal cancer, and the mother was in a debilitating car accident. Today, both parents fully accept their now-adult child's identity as a woman, and their marriage has strengthened.

> An evangelical minister faced a dilemma in his church. He discussed God's love and acceptance daily, but he wasn't sure his congregation was ready for his gender-expansive son. As he and his wife prayed for guidance, he explored ways to discuss this with his church community. This father had a deepening conviction with respect to his child. Love and acceptance must come first. His job was on the line, but he knew he was on the right track with God.

Parents can be in a day-in, day-out high state of vigilance as they face the stress of managing their family's internal path, fielding questions from other parents at their child's school, dealing with chance encounters at the park or grocery store, and worrying about the kind of life their trans child might have. Sharing a child's new identity with a church community or the child's grandparents, for example, can create higher stress and anxiety than sharing with a neighbor or family at school:

> An African American grandfather raising both his grandchildren was reticent to bring his transgender granddaughter to his Baptist church, where he served as a deacon. The church was an integral part of his identity, and rejection of his granddaughter would have huge consequences. After struggling with how or whether to discuss the matter with church leaders ahead of time, he decided to just go to church as usual with both grandchildren, this time with a grand*daughter* and a grandson. He had no idea what to expect. There were a few quizzical looks, he later said, but since then a number of the women from church have taken his granddaughter under their wing.

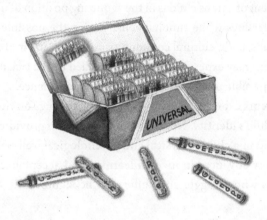

A Latino father worried about attending an upcoming family reunion with his nine-year-old trans daughter. The father knew that his child's transition was the right thing to do—she had been struggling deeply for years. But he also understood that in his large extended family, if his grandmother, the matriarch of the family, wasn't on board, then the rest would follow her lead. He finally worked up the courage to approach his grandmother to share the story. To his significant relief, she listened, nodded, and said her great-grandchild's happiness was all that mattered to her.

Both families had positive outcomes during these stressful, crucial moments. Not everyone is so fortunate. Many families go through long, arduous journeys. There are tens of thousands of families with unique, challenging circumstances to manage as they travel on the complicated path to understanding and acceptance. Parents need time to process their feelings, resources to deepen their own understanding, factual information to distinguish between real and perceived dangers, and the kinship that comes from connecting to others with a shared experience.[7]

The risks that come with supporting a trans child, including so many unpredictable reactions and situations from others, can feel unending. What others (or even parents themselves) may not realize is that this creates a unique, exhausting, and isolating experience. Unlike the death of a relative or friend, where the stages of grieving are to be expected and support from others assumed, a parent of a trans child is in the agonizing position of navigating their own complex feelings while simultaneously facing the possible loss of family members, friends, faith/cultural community members, and more. The depth of pain that a parent may experience is only intensified by the lack of acknowledgment and the invisible nature of such a significant experience.

Not all parents experience deeply conflicting feelings on the road to celebrating their child's identity. Not all will be resistant to providing the support necessary to aid in a child's physical and psychological well-being. However, until our society advances in its own learning and acceptance, the percentage of families who struggle and suffer will be significantly higher than it needs to be.

Many of these families' stories mentioned are, of course, not over. The Muslim family slowly came to a place of acceptance and love. The family who had lost most of their family was grateful when one of the child's grandmothers came to visit. Surprising them all, she attended a support meeting and told the attendees that she hoped to learn more to better support her grandson. Poppy's son was active and successful on his high school soccer team, graduated, and is now attending college with a new athletic interest in bodybuilding. Regardless of the length of time it takes—a few weeks, many months, or even years—for a parent to fully support their child's gender identity, there is one common refrain I hear: "I just wish I could have supported them sooner!"

Without a doubt, the factor that families have praised as being the most crucial in their journey to acceptance was the ability to connect with other families of shared experience. The ability to *find* those with shared experience is difficult for many. Pointing a parent, grandparent, or other caregivers to a resource like the national family support organization, TransFamilies.org, can be life-changing and life-saving.

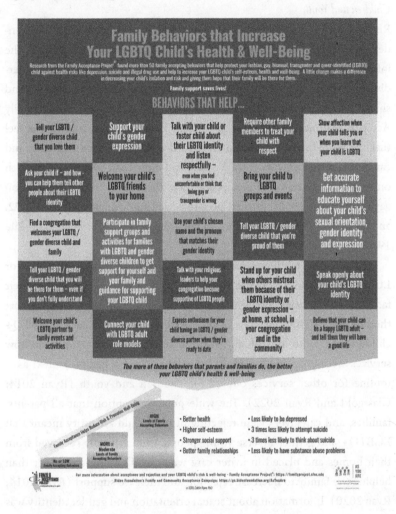

The English version of the Family Acceptance Project's General Family Acceptance Poster shows how family supportive and accepting behaviors help protect against health risks and promote well-being. See Appendix C for guidance on poster use. https://familyproject.sfsu.edu/posters

FAMILY ACCEPTANCE PROJECT

Family Acceptance: Building Healthy Futures for Transgender and Queer-Identified Children and Youth

Research and resources to help diverse families to support their transgender and gender-diverse children have increasingly become available as the information age continues to change how the lives of transgender, gender-diverse, lesbian, and gay individuals—and now children—are depicted and shared online. As Dr. Caitlin Ryan, director of the university-based Family Acceptance Project (FAP) often points out: "Although many parents may feel that knowledge about their children's sexual orientation, gender identity and care has emerged only recently, we have had more than 80 years of research on sexual orientation and gender identity. These early studies focused on gay adults in the 1950s, the first peer-reviewed study on gay youth in 1972, and the first gender identity clinic for children and youth founded in the late 1980s in the Netherlands."

Historically, families were excluded from research. Services for LGBTQ+ and gender-diverse youth emerged in the late 1970s, yet their families, seen as rejecting, were felt to be incapable of learning to support their LGBTQ+ children. As a result, services emerged to serve LGBTQ+ children and youth individually or through peer support—similar to how services were provided for adults—but not within a family context as is routine for other services offered for children and youth (Ryan 2014; Glassgold and Ryan 2022). The widespread perception that all parents, families, and caregivers were rejecting of their child's identity meant that LGBTQ+ and gender-diverse young people were typically removed from their homes and placed in foster care when conflict erupted rather than helping the family to decrease rejection and increase support (Ryan 2014; Ryan 2020). Information about sexual orientation and gender identity was also presented in terms of adult identities and older adolescence. As a result, parents, caregivers, and providers lacked resources and guidance to help them understand how to support and affirm LGBTQ+ and gender-diverse children. Instead, they were routinely pressured by families and peers to change their identities (Ryan 2014).

Dr. Ryan's groundbreaking research on LGBTQ+ and gender-diverse youth and families showed that family reactions to their LGBTQ+ children were much more varied than was previously understood. FAP's research explored the child's identity in the context of the family's cultural and religious beliefs and values. This research identified more than 100 specific family rejecting and accepting behaviors that parents and caregivers use to respond to their children's sexual orientation, gender identity, and expression, and shows how these behaviors contribute to health risks and affect well-being for LGBTQ+ young people (Ryan 2014; Ryan 2019a).

Rejecting Behaviors

More than half of the family behaviors that Dr. Ryan and her team identified were rejecting and focused on trying to change, prevent, deny, or minimize their child's identity through a range of behaviors such as not letting them learn about or talk about their identity or participate in LGBTQ+ support groups, making their child pray and attend religious services to try to change or prevent them from being gay or transgender, and physically punishing them and using hurtful words and slurs to describe their identity and gender expression (Ryan 2009; Ryan 2019d; Ryan, Barba, and Cohen, forthcoming). Family rejecting behaviors are culturally reinforced beginning at early ages with gender-diverse children and can be traumatic for LGBTQ+ and gender-diverse children and youth (Cohen and Ryan 2021; Ryan, Barba, and Cohen, forthcoming).

Accepting Behaviors

Dr. Ryan and her team also identified and measured more than fifty accepting and supportive behaviors that parents and caregivers use to support and affirm their child's identity and gender expression. These include behaviors such as getting accurate information to self-educate about their child's LGBTQ+ identity, supporting their child's gender expression, standing up for their child when others mistreat them because of their identity and gender expression, and finding adult LGBTQ+ and gender-diverse role models to give their children options for the future (Ryan 2019a, 2019b, 2019c).

Outcomes

FAP's research found that as family rejecting behaviors increase, health risks increase significantly. LGBTQ+ young people raised in highly rejecting families where they experienced many specific rejecting behaviors reported high levels of health risks in young adulthood. They were more than eight times as likely to attempt suicide, nearly six times as likely to report high levels of depression, and more than three times as likely to use illegal drugs and to put themselves at high risk for HIV and sexually transmitted infections (Ryan 2009; Ryan 2019a). Conversely, LGBTQ+ young people who were raised in accepting and supportive families reported much lower levels of risk and higher levels of well-being. They were three times less likely to think about or attempt suicide and much less likely to experience depression and to have problems with substance abuse. They had high levels of self-esteem, supportive relationships, and better overall health (Ryan 2009, 2019b, 2019c).

Resources for Families

Dr. Ryan and her team have developed a series of evidence-based multilingual family education resources in eleven languages and a family support model to decrease family rejection and increase support. This includes Best Practice resources for Suicide Prevention for LGBTQ+ young people (Ryan 2009) and a series of Healthy Futures posters that highlight common accepting and rejecting behaviors across cultures and show the importance of family acceptance and support (Ryan 2019b, 2019c, 2019d, 2019e). FAP developed an online resource for diverse LGBTQ+ youth and families to help decrease mental health risks and to increase family acceptance and connectedness (https://lgbtqfamilyacceptance.org/) and trains on this work across the United States and other countries. These resources can help diverse families learn to support their LGBTQ+ and gender-diverse children, even when they believe that being gay or transgender is wrong, as they learn about their children's identity and related needs. (See FAP's Poster Guidance in Appendix C.)

Dr. Caitlin Ryan is a clinical social worker and researcher who has worked on health and mental health since the 1970s, with a focus on children, youth, and families. Over twenty years ago, she started the Family Acceptance Project—a research, education, intervention, and policy project—to study LGBTQ+ youth and families and to develop the first family support model to prevent health risks, including depression, suicide, illegal drug use, sexual health risks and ejection from the home, and to promote well-being of LGBTQ+ young people.

References

Cohen, J. A., and C. Ryan. 2021. "Trauma-focused CBT and Family Acceptance Project: An Integrated Recovery Framework for Sexual and Gender Minority Youth." *Psychiatric News* XXXVIII, no. 6: 15–17.

Glassgold, J., and C. Ryan. 2022. "The Role of Families in Efforts to Change, Support, and Affirm Sexual Orientation, Gender Identity and Expression in Children and Youth." In *Change Efforts in Sexual Orientation and Gender Identity: From Clinical Implications to Contemporary Public Policy*, edited by D. C. Haldeman, pp. 89–107. Washington, DC: APA Books.

Ryan, C. 2019a. "Family Acceptance Project: Culturally Grounded Framework for Supporting LGBTQ Children and Youth." *Journal of the American Academy of Child & Adolescent Psychiatry* 58, no. 10: S58–S59. doi: 10.1016/j.jaac.2019.07.391. Available in English, Spanish, Chinese (traditional & simplified), Korean, Japanese, Vietnamese, Hindi, Punjabi and Tagalog, and an American Indian version.

Ryan, C. 2019b. *Family Behaviors that Increase Your LGBTQ Child's Health & Well-Being*. San Francisco, CA: Family Acceptance Project, Marian Wright Edelman Institute, San Francisco State University. https://familyproject.sfsu.edu/poster.

Ryan, C. 2019c. *Family Behaviors that Increase Your LGBTQ Child's Health & Well-Being— Conservative Version*. San Francisco, CA: Family Acceptance Project, Marian Wright Edelman Institute, San Francisco State University. https://familyproject.sfsu.edu/poster.

Ryan, C. 2019d. *Family Behaviors that Increase Your LGBTQ Child's Risk for Health & Mental Health Risks*. San Francisco, CA: Family Acceptance Project, Marian Wright Edelman Institute, San Francisco State University. https://familyproject.sfsu.edu/poster.

Ryan, C. 2019e. "The Family Acceptance Project's Model for LGBTQ Youth." *Journal of the American Academy of Child & Adolescent Psychiatry* 58, no. 10: S28–S29. doi: 10.1016/j.jaac.2019.07.123.

Ryan, C. 2020. "Family Rejection Is a Health Hazard for LGBTQ Children and Youth." *Journal of the American Academy of Child & Adolescent Psychiatry* 59, no. 10: S336. doi: 10.1016/j.jaac.2020.07.817.

Ryan, C. 2014. "Generating a Revolution in Prevention, Wellness & Care for LGBT Children & Youth." *Temple Political & Civil Rights Law Review* 23, no. 2: 331–344.

Ryan, C. 2009. *Supportive Families, Healthy Children: Helping Families with Lesbian, Gay, Bisexual & Transgender Children*. San Francisco, CA: Family Acceptance Project, Marian Wright Edelman Institute, San Francisco State University. Published in English, Spanish, and Chinese. http://familyproject.sfsu.edu/publications.

Ryan, C., A. Barba, and J. Cohen. Forthcoming. "Family-Based Psychosocial Care for Transgender and Gender Diverse Children and Youth Who Experience Trauma." *Child and Adolescent Psychiatric Clinics of North America*. https://www.journals.elsevier.com/child-and-adolescent-psychiatric-clinics-of-north-america.

FAMILY CHALLENGES

The Strain on Spousal/Partner Relationships

A child's gender disclosure can create significant tension in parents' relationships, especially if there is disagreement on how to approach or support the child's well-being. One common narrative I often hear is that of one parent being "supportive" of their child while the other is "unsupportive." To label something as deep and complex as a parent's love for, and desires to do what is best for, a child as either supportive or unsupportive is too simplistic. Parents love their children and want what's best—they just have different opinions about what that is. Individual and societal ignorance, coupled with inaccurate assumptions about gender identity, can make it difficult for parents to find common ground.

This can be especially hard on a child. Two parents I encountered were separated when I met them and soon decided to divorce. The divorce came on the heels of their young teen's recent gender disclosure. It's not unusual for two parents to be on different timetables with respect to their learning, acceptance, and affirmation of their child's gender identity. For this family, the parents' divergence of perspective and uncertainty about the next steps caused a deep polarization. The teen lived as a male while with one parent and as a female during the time with the other. Aware of one parent's initial deep resistance and deeply anguished about their impending divorce, the teen worked hard to minimize his own needs. He essentially retracted his gender disclosure to his resistant parent while falling apart at home with the other. His distress resulted in several psychiatric hospitalizations as the parents navigated their divorce.

Even in a strong marriage, when parents feel they must validate and defend their choice to support their child's gender, this external pressure can cause strain on the relationship. If parents can get on the same page, often the relationship grows even stronger for it. But sometimes that doesn't happen. A parent shared this story:

> Of course, my former wife and I deeply love our two children. Our oldest was a parenting "breeze," but our youngest struggled from a very young age. She had at least five different behavioral diagnoses, none of which really fit. At age nine, we found an article about a transgender child and instantly knew

this was the real issue at the root of it all. For so many years, we fought, disagreed on, and struggled about how to best help our youngest, not realizing that *neither of us* knew the "right" way to parent her. While we found our way to the same page in support of her and her gender, the strain on our relationship was enough that we could not remain together.

While some people may generalize or predict that mothers are more supportive than fathers, and birth parents more than stepparents, the fact is that the level of support that comes from different parents is complex, unpredictable, and shaped by pre-existing family dynamics. It is helpful, during a time of nascent and/or reticent support from parents, to start with the assumption that they all want what is best for their child. If a family begins their dialogue with this assumption, then when divergent opinions surface, they can return to this core foundation again and again.

No single family's story is the same. Many variables are at play, and outcomes are difficult to predict. However, one of the most influential factors for any parent's path is finding immediate support. This can happen when they hear another family's story, find a knowledgeable provider, gain encouragement from a close friend, or learn that a coworker also has a transgender child. The importance of support for parents, and its ability to decrease fear and isolation, cannot be underestimated.

Siblings

Parents often worry about how to discuss their trans child's gender identification with the child's siblings. Surprisingly, siblings often express the least upset of anyone in the family. Of course, siblings will have some initial questions, which are important to address in a straightforward manner and in age-appropriate ways. If parents can prepare for this conversation, they can optimize the chance for a positive outcome. When parents display anguish— through tears, anxiousness, anger, or being too solemn or stilted—siblings may mirror their reaction. Discussing a child's gender exploration in a straightforward, matter-of-fact manner will allow their sibling to ask questions and incorporate the information in the same manner.

Like any other individual, a sibling can experience a range of responses and can benefit from receiving support for their feelings. For example, a sibling may look up to an older brother as a role model. How does it affect a child when their role model says, "I am not who you think I am"? Of course, they may feel some combination of confusion, sadness, or anger. Providing acknowledgment and understanding for the sibling's feelings is an important part of helping them move through these feelings. A parent, aunt/uncle, teacher, school counselor, therapist, or any other supportive adult who can focus their attention on the emotional needs of the sibling can be helpful.

It is very common for the sibling of a trans child to get sidelined simply because the trans child's needs may be more immediate and pressing. Creating regular one-on-one time for a sibling's feelings and questions will be beneficial. Additionally, it is common for siblings to sideline their own needs indefinitely as the heightened attention on the trans child most often takes center stage. If a sibling is sidelining their needs while the "gender issue" continually, and sometimes indefinitely, takes center stage within a family, the impact on that sibling can be harmful.

A family whose teen disclosed his gender status to his family while in high school found that the gender transition consumed the minds of both parents and child for a couple of years. When the parents discussed current family issues, the comment about the younger sibling was always, "He's fine, no problem there." After the trans child was off to college, the younger child fell apart. His school grades and mental health steeply declined. One of this child's parents shared with the parent support group:

> We talked about the needs of siblings in this group and I thought our family
> was doing fine. Turns out that was definitely not the case. Our youngest is so
> angry with us for not being there for him. Now we are in full-time damage
> control.

I often recommend that the whole family take a "gender break" to have some family time that doesn't revolve around the trans child's particular gender-related needs. That break could be something as simple as ordering pizza and watching a movie as a family.

Extended Family Members

Some parents benefit from having extended families who are close in proximity and close in their bond. Others may have uncles, cousins, grandparents, and aunts who live farther away but who still maintain a close connection. Sometimes these family members serve as important caregivers for a trans child.

It is rare for a parent of a trans youth to *not* experience any pushback from extended family, and the likelihood that some family members may initially struggle with acceptance is high. An extended family member's resistance and the pain it creates can be compounded by the very things that ordinarily tighten a family's bond: sibling relationships, shared faith values, close-knit connections within communities of color, and culture-based celebrations or rites of passage. For instance, a South Asian mother who attended a support group said that she and her nine-year-old trans daughter were not invited to her cousin's huge Muslim wedding *unless* her trans daughter was willing to attend wearing traditional clothing for boys. It was heartbreaking for the mother to know that their attendance was contingent upon telling her daughter, who was so excited to attend, that her authentic self would not be welcome.

In another situation, an African American family had been raising their trans granddaughter since a young age. The grandmother was supportive early on, even though initially she knew very little about transgender children. The grandfather, while not overtly rejecting, was slow to be supportive of his grandchild. He had a pivotal turning point when he watched a particular scene in a movie where the father's angry disapproval of his young trans daughter showed clearly on his face. He said it was as if someone had held up a mirror to him. In the years since then, he has been supportive. The father of the trans girl, on the other hand, has not been able to embrace and accept his trans daughter. The biggest barrier is that his wife (not the child's mother) is not accepting of her. "God doesn't make mistakes," she told him. He feels like he must choose between his wife and his child. Because his child has love and acceptance from the grandparents who have been raising her, he opts to appease his wife. The damage to his relationship with his now-teenage daughter has been significant.

Responses from Aunts, Uncles, and Other Adult Family Members

If a parent of a trans child has siblings of their own, these family members can be of great support to that parent. Unfortunately, there is no guarantee that a parent will get that support from their siblings, or at least not early when it is most needed.

One parent shared the exchange she had with her sister, with whom her teen had a very close relationship:

> Your child is not a boy—she's just a strong young woman who is a bit of a tomboy. I was like that too. You're not thinking clearly about this. She needs to know that being a strong woman is empowering, not that she needs to change her gender just because being a boy would be easier!

The father of a trans girl heard this from his older sister:

> You know this is going to blow over. If you remember, my oldest son was always trying on my dress shoes. We nipped that in the bud when he was five. Look at him now—he's a Marine! You can't encourage him. Just lay down the law and it'll pass.

One dad's older brother said, "Just don't tell Grandpa. He's ninety. This'll kill him."

Some parents have relayed hard stories of their close sibling(s) who, reacting out of fear, made some hurtful decisions. One aunt told her sibling, the parent of a trans teenager, that she didn't want this teen "around her children." While it wasn't blatantly stated, the clear implication from the aunt was that she did not consider her sister's trans child to be a safe person to be with other children. This, unsurprisingly, placed a huge wedge between the two, previously close, families.

Grandparent Responses

The level of conflict that can occur between the parent of a trans or gender-diverse child and their own parent(s) can vary in intensity, duration, and outcome. At a time when a family could benefit from crucial familial support, they may find that additional conflict is present and support unavailable. A parent may even find themselves defending their spouse to their parents because the blame—for "making"/"allowing" a child to be trans—is more easily assigned to the in-law. Grandparents may feel deeply hurt because, from their perspective, it can feel as if their adult child is rejecting years of direct parenting experience. For a young child or teen, a grandparent's refusal to acknowledge their identity, and use the correct name and/or pronoun, regardless of the reason, may be perceived as invalidation and rejection. This can place a parent in the terrible position of feeling they have to choose between their child and their own parent.

During an early conversation with his daughter about the teen grandchild's gender-fluid expression, one grandfather shared:

> "When we encountered kids like that when I was a kid, we beat them up." After a long pause, he added, "I didn't want to but I felt that if I didn't, I would be next."

Over the span of many months, a parent attending a support group shared how much she was struggling with her mother regarding her choice to support her teenage daughter's gender identity. The parent talked of how her mother's faith as a born-again Christian was at the center of the conflict. After some time, the parent came to the support group and gave this update:

> We had gotten to the point where we were spending less and less time together. It was hard, but I told my mom that, unless she could treat my child respectfully and without judgment, including consistent use of her name and pronoun, she would not be able to spend time with her. My mother said she did *not* judge my daughter and loved her. The challenge for her was that she felt she had somehow failed in her parenting of *me*! She was worried about *our* relationship. I was floored. We talked through some things that we

had not discussed before, and it really helped us turn a corner. I am so grateful we could understand each other better. It's been a long haul to get to this
place. I love my mom and didn't want to lose her.

NOTES

1. Melinda M. Mangin, *Transgender Students in Elementary School: Creating an Affirming and Inclusive School Culture*, Youth Development and Education (Cambridge, MA: Harvard Education Press, 2020), 149.
2. This article is emblematic of some of the current backlash surrounding transgender children: "Arkansas Passes Bill Restricting Access to Medical Treatments for Transgender Children," *Washington Post* (March 29, 2021), https://www.washingtonpost.com/dc-md-va/2021/03/29/arkansas-passes-bill-restricting-access-medical-treatments-transgender-children/.
3. Diane N. Ruble et al., "The Role of Gender Constancy in Early Gender Development," *Child Development* 78, no. 4 (2007): 1121–1136, https://doi.org/10.1111/j.1467-8624.2007.01056.x.
4. "Five Stages of Grief," *Wikipedia* (May 29, 2022), https://en.wikipedia.org/wiki/Five_stages_of_grief.
5. Damien W. Riggs and Clare Bartholomaeus, "Gaslighting in the Context of Clinical Interactions with Parents of Transgender Children," *Sexual & Relationship Therapy* 33, no. 4 (August 15, 2018): 382–394, https://doi.org/10.1080/14681994.2018.1444274.
6. Tey Meadow, *Trans Kids: Being Gendered in the Twenty-First Century* (Oakland: University of California Press, 2018), 144.
7. Thankfully, there are more resources for parents now than ever. See Diane Ehrensaft, *The Gender Creative Child: Pathways for Nurturing and Supporting Children Who Live Outside Gender Boxes* (New York: Experiment, 2016); Elizabeth P. Rahilly, *Trans-Affirmative Parenting: Raising Kids across the Gender Spectrum* (New York: New York University Press, 2020); Elizabeth J. Meyer, ed., *Supporting Transgender and Gender Creative Youth: Schools, Families, and Communities in Action*, Gender and Sexualities in Education, vol. 4 (New York: Peter Lang, 2014); Ann Travers, *The Trans Generation: How Trans Kids (and Their Parents) Are Creating a Gender Revolution* (New York: New York University Press, 2018).

5

Strategies for Families

There can be no keener revelation of a society's soul than the way in which it treats its children.

Nelson Mandela

While family circumstances are unique, there are a core group of questions parents commonly express:

- Could my child just be gay?
- What if this is a phase?
- Aren't they too young to know?
- Is my child just confused?
- What if they change their mind?

- Aren't they just trying to get attention? Could peer pressure be at play?
- Will supporting my child's gender exploration "make" them trans?
- What can I do to support my child?

COULD MY CHILD JUST BE GAY?

Most people have a familiarity with what it means to be gay or lesbian—someone who has a same-sex romantic or sexual attraction. The term transgender may feel like it somehow falls into that definition. However, being transgender is not a sexual orientation. We all have a sense of our gender that is innate, even as young children. A clearer way of understanding it is to consider the language that children themselves use, for example, "In my heart and mind, I am a boy even though you see me as a girl." As humans, we *all* have an innate sense of our gender identity, which is separate from the people to whom we have an attraction.

For two decades, I have listened to parents ask questions like "Could my child simply be gay?" or "How is this different than being gay?" Many have flatly stated, "I wish my child was *just gay*." It's not surprising that parents who have no understanding of the word *transgender* latch on to the nearest descriptors they recognize—terms like *lesbian, gay,* or *bisexual*—even though these terms describe sexual orientation rather than gender identity.

Parents of gay and lesbian children from past decades would likely find the wish for a gay child a bit ironic considering the stigmatization, misrepresentation, and perceived immorality that were once strongly associated with sexual minorities. This "wish" speaks to an overall increased familiarity with, and a higher degree of acceptance of, those who identify as gay, lesbian, or bisexual.

Within the United States today, there exists a visible presence of LGBTQ+ people, and most people know and are connected to LGBTQ+ people, including immediate or extended family members, coworkers, neighbors, and friends. Unlike in the past, we no longer experience a collective cultural dissonance with respect to differing sexual orientations. We, of course, may have varying perspectives about sexual orientation, but LGBTQ+ people are now a known and visible part of our cultural mindset.

The subtext within the statement, "I wish my kid were just gay," is a desire to have that solid, culturally recognizable frame of reference for their child's experience. Parents *can* find other parents of gay or lesbian children within their communities or online. Many of their friends or coworkers would likely relate their own tales of a child, nephew, or cousin who has come out and be able to offer support and resources. The shared experience of others can provide a newly exploring parent with comfort, normalcy, and hope for their child's future.

Of course, today's improved acceptance of those who are gay, lesbian, or bisexual does not mean that sexual minority populations experience *full* acceptance in today's society. It does, however, speak to the significant *progression* of acceptance within many facets of our society—including the legal and scientific communities, medical and mental health professions, the workplace, and mainstream popular culture. For transgender people, this moment in history is akin to the widespread invisibility and stigmatization of LGBTQ+ people decades ago. The good news is that with more information, higher visibility, and greater understanding, we can shift from a place of fear of an unknown population to recognizing and accepting trans people as valued community members.

While this progress may not be linear, it is heartening to consider this forward trajectory and the positive impact it will have on trans youth. Yet, for shocked, confused parents whose child just stated, "I think I am transgender," this vision of the future may feel irrelevant and impossibly far away.

WHAT IF THIS IS A PHASE?

Gender exploration is a normal part of any child's development. Many people have had childhood interests considered outside of gender norms. Even within what is considered "typical," there is wide variation. It is normal for children to discover, engage, and *then discard* any number of interests and activities through-out their childhood. For some children, their interests are relatively gender-consistent; for others, they may be varied. As discussed earlier, these interests, activities, and preferences fall into the category of gender expression and, of course, anyone's gender expression can go through phases.

However, when a parent asks whether "this" could be a phase, they are more often referring to *gender identity*. "*This*" is when a child makes a more definitive statement like, "I am not a boy. I'm a girl."

Is it possible for a child or teen who makes a declaration about their gender identity to be going through a phase? The short answer? Yes, it can be a phase. Children can and do make statements about their gender that may not persist over time. Consider this parent's story:

> One day my three-year-old child got up from where she was playing and stood in front of me with a pretty determined look on her face. "I'm a boy," she said. I quickly scanned the room to see if there was any reason that would prompt her to make this declaration. Nothing. Should I correct her? She looked pretty serious so I just said, "Okay." My daughter turned around and went back to whatever she'd been doing. Over the next month or so, she made that statement to a few other people, again, for no particular reason that I could discern. She was never distressed when she said it. Then, it just stopped. Fast forward to kindergarten—my daughter would not wear a dress if her life depended on it. By first grade, she would *only* wear dresses. One day when she was in eighth grade, she came home and said, "I don't get girls. They get upset but can't tell you why. Will they let it go, though? No way. I like hanging out with guys. They are laid back and just want to hang out. That's me!"
>
> I realized that indeed my daughter did have a temperament more typically associated with boys. She's always been easygoing, not overly emotional. I'll never know for sure what prompted her, at age three, to tell me she was a boy. I've asked but she doesn't remember it. I'm glad I didn't try to "correct" her though. She wasn't confused, she just was taking in messages about gender like any other child her age. I certainly didn't feel like a "genital conversation" was where either of us needed to go.

The experience related above is an example of a young child's gender explora-tion. While we don't know exactly what prompted this child's statement, it was short-lived and not a source of distress for the child or the parent. Children take in information about gender at a very early age, and, again, this most often falls in the domain of gender expression—toys, clothes, hair, activities, and so on. In conversations with groups of three-to-five-year-olds, I've found that they will often say that they are both a boy and a girl "on the inside" or that they are part boy, mostly girl, or any other gender combination. It has not been my experience that they are confused; they're simply working with the manner in which gender has been presented to them up to that point. They are commenting on things like their activity interests, clothing/colors/hair preferences, or who they feel most drawn to for friendship—most of which have gendered *connotations* but are not inherently gender distinctive.

It was once felt that a true measure of transgender child's identity is that they would express their gender identity difference *insistently, persistently, and consistently*. This certainly applies to many transgender children, but not all. Sometimes parents wish for these definitive indicators so as to have a clearer understanding of the next steps. Yet many children will express gender differences and a parent will have no definitive way of knowing whether it means their child is transgender or not.

This can come across as confusion and uncertainty, and why wouldn't it? It is confusing for many of us as adults to sort out the distinctions between our gender identity, gender expression, and how we wish to engage in the world. The question of whether it is or isn't a phase is less relevant than the importance of providing a supportive environment for children *during* that exploration (as one might support *any* exploration). This support provides optimal results for a child's social and emotional well-being.

Children generally do not express disappointment in the fact that a parent was supportive of them during *any* of their endeavors. Supporting a child's gender exploration does not *make* them transgender but having a supportive environment for exploration and discovery matters, whether their gender identification difference is ultimately proved to have any permanence or not.

CONSIDERING AGE DIFFERENCES

When we consider whether a teen could be experiencing a gender phase or not, it is important to recognize an important distinction between the older child's declaration and a similarly worded declaration of a younger child. By the time a child reaches adolescence, physiological gender differences are more clearly understood. A teenager who makes the statement, "I'm not a boy. I'm a girl," understands those differences related to genitalia and is therefore unlikely to be basing that statement solely on gendered interests or activities. That teen's statement is addressing their core sense of self rather than either their gender expression or anatomical sex.

That said, parents will still wonder whether their teen's gender "confusion" is temporary. It is reasonable to ask this question—of course, teens go through phases, too. But, in this time of critical identity formation, it is important to ensure that the teen's gender identity exploration is not dismissed as an indicator of immaturity, confusion, combativeness, or peer pressure. Most teens are aware that the disclosure of their gender identity will be a challenging conversation for their parent(s). If that parent is dismissive, they risk alienating their child and creating a breakdown in communications. Even worse, if their child is in emotional distress, this dismissal could propel them toward dangerous self-harm, even death.

Parents of elementary-age children, like parents of teens, could also wonder whether their child is going through a gender phase. Yet, for many of these families, the disclosure from pre-adolescent children seems to come as less of a surprise. Often, these parents have observed gender differences over time, even years. A parent may be more likely to say, "At first, I thought this was a phase but as a few years have gone by, my gut is telling me otherwise. My six-year-old is really starting to struggle."

It is easier for people to attribute gender identity differences to a young child's "gender confusion" or to a teen's hormonal unpredictability and/or peer pressure. The age of any child is a consideration, yet it is only one consideration. There are too many factors to do more than offer up the broadest of generalizations. Children of any age may have an obvious, solid sense of their identity, others may be exploring where on a gender continuum their gender identity lands, and still others are drawn to the freedom that comes from discarding gender restrictive norms and expectations. Ultimately, the recommended course of action, regardless of age, is to listen, affirm, and support a child's path.

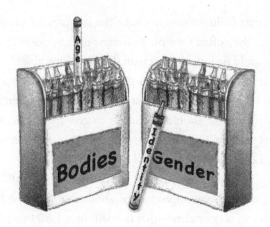

AREN'T THEY TOO YOUNG TO KNOW?

A gender transition is a huge, daunting prospect. When adults pursue a gender transition, the stakes are very high. Despite a gradual progression in societal acceptance, a person's gender transition ranks up at the top of any list of momentous life events and accompanying loss. Finding gender congruence may come at the cost of personal relationships with a spouse/partner, children, extended family, friends, neighbors, or coworkers—every individual relationship is potentially in jeopardy. Jobs, housing, and even work history are at risk. Physical safety cannot be taken for granted. Vigilance is a universal necessity. Even if a person is able to successfully minimize the personal losses, access to knowledgeable gender-related care is still a significant barrier for a majority of people across the United States.

With everything that factors into an adult's transition, the questioning of a child's readiness is quite understandable. Of course, a child is not ready to manage these potential hardships! These high-stakes considerations are the subtext for what appears to be a straightforward question: "Aren't they just too young?"

We need to look at the question in a more direct, straightforward manner. Are they too young to know who they are? The short answer is no. Do we ask that question of young children who are not transgender? No, we do not. I've often polled adult audiences to share the precise age at which they felt their gender identification solidified. The question is met with nodding heads, even laughter. The consistent response is, "What do you mean, I've always known my gender!" We can extend the same understanding to trans children. They know who they are. Trans children may not have the language to adequately *describe* their experience. They often have no awareness of the *possibility* that a person's gender identity could be incongruent with their anatomical sex. A child may not have ever met or heard of another trans person. Under these circumstances, the fact that a child is able to articulate their gender identity as being distinct from their sex-assigned-at-birth should inspire us to give their articulation an even greater degree of validity. These children state who they are even when the world tells them their existence is impossible.

Parents of gender-diverse children worry that if they talk about gender options—actually step into conversations about the idea that boys can wear dresses and girls can play hockey—that this will somehow *encourage* their child toward a different gender identity. This is not the case. The interests of children are just that, their interests. Their gender identity is what it is, the internal sense of their own gender. Exploration of interests is simply part of healthy childhood development. It is reasonable to wonder whether a child is articulating their core sense of self (gender identity) or commenting on their gender-specific interests (gender expression). Both aspects, however, can be met with validation and support. If the child's gender identification is not the issue at hand, then it will not persist over time.

Current studies on gender cognition indicate that a gender-diverse child's *awareness* of their gender is commensurate with that of non-transgender children.[1] In other words, trans children have a solid sense of their gender in the same way, and at the same time, that other children do. Although they may know that they feel themselves to be a different gender than has been assigned by others, a young child generally lacks the vocabulary to express this definitively. With no images of other trans or gender-diverse children like themselves—and with the awareness that this difference is unsettling to adults around them—a child may wait to disclose this information to parents for some time. Some children express this as early as two years old, others do not. "Knowing" from an early age does not make a child any "more or less trans" than children who express their gender at later ages.

IS MY CHILD JUST CONFUSED?

When a child's gender identity and/or expression differ from what is viewed as the norm, it can indeed be confusing for them. *Any* person may face similar challenges as they experience gender-restrictive expectations within a family, community, or society as a whole. If that weren't the case, we wouldn't have evolving discussions and debates about those gendered roles and expectations that have spanned recorded history. Gender rights—and restrictions—have and will continue to be an ongoing conversation. Not too long ago, a girl may have felt that her dream to be a police officer was an impossibility. While once a historically male-dominated profession, men in the twentieth century were either forbidden entry to nursing schools or faced an uphill, stigma-ridden career path as a nurse. But now we have women who are law enforcement officers and a growing cadre of men in the nursing field, although both may still face challenges in their fields. Representation and visibility of all genders in the full range of career options communicate *possibility* rather than the *impossibility* to children.

If we do not have these visible representations of gender possibilities—either in the way we express it in our lives or in the way we embrace our sense of self—then children's possibilities seem limited or constrained. Similarly, many educational and career paths were legally prohibited for African Americans from the time of the Emancipation Proclamation until the latter half of the twentieth century, making it virtually impossible for any child of color to pursue their dreams and interests. It takes minimal effort to imagine the confusion experienced by any child of color when presented with the reasoning and justification for these barriers.

In many respects, the child is the best one to determine who they are and how they feel about their gender. Children of all ages—whether five, fifteen, or twenty-five and beyond—will articulate their gender identity to the best of their ability with the language they have available. Yet, this does not mean that their understanding of who they are won't evolve over time. Clarity can take time. It is important to recognize the challenges that come when a child feels an incongruence within their body while perhaps also experiencing resistance from friends, family, school, and society. What a child unequivocally needs is support in finding this clarity. Traveling this path together is the single most important ingredient to achieving long-term, successful outcomes. Your child may need your support and assistance in many ways but not know how to ask. Of course, the younger the child, the more you may need to take the lead with respect to schools, gender transition-related steps, disclosing to others, and navigating any challenges that arise. DO engage your child in conversation. DON'T assume they know all there is to know. And DO strive to travel this journey together.

Rather than ask whether an individual child might be confused about their gender, it might be better to consider whether society's gender norms create a confusing cultural environment that is full of contradictions. Somehow, we expect children to make sense of these contradictions. In this time of societal discovery and increasing awareness of gender identity—both in the complexity of expression and biological origins—we might consider trusting children to know themselves.

WHAT IF THEY CHANGE THEIR MIND?

If, during a period of exploration and information gathering, a child "changes their mind," the act of supporting them has done no harm. A name or pronoun once changed, can be changed again. Hairstyles can be changed "back." Even certain medical interventions such as puberty delay and early hormonal interventions can be paused, discontinued, and/or remedied. Having the chance to explore and "try things on" is often the only way to gain salient information.

In my experience, this parental question ranks highest in both frequency and apprehension. What if a parent takes the scary step of supporting their child's gender transition (social and/or medical), and several months or even years later the child changes their mind? The possible repercussions imagined by a parent are frightening. They fear their child might eventually say:

"How could you *do this* to me? I was so young!"

"I was just going through a phase. How could you let me take *hormones*? Surgery?!"

"You've ruined me. I'll never have a shot at a normal life!"

These fears and other anticipated scenarios loom large when a parent or caregiver is in the early period of awareness or disclosure of a child's gender identity. This question of a possible change of heart can be paralyzing to a parent struggling with how, and especially *if*, they should take any supportive steps.

Parents are just as likely as anyone to mistakenly assume that a gender transition entails a single, but seemingly enormous, decision where all invested parties need to have the utmost clarity and conviction. Indeed, this misperception is at the crux of the collective angst of parents, providers, educators, and society as a whole. If there were, for example, a clear, definitive chromosomal test confirming a child is transgender (there isn't), it would likely inspire a collective sigh of relief because it would eliminate the responsibility of making what feels to be a huge, risky "gender determination." It would remove the scary decision-making away from any parent or provider, as well as from the child.

While the possibility of a child wanting to move forward with steps toward a gender transition and then stepping back is small, it does occasionally happen. After working with thousands of families, I am aware of only a handful who have reversed their course. These children received the parental love and support that was so urgently needed at the most crucial time. The fact that parent and child could navigate this path together, regardless of their end destination, only served to strengthen their bond. Supporting a child's path is not a definitive determination that they are transgender, it is an opportunity to willingly join a child, side-by-side, and defend their right to discover their authentic self.

IS MY CHILD TRYING TO GET ATTENTION OR RESPONDING TO PEER PRESSURE?

If a child makes a gender pronouncement during the time of adolescence, parents sometimes want to chalk it up to external factors, such as attention-seeking and peer pressure. The teenage years are marked by behavioral changes, stronger connections with peers, and an increased desire for independence from parents. Because teens don't often go through this time of change in the most graceful manner (more common descriptors include sullen, snide, rebellious, full of attitude, emotional, etc.), it is understandable that parents might dismiss their gender disclosure as reactive.

One parent in our support group believed his teen's behavior was directed at him:

> I have to say; my teen will do anything to get attention. He loves to piss me off, and I have to say, he sure picked a doozy this time. Gotta give him credit because I sure wasn't expecting him to go this far!

Another parent responded by saying:

> Well, it seems like a pretty tough way to go about pissing you off. Leaving
> stinky socks on the floor or an empty milk carton in the fridge seems a more
> effective way to accomplish the same thing. You mentioned your kid was
> having a tough time with some other kids at high school because he's talked
> to them about being trans. It's a pretty high price tag if your kid's only moti-
> vation is to get your goat.

As this parent pointed out, making a gender disclosure often has difficult consequences for teens. They are making this declaration at the risk of their safety,
their friendships, and their relationships with adults whose approval and love
they seek. They are unlikely to undertake this journey for any other reason than
a deeply felt search for gender authenticity.

Can a teen's peers have an influence on their gender identity? Yes, of course,
but not in the way that a parent might think. The adolescent years are a time
when youth are more actively defining who they are, identifying their interests,
and seeking a like-minded kinship among their peers. Teens who are drawn to
peers with whom they more closely identify may at the same time discover language and context that better describes who they are. They may share with each
other stories of other trans or gender-diverse youth through social media. Peer
influence does not *cause* differences in gender identity. It can, however, provide a
teen with a greater impetus to discuss their own gender with a parent.

Over the years, I've heard parents say their child didn't have any issues with gender and never brought it up until they started hanging out with a particular kid (or group of kids). Children of any age, but especially as they mature and start expressing greater independence, are typically drawn to those with whom they feel they have more in common. If a child who has gender differences finally encounters a peer with whom they feel more connected and at ease, that child may certainly embrace the language and shared perspectives that they didn't feel previously able to express or for which they lacked context.

Again, are children impacted by peer pressure? Of course! But the desire to be liked, included, or respected by others is more likely to *prevent* teens from making a gender disclosure than to encourage it. The results of acknowledging and articulating one's gender identity—at a time of such heightened social stigma—is more likely to increase isolation and rejection from a peer group. Sharing one's gender identification with any adults or peers is a courageous sharing of one's arrival at (or search for) a personal gender authenticity, even if the familial and social price tag is high.

Adolescence is a time of discovery and exploration. Children are influenced by their peers at school, as well as by their connections found on the internet (Instagram, YouTube, Tik Tok, etc.*). If your child has some gender differences, they will soon discover adults and teens who are talking/posting about their gender identity and steps related to transitioning. If a person who does *not* experience a gender difference watches a video or reads a chat thread, they will not decide that they are transgender by simply viewing or reading this content. If a person *does* experience awareness that their gender is somehow outside the "norm," this new information can be illuminating. They may see themselves reflected in others and now have the language to describe how they feel.

It isn't that they are influenced by what they find on the internet as much as they are empowered by it. It is possible that a child is exploring and expanding their understanding of gender in an effort to experience more personal freedom from society's gender expectations. They may feel themselves to be gender-diverse without a need to specifically claim a transgender identity.

---

* *I strongly encourage parents to be discerning and attentive to their child's social media engagement for reasons to do with safety and misinformation.*

WILL SUPPORTING MY CHILD'S GENDER EXPLORATION MAKE THEM TRANS?

Because this question is so prevalent, many parents feel that a "wait-and-see" approach (taking no gender-supportive steps) is a safe bet. This "wait-and-see" approach is not a passive one. *It is an action* that invalidates and dismisses a child's interests and accomplishes only one thing. It sends a direct message to the child that there is something inherently wrong with them. While that may not be the parent's intent, that is the way a child will receive it.

Of course, many children *do* go through gender exploratory phases. We *can allow and support* their exploration without fear that a child will go through irreversible gender changes in some haphazard and reckless manner. In actuality, providing support is essential to ensure that their process is deliberate and safe. A gender transition should be an informed, thoughtful process involving many gradual steps and considerations. This can accomplish much including the recognition of any potential phase and, more importantly, strengthening a child's positive sense of self and core resiliency. Many don't realize that both child and parent can benefit from an attentive approach regardless of eventual gender outcome.

Imagine a teen who, after years of inner struggle, finally finds the courage to say something about their gender to a parent. You can be sure that teens will never forget the way the parent first responds. Without a doubt, it is rare for any parent to first respond with excitement, happiness, or pride. It is simply not a likely, natural response to something that feels so intimidating. But I encourage parents to at least start with calmness and inquisitiveness. Some straightforward, noncommittal responses could include:

- Well, that's some news all right. I don't know what to think but I am glad you felt you could share this with me.
- I'm unfamiliar with the terminology you are using. Could you say more about what that means for you?
- I imagine that was not easy for you to say. Have you talked to others about this? What was their response? Are you doing okay?
- This is a lot to absorb. I may need some time. Just know that I love you!

Even if a parent has a strong, negative reaction—anger, ridicule, fear, invalidation—it is not too late to come around afterward and offer up an apology and any of the above or similar responses. The primary goal does not need to be one where immediate acceptance is magically manifested but rather one where a parent communicates their commitment toward traveling this journey together.

No one family's story is the same. Every youth has a unique experience with respect to their gender. Yet, there is a common theme underlying parental questions such as, "Is this a phase or is my kid just gay? Aren't they too young or will they possibly change their mind?" At the core of these questions is fear: Fear of the hardships a trans child might experience. Fear of making a permanent and harmful mistake. Fear of judgment and ridicule by others. Most parents may not, at first, recognize the fear that inspires their questions.

It is important for a parent to not get too invested in hoped-for, fear-based outcomes, such as their child changing their mind or outgrowing a phase. Again, parents who worry that support of a child's gender exploration is premature, impulsive, or irresponsible may adopt a "wait-and-see" approach, not recognizing the harmful effects of withholding gender-affirming parenting and health care. For a trans youth in deep distress, this immobility can be very dangerous. A teen experiencing distressing pubertal changes, for example, because a parent/ provider has decided to see if the youth "changes their mind," may interpret this over-cautionary approach as an outright rejection. With each irreversible and incongruent physical change, the teen's despair heightens and so do their risks for self-harm, depression, substance abuse, and suicide.[2] Child and parent are best served when a family can elevate in importance the shared goal of a supportive, loving journey to whatever gender outcome.

WHAT CAN I DO TO SUPPORT MY CHILD?

No matter which way parents turn, they face challenges.[3] Ignorance and bias against transgender people and the subsequent lack of family and community support often make parents feel like they have few options. They can ignore or "wait out" a child's gender assertion as a phase, or they can assume their child is confused or mentally ill and reject their child's gender assertion.

It's understandable that parents want clarity on the causes of differences in gender identification. Many parents wonder if their childrearing practices had any influence on the formation of their child's identity. Recent studies have shed light on gender cognition development and the evidence points toward neuro-biological and other physiological origins in the formation of gender identity.[4] But ultimately, as we wait for more definitive information and answers, parents recognize that their child needs guidance and support now.

Supporting a child's path of gender discovery will not somehow "make" them transgender, as is so often feared. It will, however, provide their child with a sense of safety, acceptance, and value. After a decade of witnessing families who take a supportive, affirming approach, the most predictable outcomes to report are closer family relationships and more confident children, regardless of the child's eventual gender identity.

What can parents who are taking tentative steps toward supporting their child do to improve their chances for positive outcomes? The answers are plentiful, some simple and some complex, and they will only minimize challenges rather than eliminate them. The short answer is to increase their own and others' understanding and awareness regarding gender issues to reduce fear and anxiety and to provide the space and breathing room for their child's gender discovery.

Find Support and Connections

The single most frequently articulated factor I've heard thousands of families mention as crucial to their journey is connecting with other families with shared experience. This is especially valuable when the families share deeper connections. Geographic and cultural commonalities can immediately decrease a family's sense of isolation, especially for families who don't fit the predominantly white, middle-class, urban, and coastal demographic of media-visible families with trans children. But even the most visibly represented families can feel isolated, as the paths to connection are often scarce or inaccessible. Support groups, social media connections, and organizational and community events, if available, are a place to start building connections.[5]

Finding a supportive friend, family member, or other confidant can make a difference. A knowledgeable therapist can provide immense support to a parent or caregiver. The key to a successful experience with a support person is not necessarily their level of gender savvy, (although that, if available, can be very helpful), but whether they can provide nonjudgmental support for a parent navigating a confusing time of stress. It is all the more beneficial if that person is someone who understands that the child's gender identification journey is a *process* and is willing to be present and open-hearted to that process. A support person cannot go wrong, at the very least, by encouraging rest, healthy meals, staying hydrated, exercises to relieve physical and mental stress, and assistance with gaining perspective. While parents' options will vary significantly, I encourage them to make a list of people where they feel they might find the most support. If at all possible, a parent should prioritize getting the support they need to then be able to determine how best to support their child.

Seek Couples Counseling

Parenting any child can have its challenges. The average co-parents often discover how their perspectives differ when it comes to things like faith, school performance expectations, food and diet, and approach to discipline. Because neither parent has the how-to manual on raising a transgender child, the level of parental conflict can intensify. Engaging an affirming and knowledgeable therapist for assistance, if feasible, can be of benefit and help prevent a parent from mistakes like inadvertently (or deliberately) using the trans child as a substitute for direct communication with a co-parent.

Local availability of trans-competent therapists may be scarce or nonexistent. The few providers that exist within some communities may have experience seeing only adult clients, which does not easily transfer to the specific needs of children. Or the in-demand therapist may be fully booked. It is reasonable to cast a wider net and explore the option of a therapist that works remotely through telemedicine or video conferencing. Finding the right provider can mean the difference between successfully navigating a child's gender transition as a family or damaging or breaking spousal and/or child–parent relationships.

Develop Strategies for Disclosure/Non-Disclosure

Once a child shares their gender identity with a parent, the process of disclosure is far from over. Any social transition steps taken—clothing, name, pronoun changes—are observable by others, most of whom will request some type of explanation. It can be helpful for parents to strategize in advance whether, how, when, and to whom to offer explanations. Questions that any parent can and should explore are:

- Which people should I disclose to first, and why?
- How do I determine when, or if, disclosure is of benefit to me and my child?
- Do I need to respond to a person's inquiries just because they've asked?
- Do I have time to explain?
- What legal rights are there that protect my child?
- Do I want to discuss it with this person?

- Should I write an email or discuss it in person?
- Will it be safe to disclose my child's gender experience?
- How much of the disclosure process belongs to my kid and how much do I do?

Equally important for a parent is to prepare themselves and their child to respond to both expected and unexpected scenarios. Role-playing responses for potential encounters will inspire greater confidence in both parent and child. It is important to consider a child's needs in this too. How much, when, and under what circumstances do they feel safe to disclose?

Advocate for Staff Training at School

As a parent seeks support for their trans child from their child's school, more often than not they are met with a degree of resistance from teachers and administrators. Some resistance is benign in nature and indicative of the broad-based lack of exposure to this issue. Under these circumstances, a principal may plead, "Just tell us what to do," hoping that the parents themselves may be a source of guidance. Other times the resistance is more pronounced, as administrative or district personnel are fearful of "stirring the pot" on what is often a controversial subject.

I strongly encourage parents to point their child's schools to organizations like Gender Diversity (http://genderdiversity.org/) as a staff training resource for two reasons. First, parents should not be in the position to train schools on how to support transgender children—they are often too overwhelmed, and they likely do not know enough to be able to do so. It is no more the responsibility of parents of trans and nonbinary children to train their schools about gender diversity than it is for families of color to train schools about racism or racial diversity, for non-English speaking families to train schools about cultural or linguistic diversity, or for families to train their schools about differences in cognitive function or physical ability.

Second, any family is likely to have a unique set of variables that need to be considered. Schools need a solid foundation of understanding to meet the specific needs of each child and each family and to educate teachers, other students, and the parent community. This foundation is significant and extends well beyond any specific needs of any one student.

Prepare for Anything

Our society is in the midst of a significant, volatile shift with respect to trans and gender-diverse children. A previously invisible population is no longer so. While most people are confused and some are dismissive, a small but dangerous portion are distressed enough to take more drastic action. As mentioned earlier, that action might include a call to child protective services. Some people have mobilized larger constituencies to fight against gender-inclusion policies and to introduce legislation preventing or repealing protections for these highly vulnerable children.

Some families of gender-diverse children have opted to document their child's path to protect their child in case someone questions or attacks the parents' supportive approach. A parent may compile things like an assessment of their child's gender identity by a mental health professional; a letter from a physician documenting a treatment plan; and statements from professional organizations like the American Psychological Association, the American Academy of Pediatricians, and guidelines from the Endocrine Society as a way to corroborate an affirming parenting approach. Additionally, a parent may include letters from teachers, clergy, family friends, and others who can vouch for the positive impact of gender support on the trans child's life. Having ready documentation at-hand can tip the scales toward a positive outcome when fear-based actions might otherwise cause harm to a family.

Build a Network of Support

We have some ways to go before our society will understand and fully accept trans and gender-diverse children. The stigmatization of these children is at its height in the United States (hopefully, it won't worsen). If parents themselves experience this kind of distress, so too can any family's existing support network of friends, family, and community. It may be that a family will need to actively seek out *only* those who are ready to be supportive and build new relationships with people who have a better understanding of gender differences.

If a parent cannot get the support of their extended family, they may be able to find *one* family member who is loving and compassionate. If a parent experiences rejection from their church community, they may be able to find a faith-based online group of other families who have shared experience. If a child is experiencing ongoing bullying and the school claims they are helpless to prevent it, or worse, blames the trans child for the assaults, then other supportive schooling options—albeit out-of-reach for many—should be seriously considered. Sadly, a family's usual, expected sources of foundational support may disappear. As much as a family can do to replace this support network, all the better.

It is not necessary for parents to "give up" entirely on their former relationships. I often encourage parents to leave the door open for the possibility that others may come back around. Often a friend, family member, or coworker will seek reconciliation as they move through their own learning process. Some come around quickly; others can take years. How much time, dialogue, and patience any parent offers to those within their existing sphere will certainly vary.

That said, what trans and gender-diverse children and their families need, first and foremost, is an environment in which they can expect to receive support. The mantra that many parents share with each other is "Put on your own oxygen mask first." That means first finding support for those closest to the child and, of course, the child themselves, and then addressing the needs of others when or if they're able.

A STEP-BY-STEP JOURNEY

In reality, to best support a child's gender transition or exploration, parents and any involved providers need to address the child's needs in step-by-step increments. Many factors need to be considered, but they do not need to be lumped together. A pronoun change, while awkwardly rolling off the tongue at first, is nonetheless a powerful step of affirmation for the child, and one that is easily reversed should a child's gender exploration fall into the category of "phase." Growing one's hair or cutting it short, again, is a relatively benign step that can provide children and parents with more information they would not otherwise get without that step. Decisions related to a social transition—name, pronoun, hair, and clothing choices—are completely reversible should there be an unforeseen change of heart.

It is sometimes easier to allay the fears of a parent who has a young, pre-adolescent child than those of families who have children who are beginning or partway through puberty. With respect to pre-teens and teens, the decisions about names and pronouns can go hand-in-hand with decisions about medical intervention. If anyone—parent or child—is expressing anything less than complete conviction, decisions about puberty-delay intervention or beginning cross-hormones can feel overwhelming.

Parents often express feelings of being overwhelmed. One parent said to me, "We've been struggling for some time with whether it is the right thing to start our teen on testosterone or not. Do we do this or don't we? How can we know?" I told them that this question—how can we know—is not the right question. If parents are connecting the smaller decision of whether or not to start hormones with a much bigger question—Is my child truly a transgender man?—then, in some sense, they're asking for a crystal ball to see into the future. Instead, parents can take an inventory of what they know to be true. In the case above, the parents' list included the following:

- Three months prior, their child disclosed information to them about his gender identity.
- He was currently seeking support from them with respect to his name and desired pronouns.
- He had expressed a strong interest in taking testosterone and seemed to have really struggled with the physical changes associated with his natal puberty, like breast development and menstruation.

As discussed, parents may be understandably concerned as to whether or not their child is going through a phase, whether he might change his mind, and how they can be certain it's the right thing. The short answer is that they can't be one hundred percent sure, especially not without more information. How is a teen going to know whether testosterone will be right for him if he hasn't experienced it? Both parents and child need more information. What are the physical changes that a child will experience with testosterone and how will he feel about those changes? It is one thing to read about physical and psychological changes in a book or pamphlet; it is another to actually experience them.

It's important to uncouple the decision about beginning a hormonal treatment from gaining certainty about a child's eventual gender identity. Parents should find a knowledgeable doctor who understands the importance of a gradual hormonal treatment plan. A teen can start a low dosage of hormones and see how they feel about the changes. They can do this over a period of months, sometimes longer, and still have the ability to step away from the treatment *should* they decide to change their mind. If parents are concerned that this might be a phase, then a gradual, low-dosage treatment plan will provide time for a phase to play itself out and/or for the parents and child to acquire a more informed certainty.

This is all dependent upon the capacity for parent, child, and even provider to talk consistently and openly. These adults are there to provide resources and to help the child to understand the implications of their decisions—socially, emotionally, medically—without applying direct pressure but with clarity and honesty. The child needs to feel that they are not being judged, manipulated, or controlled.

It bears repeating—gender identity is one's innate sense of their own gender. An important consideration that often gets lost in this "hormones or not?" decision-making approach is that there are many trans and nonbinary-identified people who are not interested in (or able to consider) a medical transition.

I encourage families to not worry about whether their child is transgender or not. Time will tell. After witnessing the journeys of many families over many years, one thing I can say is that I've not met a youth who regretted the *support* they received along the way. Does that mean that every child or teen who has declared themselves to be transgender continues to do so unwaveringly? No. A few have stepped away from transition-related steps of their own accord. Other parents will wait years for their child to finally "arrive" at an "end destination" (solidly identifying as a boy or a girl) while their kid is comfortable and confident with discarding binary gender labels altogether. A parent is coming at it the wrong way if they feel like the most important thing is for their child to make up their mind. The best outcome for these children comes when a family provides love, acceptance, and support for the journey itself, not the destination.

EXTERNAL CHALLENGES

Among the thousands of families that I've encountered over the years, there is a consistent initial hesitancy to absorb and accept the possibility of their child's gender nonconformity. The top questions parents ask—is this a phase, aren't they too young to know, what if they change their mind, and others—mirror the questions in our broader society. Most often these questions show up in our society as resistance to—or even hostility toward—a child's gender identity. For example, one teacher wondered whether she should start using a trans child's name or pronoun without first having a definitive diagnosis from a professional. A janitor dismissed a teen's right to privacy by informing other youth of the teen's "true" gender. During a field trip, a parent chaperone loudly refused to use the correct name for a trans student on the bus ride. One family, filling out a home rental application, was told to provide "documentation" proving the child's gender status before the landlord would consider the application.

Most families of transgender children and youth experience dozens of examples like these. Almost *everyone* feels entitled to demand unequivocal "proof" that a child is transgender. Why is this? While the answer to this question could easily be the topic of a dissertation, for the sake of brevity, I'll boil it down to a few concrete factors:

- Most of us have had little to no exposure to trans people, much less trans children. If we don't see them, we assume they must not exist.
- Most of us can't imagine the gender incongruence so often experienced by trans people. If we haven't encountered a trans person in our lives, we only have the opinions of others—who typically have the same inability to imagine—to guide us, which can result in a belief that gender incongruence doesn't exist.
- Although the body of validating research is growing, the dissemination of this information into the general populace is slow, and it pushes against the current tide of misinformed public opinion.
- It could be said that there is a transactional aspect to this need for proof. Because people are being asked to see/receive the child differently, to make accommodations that they believe run counter to how they see the world, they demand something in return—in this case "proof."

That leaves many well-intentioned people asking the same questions as any distressed, confused parent. What if this is a phase? What if they change their mind? Surely, they *are* too young to know, right?

Nor is everyone well-intentioned. Unfortunately, there are people out there with ill-intent. There are some who seek to dehumanize for the purpose of exploitation, to express dominance, or get pleasure from harming others, and they may seek to leverage that for profit or pleasure.

How does this widespread questioning affect parents and caregivers of trans children? It can place them under immediate and ongoing stress. Validating and supporting a child's gender identification is counter to the expectations of most people and antithetical to the societal norms of our time. Any or all of a parent's relationships with others can be affected or even threatened. Some frequently recurring discussion topics in parental support groups include conflicts with spouses; judgment from grandparents; hesitancy or resistance from extended family; and fear of rejection by family friends, coworkers, faith communities, and neighbors. This can be a frightful predicament for a parent—feeling as if they must choose between their child and *everyone else*—and can have destructive consequences for a vulnerable child.

COMMUNITY CHALLENGES

Imagine the predicament for parents of a gender-exploring or transitioning child. The parents, struggling with their own feelings and learning curve, are then in the unenviable position of navigating the uncertainty all around them, including a spouse, other children, and any number of extended family members.

Now imagine how that predicament would be deeply compounded by the likelihood that the communities to which that family belongs are unfamiliar with diverse gender identities in children. During any given support group meeting, I hear parents' fear-tinged questions about how they might approach the overwhelming task of talking about their child with those in their neighborhoods, church communities, ethnic communities, and circle of friends.

During most other life events, parents could reasonably expect to seek and receive support from their communities. If a family member experiences a lengthy illness, church members might organize to help the family with chores, deliver meals, or look after children. If a parent is injured, a neighbor might take out the garbage. If a teen were experimenting with drugs, for example, a parent could seek guidance from a school counselor, community elder, a church pastor, or other parents.

This network cannot necessarily be counted on when it comes to supporting a trans child. It is a little too easy to chalk up this community's "unavailability" solely to bigotry and prejudice. While this may sometimes be the case, what is more likely is that the majority of people lack reliable information or societal context. As discussed earlier, most people will assume a child's gender identification has something to do with their sexual orientation. If a particular ethnic, faith, geographic, or political community has a stated or implied stance against sexual minority people, then that same stance is often mistakenly applied to gender identity. As a result, community support is often immobilized before it can even be requested.

One family took the drastic step of leaving their family and community entirely to find a more supportive place for their son:

Our trans boy's masculine gender expression was obvious from a very young age. Gender expectations from our Mormon church and community were clearly delineated. Many felt that we were encouraging him to be gay. Of course, we weren't! He was so young, we didn't worry about it at first. Whenever we tried to encourage more feminine clothing and hair, however, he would get so upset. We felt so much at a loss. We felt our choice was to have a happy kid and an unhappy community, or the other way around. By the time he was five, it didn't matter how understanding we, as his parents, were. He was more and more aware of the disapproving looks from adults and the insensitive comments from the other children. I've never seen a child so young be so despairing. I finally called my husband at work one day and said, "Honey, you have to get us out of here!" Once he found a job, we left everything—family, friends, and community—and started over. It was painful and isolating for the first couple of years. We were so scared. Yet, I know we made the right decision. I see it every day in his eyes!

Certainly, one of the harder stories I've heard had to do with a white family that lived in a politically conservative part of the southeastern United States. When community members learned that this family was supporting their trans child's gender, the family began to lose friends and were shunned by their small-town community. Their fear heightened when anonymous death threats came. One terrible morning, they awoke to find the family dog dead and nailed to a fence. On the fence was a note, "Your kid is next." The family fled their home of many years the same day.

Obviously, as evidenced in this family's experience, community response can be unpredictable and volatile. Yet some families experience a much greater degree of compassion from their community despite the lack of exposure to trans people.

While it is hard to predict any particular community's response, in my experience there is an important variable that seems to make a difference and that is acknowledging that most people are in the same place. Until recently, we have not made a place in our communities for gender-diverse children. Today, we are. Our awareness of the need for support of these children is becoming better understood but the pathway forward is only now being created. If any community—church, school, or town—can recognize this, and make a *proactive* commitment to further establish this pathway, greater progress can be made.

A city council member of a small, conservative town shared this story:

> We have a close-knit, rural community but that doesn't mean everyone agrees on everything. We pride ourselves on solving our problems together. When our school board began to discuss gender-inclusive policy for our district, we realized pretty quickly that we were *all* in need of learning more regardless of whether we were "for" or "against." We decided to really dig in. We hosted community "house" parties, formed an advisory committee with a cross-representation of people, and hired an educator to guide us in the process. Meetings were open to the entire public, not just families within our district schools. By the time we finished, the majority believed—regardless of whether they were originally "for" or "against" the policy—that having a policy to address *any* issue that might come up was better than having nothing at all. The time and effort that we put in were well worth it. We're pretty proud of our town!

SCHOOLS

After a parent's realization that their child is gender-diverse—but often before they have had a chance to catch their breath—the question of how to navigate schools looms large and immediate. Teachers, administrators, counselors, and even other parents may put up some resistance to a child's gender journey. Home-schooling communities are often no exception. Educators and administrators may struggle to understand the school's role in the transition process. Principals may say, "Why should we do all this for one student?" Or, as stated previously, they may inappropriately ask a parent for leadership and direction. A teacher may directly or indirectly blame the gender-diverse student for any bullying that they might experience. Faith, political, cultural, and geographical differences can complicate the conversations even further. It is not appropriate for a school to ask a single family to shoulder the burden of educating everyone. We will discuss this further in Chapters 10 and 11.

The visible presence of trans children in today's schools is increasing at a pace far faster than we are able to adequately address. It is logical for school personnel to look to the family members of a trans or gender-diverse child for guidance. While some of these families may be able to assist schools to some degree, the vast majority are in a state of upheaval as they seek to mitigate the conflict within their immediate circles. While a child's gender exploration and/or transition is not the same as a death of a loved one, the experience can easily mirror the stages of grief that comes with such a significant life event.

There are so many questions coming from everywhere a parent turns—is this a phase; aren't they too young to know; what if they change their mind? Finding answers is not easy. The learning curve is steep, and distinguishing accurate information from outdated/inaccurate sources is difficult. Some parents wish they could speed up time or discover a crystal ball with definitive answers to the "gender question." Advice from others abounds, but the lion's share of that is often no more informed than what little a parent already has available.

School administrators, teachers, counselors, and other staffers are better served if they do their own search for education and guidance especially as it pertains to the school's responsibility—that of creating a safe, inclusive learning environment for all students. While questions about gender diagnoses, medical interventions, and inquiries about genitals might feel urgent, the reality is that these lines of inquiry—regardless of intent—are almost always invasive and disrespectful. Looking to a beleaguered and distressed parent for advice will only add to their already full plate. It can even set the stage for deeper conflict and higher emotions within the entire school community if a family feels under attack. I'm not advocating that educators strive for complete independence from the family in this process—just that school districts recognize that they have a responsibility to address gender inclusion within their schools and that they can seek information from an individual parent in understanding the specific needs of that child. The school has the responsibility to understand those needs and provide appropriate support. Schools can do too little, but they can also be too eager to do too much, sometimes placing the child in difficult situations with other students, staff, and parents.

INTERACTIONS WITH AUTHORITIES

Families of gender-diverse youth can encounter dozens of stumbling blocks that hinder or prevent them from creating optimal environments for their children. When an uneducated or unsupportive person is in a position of authority, the stakes can be even higher. For instance, the landlord mentioned earlier in this chapter exercised a discriminatory overextension of power when he demanded "official" documentation of a child's gender diagnosis during the rental application process. Misuse or abuse of authority becomes even more dangerous when factors such as race are present. For example, black respondents of the 2015 U.S. Trans Survey were found to be *six times* more likely to be attacked by police officers than white respondents.[6]

An unfortunate number of families have had harrowing experiences when a neighbor or other community member decides to make a report to child protective services (CPS), mistakenly assuming that the gender-supportive measures taken by a family are actually indicators of child abuse. Because most CPS agencies are still lacking in training, knowledge, or policy about gender differences in children, any outcome of an investigation may hinge on the level of awareness of the individual investigator assigned to the case. If a child is taken from the home while an investigation occurs, it could take a significant amount of time—weeks, sometimes longer—for the agency to investigate and determine that nothing is "wrong" and that a supportive approach is actually considered "best practice" in today's society. Sadly, a number of trans children have been separated from supportive parents by some child protective service agencies across the United States and become wards of the state or placed in foster care because agency investigators, judges, and child experts are unaware or resistant to current-day professional "best practices" for trans youth.

MEDICAL PROVIDERS

Even medical providers may present barriers for families striving to support their children. Many parents do their own research, seeking information about current medical interventions and options for their trans child. As they seek to support and advocate for their trans child, they may want to maintain the relationship with their child's existing pediatrician or primary care provider. When a parent approaches their child's doctor to discuss the gender issues, the outcome of that disclosure can be highly unpredictable because the average family physician has no professional education or training related to gender-identity issues.[7] In lieu of knowledge and training, doctors may instead fall back on their personal perspectives, beliefs, experiences, and opinions.

When one family sought medical support for their trans child, they shared their experience with other parents at the next support group meeting:

> When our youngest child told us she wasn't a boy, but really a girl, we had a lot to learn. And, we had to learn it fast! She was just starting puberty. We had learned about puberty suppression as an intermediary beneficial step. My wife is someone who does extensive research on any number of things, and this was no exception. What she learned about puberty-delay intervention was really helpful . . . and relieving . . . for us. It would allow our child to not have to experience changes associated with a male puberty while it relieved the pressure on us as parents to make what felt like a huge decision before we were ready. We—my wife especially—were then quite stunned when we asked about medical intervention for our child and our doctor simply said, "There's no such thing as puberty delay medication!" and was unwilling to discuss it any further.

Another family brought their trans teenage son to the local children's hospital for the required assessment visits preceding cross hormone care:[8]

> Our son was so happy knowing he was finally starting his transition and couldn't wait for the visit to the psychologist. He'd struggled for years before finding the courage to share his truth with his parents. However, the assessing psychologist determined that he must *not* be transgender because he was "too happy and well-adjusted." The criteria, she said, was that the youth

should be exhibiting consistent, intense distress. The teen was devastated and the parents were furious. "He's rejected because he's excited to move forward?!" his parent said incredulously. "Where was this psychologist when, for a full year, we thought at any moment we might lose our child to suicide?!"

OTHER CONSIDERATIONS

Other barriers present themselves regularly. Some are expected, and some pop up in the least expected places. For instance, one family pursuing a legal name change for their child was congratulated by a smiling judge while another family, seeking a name change within the same county, was chastised by a different judge for not providing "proof" of a gender change, even though no additional legal documentation was required for either family.

There will increasingly be a time where greater acceptance and understanding of gender-diverse children is present. Parents and caregivers will be better served if they understand the significant landscape they must navigate so that their child can focus on being a child.

NOTES

1. Jessica J. Glazier, Selin Gülgöz, and Kristina R. Olson, "Gender Encoding in Gender Diverse and Gender Conforming Children," *Child Development* 91, no. 6 (2020): 1877–1885, https://doi.org/10.1111/cdev.13399.
2. Samskruthi Madireddy and Sahithi Madireddy, "Supportive Model for the Improvement of Mental Health and Prevention of Suicide among LGBTQ+ Youth," *International Journal of Adolescence and Youth* 27, no. 1 (December 31, 2022): 85–101, https://doi.org/10.1080/02673843.2022.2025872.
3. Owl Fisher and Fox Fisher, *Trans Teen Survival Guide* (London; Philadelphia: Jessica Kingsley Publishers, 2019), 214.
4. Kristina R. Olson, Aidan C. Key, and Nicholas R. Eaton, "Gender Cognition in Transgender Children," *Psychological Science* 26, no. 4 (April 1, 2015): 473, https://doi.org/10.1177/0956797614568156.
5. Elizabeth P. Rahilly, *Trans-Affirmative Parenting: Raising Kids across the Gender Spectrum* (New York: New York University Press, 2020), 29.
6. S. E. James, C. Brown, and I. Wilson, *2015 U.S. Transgender Survey: Report on the Experiences of Black Respondents* (Washington; Dallas: National Center for Transgender Equality, Black Trans Advocacy, & National Black Justice Coalition, 2017).

7. This is changing, of course, but it is not consistent nor is it comprehensive: "U.S. Medical Schools Boost LGBTQ Students, Doctor Training," *AP News* (April 20, 2021), https://apn ews.com/article/ky-state-wire-health-us-news-ap-top-news-medical-schools-985d50d0a 7b1b593acd0dd791e8c3118.
8. Rachel Baxter, "What Is Cross-Sex Hormone Therapy?" *ISSM*, https://www.issm.info/sex ual-health-qa/what-is-cross-sex-hormone-therapy/.

6

Transition Considerations for Children

The journey of a thousand miles begins with one step.

Lao Tzu

In 2000, I saw a television interview with a family of a young, white trans girl. This was one of the first depictions of a child's experience of being trans shown during mainstream television programming. The child and her family were queried about their thoughts and experiences. After a commercial break, I was shocked when, as they returned to the interview, the banner across the bottom of the screen said, "9-Year-Old Wants Sex Change." It was a sensational headline that played into a broad-based, uninformed notion that genital reconstructive surgery is the ultimate goal of all transgender people. Whether intentional or not, the banner implied that this family was already, or soon would be, pursuing genital surgery for their young child. It was disappointing to see these misconceptions perpetuated in this headline designed to titillate an uninformed audience.

How do we, as a society, begin to understand what it means to be transgender? We must begin by having a willingness to learn. While it was disappointing to see the TV banner, the fact that millions of people were able to hear one family's direct experience means that those who viewed the show have likely gained greater awareness and empathy.

As I lead staff training throughout a wide range of communities, it is quite common for people to inquire about possible gender transition steps a child might pursue. Most of the time, these questions are often far more intimate and extensive than what any particular educator *needs* to know to effectively do their job. It is helpful to recognize and acknowledge that the concept of a child transitioning is a loaded topic—fear, strong opinions, and conjecture often drive these heated conversations.

My hope for this chapter is to find a balance between addressing the curiosity that exists for so many while also highlighting *relevant* information that could be helpful to a parent as well as a teacher, principal, coach, or counselor. As we find this shared understanding, we will then be able to act with a common purpose—that purpose being the informed support of gender-diverse children.

CULTURAL NORMS AS THEY RELATE TO GENDER

Gender and all that the word encompasses is complicated, elusive, and interdependent on many factors. Gender expectations interrelate with a person's economic/class status, their racial and/or cultural identity, the cultural norms of their generation, and so on. The more we seek to find definitive answers, the more intricacies, and intersectionality we uncover. Understanding this complexity is an exploration we can embrace and celebrate.

We would be hard-pressed to name aspects of our identities that are not influenced by, or fraught with gender constructs. Yet so many of us are unaware of these elements and accept many of them as immutable. Perceptions and expectations vary from culture to culture and generation to generation and are subject to the passage of time.

Consider the high-heeled shoe. Many would say high heels are inarguably within the domain of women's clothing. If we survey history, however, we see that this was not always the case. High heels date back to ancient times in Persia for use by warriors on horseback. Many centuries passed before they were appropriated by European men. Not only did they, like the Persians, find high heels helpful in their equestrian adventures, but high heels were then incorporated into fashion, and they became an indicator of class status. These men also enjoyed the way high heels enhanced their physical presence among other men. Some women, subsequently, began to adopt the wearing of heels as a gender-transgressive expression and, as time progressed, heels worn by women became a symbol of class status. In the twenty-first century, high heels symbolize femininity, transgressive femininity, and hyper-femininity depending on who wears them and how they are worn. This is just one example of how an item's strong gender association can evolve over time, geography, class, and culture.[1]

Indigenous cultures within the United States, and other countries around the world, have historically viewed gender roles in a more expansive way. Many indigenous tribes in North America have recognized people who experience gender fluidity—with respect to identity, expression, and sexuality—with the encompassing term *Two-Spirit*. The term Two-Spirit was often considered to have a spiritual and/or ceremonial element as well. Today much of the indigenous Two-Spirit culture has been damaged, erased, simplistically reframed, and even appropriated through a colonial lens.[2]

The continued influence of Western-European dominant culture perpetuates a pervasive insistence on achieving gender certainty within a definitively binary framework. This results not only in stifling or eliminating any individual's gender expansiveness but also in the destruction of cultures and their history. A binary framework seeks to move us to quick, permanent "solutions" to gender diversity that are historically grounded in stigmatization, institutionalization, or surgical "fixes."[3]

A number of years ago, the long-running Gender Odyssey conference (https://genderodyssey.org/), an event providing learning, support, and resources for families of trans and gender-diverse children, hosted a keynote speaker, gender activist Eli Vásquez. Vásquez is an Ecuadorian attorney and the founder of Proyecto Transgenero (Project Transgender), an organization in Quito that has led the civil rights movement for transgender and intersex people in Ecuador.

Vásquez discussed a particular Ecuadorian coastal community where approximately *one-third* of the population is comprised of gender identities other than male or female. These other genders were acknowledged, and *not* stigmatized, within this culture. While the dominant culture within the United States might view them as transgender, they are largely unfamiliar with the term and do not pursue the medical interventions so commonly associated with the experiences of transgender people within the United States.[4]

While it is difficult to make any unequivocal statements, the existence of this Ecuadorian community and others like it offer a window of potentiality regarding trans/nonbinary identities and "treatments" that may or may not involve body-altering procedures. However, the unquestioning social acceptance within this particular South American coastal community is unique. American families, within the dominant culture's rigid gender roles and expectations, are tasked with sorting through complicated, and contradictory personal, familial, social, and systemic constructs and must navigate paths of treatment within these constructs.

Parents of trans children and others often ask me, "What if there were no rigid gender roles or expectations within our society? Would trans people still feel the need to pursue physical changes through hormones or surgery?" I do believe that if trans and gender-diverse people were not deeply stigmatized and challenged to defend who they are, fewer people would feel the need to take body-altering steps to be "seen" and accepted.

GENDER DIVERSITY IN CHILDREN IS NOT A ONE-SIZE-FITS-ALL

Even if we were able to wave a magic wand and remove the apprehension from the minds of each and every person, the entrenchment of gender misconceptions would remain archived in the media and within systems like schools, courts, agencies, politics, and corporations.

It is with this in mind that the following "transition" information is provided. I offer it based on questions most often asked of me during trainings. My primary caveat is to encourage the reader to be ready and open to considering the complexities that present themselves. Do not assume that one-size-fits-all.

Even the word *transition* implies that some kind of movement is necessary. If I were to simplify the wishes of any trans person, with respect to their gender, it is that they would like to be seen and validated for who they are and accepted without stigma regardless of any transition-related steps, medical or otherwise.

THE TRANSITION PROCESS

Transition is the term typically used to describe steps toward gender identity authentication. This is not a fixed series of steps applicable to all, nor are these steps required by any authorizing entity. Yet there is an erroneous belief that there is a set, required path which requires professional approval before being allowed to take any action toward transition. Professional help and support *can be and often is* part of that path depending on variables unique to each person's circumstances and needs. For a child, a few of these variables would include their age, level of parental support, access to resources and knowledgeable professionals, school environment, and community receptivity—all of which will require careful consideration as they can and will influence decisions made along the way.

Before discussing various aspects of transition, it's worth emphasizing that there is a general societal impression that transition is one single decision; that once a person takes a tentative step there is no "going back." This is simply not the case. As outlined in the next pages, we can see that it is the initial foray that helps to illuminate the correct path. Because we can't see the future or know how we might feel about *any* upcoming changes until we begin to actually experience them, it is reasonable to think of the beginning stages of transition as *exploratory*. Any social transition step is completely "reversible." Puberty delay medication, which may or may not be a precursor to hormone therapy, can be stopped at any time with no irreversible effects. Even beginning a cross hormone regimen can be stopped if it is discerned that it is not the right course.

While transitions can have commonalities, each is also unique. It is reasonable to recognize that "transition" is a series of steps that then lead to other steps. Sometimes there might be steps "back," or efforts to slow things down or speed them up. Occasionally it is helpful to pause for an interim period of time. Embarking upon these transition-related steps is often the only way to obtain crucial information about whether to consider any next steps. Exploration *will not make* a child transgender if they are not. Allowing room for a bigger, more informed conversation provides everyone—child and parent alike—with vital information. It becomes a more informed path rather than a guessing game.

Gender transition steps can be separated into several broad categories: internal, social, medical, and legal. It must be emphasized again that there is no one particular transition process for all, no general timeline, and no assumption that any person would/should pursue all aspects of transition.

INTERNAL AWARENESS

All people have an internal sense of their gender. For most, their sense of self aligns with what can be called *sex assigned at birth*. This assignment is based on a baby's genital configuration. In births in which there is a clearly defined penis the baby is designated a male; a baby with a clearly defined vulva is pronounced to be female. But a person may have a sense of themselves that falls outside of this norm. They can have a feeling that who they *are* is distinct from the body into which they have been born. There is no definitive time frame in which a person may discern this incongruity. For some, this is a growing realization. Other children have this sense very early on. A child may use language such as:

- I'm not a girl, I'm a boy.
- God made a mistake when he made me a boy.
- When I grow up, my penis will grow in like daddy's.

Statements like these are straightforward and are often what providers and caregivers expect or hope to hear from transgender children as it has a very definitive quality. When a child makes a guileless declaration at an early age, it can be quite startling. Many parents, believing that a child is "too young to know," wait until the child repeats this pronouncement with frequency. This repetition seems to make them feel more certain that it isn't a passing phase. Some professionals have even created a guiding mantra—trans children will assert their gender identity *consistently, insistently, and persistently* over time. While this guidance can provide a level of comfort to some providers and parents, it is not a *de facto* indicator that a child is truly transgender. It is too simplistic to be relied upon for all cases of gender identity difference.

For many children, the internal recognition of their own gender can be less straightforward. From the earliest ages, children experience life with what appear to be fixed gender expectations in practically every aspect of their surroundings. Many will be unable to articulate their internal sense of gender because having a gender identity different from the sex assigned at birth is still largely considered to be an impossibility. As a result, there should not be an expectation that all children will make an early, definitive gender declaration. It can be helpful to understand some of the variables at play for children.

Young Children

Hearing the stories of thousands of families, I've found that indeed some trans children will proclaim a gender identity difference as soon as they are able to talk. Others may not experience distress until they become a little older. This might occur between the approximate ages of four and seven when those around them, especially peers, begin to expect gender conformity. Any out-of-the-ordinary behavior that was previously viewed as just an innocuous phase is now expected to disappear. A preschool-age boy may have few repercussions from his peers for his interest in wearing dresses and pink clothing, or playing with dolls. But, as he enters first or second grade, he will receive greater pushback and teasing from students who more strongly begin to enforce gender stereotypes. The expectations of gender conformity from others (including teachers, parents, and other adults) become more pervasive as the child ages, and what was considered to be a "phase" of his gender expression begins to be viewed as more and more problematic. The resulting intensity of this scrutiny, and sometimes punishment, creates anguish for the young child and is often what motivates a parent or teacher to reach out for help and information.

A two- or three-year-old may insist they are a boy while the reaction of a parent may be one of amusement, annoyance, or correction. One parent finally reached out for support with respect to her four-year-old who had been insisting for over a year that they were a boy. "I tried any way I could think of to explain to my daughter that she was a girl and, all the while, she insisted otherwise. I talked to her about the fact that boys have penises and girls have vaginas, so, therefore, she was a girl. She looked at me like I was from another planet and simply said, 'Mama, I'm a boy. My penis just hasn't grown in yet.'"

Older Children

As a child with a gender identity difference matures, it is common for us to notice behavioral changes and/or emotional challenges. Children ages eight to eleven, like their younger counterparts, may still have difficulty articulating their gender discomfort or may feel that they simply cannot express themselves because they recognize that most people will not listen to or believe them. At this age, children are more capable of critical thinking. A nine-year-old may fully understand the anatomical nature of sex, and the accompanying gender expectations, and feel at a loss with how to manage their own frustration, despair, and sense of incongruity.

Another factor coming into play for these older children is the awareness of their impending pubertal development or, for some, pubertal changes that have already begun. A child's struggle with what feels to be an inevitable physiological incongruity can manifest in a number of ways, including anxiety, depression, anger, being increasingly withdrawn, and the threat of, or actual, self-harm. Families with children in this age range may seek professional help to address the behavioral challenges they witness. For some children, this run-up to puberty is the catalyst that finally pushes them to express their gender concerns. Others will struggle to openly articulate their gender disconnect. Often, parents and providers will focus on addressing the child's resulting behavioral issues but be hesitant, resistant, or unable to recognize that gender incongruence is very likely to be at the core.

One family brought their nine-year-old to a parent support group. The mother related the intense, angry outbursts her child was experiencing and the difficulties this was causing in school. She was not yet ready to embrace that her child was a transgender boy and was struggling with how to deal with his defiance. She shared that she was in a constant state of bargaining with him, acceding to his insistence on getting his hair cut short on the condition that he wear earrings so that others would perceive him as a girl. "If she really is a boy, she can transition when she's nineteen," she said. Meanwhile, during this first group, the child was quite guarded with the other tweens.

When the children were asked to play a sharing game that asked what kind of superhero they would be, he would not engage with anyone beyond laying on the floor repeatedly stating, "I'm dead, I'm dead."

After attending several groups, both parent and child progressed in a positive way. The mother more fully understood that delaying any validation of her child's gender identity and that her notion of waiting for a decade or more was too extreme for a child who was in obvious, immediate distress. As they took the beginning steps of a social transition at school, his teacher observed a positive, transformative shift away from his challenging, combative behavior that had been going on for over a year. His mom was astounded to see her child making friends, laughing and playing, and rapidly improving in school.

Teens

For teens, the capacity for critical thinking continues as does their pubertal development. What makes the internal process so distinct for teens is their increased access to gender-expansive language, information, and resources, as well as a broadening understanding of gender identity that is more and more embraced, especially by younger generations. This is a powerful time for many teens in their path to self-discovery. The terminology available at their fingertips is plentiful and helps them better understand their own experiences. Their ability to conceptualize gender identity and gender expression, and how these are distinct from sexual orientation and anatomical sex, typically exceeds the more binary conceptualizations of their parents, teachers, and other adults. Hearing the stories of other teens via YouTube, TikTok, and other social media sites is often cited as a significant factor that influenced their decision to disclose as well as giving them the language identifiers to claim as their own.

While they are gaining a better understanding of themselves, these teens are already aware of the stigmatization and marginalization experienced by trans people in society. Lifelong expectations of gender conformity paired with the societal contempt for gender-diverse people are notions that youth of any age will encounter and internalize. They may have directly experienced, or certainly observed, negative treatment toward others as a result of identity or expression differences.

This onslaught of negativity is pervasive. Children have an incredible capacity to absorb this informational onslaught. On the other hand, their ability to process, integrate, and reflect it back to others is more difficult. Because of their age, they may not have the developmental capacity to clearly articulate what is going on for them.

As a teen acknowledges and shares their gender identity with others, it can inspire a huge internal conflict. This disclosure, instead of an empowering time of self-discovery, is instead a struggle with an understanding that to be who they are means they are also an unvalued and reviled outsider in society. The resulting inner conflict can be agonizing to reconcile within oneself, much less speak aloud to family or friends.[5]

SOCIAL TRANSITION

Most of the initial steps to affirm a child's gender identity are known collectively as a "social transition." These steps can include disclosure to others, a name change, pronoun change, and changes to gender presentation. This might include changes to hairstyle, wearing a different wardrobe, engaging in different activities, and other choices more typically associated with a specific gender like certain toys, makeup, accessories, and even access to a wider array of colors!

A social transition can often be a highly intimidating step for families. By the time the child is able to express themselves, the need for these steps is very often high and urgent. For an uncertain family, it can feel like a decision with huge, permanent ramifications. Again, the assumption is that, once a social transition is started, it must continue forward culminating in a full-on medical intervention. The reality is that a social transition is "reversible" and moving forward with it, even with uncertainty, accomplishes a number of things:

1. It acknowledges and supports the child's sense of self.
2. It allows all involved to gain time while gathering information as to the positive impact of the social transition steps on the child.
3. It allows a family to adjust and adapt to changes affecting the family.
4. It reinforces for the child that the family's love and acceptance is unconditional.

A social transition allows the child (and family) to "try it on." How does it feel for the child to be called by a name or pronoun that feels more resonant to them?

Does being allowed to wear the clothing they choose—outside of the home—provide them with a greater sense of authenticity? Does family support allow them to more fully embrace their budding selves?

Taking these fledgling steps is simple but not necessarily easy. Information to be gained through social transition is invaluable, but it is also an intimidating process for parents. What if their child is indeed transgender? The prospect is daunting for most. So many parents worry about making a mistake. It can be reassuring to keep in mind that, if a child is experiencing a *phase* or *changes their mind*, then names, pronouns, clothing, and haircuts can all be *reconsidered*—none are inherently permanent.

Disclosure

Disclosing a child's gender identity to others ranks high as one of the most challenging aspects of a social transition. Almost everyone within a child's immediate periphery, *as well as the child themselves*, will be expected to offer explanations, and address questions from others, many of which are inappropriate and deeply personal.

Each family's path will be unique to them. Some families will feel comfortable being public about their child's gender journey while others will feel this to be a very private family matter. Furthermore, because the path is unknown, a parent may not know how they will feel (besides being overwhelmed) at certain points along the way. It's one thing to talk with an extended family member about a child's gender exploration and quite another to answer queries from an acquaintance in the grocery store check-out line. A parent can feel put in a position of defending their parenting practices. A number of parents have said, "I don't have a problem allowing them to express themselves at home, but how am I supposed to let them out the door! How do I explain this?!"

There is no one way to share the transition journey of a child. A teen may have input regarding how the information will be shared. Some teens prefer to tell certain people, while asking parents to *not* disclose to others. A young child may ask that their gender transition is not discussed with anyone only to turn around and tell their classmates a week later. Some children will not understand why an explanation is needed at all. Other children will shoulder the full burden of disclosure on their own because they do not have parental support.[6]

It is important for any parent to be very discerning with respect to how, to whom, and when disclosure is pursued. The child's wishes should be considered, yes. But, for example, if the child wishes to disclose in their own way, there will be gaps in their understanding. Having little awareness of school as an institution, a child may expect the school to respond quickly and easily. This is rarely the case. With no facilitated discussion with school staff, teachers, administrators, and other students, it can result in an unpredictable outcome that could be deeply detrimental to the child.

Of course, gender-diverse children themselves are regularly in the position of disclosing their gender status to peers and adults. Having to shoulder the complexity of societal ignorance and resistance as they disclose is hardly a task that children of any age should have to take on by themselves, yet that is the current day reality for the majority of youth.

For any child experiencing marginalization, such as being a person of color, an immigrant, or having physical or intellectual differences, being trans intensifies feelings of being an outsider and makes disclosure all the more strenuous.

Daria, a teenage trans girl, had this to say about finding connections based on shared experience:

> I like to include myself in the main group [of trans youth], but I also like talking to POC [people of color] . . . about POC issues. I want a balance of both. [I've been talking] with people about how being a person of color in the LGBTQ+ community is different than being white in the same community. There are not a lot of resources for people of color. [There should be] a place for everyone to talk about things. It's kind of hard for me to talk about POC issues in front of white people because I don't want to offend people.

A teacher with a strong understanding of intersectionality is likely better prepared to engage students in discussions of gender diversity but will surely need initial guidance. Students can be encouraged to relate their own unique qualities with that of a trans student, but this often needs to be modeled initially. Because of our society's broad-based unfamiliarity with, and stigma attached to, trans and nonbinary people, it is imperative that school personnel be educated in gender diversity and the needs of trans students. With this knowledge, they are powerfully influential in how any child's gender disclosure is received, not abdicating their responsibility for the care of the child by allowing the child to fend for themselves.

Just as we would not expect a child with differences in language, culture, and ability to optimize their own school experience without support, nor should we expect that of a child with gender differences.

There is no such thing as a single struggle issue because we do not live single issue lives.

Audre Lorde

Name Changes

One of the first gender-affirming steps that a child may request is that of a name change.

On the surface, this is a simple, straightforward step. Joey wants to be called Johanna. This can be done within a family, school, youth program, or with peers at any time. No diagnosis is needed nor does a legal name change order need to occur. Many students go by names other than their legal name and we scarcely notice. Some use a middle name, a nickname, or go by initials like P.J. Birth order might mean a child goes by "Junior" or a lengthier name, like Nicolette, may be shortened to Nicky. Someone with an ethnic-specific name like Jorge may change it to George. A family who immigrates from another country may adopt a more "Americanized" name for their child to ease their entry into a community.

There are numerous reasons why someone may change their name and, in general, we are relatively unconcerned and unquestioning about these scenarios. Yet, the request for a gender-related name change can inspire a significant degree of consternation for many. For an apprehensive parent, a name change can represent a big, scary step into an unknown transgender experience for their child. Most parents I've encountered experience a degree of sadness and frustration at letting go of the name they gave their child at birth. One parent had this to say:

> I named my first son after my grandfather who I was really close to as a child. He passed away when I was a teen. I knew then that, if I had a son, I would name him after my grandfather. Now my child wants to go by the name Ariel. I would never have named any child, boy or girl, after a Disney character!

Another parent pleaded:

Do I have to agree to the name my five-year-old trans daughter chooses? She wants to be called Rapunzel.

Yet another:

I named my child Riley. It was really important to me to give my child an androgynous name. Now, they identify as nonbinary, whatever that is, want me to use gender-neutral pronouns, and to call them Quinn. What's wrong with the gender-neutral name I gave them?

Some parents will sit with their child and discuss the importance of how a name is selected perhaps mentioning that the naming of a child is usually a parent's responsibility. They may give a child a choice of two or three names that might have been selected had their child been born a different gender. Other parents will agree to the name selected by their child or collaborate with the child on name choice.

A trans girl had decided to name herself Rose, after the beloved family chicken! Her mother and she discussed changing her name to that of her favorite aunt, a choice that appealed more to Mom. But the child was adamant. They combined the two names and both mother and child were happy with the name Rosemary.

For the child, a new name reflects a new (or acknowledged) self. A name of their own choosing can feel empowering. A child may want to change their name numerous times, much to the dismay of a parent! It is a natural part of exploration. Regardless of how a new name is selected, there is almost always a time of adjustment for families, peers, and teachers, and that adjustment is often more prolonged than the child would prefer. Some teens and young adults will refer to their former name as their "dead name" which can be *both* distressing to their parents *and* a testimony to the importance of the name and how it relates to their identity. While there is no right or wrong way, I've seen a greater sense of closeness occur when a family engages in name selection together.

It is not an easy task for most people to switch names for a person they've known for a long time, perhaps their entire life. A combination of persistence and patience is helpful for this transition-related step. In general, children and teens seem to have an easier time adapting to name changes. A teacher can be instrumental in facilitating a student's name change by simply presenting it in a positive, matter-of-fact manner.

PRONOUNS

Pronouns are some of the shortest words in the English language. So why is it that the act of changing a pronoun is met with significant collective resistance? Some years ago, I led a staff training for fifty wonderful people who offered outdoor programs for children and teens. One of the youth leaders was a young trans-identified adult who was exploring possible gender transition-related steps. At the time of the training, this youth leader was clear that he expected others to use the pronouns he/him/his when referring to him. He did not expect anything of others beyond this pronoun request and simply took it upon himself to make a note of it on his name tag.

As individuals—and as an organization—they prided themselves on the diversity of the youth that engaged in their programs as well as their commitment to creating an inclusive environment for everyone. That said, this simple act of placing his pronouns on his name tag, challenged them more deeply than they expected. The group felt if this youth leader would also change his name from Abby to a more masculine-sounding name, that their hesitancy to use the pronoun would be lessened. We discussed this honestly and in-depth. Digging into the heart of the matter, we explored whether or not Abby *should be expected* to change his name for the sole reason of making it less complicated for others. Eventually, they all agreed that Abby should *not* change his name just because they wanted him to. But, they said, it sure would make it a lot easier!

Switching Pronouns

Until recent years, it was very rare for anyone to have to accommodate a person's pronoun change request. There were so few visible adult trans people and certainly next to no youth. Therefore, for the vast majority of people, making the mental shift to a new pronoun is unfamiliar terrain.

As is the case with any new activity, the learning curve is the steepest at first and then gets easier and more natural with practice. When a person learns a new language, there is much to master—vocabulary, syntax, pronunciation, conjugation, and more—and many will tell you the hardest part is the concentration and recall needed for the most basic conversations. This is not unlike the attention needed to consistently recall a person's new pronoun. With practice and time, we can all become proficient. Our early efforts will not only be a validating, supportive acknowledgment of a person's identity but will enable us to more easily adjust pronouns for anyone else in the future:

> One mother shared with the parent group that she practiced using her child's new pronoun in private. While ironing and folding laundry she would repeat—my son Sam, *he* is an artist, *he* likes to read and write poetry, *his* favorite food is avocado—until the new pronouns came more easily to her.

The following are a few tips for using the correct identity-based pronouns.

1. **Take the request seriously.** It takes a courageous child to push against the norm. This child is not oblivious to the resistance of adults and peers and is making their request despite this pushback. There is no harm in using a different pronoun than was once used. Again, an affirming approach is not going to "make someone trans."
2. **Practice, practice, practice.** When you have a free moment to yourself—in the car, on a walk, etc.—picture the child in your mind, say their name aloud, and use the new pronoun. For example, Caleb-he, Caleb-he, Caleb-he. The internal visualization coupled with the vocal and auditory reinforcement is one of the best, quickest ways to become consistent.
3. **If you make a mistake, a quick apology and correction** are the best ways to respond. Over-apologizing, explaining, and justifying your error can result in greater harm than the initial slip itself.
4. **Recruit help!** If you are struggling with consistent pronoun usage, or even getting started, ask those around you for help. If others are consistently using the new pronoun, it provides helpful auditory reinforcement.
5. **Find additional motivation!** Some parents have opted for a modification of the "swear word" jar. In an effort to avoid cursing in front of the children, parents agree to a monetary deposit for any infraction. The

same can be done for pronoun slips. Money can be a great motivator and adds a bit of fun for the child (aka beneficiary).

6. **Minimize mistakes while you get there**. Some people will opt to avoid pronoun use altogether because of the early difficulties to adapt. They may instead substitute the child's name where a pronoun might otherwise be. *I asked Amiyah to clean Amiyah's room because it looked like a tornado went through it.* While this can be a reasonable step, it should be a short-term one,* especially if a different pronoun has been clearly requested.

Of course, there are a number of ways to get to consistent pronoun usage. Just know that you will become more proficient with time and practice.

Gender-Neutral Pronouns

THEY/THEM

Many young people today are laying claim to the use of *they/them/theirs* as a singular pronoun. If they feel themselves to be neither male nor female, somewhere in between those poles, or a mix of these two commonly acknowledged genders, *he* or *she* as a pronoun feels limiting and inaccurate to reflect their experience. Using *they/them/theirs* can also be an interim pronoun while a person is continuing to explore their sense of self and identity and may be switched out for a conventional pronoun later. Many, many people struggle with, and even reject, the idea that this is a reasonable or valid consideration.

Teachers, in particular, struggle with the use of plural pronouns to refer to an individual. *It's not grammatically correct!* is their refrain. It is helpful to recognize that new words come into usage, old ones fade away or take on a new context, and each generation both resists *and* creates them. Some people will not know what it means to *Xerox* or *mimeograph* something but readily know how to make a print copy. We may still *dial* a number even though many have never used a rotary phone. Supernatural occurrences might be considered to be a bit *woo-woo*. A train wreck describes derailed railroad cars but a *train wreck* may more often describe that short, mismatched relationship we wish we had never entered! Today, we *Google* for more information and *Tweet* our thoughts to others including this ironic tweet from user *@Yes2Homeschool:*

---

* Some children *do* request that others use only their name in lieu of any pronoun usage.

Any English teacher who uses "they/them" as a singular pronoun should lose <u>their</u> teaching license.[7]

We use the singular application of *they/them* pronouns regularly—probably every day! It is used when a person's gender is not known. In addition to the above tweet, someone may say, "My friend has recommended a dentist to me. *Their* office is just around the corner." Or you may find yourself on the phone with a customer service representative. For an unresolved issue, you may ask to speak to *their* supervisor. We may not realize that the singular employment of *they/them* pronouns does have a precedent with which we are all familiar.

Regardless of our familiarity, the reality for most of us is that consistently using *they/them* as a singular pronoun for a person—as it relates to their gender identity—does not come easily. It is new. With any new task, practice makes perfect.

Merriam-Webster and other arbiters of the English language are weighing in. In September 2019, the Merriam-Webster dictionary added an entry to the definition of *they* providing the official stamp of approval for usage in describing a singular person, specifically a nonbinary identified person. While the singular, more archaic, usage of they/them has been documented as far back as the 1300s, this present-day acknowledgment returns this pronoun into twenty-first century, grammatically correct usage.[8]

As society becomes more progressively confident with the singular usage of *they/them* for nonbinary people—and others who simply prefer it—it will dispel current feelings of awkwardness and replace it with a matter-of-fact and even ho-hum status.

OTHER ALTERNATIVE PRONOUNS

Some children, teens more often than younger children, may request pronouns other than *she*, *he*, and even *they/them*. Recent times have seen the creation of completely new and different pronouns. The usage of these alternative pronouns varies, with some enduring and others falling out of use over time. A person hearing an alternative pronoun for the first time is likely to look quite puzzled. "Come again?" they might respond. Not surprisingly, using these consistently in one's speech is also a challenge for most.

Zie is at the mall with hir (pronounced: heer) dad watching a movie.
I went with zem to get zer haircut this weekend.

Some additional variations include *xe, ze, zir, it,* and *s/he*. It is important to do one's best to use the pronoun requested by the individual and not assume that because something works well for one person, it will work well for others. I've met one person that wished to be referred to as "it." Many others would find that deeply offensive. *S/he* can work well as a written option but how to best verbalize it varies. Some will say *she-he* (others consider this a slur) or pronounce it as "she-slash-he" which is a bit cumbersome for regular pronoun usage.

GENDER PRESENTATION

It can be helpful to families, educators, and professionals to have an awareness of how society's gendered expectations affect a child's expression and presentation. Trans children will express unique gender differences. That uniqueness needs to be honored.

All children experience a kind of "social transition" over time. We consider their changing interests, evolving clothing preferences, and presentation changes as they come into themselves to be a natural process of self-discovery—a normal part of childhood development. Yet, when it comes to gender norms and expectations, we do not always recognize that a double standard exists. Girls have a greater latitude for expressing masculinity compared to societal intolerance for boys expressing femininity.[9] Any child, not just gender-diverse children, would benefit from an equitable opportunity for stigma-free self-discovery.

An important social-transition step for trans children is aligning their outward gender presentation with their innate gender identity. Changes related to presentation may include the selection of different clothing, new hair length and/or styles, and accessorizing in ways considered gender-typical. This may be the time when a trans girl starts growing her hair longer and wearing dresses, skirts, leggings, and accessories we consider to be feminine. Trans boys will often lean toward clothing considered masculine and/or opt for a shorter haircut. Offering support for gender presentation changes provides an opportunity for a child and their family to gain more information that they might not otherwise get.

Any parent can struggle with the daunting task of supporting a child's gender transition. Add to that the complexity of how their child's gender identity relates to their gender *presentation*. It seems as though it would be "easier" if a child would express absolute "cross-gender" identification and then choose to also present in a way consistent with what society presents as the norm for that gender role. One couple recently said:

> My wife and I are physicians. We've both had trans people in our respective practices. We "get it" intellectually, but it is hard for us emotionally. Our fourteen-year-old trans daughter resists clearly defining or presenting herself as female but wants to start estrogen. We consider ourselves progressive people but somehow it seems like it would be easier if she would just clearly, confidently state that she is a woman. Then we could just get on with it.

There is no one way to enter into gender presentation changes. Nor is there a need to make any presentation changes to prove the validity of one's gender identity. Yet, the societal expectation to see a definitive congruence between gender expression and gender identity is still the prevailing one. Gender presentation does *not* need to be "gender-aligned." A trans girl, like any other girl, may be more comfortable in jeans and a t-shirt and hoping to join the track team. A trans boy may continue to express his individuality by wearing make-up and doing his nails. These kids may have a very clear sense of themselves as a boy or a girl yet not feel obligated to satisfy anyone else's notion of what that should look like.

Some trans children, especially at the younger ages, may experience a "pendulum swing" with respect to their gender presentation preferences. For a trans girl, this might include an insistence on wearing dresses at *all* times, that pink is the predominant color choice for every stitch of clothing, and that all "boy things" should go away. A trans boy may feel that he should no longer play with dolls or have an interest in makeup. One parent said that her ten-year-old trans boy started telling sexist jokes because "that's what all the other boys do." These more polarized gender presentation leanings typically soften over time, especially when trans children realize that the gender preferences of other children are not so rigid. After all, princess dresses can be impractical at times and a lot of boys like to play with dolls.

The outward presentation choices of a nonbinary child can be challenging as well. While a child's identity may or may not remain in what is viewed as a place "in-between genders," their presentation may or may not be consistent as well. They may feel confident to choose as they like from all options of dress, colors, clothing, and hairstyles as a way to express their identity. This is particularly challenging for parents. I've seen a high degree of the angst of more than one parent as their nonbinary trans boy headed out the door to school wearing makeup and a scarf while sporting a buzz cut and facial hair!

A less experienced medical provider may assume that a trans child is *required* to adopt a gender-specific expression to *qualify* as transgender. This provider may then withhold transition-related care such as puberty suppression or early hormone intervention until the child's expression satisfies the provider's personal expectations.[10] The mother of a teenage trans girl shared this experience with other support group parents:

> My trans daughter socially transitioned over two years ago. We all felt ready for her to begin the next step of entering puberty. The doctor refused to prescribe estrogen for her until she got her ears pierced! My daughter was so livid! I didn't know how to fight the doctor on this at the time and didn't want to jeopardize the relationship as he was the only available provider in our town. My daughter took matters into her own hands. She grabbed a friend and they pierced each other's ears, old school style, with a needle and god knows what or how. Who has to get their ears pierced before getting medical care?!!

Barriers that prevent a child from pursuing gender transition steps are plentiful. The steps, whether available or not, may look different than another child's transition steps. Any family raising a trans or nonbinary child within a community unfamiliar with and resistant to gender-diverse expression in children will be aware of the potential impact of this environment on their child. The following example highlights the complexities faced by one family and how they decided to address them:

We live in a rural community with jobs, family, and friends all within a few miles of us. My wife and I grew up here and started our own family. As far as we knew, there were no transgender people and certainly no children. Our eight-year-old son told us he was a girl on the inside. What are we supposed to do with that? We knew our community have no understanding of his experience and would be deeply resistant. We were not in a position to move, we'd have to leave everything we've ever known. Our child didn't want to move either. After many conversations all the way around, we decided our child could live at home as a girl but continue to attend school as a boy. As her parents, we struggled with this and felt a lot of guilt. Our trans daughter said she would be okay with it so we crossed our fingers and kept on with our lives. We are making sure that we line up pubertal suppression with a doctor in the nearest city so when that time comes, we'll be ready. I don't quite know how we'll figure this out in the long run but I guess we'll take it a day at a time.

While far from what most would consider ideal, this seemed like the choice that would cause their child *the least* distress. The parents understood the importance of puberty suppression to minimize the physical changes of adolescence knowing that an eventual gender transition was likely. While this family's situation is more complicated than others, it highlights the importance of weighing all factors with thoughtful consideration.

ID DOCUMENTS

Changing identity documents and legal records is often part of a child's transition-related process. The most common of these is a legal change of name, amendments to a birth certificate, and passport and social security updates. For older children, document changes can also include updates to a driver's license. Federal identification documents, such as the Social Security Administration and the U.S. Department of State, will have a more consistent process regardless of the state of birth or residence while driver's licenses, state ID cards, and birth certificates are issued by individual states, and the processes to do so could vary widely. In some states, the process for changes will be straightforward and in others, the process may be prohibitive or nonexistent. Minor children will most often need parental consent for changes to legal documents. For up-to-date information, the website for the National Center for Transgender Equality (NCTE) can provide a state-by-state breakdown of the requirements needed for changing a variety of documents. NCTE also provides information for immigration document updates to a Permanent Residence Card, Employment Authorization Card, and Naturalization Certificate.

PERMANENCE AND CERTAINTY

There is the continued perception that once a transition of any kind has begun, it is headed down a road from which there is no return. We need to *remove the notion that achieving unequivocal permanence and certainty is a requirement* before considering social transition.

The steps of social transition can be gradual, incremental, taken all at once, or parsed out in any manner best suited to the child and family. They are not part of an unequivocal march toward hormones, surgeries, and a permanent life change. If a parent has disclosed to the whole world that their child is transgender, and their kid eventually says, *Hmm, I guess I'm not trans*, the parent simply needs to say: *We supported our child as they were exploring their gender. We will continue to support them now.*

If all social transition-related steps, decisions about hormonal intervention, and surgical procedures are viewed as one single package—requiring a definitive yes or no decision—this will place undue pressure on the child to convince a skeptical audience of a future that they cannot yet envision. The desire for certainty in advance is rooted in the fear of making an incontrovertible mistake and the child is the one most likely to suffer.

MEDICAL TRANSITION

A medical transition—like a social transition—includes a number of possible interventions. Medical providers who are competent in working with gender-diverse youth recognize that medical intervening steps require attention to the unique needs of any particular youth. What are some of these unique considerations? The list below will give you an idea but is nowhere near exhaustive. Some have to do with medical care, others have to do with a child's psychosocial experience. A competent provider will consider these variables in totality and recognize that additional variables may arise in ways that call for continued evaluation and possible adjustment.

1. Age of child
2. Stage of puberty
3. Length of time since first disclosing their gender or "coming out"
4. Level of discomfort with pubertal changes or anticipated pubertal changes
5. Gender identification of child
6. Insurance considerations or barriers
7. Co-occurring factors

8. Awareness and understanding of youth
9. Level of familial support
10. Any urgent or time-sensitive considerations

The youth, their provider, and their caregiver(s) comprise the team that will consider these factors so that informed decisions are made that optimize the physical and mental health of that youth. There is much to discuss, too much to address fully in this book, but the following paragraphs will provide a beginning overview.

My hope is to facilitate a process of discernment for those who are in the decision-making position for a child. For others hoping to deepen their learning, we can begin by demystifying what feels to be unchartered terrain.

THE PROCESS OF MEDICAL TRANSITION

The two primary medical options available to trans youth are *puberty suppression* and *cross hormone therapy*. These interventions are sometimes used separately, and sometimes in tandem.

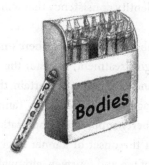

Puberty Suppression

Puberty suppression is a treatment that uses a type of medication referred to as GnRH agonists (gonadotropin-releasing hormone agonists) or more commonly known as *puberty blockers*. GnRH agonists have been used for decades to treat a variety of conditions, such as hormone-sensitive cancers, fertility treatments, endometriosis, and early "precocious" puberty in very young children.[11] In recent years, puberty suppression has been used to temporarily suppress pubertal development in pre-adolescent trans children. It is sometimes used in combination with cross hormone treatment in trans *adolescents* who may have already had some pubertal changes. Parents are sometimes hesitant about this first step of medical intervention:

> I don't know if my child is truly transgender or if they are just experiencing a phase. They are so young—shouldn't we wait before taking any medical steps?

The benefit of this early intervention is significant *because* of the very fact that the children are young. Puberty suppression is a medical intervention that *only serves to pause puberty* so that no further pubertal development occurs—providing a temporary reprieve to those families who *are* uncertain about their child's gender identification. It provides deep relief to a child who knows that puberty will bring unwanted, incongruent changes to their bodies. Essentially, blockers are an ideal solution to a parent's hesitancy because it buys that family time to continue the process of discovery and learning. With more time, a childhood phase can play out with no physical changes to overcome. If it is not a phase, the use of blockers can prevent significant pubertal changes from occurring *while* the adults in that child's life—providers and parents—can observe the gender identity consistency that will instill greater confidence for all.

When considering puberty suppression there's no need to arbitrarily predetermine the age to begin treatment. Instead, the stages of pubertal development are monitored and assessed to ascertain the right moment for the individual child. These stages are referred to as Tanner stages of puberty. The optimal time to begin puberty suppression medication, commonly referred to as puberty blockade, is at the onset of Tanner stage two. Stage two typically occurs between the ages of ten and fourteen, although it may be as early as age eight or nine. Other children can have a much earlier pubertal onset (precocious puberty), while still others might fall into the category of late bloomers. Family history, genetics, obesity, nutrition, racial differences, and other factors may influence the time of pubertal onset as well. For example, studies show that African American and Hispanic children with ovaries may start puberty up to a year earlier on average than their white counterparts.[12]

Regardless of whether a child is trans, or just experiencing a stage in their gender exploration, puberty suppression allows the parent, the child, and any involved provider a chance to gain greater clarity and confidence in their path without the feared risk of permanent changes brought about by puberty. More importantly, it can decrease the understood risks of possible self-harm or suicide that are associated with unwanted, incongruent puberty.

It is important to note that the use of puberty suppressing medication has minimal side effects. These are understood and monitored by the administering physician. The most recognized side effect is a potential temporary decrease in bone density, which can be mitigated with calcium and vitamin D supplementation and engaging in weight-bearing exercise.

Puberty suppression is a very useful treatment that is completely reversible. It can be easily discontinued if it is not the right step for a gender-diverse child. The pubertal progression picks up from the stage at which it was initially "paused." Bone density and growth return to their original path. For an exploring child— one that may not ultimately continue toward a gender transition—the treatment is a welcome moment to pause and collect more information; for the child who goes on to make other medical transition steps, it is crucial and lifesaving.

WHAT IF PUBERTY DELAY INTERVENTION IS URGENT FOR THE CHILD BUT THE PARENT IS NOT READY?

A child may be starting pubertal changes while their apprehensive parent struggles with fear, misinformation, and confusion. The emotional period of learning can take months, sometimes longer, during this crucial time of irreversible pubertal changes. Understanding that pubertal blockade buys time is paramount. Again, blockers *temporarily halt* further pubertal development and are noncommittal toward any specific gender path. Everyone gets a chance to catch their breath.

Hormone Therapy: Getting Started

While it can feel equally or more challenging for a caregiver to consider hormonal treatment for their teen, this medical intervention is nuanced as well. It is not an "all or nothing" decision.

Unlike puberty blockers, beginning an initial treatment of estrogen or testosterone will bring about gradual physical changes. For a teen experiencing distress related to pubertal changes, it can provide immediate relief by simply providing them with the knowledge that their needs are heard and validated. We can shift our perspective from viewing hormonal care as an irreversible path to an end gender destination and, instead, recognize it as a step-by-step part of a young person's gender exploration and discovery. Then, we have validated a youth's experience in the *present* and provided a vehicle for gaining a more accurate view into the future, while simultaneously providing them with validation and perspective.

Like puberty blockers, it is crucial to understand that *beginning* hormone intervention is NOT a full commitment to a gender transition. It affords a teen the immediate relief that comes with moving toward their objective, even though initial physical changes are often imperceptible to others. These slow and gradual changes provide them with important information that they cannot get otherwise. What does estrogen feel like? What changes, what stays the same? What do I like about testosterone, what don't I? Does it feel like things are going too fast? Too slow? Do the changes I experience resonate with who I am? Do I feel a relief to be on my way or are there some doubts now that I've begun my gradual dosage? Any attempts to answer these questions *before beginning hormonal intervention* would just be speculative. They need real information.

It is critical to give weight to the tenuousness of a child's mental stability when making a decision. By the time many teens disclose their gender identity to another person, they do so because their suffering has ramped up in urgency. The need for movement has taken priority over any other concern. Some experience it as a life-or-death situation. Beginning a hormonal intervention is low in risk, it's an important information-gathering step, and it plays a critical role in minimizing some of the risks associated with mental health distress.

If a teen, as parents so often fear, has a change of heart about their gender trajectory, a knowledgeable, informed medical provider can adapt, adjust, or even halt a treatment plan. These adaptations may be temporary, permanent, or not be required at all. While it might seem illogical that a parent would view early hormonal intervention as an unequivocal, permanent path, nevertheless, many of them do. Moving forward on a hormonal regimen is not a mandate requiring youth to unwaveringly pursue a gender transition. Physicians with expertise in this area will understand the complexities involved. With suicidal ideation, and other possibilities of self-harm, withholding hormonal intervention for a distressed teen is an unnecessary and dangerous risk. Forward motion, not stagnation, is often needed, if only for the teen and parent(s) to gain more information.

As medical knowledge increases and societal awareness deepens, more trans and gender-diverse children will likely have access to this important intervention. Current and future research studies validating this supportive intervention will certainly be a factor in increasing the accessibility of this option.

Blockers and Hormones

While it may be ideal to "catch" a child at the onset of Tanner stage two puberty to prevent any unwanted secondary sex characteristics, medical providers are recognizing that a youth that is partway into puberty can benefit from the concurrent use of blockers and hormonal treatment. The blockers will suppress the further progression of the natal puberty so that the administration of cross hormones can be at a lower dosage and still achieve the desired changes.[13]

Adolescent youth who did not disclose their gender status in time to avoid pubertal changes yet know that their natal puberty will provide *continued* unwanted changes can benefit physically and psychologically from the combined use of blockers and hormones. The natal puberty is arrested while the gender-validating puberty is beginning. An added benefit to this combined approach is that a medical provider can facilitate a more measured pubertal progression that is more gradual than one solely reliant on hormones alone.

Pubertal Development and Medical Decisions: Parental Discernment and Responsibility

Trans and nonbinary children often experience apprehension about the onset of puberty, yet they may not have the ability to verbally express it to those around them. Their inability to express this apprehension does not mean they are not struggling.

Some children may be unaware of upcoming pubertal changes. They may have never considered the possibility of their own body changing, feeling perhaps that it was a more abstract notion of something that happens to other people. Others have a much clearer understanding. Regardless of their comprehension level, the onset of physical changes can bring about feelings of helplessness—including shame, despair, disgust, dissociation, and increased body dysphoria. Many of them will struggle to understand what is going on internally and have an even greater difficulty verbalizing it to others!

At this stage of adolescent development, young people are developing the ability to engage in more abstract thinking. They will be more introspective when considering their own identity, and increasingly sensitive to how others, especially their peers, perceive *and receive* them. It is a time of increased independence from parents and where their own values and interests are elevated in priority. As a result, they will want—and should have—a role in their own gender decisions. But there is more to it than that. The supportive, discerning role of a parent or caregiver is crucial.

When considering the convergence of physical changes, psychosocial growth, and gender identity development in gender-diverse children, the significance of the challenges these youth face becomes clear. It is not uncommon for trans children to develop an eating disorder; experience anxiety attacks; and engage in coping mechanisms such as cutting, isolating, and being uncommunicative. Expecting a child to fully understand these new, interrelated experiences and then succinctly articulate a request for blockers or hormones is unrealistic. Some may be able to articulate their struggle, and possibly even ask for puberty suppression and/or hormones if they understand these options exist. Others, fearing parental rejection or resistance, will minimize their struggle or not ask at all. The conflict between parents, especially if gender-related, will add to the child's burden. The child may greatly diminish their own needs to keep the peace.

Do Parents Have a Role in Medical Decision-Making?

Even under the best of circumstances, a supportive parent may take their child's silence, nonchalance, or indecisiveness as a reason against the pursuit of transition-related care. It is crucial for parents and providers alike to understand the developmental, psychological, emotional, and physical complexities that come with making gender-related medical decisions. It is unrealistic, even dangerous, for an adult to rely solely on a child's ability to "ask" for medical care before intervening. Many are unaware that medical intervention is a possibility at all, so asking for intervention will seem to fall into the category of fantastical thinking. As one youth said, "I might as well have wished for a pot of gold under a rainbow."

In other situations, a young person may have accessed the internet for transition-related information well before they disclose their gender identity to anyone. As a result, some parents rely on their child's internet foray as the source of their own knowledge. It might be obvious to an outsider that a child should not be the sole source of a parent's understanding but when you factor in a parent's initial shock, a dearth of knowledgeable providers, and a young person who has had a significant head start, the temptation for a parent to initially rely on their child is better understood. In some cases, this can even prevent transition-related care from happening:

One member of a support group shared that her child was in crisis about beginning pubertal changes yet when asked by the parent, the ten-year-old said she "did not want to" move forward with puberty suppression. As the parent shared, it became more clear that what her child did not actually want was to go to the doctor for an injection! This child had always expressed her fear of needles when in a doctor's office. But, she had much less ability to understand something that was just beginning (puberty), and that medical intervention could stop that progression. All she heard was that she would need to get a shot! If the question is, "Do you want a shot, or not?" it's not hard to imagine that any child's first response would be anything other than an emphatic NO!

Another teen had attended a trans youth group for years. His youth group friends knew he wanted to begin hormones, but it just didn't happen. He would just shrug when others would ask why his parents wouldn't help. "I don't know, they just won't." His parents shared a different story:

> We have a child through transracial adoption. He's seventeen now and came out as a trans three years ago. He's really quiet and does not advocate for himself. We figure that he has to learn how to stand up for himself someday. So, when he can ask us directly if he can start testosterone, we'll go for it!

This teen *had* clearly and repeatedly expressed his desire to begin hormones at his youth support group but had difficulty making a direct request of his parents. Rather than recognizing that starting testosterone, and achieving greater gender congruence in the process, might make him a more confident young adult, they held off. It was hard enough for their son to order from a restaurant menu and more dismaying to know that they would withhold medical care to teach him a lesson.

In another situation, a father suggested that his child needed to exhibit a higher degree of responsibility for them to *earn* the use of hormones. She had been on blockers for almost four years:

> My fifteen-year-old trans daughter is still having behavioral outbursts. She does not have her act together! I don't think it's gender-related though. Now she says she wants boobs because all her friends have them, and to bleach

her hair platinum blond. When she starts taking care of her responsibilities at home and acting more mature, then I'll consider the hormones!

Taking a step back to consider the overall situation can be helpful in providing a parent better perspective. What teen is expected to get their behavior in line to begin puberty? None. Puberty happens when it happens. Young people awkwardly navigate puberty and behavioral changes are part of it. Gender-related medical treatment should not be withheld as a punishment nor put forth as a reward for good behavior. This teen observes her peers moving forward in their pubertal development while she is stuck in a pre-adolescent's body due to lengthy suppression of puberty. At age fifteen, she is being more and more excluded from her peer group as a result. What a truly frustrating position for her—no wonder there are some emotional outbursts. Even parents can struggle with the understanding that medical decisions are appropriate interventions for trans children, not a choice to pursue cosmetic enhancement that could then be considered a reward or privilege.

Hesitancy and Silence

Children rely on parents and caregivers to make medical decisions for them. We don't ask a child if they want their tonsils taken out, or what course of treatment they would like to pursue to address their diabetes. There is a legal requirement that each decision-making parent is responsible for the basic needs of their child including housing, education, food, *and medical care.* While that sounds straightforward enough, it isn't always so clear-cut. The youth's voice is a crucial component, yes, but they still need adult guidance. Discernment is vital.

The parents of Sean, a seventeen-year-old trans boy who had socially transitioned three years before, were regular parent support group attendees. They had been in a wait-and-see mode, regarding chest reconstructive surgery for their large-chested son: "If he wants top surgery, all he has to do is ask." The parents admitted they were terrified of this step and, as long as their son wasn't asking, their fears could be pushed out to the future. The next time they came to a group, one of the parents had more to say:

After sharing our fears with all of you, my wife and I had a good long conversation. We realized how easily our son might recognize *our fear* and how that might prevent him from coming to us. So, we sat our kid down and had a face-to-face. We told him we were ready and, if he wanted chest surgery, we'd support him 100%. The relief on his face was immediate and he did say he wanted to move forward.

A year later, after the surgery and recovery, the father shared again in the group:

> It pains me to know that I let my own fear get in the way of something that my kid truly needed. He needed *me* to take the lead, while I was dragging my feet and expecting him to do it. He is doing so well. He stands taller, jeez, he's just got a light coming from him now. I just wish I'd showed up for him sooner.

One reframing that has helped many parents gain better clarity is to consider this question, "If my child had any other medical condition in which I knew the recommended treatment, would I sit back and wait for my child to find the courage to ask for it?"

A parent may recognize that their child is in pain, but it can be difficult to determine the source of that distress if that child is unable or hesitant to articulate it. Even recognizing a child's difficulties as gender-related may not be enough if the *providers* in a child's life are unable or unwilling to recognize the presence of gender dysphoria. A parent's ability to advocate for their child may be severely hindered as a result.

A mother and her trans son shared their story with me.

> Son: I really hated it when I started developing breasts. I didn't know what to
> do. What I thought was, *my body made these breasts so I should also be able*
> *to make them go away.* When everyone went to sleep at night, I would go
> into the bathroom and take my shirt off. Night after night, I pounded my
> breasts with my fists so hard that I was black and blue from the bruising,
> but they never went away. I told no one.
> Mother: I took my son to so many providers in an effort to get him help.
> I was desperate. Each one latched on to anything and everything besides
> his gender. *It's because he's adopted. It has to do with his low birth weight. He*
> *has a learning disability, etc.* I kept telling each of them that I thought that

gender was part of his struggle, but none would listen. It took forever for me to find someone who could truly help.

Health care professionals and caregivers should recognize that, while steps to undertake puberty intervention require thoughtful consideration, it is crucial to not depend solely on a child to steer the ship. Gender congruence, peer concordance, and adult support for the child are critical factors that must be included.

LACK OF PARENTAL OR CAREGIVER SUPPORT

The importance of parental support in a trans child's life is impossible to overestimate. Yet, parents worry. *If I support my child's gender and then my child changes their mind, will I have caused harm? Why should we expect literally everyone to make all these changes when it may surely be a phase?* Most families are unprepared for supporting their gender-diverse child and feel deeply challenged when considering if, how, and what they should do about their child's gender.

Today, we better understand that supporting a child's gender pathway will cause less harm than taking a passive or resistant stance. It is important to recognize that caregivers, educators, and society are now being tasked with creating and implementing more supportive environments. By doing so, we can decrease the harm to a child's physical and psychological well-being. As understanding and inclusivity increase, we still have many children who will not receive support. While numbers are difficult to estimate, trans youth who lack support for their gender identification still likely outweigh those who do have support. Youth who are in foster care, the juvenile justice system, and those lacking consistent adult advocates in their lives are going to have an even harder time receiving the needed support due to ignorance, stigma, and a lack of continuity within health care and educational systems.

There is no certainty that divorce courts will rule in favor of a gender-affirming parent over a resistant parent. Misinformation is still a significant contributing factor. In recent years, however, court systems throughout the United States continue to progress in the number of gender-affirming decisions. Their data-driven findings support that withholding medically necessary, gender-based care constitutes discrimination.[14]

Without parental/guardian consent, it is difficult for youth to access affirming medical interventions of any type, including non-permanent puberty suppression. Exceptions can include foster youth, wards of the state, and emancipated minors, but their success will likely be dependent on the presence of informed adults advocating on their behalf.

Parents often lack awareness of current research detailing the high risks factors for unsupported trans youth. They may only find outdated, dangerous parenting recommendations like conversion/reparative therapies (currently being outlawed in many states). Parents are aware of the stigma associated with being transgender and they fear that their children will be in danger throughout their lives. Cultural and faith differences can complicate a parent's experience. It's no wonder that parents have difficulties when considering how, when, or if to be supportive of their child's gender. This creates an unpredictable environment for any gender-diverse youth. At the same time, the visible and vocal presence of nonbinary and trans youth is increasing nationwide.

For hesitant parents and caregivers, it may feel impossible to think that they will one day consider this challenging time to be one of their life's greatest blessings, yet so many do. Unlikely, too, the notion that a child, regardless of whether they will pursue a gender transition or not, will say, "I really wish my parents had NOT supported me on my gender journey."

CAN A CHILD GET GENITAL SURGERY?

A six-year-old may ask when their penis is going to "grow in" but the pursuit of genital surgery is definitely not in that child's near future. Genital surgery is not medically recommended for young children. In some situations, older teens, particularly those with parental support are able to successfully pursue genital surgery. For the majority, however, it is still largely unavailable. Older youth desiring genital reconstruction will likely not pursue surgery until adulthood.

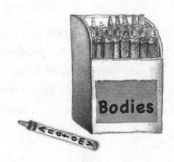

There is a presumption that genital surgery will be an inevitable transition step. This is not, nor has it ever been the case for many transgender people.[15] While it is difficult to determine the precise percentage of people who have genital surgery, the actual number is much lower than most would anticipate. Some people are simply uninterested in surgery, concerned about the sexual function of reconfigured genitals, or don't feel that their "parts" need to be changed. Social transition, hormones, and perhaps some surgery, but not *all* available surgeries, may be what is necessary for them to feel more at ease with their bodies. For many, insurance and/or financial barriers are present, and still others have no access to skilled surgeons.

Recently, the father of a young trans girl related this experience:

> I've been coming to this support group for five years. My daughter socially transitioned when she was four-and-a-half. She's nine now. I've prepared myself for what I assumed would be her inevitable need to have genital confirmation surgery. The other day she told me, *I like my penis. I'm going to keep it.* I was completely floored. Then, I felt a little silly about my own assumptions!

It is too early to identify surgical trends with respect to children who've transitioned at early ages. Factors that may contribute to any young person's later surgical pursuits include a level of body congruence versus body dysphoria; validation of gender identity and support from family, peers, and community; whether or not a child's gender history is known or kept private; and many other considerations.

CHALLENGES AND BARRIERS TO MEDICAL CARE ACCESS

The increased societal trajectory of visible trans and gender-diverse youth is in stark contrast with society's ability to meet the needs of these youth and their families. This makes the present time a true state of transition, not just with respect to a child's gender but to our overall societal response as well. This means that any particular child's experience can be unique, inconsistent, and oftentimes not in the child's best interests.

Lack of Knowledgeable Medical Providers

When encountering an unknown health issue, the logical inclination would be to seek out an expert, perhaps getting a second or third opinion. However, providers experienced in gender care are still difficult to find, especially outside urban areas. Finding those who are familiar with care for children is harder still. Medical school curriculum content addressing gender identity is often unavailable, outdated, or so brief in duration that it is largely ineffectual for the medical students hoping to learn more. This is changing as medical programs across the nation add gender-specific content to required and elective course offerings for future providers. In the interim, knowledgeable care can be difficult to find. Some families have traveled out of state to find care. This is not a viable solution as it only deepens disparities already experienced by families of color and others for whom this option would not be possible.[16]

General care practitioners, physicians' assistants, naturopathic doctors, and other care providers can and do provide hormonal support and pubertal intervention. It does not require a sub-specialty. To reduce existing inequities, accessible gender-affirming health care is essential. All medical care providers should address ways they can make their practices more welcoming and inclusive, make their staff knowledgeable and confident, and address any barriers encountered by these youth within the larger health care system.[17]

Like anyone else, medical professionals are not immune to the negative misrepresentations of trans people in society. They may feel intimidated at first, getting tripped up by their own lack of knowledge. For these providers, the recognition of the need to offer care came only when they first encountered a trans patient. Despite their initial inexperience, this moment provided many of them with the impetus to pursue additional learning, consult with experienced providers, and delve into available resources. It does not take long for their confidence to increase as they recognize that their previous medical training has already provided them with most of the tools they need.

Insurance Barriers

In the past, all gender-related care for trans individuals regardless of age was specifically excluded from insurance coverage. It was considered to be "elective" rather than necessary medical care. As of 2021, it is now illegal in most situations to deny coverage based on a person's transgender status. While blanket exclusions are no longer a given, adequate and barrier-free coverage for everyone is not in sight either. Some insurers are still clinging to gender exclusions and approximately twenty percent of U.S. states continue to deny coverage.[18] Disparities in coverage are rampant. One family was horrified to learn that, while their child's puberty blocker was approved, the hospital had billed their insurance company a whopping $80,000! This outpatient procedure typically falls into the $3,000 to $4,000 range. This is a less common example but highlights how unpredictable and inconsistent the process can be.

Many claims are initially denied, and some are reversed upon appeal—or multiple appeals! There can be widely divergent experiences with insurance representatives who are unfamiliar with their own policy changes, or who may have their judgment clouded because of their own discomfort and ignorance. An uninformed or resistant individual that is part of the health care and insurance systems can present blockades within the process that may end up being insurmountable for a family. Even if the family has the resources to prevail, critical time is dangerously wasted, placing the child at much greater risk.

Families are advised to be as timely as possible with their health care planning. Unfortunately, it can take months or longer for a family to navigate the coverage denials and appeal process, with no guarantee of prevailing. These delays can be extremely difficult for youth when they are experiencing incongruent body changes. It can also mean the difference between later surgical interventions, such as chest reconstructive surgery or facial feminization surgery (if puberty has already begun), and having no need for some of these surgeries at all (if they had timely access to puberty suppression).

Trans medical care is still considered controversial, especially for children. Until recently, there was little attention given to the needs and lives of gender-diverse children. It bears repeating that there are long-term studies and projects underway confirming the positive impact of familial support *and* gender-affirming care offered by informed providers.[19] As these studies continue to add to the body of knowledge, the access to this care will be more consistent and less fraught with subjectivity.

Gender Dysphoria Diagnosis

Accessing gender-affirming medical care typically requires a diagnosis of *gender dysphoria*. Gender dysphoria (GD) refers to the distress a person feels due to the incongruence of their assigned sex at birth and their gender identity. The diagnosis was modified from the previous *gender identity disorder* to gender dysphoria in

2013.[20] The name and criteria revisions were established to reflect the increased understanding of gender identity differences and to remove the stigma associated with the label of disorder. According to the American Psychiatric Association, one of the critical elements of gender dysphoria is the "presence of clinically significant distress," and the goal of treatment is to address this distress.

One of the conundrums associated with a gender dysphoria diagnosis is that many gender-diverse children do *not* present a "clinically significant" observable level of distress. Why is that? Family support! Gender dysphoria does not only encompass a gender incongruence with one's body, but it is also the distress that comes from walking through a day-to-day life experience where trans children experience invalidation, exclusion, and rejection from the world around them. If factors such as family support, peer acceptance, and gender inclusion in schools are present, there is much less gender pushback to feel "dysphoric" about.

Many trans children do not fit the expected gender assessment criteria because much of the criteria (including the way providers interpret them) itself is arbitrary or flawed. For example, to be diagnosed as transgender, children are expected to have exhibited a long history of gender nonconformity. This would include a boy who likes the color pink and plays with dolls or a girl who wants short hair and is interested in trucks and sports. These notions about how girls and boys should behave may seem antiquated and yet they persist. Many trans girls may not exhibit enough interest in what is deemed "feminine" and trans boys may not present some level of "masculinity" that is deemed necessary to be entitled to the diagnosis. We know that a child's *gender expression*, in and of itself, is not a direct, undeniable indicator of a child's *gender identity*. Yet this is still used as a qualifier.

A sixteen-year-old, despite support from her family and therapist, continued to be denied access to gender-affirming hormone care. The family, First Nations people living in British Columbia, had been referred to a gender specialist and, time and time again, were turned down despite the teen's years-long social transition and consistent identification. The helplessness felt by both mother and child was only deepened when the physician shared that the teen just wasn't "feminine enough" in her behavior to be trans:

> My daughter, like many tomboys, loves sports, being outside, and her interests are the same as all of her female friends. The doctor, he just doesn't get it!

The mother felt that being First Nations, a single parent, and a woman were all at play in his refusal to listen and provide care at such a crucial time in her daughter's life.

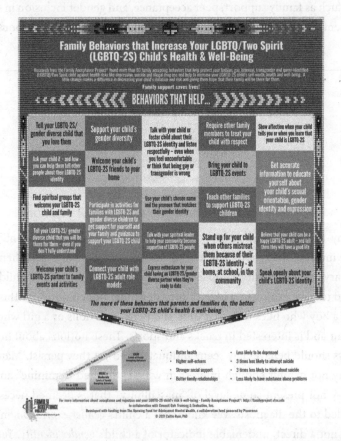

This version of the Family Acceptance Project's General Family Acceptance Poster for American Indian families and communities shows how family supportive and accepting behaviors help protect against health risks and promotes well-being. See Appendix C for guidance on poster use (https://familyproject.sfsu.edu/posters).[21]

Because the content in medical schools and residency curricula is lacking in transgender health education, physicians often lack the competence, and subsequently the confidence, to provide needed care to gender-diverse patients.[22] Some providers may erroneously conclude that a diagnosis of gender dysphoria implies that there will always be coexisting issues such as anxiety or depression. This is sometimes true, but not with all children. What happens if a trans youth exhibits none of the expected dysphoria criteria?

> One teen, dangerously suicidal during the previous year, finally found the courage to tell his parents that he was transgender. The parents pulled out all the stops to support their child, setting aside any personal conflict they may have felt as they knew his life was in jeopardy. His school supported his social transition and helped facilitate the disclosure to his peers. All went very well and his mental health dramatically improved. Even the six months-long waiting list at the Children's Hospital adolescent gender clinic did not dampen his spirits. He knew he was on his way. The day of the appointment came when he and the psychologist would discuss beginning hormonal treatment. He had no problem telling his parents, and the psychologist, that it was one of the happiest days of his life. Imagine this teen's shock when the psychologist decided that he must not be transgender because he was not exhibiting the symptoms of gender dysphoria (ex. depression). "He's just too happy." The parents felt rage at this dismissal: "Where was this psychologist when, last year, our child was on a suicide watch every fifteen minutes! How dare she play games with our child's life!"

This psychologist dangerously ignored and disregarded this teen's mental health history. It is also possible that she concluded that because the deep depression went away so too did the gender identity incongruence that he had been feeling all along. The lack of judgment and discernment could have been dangerous, if not fatal, were it not for the strong advocacy and immediate action of the parents to find a more competent provider.

While this teen had a history of depression, some trans and gender-diverse children don't. If a child's gender identity is recognized, understood, and embraced, they may not experience the expected levels of mental health distress that far too often are *assumed must be present to assign a diagnosis*. We need to consider that a supportive home and school environment for a trans child will significantly lessen or eliminate the social dysphoria these children might otherwise experience.[23] Reducing the dysphoria that comes from a more optimal external environment could then have a positive effect on reducing the degree of internal body dysphoria that a child experiences.

It is common for gender-diverse children to have acquired other mental health diagnoses on their journey to gender recognition. In addition to depression and anxiety, higher rates of things like autism, sensory issues, obsessive-compulsive disorder, and eating disorders can occur as well.[24] When the core gender issue is recognized, and support offered, these co-existing factors are diminished, some even disappear. Some remain.

Whether there is a gender dysphoria diagnosis or not, medical and mental health clinicians may delay or ignore treatment for a youth's gender incongruence for many reasons. Some will simply not recognize a child's gender identification difference, some will lack the knowledge to address it, and others will lack the confidence to step in and learn. Regardless, the result is a provider who is more inclined to treat symptoms—like those associated with anxiety and depression—by providing coping strategies. Coping strategies are good, yet the underlying core gender issue remains unresolved. They may focus on co-occurring diagnoses only simply because they are more familiar. However, if the source of a child's anxiety, depression, or other concern has to do with, or is exacerbated by the gender incongruence, how can these challenges stabilize and decrease without simultaneously incorporating gender-affirming care?

We are learning how to best support gender-diverse children of any age. It is not a simple task. One person can deeply impact a trans child's future, especially if they are in positions of decision-making authority. While society moves from ignorance to understanding, the lives of today's gender-diverse children are significantly, and sometimes dangerously impacted. Parents may be supportive, or they may not. Physicians may have a grasp on appropriate medical care, or they may not. There are many others who can support—or devastate—a child's life path simply out of ignorance.

One single parent had a years-long, tiring struggle as she fought for gender-affirming care for her young adult child with Down's Syndrome. He consistently articulated his male identity with his mother, teachers, his peers at school, and within his extended community of peers with Down's. Her support of his gender identity came with a hefty price tag. The family lost the community of Down's Syndrome parents that, until then, were an integral part of their lives. These families were just as intimidated and uninformed as are so many others. The mother's guardianship authority came under intense scrutiny as the state explored whether the gender-affirming support she provided for her child might be a form of caregiver abuse. The mother patiently, persistently assisted any concerned state agency representative along the way by providing medical documentation of his diagnosis, and other resources to deepen their understanding. She was transparent about the care options available to her son, including the challenges and barriers to accessing competent providers.

When, years later, it was time to schedule his chest reconstructive surgery, she was unable to find an experienced surgeon in her state. She instead chose a skilled out-of-state surgeon to provide her son with the best possible outcome. This action, despite her transparency about it, caused an unexpected investigation which, among other things, placed a significant focus on her character and intent. If the adult protective services investigator assigned to the case had little to no knowledge about the recommended best care practices for transgender people like her son, the mother could lose her guardianship. Fortunately, the investigator did take the time to review all the materials and documentation for the case. He spoke at length, one-on-one, with the son and made the determination that the mother was indeed looking out for the best interests of her son and that he was in good hands.

Acquiring a diagnosis of gender dysphoria for a trans or nonbinary child does not fall into the category of "should we?" or "shouldn't we?" It presents barriers while removing others.

What would help us better determine the best courses of action, treatment, and support for children of different ages and circumstances, is to realize the importance of deepening the understanding of gender identity differences. It is not just an internal sense of physical incongruence that is difficult to navigate, it is the reality of being excluded from a world because of it. Gender transition steps are just that—steps. For trans or nonbinary youth, some/none/all of them are part of their bigger step-by-step journey that allows room for the discovery and authentic expression of their gender. Finding the courage to embrace one's gender identity would not be so difficult if we created a society that could embrace it as well, rather than one determined to push so hard against it.

NOTES

1. Summer Brennan, *High Heel*, Object Lessons Series (New York: Bloomsbury Academic, 2019).
2. Sabine Lang, "Various Kinds of Two-Spirit People," in *Two-Spirit People: Native American Gender Identity*, ed. Sue Ellen-Jacobs, Wesley Thomas, and Sabine Lang (Urbana: University of Illinois Press, 1997), 100–118.
3. Cindy L. Griffin, *Beyond Gender Binaries: An Intersectional Orientation to Communication and Identities* (Oakland: University of California Press, 2020), 18–21.
4. Elizabeth Vasquez, "Project Transgender—Various Bodies, the Same Right," *World Issues Forum* (February 2, 2011), https://cedar.wwu.edu/fairhaven_wif/2010-2011/2010-2011/13.
5. For stories from these teens perspectives, see Owl Fisher and Fox Fisher, *Trans Teen Survival Guide* (London; Philadelphia: Jessica Kingsley Publishers, 2019); Susan Kuklin, *Beyond Magenta: Transgender Teens Speak Out*, 1st ed. (Somerville, MA: Candlewick Press, 2014).
6. This chapter discusses the ins and outs of disclosure from the perspective of the teens themselves: Owl Fisher and Fox Fisher, *Trans Teen Survival Guide* (London; Philadelphia: Jessica Kingsley Publishers, 2019), 22–40.
7. Conservative Self-Owns [@ConSelfOwns], "Https://T.Co/7FQv0xuxa2," Tweet, *Twitter* (December 12, 2021), https://twitter.com/ConSelfOwns/status/1470160305338597377.
8. "Singular 'They'," https://www.merriam-webster.com/words-at-play/singular-nonbinary-they.
9. This, too, is subjective and changes across generations, cultures, and ethnicities. See Sally Hines, *Is Gender Fluid? A Primer for the 21st Century*, The Big Idea Series (London; New York: Thames & Hudson, 2018), 72.
10. Jen Hastings et al., "Medical Care for Nonbinary Youth: Individualized Gender Care Beyond a Binary Framework," *Pediatric Annals* 50, no. 9 (September 2021): e384–e390, https://doi.org/10.3928/19382359-20210818-03.
11. "Precocious Puberty," John Hopkins Medicine (November 19, 2019), https://www.hopkinsmedicine.org/health/conditions-and-diseases/precocious-puberty.
12. For discussions of the early onset of puberty in girls, see Frank M. Biro et al., "Pubertal Assessment Method and Baseline Characteristics in a Mixed Longitudinal Study of Girls," *Pediatrics* 126, no. 3 (September 2010): e583–e590, https://doi.org/10.1542/peds.2009-3079; Brian Handwerk, "Puberty Is Beginning Earlier in Girls, So What Can

Parents Do?," *Smithsonian Magazine* (December 26, 2014), https://www.smithsonian mag.com/science-nature/puberty-beginning-earlier-girls-so-what-can-parents-do-180953 738/; Pat Etheridge, "Early Puberty: Growing Older Sooner," *CNN* (November 1, 2013), https://www.cnn.com/2013/11/01/health/early-puberty-girls/index.html; also see Joan Jacobs Brumberg, *The Body Project: An Intimate History of American Girls*, 1st ed. (New York: Random House, 1997).

13. Rachel K. Jensen et al., "Effect of Concurrent Gonadotropin-Releasing Hormone Agonist Treatment on Dose and Side Effects of Gender-Affirming Hormone Therapy in Adolescent Transgender Patients," *Transgender Health* 4, no. 1 (October 29, 2019): 300–303, https://doi.org/10.1089/trgh.2018.0061.

14. "Transition-Related Health Care," *Lambda Legal*, https://www.lambdalegal.org/publicati ons/trt_transition-related-health-care.

15. German Lopez, "Myth #5: All Trans People Medically Transition," *Vox* (May 13, 2016), https://www.vox.com/identities/2016/5/13/17938114/transgender-people-transition ing-surgery-medical.

16. David C. Call, Mamatha Challa, and Cynthia J. Telingator, "Providing Affirmative Care to Transgender and Gender Diverse Youth: Disparities, Interventions, and Outcomes," *Current Psychiatry Reports* 23, no. 6 (April 13, 2021): 33, https://doi.org/10.1007/s11 920-021-01245-9.

17. Jason Rafferty et al., "Ensuring Comprehensive Care and Support for Transgender and Gender-Diverse Children and Adolescents," *Pediatrics* 142, no. 4 (October 1, 2018), https://doi.org/10.1542/peds.2018-2162.

18. "Transgender People Report Years of Battles for Health Insurance Coverage," *NBC News* (September 22, 2021), https://www.nbcnews.com/nbc-out/out-health-and-wellness/tran sgender-people-report-years-battles-health-insurance-coverage-rcna2145.

19. For a fun exploration into how impactful these long-range studies are, watch this account from the author of *How to Be a Girl* by Marlo Mack: https://youtu.be/lU_k4rCnPJI.

20. American Psychiatric Association and American Psychiatric Association, eds., *Diagnostic and Statistical Manual of Mental Disorders: DSM-5*, 5th ed (Washington, DC: American Psychiatric Association, 2013), 451–459.

21. *Family Behaviors that Increase Your LGBTQ Child's Health & Wellbeing for American Indian Families & Communities* [poster for multiple settings with guidance for use] (San Francisco, CA: Family Acceptance Project, Marian Wright Edelman Institute, San Francisco State University, 2021), http://familyproject.sfsu.edu/posters.

22. There are efforts to change the medical school curricula to include transgender content. See Joshua D. Safer and Elizabeth N. Pearce, "A Simple Curriculum Content Change Increased Medical Student Comfort with Transgender Medicine," *Endocrine Practice* 19, no. 4 (July 1, 2013): 633–637, https://doi.org/10.4158/EP13014.OR.

23. Kenneth H. Mayer, Robert Garofalo, and Harvey J. Makadon, "Promoting the Successful Development of Sexual and Gender Minority Youths," *American Journal of Public Health* 104, no. 6 (June 2014): 976–981.

24. John F. Strang et al., "Increased Gender Variance in Autism Spectrum Disorders and Attention Deficit Hyperactivity Disorder," *Archives of Sexual Behavior* 43, no. 8 (November 1, 2014): 1525–1533, https://doi.org/10.1007/s10508-014-0285-3.

7

Challenges Faced by Trans Children

We want to be part of something, but we need it to be real—not conditional or fake or constantly up for negotiation.

Brené Brown

Today's trans children face a significant set of challenges that can prevent them from achieving one of the most crucial and basic of human needs—a sense of *belonging*. What is at stake for them is whether or not they have a place in society, are welcomed among their peers at school, experience support and inclusion within their own families, and even have a sense of *belonging to their own bodies*. Any child may experience one or more of these challenges but trans children experience these challenges with increased intensity and may even face all of them simultaneously.

A strong sense of belonging is necessary for human development. We know that one of the most punishing actions we can take toward a human being is to separate them from the group. Children are given "time-outs" for misbehavior and criminals are removed from society when sent to prison. Even within prisons, an inmate who breaks a rule is then sent to solitary confinement.

When a child's gender differences are such that separation is deemed an appropriate course of action—separate restroom and locker room facilities, for example—what is the toll on their developing psyche? Experiencing ostracism at school or punishment within their family will only exacerbate the damage. Belonging to a group(s) and society is essential to the proper development of self, feelings of worth, and improved ability to be a self-confident, contributing member of society. The sense of safety that comes with inclusion fosters resiliency and further develops skills to manage the ordinary physical and mental demands of a child's everyday experience. A child can become a vibrant, participatory community member with societal support. When some or all these areas of belonging are absent or compromised, as so often happens with gender-diverse children, they become extremely vulnerable.

When children are told they are confused, wrong, sick, or combative because they are trying to articulate their internal gender identity, they will make efforts to repress their true selves to gain or preserve that crucial sense of inclusion. This repression has resulted in members of the health professions believing that the gender identity of these children was malleable—that it could be "changed" by sex-aligned parenting practices—and that eventually, the child's gender identification would "desist." What more often occurs is a child's *unwillingness* to express their true selves. They will hide or deny their true gender for years, decades, or even their lifetime because the need for acceptance and belonging is crucial to their survival.

Society is still in the early stages of fully understanding gender identity differences in children. We are hindered by professionals who have taken their cues from outdated sources and who have not yet accessed more recent research addressing the needs of today's trans youth. Without these current studies recommending validation for the support of trans children, many people may still feel it is logical to deny, ignore, or delay affirmation of a child's gender identity. We once believed that these tactics would even allow a child's gender "confusion" to straighten itself out. Current studies show this inaction to be harmful and ineffective, yet many families and providers are simply unaware of this progression in understanding. This erroneous approach ignored, and misinterpreted, *the lengths to which a child might go* to gain that crucial sense of belonging at home, in school, and within society.

Present-day scientific understanding has provided us with a more informed understanding of gender identity, linking it to origins in the brain rather than the supposition that genitalia is the ultimate determiner of gender. What this understanding tells us is that a child's internal sense of gender can be distinct from the genitalia we typically associate with a particular gender. Until we can better determine how to support a child's identity, rather than proscribed pathways based on body parts, we can expect that these children will have to navigate significant barriers to belonging.

But first, it can be helpful to better understand the complicated relationship that trans children have with their physical bodies, bodies that, to varying degrees, are incongruent with their gender identity.

A SENSE OF BELONGING TO ONE'S OWN BODY

Gender "Proof"

In general, many adult trans people describe experiencing a degree of incongruity—or difference—between their physical bodies and their gender identity. They often share heartbreaking stories of rejection, invalidation, ridicule—even violence—when, as young children, they attempted to articulate their gender incongruence to their families or friends. Upon reaching adulthood, they then took steps toward a physical gender transition, including hormonal and surgical interventions.

While there are more resources available today than in generations past, children still erroneously learn that gender is definitively based on anatomical differences. If a trans girl is told that she can't be a girl because she has a penis, it is understandable that she could develop a sense of body incongruence. Many parents of trans girls have reported harrowing experiences when their four- or five-year-old child thought about or tried to cut off their penis. These children have been told that the penis is the organ of the body that *"proves"* that they are not a girl. Tragically, these children conclude that, if they can remove this invalidating body part, they will have no further barrier to being the girl that they know themselves to be. The degree of despair expressed by these children, and at such young ages, warrants both attention and solutions.

Trans children typically find themselves in this confusing juxtaposition very early in childhood. The child innately senses their gender identity but is surrounded by still more "evidence" to the contrary. This "evidence" begins with their gender being assigned at birth (based on genitalia) and continues with societal limitations on gender expression—toys, hair length, play activities, etc. The most immediate step that we as a society can take, and the one that causes the least harm, is to simply acknowledge that a child's gender identity can be distinct from their physical anatomy.

Emulating Gender: Identity, Expression, or Body Parts?

We expect a child to emulate the mannerisms and expressions of people of the same gender. A daughter emulates her mother by trying on her heels and getting into her makeup. A son may use a toy as a hammer to imitate his father's work on a backyard project. Parents find this entertaining, delightful, and a normal part of child development. Yet, as we observe this gender development, we do not consider the separate components of gender—specifically anatomy, gender expression, and gender identity. Do we believe that a toddler recognizes that he and his father both have penises and, therefore, he should copy his father's actions, interests, clothing, etc.? No, a child might not even see his dad's genitals until he is much older. This toddler is emulating who he relates to and the things he is interested in. This does not mean that every cisgender (not trans) child emulates a parent of the same anatomical sex, we just *expect* them to.

A trans child, too, will emulate the behavior of the parent with whom they most closely identify and/or with whom they share interests. That may or may not be the parent with the same genitalia. A parent with different genitalia may ignore or tolerate this at first, but as the child matures, those parents will typically tolerate this less and less, experiencing consternation and resistance. The cisgender child's experience is seen as normal and playful, while the latter gender-diverse child's expression is quashed at an early age. The child experiences pressure to conform both at home and school with that pressure steadily increasing with time.

Conversely, there are many trans children who engage in gender-typical behavior. Caregivers are bewildered when this child discloses a gender identity difference. "But there were no signs! My child has always been a girly girl, how can she say she is a boy?" Just as there are young boys who like dresses and dolls and older boys who like makeup and skirts, there are also trans boys who have an atypical gender expression as well. A parent struggles to accept their child's identity as a trans boy who wears dresses because, as we've addressed earlier, it can be difficult for parents to delineate the distinctions between identity (who I am), expression (how I present myself to the world), and sexuality. It is understandable that parents and others inadvertently intertwine these concepts. For a child whose parent does not have a conceptual understanding of gender identity, this lack of distinction and understanding creates one jumbled mass of contradictions.

If kids can't explain it clearly, it's not their fault. Parents, as well as providers, have an unrealistic expectation that the child will be able to explain these complex concepts with language that clearly doesn't yet exist for them. That makes it extremely difficult, if not impossible, for trans or nonbinary children to clearly articulate their gender identity in a way that can be understood. More than one parent has been completely flummoxed as their trans child first attempted to explain their gender identity. "Mom, I know you see me as a girl (*sex assigned based on genitalia*), but I am actually a trans boy (gender identity). I'm gay (sexuality) and I love skirts and makeup (gender expression)." Many parents are bewildered by this: why not just "be" a girl, wear skirts and makeup, and find a boyfriend? What the parent is lacking is an understanding of the crucial concept of *gender identity*, simply because they have had no introduction to it.

Furthermore, gender expression in children can vary considerably over time. We easily assign the label of a *tomboy* to a girl if she likes climbing trees or sports. When that tomboy begins to explore more feminine behaviors or attire, we are unconcerned. We take that in stride as a "normal" exploration and progression. Yet, when a trans girl who was insistent on wearing dresses for so long then dons a pair of jeans and a t-shirt for a day, the parent can immediately question their choice, perhaps thinking hopefully, *maybe she is really a boy and not transgender after all!* A t-shirt is not proof of anything other than a preference for wearing a comfortable, practical article of clothing. What this divergence demonstrates is that trans children are under significant pressure to consistently *prove their gender* through choices in hairstyle, clothing, and style preferences. The parent of a trans kid wants to seize on any variation in presentation as possible proof that their child may not be trans. Ironically, most people today would agree that demanding that level of feminine constancy (no jeans and t-shirts) of all girls would be not only unrealistic but also very sexist. What is the difference between a tomboy and a trans girl? One identity, tomboy, is societally acceptable and the other, trans girl, is stigmatized.

The Negative Impact of Societal Stigma

From childhood forward, most of us have experienced both conscious and subconscious stigmatized representations of gender-diverse people. Many of these images, stories, and portrayals bring up feelings of discomfort, fear, or even repulsion toward those who transgress gender norms. Children, too, perceive these negative representations as well as the reactions of those around them and, as a result, internalize that negativity. This gives rise to shame, confusion, and physical and emotional distress. This conflict can manifest in many ways. A few of these include:

- Low self-esteem,

- Self-harm,
- Eating disorders,
- Sensory issues,
- Behavioral outbursts,
- Depression,
- Anxiety,
- Isolating, and
- Hypervigilance.

By and large, young children are not yet developmentally capable of under-standing or fully articulating the *internal and external* gender conflict they feel. A supportive parent may wonder why their child "still" struggles even after coming out. They fail to consider the negative, daily intensity that comes from living in a world of gender instability. Even older teens, who have a better understanding of society's gender rigidity, will not get by unscathed. While a trans teen, like younger children, will benefit from any gender support they receive, it will not be enough to counter the onslaught of negativity they receive from every angle. It is not a question of how we prevent a child or teen from internalizing this negativity. They will internalize it to a degree. Rather, how do we instill a greater sense of confidence, coping skills, and resiliency in these children while simultaneously advancing the understanding and accept-ance of society?

IF GENDER IDENTITY IS OVERLOOKED, MISUNDERSTOOD, OR MINIMIZED, THE IMPACT CAN BE DEVASTATING

Families, and even the health care providers they seek out, have been ill-prepared to accurately identify a child's underlying gender issue. Providers receive little to no training from their universities and mainstream parenting books don't make mention of it either. Parents and professionals can recognize a child's distress but will focus on managing the symptoms rather than realizing that gender incongruence is at the core. This is gradually changing but that change is not fast enough for the majority of today's gender-diverse children.

Parents attending gender support groups often relate that their trans child had received multiple behavioral diagnoses before the gender identity aspect was understood. If a provider does not understand the foundational elements of gender identity, cultural dissonance, and gender bias—and what occurs when they intersect—they may interpret a child's behavioral outburst as an attribute of some other condition. For example, children with a gender identity difference sometimes struggle with getting dressed and the clothing options available to them. So do some children with ADHD. The therapist, having greater familiarity with ADHD, diagnoses treatment for ADHD. The trans child, however, may be struggling with clothing choices because they recognize them as "boy clothes" or "girl clothes." One father shared how his four-year-old trans boy became so upset every time he had to put on underclothes. Nothing ever "felt" right. When the family finally recognized their child's gender and purchased "boys" clothes, the meltdowns all but vanished.

When the core issue of gender is overlooked or ignored, it allows the distress to continue unabated. The harmful outcomes of misdiagnoses or non-support are made evident in:

- Being at an increased risk for drug or alcohol abuse, suicidal ideation, and other factors;
- Poor performance in school;
- Being a victim of bullying and harassment;
- Being blamed for hardships, violence, and other struggles;
- Receiving punishment for their gender expression; and
- Being at greater risk of being targeted by sexual predators seeking vulnerable children.

IF SOCIETY WERE DIFFERENT, WOULD TRANS CHILDREN EXPERIENCE BODY DYSPHORIA?

The ignorance of a society experiencing its own steep learning curve regarding gender should not be the burden shouldered by young children or teens. This brings up a key point: Would trans children experience a disconnect in relation to their bodies if society were fully accepting of gender identity and gender expression differences? From a U.S. and Western European standpoint, it may feel impossible to imagine a society released from gendered expectations, roles, and rules. However, as we examine nonbinary gender identities around the world, as well as throughout history, we do find examples of a more expansive mindset in which identities and roles have extended beyond those that are strictly male or strictly female.

Global history shows that we have had, and indeed are capable of returning to, a world of greater gender diversity. A trans child that experienced a greater sense of belonging and felt valued in today's world might indeed experience a decrease in emotional, psychological, and physical distress. If society chose to elevate an integrated, holistic-based approach to supporting the identity of these children, rather than our present-day genitalia-focused lens, we might alleviate some of the intense body dysphoria experienced by so many. We could provide gender-diverse children a greater sense of body congruency if—first and foremost—*we agreed that a child's gender identity has validity*.

We must be willing to find a way to confidently support these children or we will continue to place them at significant risk—emotionally, psychologically, and physically. Most of them will be too young to fully recognize the impact of societal pressures and rejection, but they are not too young to suffer from it. If we are unwilling, or as yet unable, to take ownership of the distress it heaps on trans children, we will continue to lose many of them to suicide, violence, homelessness, Adverse Childhood Experiences (ACEs), related illness, and more.

Children are not born with an understanding of expected gender roles; these are learned over time and from the earliest of ages. Gender roles and norms are deeply subjective and vary by generation, culture, ethnicity, and geography. If we can declare any certainty, with respect to these norms, it is that they will surely change with time.

We still have much to learn about gender identity and body incongruencies in trans children. We've been resistant to making necessary, gender-expansive changes concerning child-rearing practices, inclusivity steps in schools and activities, and better educating our medical and mental health providers. We feel stymied to address gender binary-based protocols within systems. We resist making change because the change *feels* monumental. Many will ask, "Why should we do all this work for just one kid?" The lack of safe and affirming environments perpetuates harm and adversely affects everyone. Addressing society's gender rigidity benefits everyone, as few people fully adhere to the extremes of the binary continuum.

GENDER EXPECTATIONS

The Stage Is Set Early: Gender Expectations from Birth and Onward

Throughout the United States and other parts of the world, the immediate gender determination of a child is culturally ingrained and essential. Pre- and post-birth gender-specific rituals are the norm in many cultures, including the "gender reveal" party to announce the results of a pre-birth ultrasound or gendered gifts bestowed at a baby shower.

Establishing this early gender acknowledgment is considered to be a crucial aspect of defining a child's place within family and society. Within those first moments, expectations are formed. "You are going to have another brother to protect you! "He's going to be a jock like his dad." "I can't wait to paint her room pink." "She's going to break some hearts with those eyes."

Pervasive gendered expectations coupled with minimal exposure to, or discussion of, gender expansiveness in children place caregivers at a great disadvantage. Parents can expect difficulties at every turn if their child expresses noticeable gender identity or expression differences, and they will often discourage these differences in an effort to decrease these difficulties. They are not trying to be insensitive or uncaring. Parents do not have much in the way of a roadmap for raising a trans child in today's world.

Few families are deliberately setting out to harm their children. Even those who may verbally or physically punish their child for their gender differences are often doing so out of the belief that it is in their child's best interests, whom they misinterpret to be "willful" or "confused." These parents are unaware of today's recommended supportive practices embraced by leading medical and mental health associations. What they are acutely aware of, however, is the harsh stigma associated with *being* transgender. While it is understandable that this stigmatization might cause parents to withhold gender-affirming support, they do not realize the harmful impact that can occur.[1] Gender-diverse children will struggle; the only question is how much.

Most parents will, or at least be tempted to, discourage gender-atypical behavior. They will "correct" a child. *You are not a girl, you are a boy* and encourage or insist that their child engages in gender congruent play, clothing, activities, and friendships. *You don't want to wear that, do you?!* or *I signed you up for T-ball, won't that be fun?* These efforts originate from a parent's hope they will reduce the likelihood of a child persisting in their differences. A parent also fears the negative attention their child could receive. While the intent may be well-meaning—*I've got to work this out of him so he doesn't get bullied*—the impact of withholding support is quite different.

Misunderstood Gender Differences Disrupt the Family

A child's gender differences often take center stage within a family, causing potential conflict among family members. This can be exacerbated by parents whose opinions diverge as to how to address gender differences. Siblings can feel sidelined as the issue consumes the family, and grandparents and other family members may feel significant distress for their own reasons. Separated or divorced parents can be so bitterly at odds that lengthy, expensive court battles ensue. Because the trans child is the focal point of these conflicts, the parents may, directly or indirectly, blame the child. Regardless of whether direct blame is verbalized or not, trans children sense it and can internalize the blame—and resulting shame—for any family turmoil.

What are some of the results of familial conflict? A few include:

- Depression, anxiety, and self-harming behaviors;
- Isolating at home;
- Poor scholastic performance;
- Behavioral outbursts;
- Loss of interest in favorite activities; and
- Difficulty making friends.

As time goes on, so does the list of long-term risk factors. Trans youth experiencing conflict at home are at higher risk for homelessness, drug and alcohol abuse, and social media/gaming addictions. Eating disorders, suicidal ideation, HIV, and STIs are risk factors that skyrocket when gender support is withheld or delayed. These vulnerable youth can experience a much higher incidence of sexual assault and/or physical violence. The risk factors for trans youth of color are heartbreakingly higher still:

Valentina, a Filipina mother, was a regular at a Trans Families support group. Her trans daughter Toni, a high school sophomore, had finally come out to her after years of increasing behavioral outbursts and conflicts at school. Valentina was exhausted and her spouse—Toni's stepfather—was angry.

"Her mother supports her gender but Toni is so disrespectful. She causes my wife so much heartache!" Even after two years, Toni's behavior didn't improve. She was expelled from school for drugs and engaging in sex work on the school campus. Valentina confided, "By the time she said something to us, and by the time we got on board, it was just too late. We'd already lost her." Toni died of an accidental drug overdose shortly thereafter.

Teenagers Need Support—Don't Use It as a Bargaining Chip

It is important to note that parents of recently disclosed trans teens can have an even deeper struggle in ways that parents of younger children often do not, or at least not to the same degree. Teen years are known to be a time of identity exploration and increasing independence from parents. It is a time of emotional, hormonal turbulence for any youth. Parent/teen relationships are known to be rocky during this developmental state. It is an especially confusing time for the parent of a gender-diverse teen. They wonder if behavioral problems are the result of a gender identity issue or simply being a teen? Both? How can they know?

A parent may use gender-affirming care or transition-related events as a bargaining chip with their child. They may invalidate or hinder their teen's gender path because of normal developmental changes associated with adolescence.

- "You need to clean your room and get your grades up. Then we'll talk about hormones."
- "We need to get your anxiety under control first, then we'll consider your transition."
- "You've never said anything about your gender until you started hanging out with those freaks at school. I don't want you to spend so much time with them. What is the matter with your friends at church?!"
- "I will never use they/them pronouns for you. Next, you'll be wanting me to call you "It." When you can lose the attitude, we'll talk but just know that those pronouns are grammatically incorrect and that just won't fly."

A parent may find themselves unknowingly playing a dangerous game with their teen's mental health by assuming the youth's behavioral issues are *only* the result of being an obstinate teen. What are some of the harmful behaviors that trans children and teens experience? How can families turn this around to better provide support? Consider the following guidance from the Family Acceptance Project (FAP).

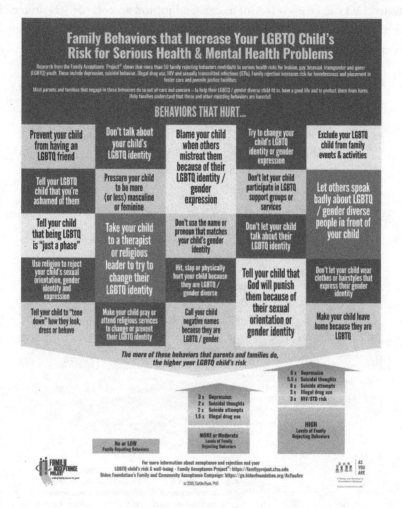

The English version of the Family Acceptance Project's Family Rejection Poster shows how family rejecting behaviors contribute to serious health risks. See Appendix C for guidance on poster use (https://familyproject.sfsu.edu/posters).[2]

Because society has yet to broadly embrace the gender-affirming practices that are so crucial to the well-being of trans youth, the majority of youth are at the mercy of their parents' willingness or ability to understand. Unfortunately, these adults, having little to no exposure to the subject, are hindered by their own ignorance, and, unfortunately, the health professionals to whom parents might otherwise turn are often in the same boat. One of the most significant challenges a trans child can face—a lack of understanding and acceptance—is situated in the place that is most important to a child—their home. What does the Family Acceptance Project have to say to parents about ways to be supportive?

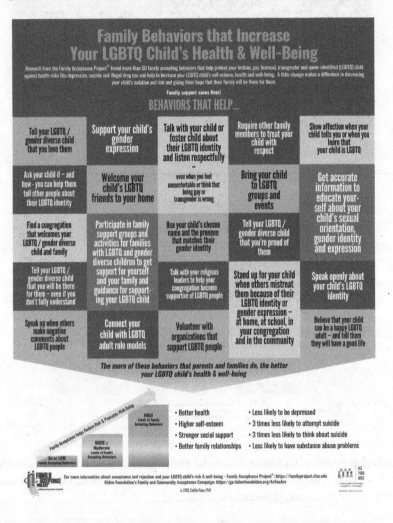

The English version of the Family Acceptance Project's Family Acceptance Poster for Conservative Settings shows how family supportive and accepting behaviors help protect against health risks and promote well-being. See Appendix C for guidance on poster use (https://familyproject.sfsu.edu/posters).[3]

The Family Acceptance Project and other recent research show us the positive impact on children when parents support their child's gender identification. This newer understanding will advance gender-affirming parenting practices. Child-rearing practices change over time as we better understand the impact on children. It was once felt that children with physical and neurobiological differences were better off segregated away from the mainstream. Today we recognize the positive effect of integration and the enrichment it provides to the lives of all children regardless of physical or cognitive ability. We have the validation we need. We can find our way forward toward gender inclusion as well.

These families need resources that will help them support their child, they need a better understanding of their child's experience, and they must begin a process of understanding gender in a more expansive way. Yes, it feels like a complex process to delineate the concepts of gender identity, sex assigned at birth, and sexuality. Most of us were never presented with this delineation. As with any new undertaking, what we once experienced as complex and unfamiliar will soon be adopted with greater ease and simplicity.

PUSHBACK AT EVERY TURN

Challenges experienced by trans youth extend beyond the personal and familial. Whether or not there is familial support at home, society's resistance to change can take an unrelenting toll on a child's well-being. It may be hard for some to imagine the impact on a child's psyche. It is relentless.

Their expression of self is often perceived by others as willful, even deviant, bringing about daily repercussions. Trans children are often blamed for bullying that comes their way; excluded from church activities with their peers; denied access to facilities; and have their core gender identification repeatedly "corrected" by teachers, friends, or strangers alike. In one case, a school janitor strongly felt the need to inform a group of students that they should stop referring to their friend by her more recently adopted name. "That's not really a girl, he's a boy and his name is Jamal."

Name calling is a family rejecting behavior that undermines self-worth and contributes to health risks. Find information and resources at FAP's family website at https://lgbtqfamil yacceptance.org/.

This ongoing hyper-attention, identity invalidation, invisibility, exclusion, ridicule, and bullying place gender-diverse children at extreme risk for victimization and harm. Their very core sense of self is in jeopardy.

As trans youth become more visible, our society struggles to adapt. We resist, we push back. A visible, inclusive environment—and how to create it—still feels like uncharted territory. Some people wonder whether we should make any efforts toward change assuming, instead, that we are in the midst of a youthful, anti-establishment *trend*. For others, it feels more ominous than that—going as far as describing an amoral *agenda* with the end goal being the erasure of wholesome family values. It is neither.

While it appears that the number of trans youth is growing, the only thing we can say for sure is that the visibility of these children is growing.

The fact is that we are finally giving attention and validity to an aspect of human identity—gender identity—that we previously did not consider. It is a game-changer.

Gender-diverse children, teens, and adults have always existed but, today, we see them. We hear their stories. We are giving attention to gender identity in ways that we couldn't, or wouldn't, before. We now have descriptive language and terminology, positive representations in the media, and advanced research progress in the field of neurobiology, including a greater exploration of the role of genetic and chromosomal differences. Perhaps more importantly, we more clearly understand that ignoring, invalidating, repressing, and excluding gender-diverse people has had devastating consequences.

A better understanding of gender identity now exists, yet our culture is slow to change. The increased presence of trans youth in society means that today's children find it deeply challenging to find a sense of belonging and acceptance within their communities, families, and schools. Their very presence is juxtaposed against a societal framework that still clings to birth sex as an immutable designation that dictates an individual's life path from birth onward. We see them, yes, but still have a lot of work to do before they will feel fully embraced and included.

Gender Binary or the Highway—Society Clings to the Perceived Immutability of Gender

Trans children and their families are often stymied as they seek care from doctors who have only learned the stages of child development through a binary gender lens. Children receive instruction from teachers who ascribe to the notion that "boys will be boys, girls will be girls." Teasing and bullying of a child's gender differences happen in schools, on playgrounds, and during extra-curricular activities. The fast-food drive-thru employee asks, "Would you like a boy toy or a girl toy?" A toy store clerk will redirect a child, "The girl's toys are on the other side of the store." Nonbinary children likely have no other option than to engage in religious activities and other rites of passage—such as a bat/bar mitzvah, altar boy/girl—that insist on gender conformity in dress or comportment. One dentist snidely told a young trans girl that she had "a really big mouth for a *girl*."

Transgender children were, and still are, expected to adapt, repress, and deny their identities to best fit within their respective communities. While we are moving toward greater inclusion, these young children are caught in the middle, situated between the rigid gender norms of the past and those of a more expansive future. As we negotiate this emergence of trans youth, it is crucial to consider the impact of this moment in time on their lives.

You're Trans?? Prove It!

The prevailing tendency of the past was to view the gender experience of trans children as an aberration—a strange oddity that, if it does exist, should be changed by any means necessary. This is no longer the case. Despite our present-day advances in understanding, it is intimidating to move forward. What if we make a mistake? What if this child is not really transgender—not really an "aberration"—the word that lingers still for so many?

This apprehension creates an expectation wherein a child, regardless of age, is tasked with the responsibility of clearly and consistently articulating a cross-gender identity to *prove to everyone else* that their experience is worthy of validation. For example, health care providers, who, in theory, are willing to support a trans child, create barriers by having expectations that are too high. The expectancy is this—that all trans youth will have a pronounced, consistent gender experience *and* be able to unambiguously articulate it.

Not only is a gender-diverse child expected to unequivocally "convince" their family and care providers of the validity of their gender identity. Yet it seems that everyone else, whether directly connected to the child or not, expects this "proof" as well. This plays out in a number of ways:

- An admissions staff member may refuse to change a child's name until presented with a legal name change document. They may demand an amended birth certificate before agreeing to any gender update on the student's records. Some will refuse even if documentation is presented.
- A teacher might dismiss a student's name or pronoun request stating how "hard it is to remember," that using an alternative pronoun is "grammatically incorrect," or flatly refuse because they "don't believe in it."
- A principal may feel it is their duty to break student confidentiality expectations regarding a child's gender history, even if it is against the child or the family's wishes, because, to not do so would be "deceptive."

- While deeply inappropriate, it is not uncommon for a school nurse to directly ask a trans child about their genitalia, or even require them to expose themselves.
- Trans children are routinely expected to use a nurse's bathroom or other facilities—that draws unwanted attention to the child—because the underlying notion is that the child's gender identity is invalid.

No matter where the child turns, the relentless message they receive is that they are confused, that their identity is "wrong." How can a child—lacking any power or authority—convince anyone else to the contrary? How do they prove to the most skeptical of audiences that they are, indeed, who they say they are? Even the most insistent child may not have the available language to adequately describe their experience to a world deeply resistant to hearing them.

It's Your Own Fault: Blaming the Victim of Bullying and Conflict

Gender-diverse children experience restrictions from accessing clothing, activities, programs, toys, and other areas of engagement because parents, teachers, and others assume these things are the "source" or "cause" of the gender identity difference. One school counselor instructed the parents of a trans youth to not let her wear dresses at home, play with dolls, or use pink and purple crayons for any art projects. The counselor said, "It's only encouraging the fantasy."

When bullying or harassment occurs toward gender-diverse youth, the victimized child is blamed for causing the behavior. A nine-year-old boy experienced daily bullying due to his gender-diverse expression. When the child's parent reported it to the school, the school counselor suggested the student was provoking the bullying by carrying his My Little Pony backpack to school. The counselor suggested that the parents hide it from the child. When the bullying continued, the school's principal banned the child from bringing the backpack to school.[4]

Children are sometimes shamed and/or taunted by teachers and other adults for their gender expression or identity. One teacher refused to use a student's name and pronoun instead, announcing to the class, "Well, I don't know what to call her or him! Maybe he'd prefer 'it' instead!" Many trans children have had other kids insist that they "prove" they are trans by showing their genitalia. They say, "I don't believe you. You have to show me!"

Exclusion and Spotlighting: Trans Children are a Lightning Rod for Society's Dissonance

In a school environment, where we naturally assume that all children have the same right to safety and education, some school staff instigates the problems unnecessarily:

> A transgender girl in Virginia was denied access to both the girl's and boy's locker rooms during an "active shooter" drill at school. She was forced to sit in the hallway for the duration of the safety drill as the teachers debated as to whether *the other students' safety would be compromised by her presence.*[5]
>
> At another school, a trans male student was not allowed to room with his male friends during an overnight field trip. He was instead forced to stay in a cabin by himself. He said it was very upsetting and felt he was being "quarantined."[6]

Sometimes a child is singled out in a highly visible way. One school insisted that a trans girl (whose gender history was not known to her classmates) get in line with the boys to be tested for color blindness. This caused many unanswered questions from her classmates and jeopardized her right to privacy.

Any trans child, unfortunately, can end up being the lightning rod for our society's state of dissonance concerning gender differences. Regardless of a school's degree of supportiveness, the spotlight often glares directly upon a single child. Consider this principal's well-meaning but misguided approach:

> One school took what they felt was a very supportive approach toward the family of a nine-year-old trans girl. At the time, the principal did not feel that her staff needed training. She did, however, ask the parents of this child to speak to all the parents within the school community at the beginning of every school year. For three years, the parents discussed their child's experience and addressed questions from the other parents. Their trans daughter, a quiet, reflective child, struggled with the added attention each year as it inspired many questions from her peers and adults alike. She told her parents, "I just want to be a girl like all the other girls." Another child's parent stopped the trans girl after school one day and inappropriately asked, "When are you going to have 'the surgery'?"

This adult's voyeuristic inquiry violates a child's right to bodily privacy and cannot be ignored, regardless of the adult's intent behind that inquiry. So, too, the principal should not require the parents of that child to educate the school community every year and deny the child's right to privacy.

Ultimately, the teachers at this school insisted to the principal that they would benefit from staff training beyond hearing one family's personal story. As we moved through the training, one teacher explained, "We wouldn't expect a family from another culture or religion to come in every year and educate everyone. Why are we doing it in this situation? And, what happens when this trans student graduates? Will we be ready for the next one?"

The Debate and Devastating Impact of Religious or Cultural Ideologies

These children (and their families) are often viewed through a tainted lens where a child's most basic sense of self is viewed as immoral, broken, or nonexistent. This normal aspect of human physiological diversity is put forth as a debate within the community. So often, the resulting collective agreement of the community points to the presence of a psychological deviancy. The community concludes there is some level of choice to this identity or perhaps the result of some undue influence. What many feel constitutes the "truth" should not be up for a majority vote, yet that is often the case for a society still deeply uninformed on the subject.

For many communities—be they geographically or ethnically diverse, or of a particular faith or political leaning—the presence of a trans child leaves many within those communities feeling conflicted and distressed. The presence of a trans child is not something that occurs within only certain communities. Gender-diverse children are everywhere. Yet, the willingness and ability to support these children are inconsistent. The receptivity of any community can have a deep impact. It is no exaggeration to say that it could be a matter of life and death for a gender-diverse child:

One mother from a mixed-race family, raising a trans teenage girl, spoke of the anti-trans legislation introduced into her state's legislature. These bills, unofficially named "bathroom bills," caused many within her rural community to fear for the safety of girls and women in gender-segregated places of public accommodation. It was all too easy to equate transgender people with sexual predators and this caused many in her predominantly white community to become politically engaged. This mother said, "As a person of color, I work very hard to keep my children safe in my conservative community. If I didn't have a transgender daughter myself, I most certainly would have been organizing and protesting with the people who were fighting *against* protections for trans people."

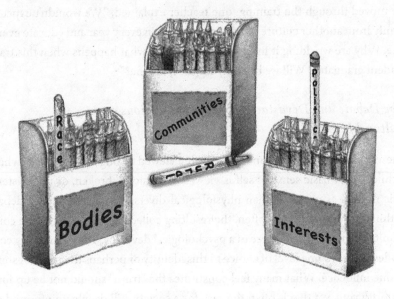

Or, in the case of certain religious communities, a trans identity can mean "eternal" punishment:

A fundamentalist Christian family of a trans child felt tormented by the conflict that presented itself when their seventeen-year-old trans son told them of his gender identity. Their church community, and the way they understood the tenets of their faith, made clear to them that their child's identity was an issue of deviation from the upright moral path expected by God. Even when they came to a parent support group, the expression of love and support by the other parents for their children caused one of the Christian parents to speculate whether the encouragement to be supportive was just ". . . Satan sitting on my shoulder whispering in my ear."

It's not just faith beliefs that inspire fear:

One Latino father struggled long and hard to understand his trans daughter's gender identity. He feared the reactions of his Latino community. He grieved the hopes and dreams of the child he thought was his son. Because his community takes pride in strong masculine roles, he feared that his own identity as a father and a man would be questioned. While navigating his own grief and conflict, he also felt that the entire family was at risk of ostracism and ridicule.

No Such Thing—Denial

One family related their recent experience of going to see their child's pediatrician. They wished to address pubertal delay intervention in preparation for their ten-year-old child's upcoming puberty. Despite the usage of GnRH analogs (puberty blockers) in children for decades, the doctor insisted that this medical intervention *did not exist*. "There is no such thing," he said.

While most medical providers would not make such an obviously refutable statement, this physician isn't the only person to offer up a denial. The denial of diverse gender identification in humans is pervasive across the nation despite scientific evidence to the contrary.[7] Many people, armed only with strong feelings, provide no justification for their opinions.[8]

One family shared this experience:

We have two sons, one in high school and, the other, our trans son, is already graduated. Our high schooler came home from school angry and frustrated. A guest speaker came to one of his classes to discuss "life skills" and asked the students to identify the "things they could change" about themselves and the things they couldn't. As an example, the speaker named gender as unchangeable. When our son said that that simply wasn't true, that he had a trans brother, an argument ensued. The speaker steadfastly refused to acknowledge the experiences of trans people and the reality of our family. Instead, the speaker opted to shut down our son—end of discussion!

These stories highlight the challenges and obstacles trans children and their families face. As we can see, if we want to optimize the positive health and life opportunities for these children, we first need to address the origins and impact of our own hesitancy. Rather than insisting on the impossible task of completing a definitive checklist that ensures a "correct gender diagnosis," providers, teachers, parents—anyone at all—would be better-served understanding that they are instead facilitating a child's gender exploration and discovery. The journey of gender exploration in schools and in our society is uncharted, but one worthy of a respectful, thoughtful, and informed approach.

SCHOOL ENVIRONMENTS PERPETUATE THE DISTRESS

A gender-diverse child's school environment is an ecosystem where the challenges these children experience—the struggle with the sense of self and/or physical body, disruptions or strife within their home life, and the isolation they experience because of cultural/societal rejection—converge in a way that is hard for others, especially the child themselves, to fully comprehend. If we gain a greater understanding of the impact these converging experiences have on a child's life, we have a clearer pathway to not only finding solutions but determining who should take responsibility for those solutions.

Is Mistreatment Inevitable?

The unfortunate inclination of family, educators, and so many others is to assign responsibility, or even blame, to the gender-diverse child for any hardships they experience. A gender-supportive family may "allow" a child to wear certain clothing, go by a different name or pronoun, or adopt a new hairstyle, yet it does not mean that a parent fully comprehends the burden their child is shouldering in their day-to-day life.

People can assume that the difficulties the child encounters are the "fault" of the child or, at least, that all the hardships are inevitable. After all, if the child were not trans, they wouldn't experience these difficulties. A teacher may not come right out and say, "This is your fault" but they could say, "Well, you have to expect this because of how you look, your pronoun expectations, the way you dress, etc." Parents can feel intimidated and at a loss for the hardships their child experiences:

> During a parent support group, one mother shared her fourth-grade child's struggle at school. The child told her mom about the constant belittlement and dismissiveness she experienced coming from her teacher. When the

mother attempted to talk to the teacher about it, the teacher immediately denied any mistreatment. However, the mother couldn't help but feel that the teacher's actions were a result of gender bias. She had noticed that the teacher made a few offhand comments at the beginning of the school year. As her child's performance at school steadily declined, the mother was hesitant to take this situation to the school principal. She "didn't want to make waves." I knew this family had a sibling in the same school. I asked her, "If your other child, the one who is not transgender, was experiencing this kind of treatment from his teacher, what would you do?" Immediately, the mother said, "I wouldn't put up with it for a second!" She added, "I wouldn't expect my other child to put up with that kind of treatment, why should I expect my daughter? I hadn't thought about it before but part of me feels guilty for asking for more since the school was willing to use her correct name and pronoun."

This parent had not realized that her hesitancy (feeling guilty for asking "too much" of the school) was directly tied to her child's gender difference. While she wasn't directly assigning fault to her daughter, this mother had been inadvertently expecting her child to tolerate the unsupportive classroom environment solely because of the fact that her child was transgender.

Another parent found himself in a similar situation where he knew his child was being bullied every day. He understood his child was struggling but felt unable to do anything about it except request a referral for a counselor. The therapist, he hoped, could help his child better *cope* with the bullying. The father's assumption was that there was no responsibility on the school's part to *stop the bullying* in the first place. He just hadn't thought of it.

Very few people say that a trans child is *deserving* to be mistreated, but they do feel as if the mistreatment is inevitable. That said, there are some who will go as far as advocating for mistreatment. One such example occurred at a school district meeting that had been requested by some local clergy:

There were about a dozen pastors who had asked to meet with the school district superintendent to discuss recent policy adoption addressing gender inclusion. One man dominated the conversation and was not interested in hearing assurances from the superintendent that poor behavior from any student would be immediately addressed. He went on to talk about the rights of the students who were not transgender. He shared this example, "Suppose there is a student who feels compelled to let a trans student know that they are a sinner and going to burn in hell?" The superintendent said that the student would be asked to not impose his religious beliefs on another student and that all students were expected to treat each other with respect. The minister responded angrily, "He should be allowed to say that any time he wants! What I hear you saying is that we are just S.O.L.,* right?"

Teacher and Struggling Parent at Odds

A frequent question raised by teachers and counselors concerns what they might do in situations where the gender-diverse child does not have parental support for their gender identity. A parent may be adamantly resistant to any name/pronoun change. Workplace expectations and/or legal obligations (requested pronouns, for example) of school staff may place that educator in direct conflict with a parent. In situations like these, the educator may be tempted to find the path of least resistance—acquiescing to the parent's demands—as the least intimidating response even as they recognize that the student is likely the one most negatively impacted. Just as parents might make choices to avoid conflict with a school, so can teachers set aside the needs of a student to avoid making waves with a parent. The best interests of the child are not fully considered or viewed as dispensable because we have not yet learned how to best advocate for gender-diverse children.

Peer to Peer

The importance of positive peer relationships is important to any school-age child. It is understandable that these relationships are among the top concerns expressed by gender-diverse children when considering and/or pursuing gender transition. If these relationships suffer, so too will the trans child's likelihood of interpersonal and academic success in school.

A school that takes a passive approach to a student's social transition, meaning one that occurs without any pre-established systemic foundation for gender inclusion, is one that directly (even if intended or not) makes the trans child responsible for any hardships that occur because of their gender.

---

* Shit Out of Luck.

What are some examples of a passive or reticent approach by schools?

- Making the child solely responsible for ensuring that peers use the correct name and pronoun.
- Avoiding or shutting down the inquiries of students who are unfamiliar with gender-diverse identities.

Silence and secrecy are family rejecting behaviors that contribute to health risks. Find information and resources at FAP's family website at https://lgbtqfamilyacceptance.org/.

- Shrugging off instances of deliberate outing, misgendering, bullying, and other misbehaviors by other students and, in doing so, sending an implicit message to students that bullying behaviors can continue unchecked.[9]
- In more extreme situations, implying that the trans student is dangerous, unsafe, or unstable and therefore unworthy of inclusion in school or protection from harm.

If a school does not take an active approach to educating teachers, parents, *and students*, it is leaving positive outcomes up to chance and solely dependent on the student, no matter how young. Of course, safe learning environments can be challenging to achieve, and addressing student bullying becomes an ongoing endeavor. Discriminatory harassment does not have to include *intent* to harm, be directed at a specific target, or involve repeated incidents. Nor is it effective to simply tell a bully to stop. If it were, we would have solved student bullying some time ago.

WHAT ARE SOME WAYS TO ENSURE POSITIVE STUDENT ENGAGEMENT?

- Do not presume that the trans child, or their parents, should be the ones to shoulder the burden of educating everyone else.
- Do not blame the child for hardships they experience because of their gender difference.
- Do provide students with opportunities to learn about diverse identities and experiences throughout their K–12 education. Gender diversity accurately fits into broader discussions of human diversity including differences related to bodies, experiences, family composition, and culture.
- Do have student conversations in advance of any particular student's gender transition to avoid spotlighting a singular experience.
- Do provide factual, positive representations of gender-diverse people throughout history, geography, and culture.
- Do employ tools from anti-bullying resources and learn how to apply them to the experiences of gender-diverse children. In my experience, I've found that educators already have most of the tools they need.
- Do not tolerate bullying for any reason. Expect respect.

While schools are responsible for safe learning environments, the whole school community needs to be engaged. Does this mean that a trans child, or their family, has no responsibility? No, but it is not their responsibility to single-handedly change school systems. For example, a child may need to understand that not everyone can remember to switch a name or pronoun overnight. The child's ability to accept the disappointment when a mistake is made is greatly improved if

(1) the child knows that those mistakes are temporary, (2) teachers will immediately address deliberate instances of misgendering, and (3) the expectations within a classroom are to remedy any misgendering as quickly and consistently as possible.

There are ways to guide student reactions to achieve more positive outcomes. Consider this school's approach:

> A school I worked with a number of years ago had a sixth-grade student who would soon be disclosing his gender to his classmates. The educators agreed to take a whole-community approach to gender education by starting with teachers and staff, then following up with a parent learning event as well. To address the impending disclosure to the student's peers, we took a two-part approach. The second part was to set aside time for classroom discussion for all the students in his grade. Prior to this, however, we decided to pull together six of this student's close friends. The trans student and I worked together to share his story with these friends, offer them a chance to ask questions, and then let them know about the larger discussion that would occur the next day. He was able to share that he wanted to tell them first because they were important to him. I asked them if they would be willing to show their support for their friend with the remaining students the next day. The school had let the parents of the six children know about the advance request so that if there were any hesitations, additional questions, or other concerns on the part of the students, they would know that they would not be pressured in any way to do something in which they did not feel comfortable. His close friends responded in such a positive way! He was visibly relieved, and his friends felt honored to be asked to support him the next day. The next day's conversation with the entire sixth grade was amazing. The trans student shared his story with much greater confidence while his friends readily shared their support for him in front of the others. The show of empathy and support from all of the students was unanticipated, but nevertheless welcomed, by the school teachers, and resulted in much greater confidence for them as well.

This school took a proactive approach with its students rather than waiting to see how it all played out. With a small amount of preparation time, the outcome for all was exceptional.

Large or Small, Experiences Add Up

It is not often clear to family members or educators, that even the smallest of gender invalidations can have a cumulative, detrimental effect on a child. A comment about hair length, clothing choices, a pronoun or name slip, or a joke at the expense of a gender-diverse person, clearly communicates gender bias to a child and reinforces feelings of marginalization even if the comment or joke is not intended to be harmful. While many school counselors are familiar with the consequences of *microaggressions* in relation to other marginalized populations, they may not recognize the unique ones that impact gender-diverse children. If that is the case, then each instance experienced by a child is viewed as a singular event. The expectation of the child is "let it go," "toughen up," "get a thicker skin," or accept that "no harm was meant by it."

Cumulative stress experienced by marginalized populations, (also known as minority stress) is understood to have a negative impact on health, both in the short term and, if unabated, in the long term as well. For example, it may seem like a win–win for a principal to offer the use of a staff bathroom to a trans child—no need for uncomfortable conversations with other parents, and the child is not forced to use a bathroom that does not align with their gender identity. Except that, for many trans children, the staff bathroom can feel just as uncomfortable and bring unwanted attention. Children may ask, "Why are you using the nurse's bathroom? What is wrong with you?" The only choice that feels available to many of these students is to avoid using the bathroom all day. These children will minimize their food and water intake and experience deep discomfort throughout every day. Urinary tract and kidney infections are common occurrences, as is dehydration.

It takes little imagination to recognize how profoundly health issues like these would impact a child's ability to learn. If not addressed and resolved, a child, in addition to medical health issues, can experience long-lasting mental health issues, including an increased risk for suicide, self-destructive behaviors, and other stress-related illnesses related to external and internal transphobia.

To better address the needs of gender-diverse children, recent research is incorporating gender identity differences into the present-day study of Adverse Childhood Experiences (ACEs), minority stress, and microaggressions.[10] When educators have a foundational understanding of the impacts of being a marginalized minority, they are better able to apply the concepts and use existing tools to also support trans and nonbinary children. This increased understanding is crucial as it supplies much-needed *context and motivation* to implement that support. If a principal, teacher, or parent understands that the lifelong well-being of the child is potentially at stake, then they are better able to make informed decisions.[11]

FACTORS THAT SERVE TO MAKE SCHOOL ENVIRONMENTS HOSTILE FOR TRANS CHILDREN

- Shaming and blaming a transgender child for hardships experienced

- Punishing or isolating transgender children because of their gender identification or gender expression
- Reduced ability to engage or exclusion from school activities such as sports, overnight trips, etc.
- Inaction or resistance from school staff to address bullying
- Inaction or resistance on the part of administrators to firmly set expectations of faculty/staff regarding consistent usage of pronouns, names, respectful student engagement, etc.

POTENTIAL STUDENT OUTCOMES

- At greater risk for unsafe behaviors because of peer pressure or peer rejection
- Additional challenge for siblings
- Unsupportive parents leading to a real hesitancy from educators
- Poor performance in school
- Uninformed medical and mental health providers and the lack of educational opportunities for them
- Lack of adequate resources, support systems, and research data
- Teasing, bullying, or harassment
- Increased risk of dropping out of school or expulsion
- Increased possibility of being targeted by predators
- A feeling of powerlessness and/or a sense of obstacles being unsurmountable because of barriers presented by authority figures (e.g., name change because of registrar's lack of understanding)

We mistakenly view any challenges or hardships experienced by a trans or nonbinary child to be a direct result of their gender rather than society's reaction to it. I receive many calls from parents, for example, who are seeking a therapist for their child's anxiety or depression. When more of the story unfolds, it is apparent that their child's struggle is due to daily bullying from fellow students and inaction on the part of the school staff.[12] Even a loving, supportive parent can believe that the destructive school climate is somehow unavoidable. Parents assume that their only course of action is to enlist a therapist to help their child cope with the distress caused by the bullying rather than addressing the issue at its source—student bullying coupled with administrative inaction.

Today's gender-diverse children are living in a time when their very presence in schools is a source of turbulence. We've addressed related times of turbulence with other invisible, marginalized, and oppressed populations throughout our U.S. history. Each time, we discover and rediscover the value of inclusion and the continual striving for equity. These times of sociological and systemic change require ongoing attention and persistence. Each and every child who embodies these social justice movements pays a price, and, we hope, reaps some of the rewards.

Visibility and affirmation of gender-diverse children are still new, yes. Children needing love, acceptance, and nurturing are not. The latter understanding is not one of national debate. Despite our differences, we all can agree on the fundamental importance of looking after children within families, schools, and society. How might families best support their children? How can schools address the questions that arise? How does society embrace the value of all its children, even the ones we didn't know existed?

We know any child needs to feel safe, loved, and protected. We understand that gender-diverse youth can experience challenges finding congruence with their bodies—especially in a world where those with shared experiences are difficult to see. When we send children out the door to school, they need to feel safe and included there as well. It is vital for their healthy development—physically, emotionally, and mentally—and their place within society.

As adults, it is our responsibility to minimize the obstacles that children encounter. The first step is to acknowledge our need to better understand. That is the moment in which we currently reside. As with any new endeavor, we draw from any existing knowledge that might be helpful, we expand our view to incorporate things not previously considered, and we seek guidance from those who may better illuminate the pathways. Sometimes that is the children themselves.

NOTES

1. Jake Pyne, "Health and Wellbeing among Gender Independent Children: A Critical Review of the Literature," in *Supporting Transgender and Gender Creative Youth: Schools, Families, and Communities in Action*, Gender and Sexualities in Education, vol. 4, ed. Elizabeth J. Meyer (New York: Peter Lang, 2014), 26–40.
2. C. Ryan, *Family Behaviors that Increase Your LGBTQ Child's Risk for Serious Health & Mental Health Problems* [poster for multiple settings with guidance for use; available in 11 languages] (San Francisco, CA: Family Acceptance Project, Marian Wright Edelman Institute, San Francisco State University, 2019), https://familyproject.sfsu.edu/posters.

3. C. Ryan, *Family Behaviors that Increase Your LGBTQ Child's Health & Well-Being—Version for Conservative Settings* [poster for multiple settings with guidance for use; available in 11 languages] (San Francisco, CA: Family Acceptance Project, Marian Wright Edelman Institute, San Francisco State University, 2019), https://familyproject.sfsu.edu/poster.

4. Lori Grisham, "School Bans 9-Year-Old Boy's My Little Pony Backpack," *USA TODAY* (March 18, 2014), https://www.usatoday.com/story/news/nation-now/2014/03/18/my-little-pony-backpack-banned-school-north-carolina/6565425/.

5. "Virginia School Allegedly Barred Trans Student from Active-Shooter Drill," *NBC News* (October 9, 2018), https://www.nbcnews.com/feature/nbc-out/virginia-school-allegedly-barred-trans-student-active-shooter-drill-n918216.

6. "Student v. Arcadia Unified School District," *National Center for Lesbian Rights*, https://nclrights/our-work/cases/student-v-arcadia-unified-school-district/.

7. Simón(e) D. Sun, "Stop Using Phony Science to Justify Transphobia," *Scientific American Blog Network* (June 13, 2019), https://blogs.scientificamerican.com/voices/stop-using-phony-science-to-justify-transphobia/.

8. "OPINION: There Is No Such Thing as 'Transgender'," *Courier News* (July 27, 2018), https://www.mycentraljersey.com/story/opinion/readers/2018/07/27/opinion-thing-transgender/37152283/.

9. Stephanie Julia Kapusta, "Misgendering and Its Moral Contestability," *Hypatia* 31, no. 3 (2016): 502–519.

10. Brian A. Rood et al., "Expecting Rejection: Understanding the Minority Stress Experiences of Transgender and Gender-Nonconforming Individuals," *Transgender Health* 1, no. 1 (December 2016): 151–164, https://doi.org/10.1089/trgh.2016.0012.

11. Many of the factors listed below are reflected in the GLSEN school climate survey data: "The 2019 National School Climate Survey," *GLSEN*, https://www.glsen.org/research/2019-national-school-climate-survey.

12. For a discussion of the importance of recognition and for the compound impact of macro- and microaggressions against transgender youth, see sj Miller, *Teaching, Affirming, and Recognizing Trans* and Gender Creative Youth: A Queer Literacy Framework*, Queer Studies and Education (New York: Palgrave Macmillan, 2019), 5.

How to Talk to Children about Gender

If we teach today's students as we taught yesterday's, we rob them of tomorrow.

John Dewey

After leading hundreds of school educator trainings all over the United States, there are two consistent questions that arise. The first is how do we talk with our *students* about their transgender classmates? The second question is how do we then talk with our *parent community* about those discussions with children? We can't address the second question if we have no idea what to say to children in the first place. Educators often feel at a loss as to how they should engage children in age-appropriate conversations about another child's gender experience or, more broadly, the topic of gender diversity. Just getting the conversation going feels uncomfortable. Perhaps more intimidating, however, is not knowing what reactions may come. How will the children respond? What will they say to their parents? And, more importantly, how will the parents react? As one teacher put it:

> I really appreciate [having] the language to talk about the lives of trans students, the ways to focus on our internal gender (identity), and the many ways we express ourselves. I got it! The examples you've given of how students respond, yes, that sounds exactly like what my students would say. I feel great about this . . . as long as I can keep the kids in the classroom 24/7! But I have to send them home every day. And the parents . . . well, that's the challenge, isn't it?

How do we address the fears and concerns that come from parents who are largely unfamiliar with the subject of gender? How might an educator respond to an angry parent demanding to know how and why the teacher thinks this "mature, graphic content" is appropriate to discuss in grade school? Educators are often relieved to know that they are not alone in these worries and that, yes, there are concrete ways to respectfully address parental concerns.

Educators will discover greater confidence as they recognize that they already have tools that will help them, and as they gain mastery over the terminology and language of gender. There is more to these classroom discussions of gender diversity than just relaying the personal experience of a gender-diverse student. These discussions need to extend beyond name, pronoun, and presentation changes. Students will be better served if the scope is expanded to include elements of diversity, inclusion, empathy, respect, and celebration. This chapter focuses on engaging children in these important conversations. Discussions with kindergartners should be straightforward and simple. Conversations with older children can build on a beginning foundation in ways that are suited to their age and developmental maturity.

HOW DID WE FIRST FORM OUR UNDERSTANDING OF GENDER?

If we are to learn ways of engaging children in conversation about gender diversity, we should first ask ourselves why we struggle with it in the first place. In part, it is because we've forgotten how simple and straightforward gender was when we were children. How does a child's initial understanding of gender occur? The same way it did for any of us—through observation and experience. When recalling our earliest experiences of gender, we predominantly remember things that fall into the category of gender expression even though we were too young to understand the term itself.

We were dressed by our parents in a certain way, given certain toys to play with, and even spoken to in gender-related ways. *You're so pretty. You're so strong.* We learned that there were expectations of us because of our gender, too. *Sit with your legs crossed. Put that down, you'll hurt yourself. Quit crying. You can't wear that!*

These kinds of messages were only part of the story. We observed the gender expression of others—parents, siblings, friends, and even strangers—and incorporated these observations into our personal understanding. If we were drawn to that expression, we tried to emulate it. Then, others reacted. If a child wanted to try on high heels, for example, the reaction would vary widely depending on the gender of the child: *Aww, isn't that sweet, but be careful* (girl). *Take those off right now!* (boy). The same action with very different reactions. Sometimes we were punished for our interests and behaviors, sometimes we were praised. While the expectations may have varied based on our social or geographic environments, racial or ethnic communities, respective family values, and even the generation to which we belonged, we all have a set of experiences originating from these expectations. We may have conformed to these expectations, or we may have pushed against them.

Regardless of punishment or praise, it is not difficult to recall how we felt. If we were praised, our feelings could have included joy and pride. If we were punished, we felt shame, frustration, anger, and sadness. Many children, over many generations, have a shared lament—it's UNFAIR! Why did we feel this way? As children, we innately understood that clothes are clothes, toys are toys, and our interests are just that—our interests. We recognized that clothes, feelings, strength, and beauty are not gendered. How and why did we, growing into adults, acquiesce and enforce the very gender norms that frustrated us as youngsters?

ADDING LAYERS OVER TIME

As we journeyed into adolescence and toward adulthood, our experiences with gender became more complex. We learned about puberty, sex, and sexual reproduction. Of course, our bodies began to change with the onset of our own puberty. We learned that chromosomes and hormones direct our physiological development, and how that development then directs our paths into adulthood. We understood that our reproductive capacity was the key to humanity's continued survival. The complexity of maturing bodies, reproduction, and human interdependency was piled on to our understanding of gender, but that wasn't all. Our social relationships expanded in both scope and complexity. We got crushes, fell in and out of love, and began to explore our own bodies and physical relationships with others. We developed strong feelings and were then taught how to feel about those feelings.

We inherited social mores, expectations, and roles from prior generations even as we began to understand that geographical location, culture, and the environment were just a few of many, many influences that expanded our understanding of gender. Layer after layer was added in rapid succession.

WE WERE NOT PRESENTED WITH A COMPLETE, ACCURATE PICTURE

Despite the added layers as we matured, important facts were ignored. Perhaps it was inconvenient to teach students that human chromosomal variations extend beyond the most common XX and XY designations. Maybe it is uncomfortable to acknowledge that we've oversimplified human genital development. While a pairing of penis/testes or vulva/ovaries is most commonly recognized, other configurations and combinations exist as well. People with intersex differences are part of our everyday world. Society prohibited, and even outlawed loving relationships between people of the same gender and denied their validity despite their existence throughout history. This denial still occurs in many parts of the world. We allowed assumptions and denials like these to continue unchallenged despite factual evidence to the contrary because it seemed to suit the majority.

We impose a binary understanding of gender on children because it was imposed on us. We expected children to engage in the world according to an anatomically informed gender role because we felt, in part, that our societal "ecosystem" depends on it for survival. It doesn't. We left out crucial information. Ignoring inconvenient facts, however, does not mean that these misrepresentations of human biodiversity are actually true. If society continues to cling to an inaccurate understanding of gender, suppressing factual information available today, it must consciously—even desperately—deny the existence of the people who embody and experience these differences.

A FRESH START FOR CONVERSATIONS WITH TODAY'S CHILDREN

As we consider how to begin more gender-expansive conversations with children, we need to know how to step into new conversations while negotiating our own hesitancy to do so. We can start by realizing that it doesn't have to be as complicated as we imagine. There are a few immediate steps we can take with children regardless of age:

1. What is it that is familiar? Expand conversations regarding gender expression.

2. What is new? Incorporate the concept of gender identity.
3. What needs repairing? Provide an accurate, unbiased framing of trans lives.

The Familiar—Gender Expression

Discussing a person's gender-related interests, roles, appearance, and behaviors are all part of one's gender expression. Messages about gender expression are abundant and are part of a child's earliest experiences. Knowing how and where to start conversations about gender expression with children—and then hearing what they have to say—will help all of us find our way to a more expansive understanding that includes their gender-diverse peers.

The New Element—Discussing Gender Identity

It's helpful to acknowledge that conversations about gender identity are new for most people. With each passing year the visibility of trans and nonbinary people in society increases—of course, this includes our nation's schools. Parents and teachers are often surprised to discover that the children's understanding surpasses their own. Regardless of whether the information is new or not, a crucial first step for any teacher is to *initiate* a conversation. We can't address it if we don't talk about it!

The Reparative Work—Destigmatizing Trans Peoples' Lives

There are several reasons why people feel intimidated about having gender-expansive conversations with children. One, most have learned about the existence of trans and other gender-diverse people later in life, not as children. If something was overheard as children, concerning trans people, it was likely in hushed tones or in a disparaging, inaccurate context. Two, we had a limited framework for contextualizing gender expansiveness. It was understood that there is a range and variation associated with "gender expression" but there was no consideration or awareness of "gender identity." As a result, we've had limited ability to describe the experiences of people with diverse gender identities. Lastly, for many, especially those of older generations, the understanding of what being transgender meant was likely conflated with some sort of vague, fringe sexuality. Even the now lesser-used term, trans*sexual*, served to reinforce this.

Today we are presented with a more accurate understanding of gender, one that is not hidden and stigmatized, one that has been recognized within the scientific community, and is separated from sexuality. As this current understanding increases, educators and parents will better grasp that the optimal way to engage children is to meet them where they are *now*, not where they once *were*.

GETTING ROLLING: BEGIN WITH GENDER EXPRESSION

The mistake we make, when considering conversations with kids, is believing that we need to bring in our adult perspectives. We don't. We assumed that what we were taught about gender was a complete picture. It wasn't. Gender identity was not yet understood, chromosomal variations were ignored, and genitalia differences were stigmatized so that we could prop up a binary framing of gender.

Let's continue, as we've always done, to have conversations about gender with all children. We can tell them that, in the past, girls could not wear pants to school and, today, some people think boys aren't supposed to wear skirts. Let's ask their thoughts about this. As children deepen their learning of biology, health, and science, we can discuss the physiological diversity within humans rather than omit it. From preschool forward, children learn about relationships. We can discuss the important qualities of these relationships without delineating between boys and girls. We teach them about respect, inclusion, and the desire to belong. All children, regardless of gender, desire this. Then, we make space for the learning we gain *from children*. As adults, we can embrace this new information. In doing so, we can provide a great gift to children—an environment where learning is emphasized and acceptance is celebrated.

So, how do we get moving on this?

Here is an example of a discussion with 1st graders:

Class, I have a question for you. How do you know if someone is a girl or boy?

The children engaged right away, excitedly answering the questions. Each response led to another, often challenging whatever statement was just made. There is no need for a teacher to point to "right" answers, or to correct "wrong" ones. What is important is to simply begin the dialogue:

TEACHER: "How do you know if someone is a boy or a girl?"

FIRST GRADER: "Boys have short hair, girls have long hair."

TEACHER: "What do the rest of you think about that?"

ANOTHER FIRST GRADER: "No! My aunt has really short hair and she's a girl."

ANOTHER STUDENT: "Girls paint their fingernails, boys don't."

STUDENT IN RESPONSE: "No, that's not true. My cousin paints his fingernails and he's a boy."

It continues . . .

STUDENT 1: "Girls wear dresses, boys don't."

STUDENT 2: "My uncle wears a skirt called a kilt. He's a boy."

STUDENT 3: "Boys play football and soccer."

STUDENT 4: "Soccer is not a boy's sport! Four of us are on the soccer team and we're girls."

Sometimes the conversations can bring about some unexpected responses! A teacher may be uncertain what to do or say. The impulse to explain or correct may be strong but also unnecessary. Why not continue to solicit student responses and see where it goes? The engagement and reflection among the students are what matters. Consider the volley of thoughts from the children as the conversation continues:

STUDENT 5: "Boys like to blow up things, girls don't."

Longer pause. A hand shoots in the air.

STUDENT 6: "I like to blow up things and I'm a girl!"

THEN, ANOTHER CHILD SAYS: "Men have gray hair and women don't."

Now, at this point, should a teacher dive headlong into a conversation about society's disparate standards for beauty and aging, and how these are applied to men in certain ways and to women in others? Should the teacher point out that the expectations of older men to stay fit and wrinkle-free are much lower than the standards expected of women and how the entertainment industry exaggerates this even more?

A teacher *could* offer those thought-provoking points, but it may depend on available time and how much room there is for these tangential conversations. For this initial conversation, it could be better to stay with the discussion at hand. Instead of intervening with more layers to consider, a teacher can continue to invite further thoughts from the students. It is important to set the expectation of being observational, not judgmental:

TEACHER: "So, men have gray hair, and women don't? What does everyone think about that?"

The extra invitation prompted this comment from a thoughtful-looking child.

STUDENT: "No, women have gray hair too. It's just all right here!" and with that, motioned down the center part-line of his hair.

When children describe gender expression differences, their observations are insightful, humorous, and straightforward. When asked to discuss things that only boys can do or things that only girls can do, their comments typically center on toys, colors, sports, clothing, hair, and behaviors. Is pink really a color only for girls? Is it only girls who play with dolls? Are "action figures" also dolls? Is it okay if boys like to cook? Can girls play soccer, wrestle, or play football? Who gets to wear skirts and dresses? By engaging children in these discussions, teachers have a wonderful opportunity to encourage observation, discernment, and reflection.

A Picture Is Worth a Thousand Words

One elementary school teacher decided to share some images of people from various print and online sources, in the hopes of spurring the discussion. These were of people who did not adhere to a gender expression considered typical—a female Olympic athlete who competes in the hammer throw, a male rap singer who wears a skirt, a female actor wearing a top hat and tails, a male ballet dancer, a female firefighter, and images of alternative gender roles around the world. She spread these pictures across a big table and asked the children to take a few seconds to look at all the images. Then, she simply asked, "What do you think?" The second graders excitedly shared their thoughts.

They related experiences of how they themselves transcend gender stereotypes. Some incorporated other differences into the discussion—skin color, body shape, hair color, and of their favorite media characters and avatars. They discussed the interrelationship of geography, culture, and ethnicity and how it informs what is considered "normal" and what is viewed as "bad" or "wrong" when outside the norm. It was an easy and exciting conversation for these second graders and it was easily guided by the teacher as they delved into themes of difference, inclusion, privilege, possibility, and celebration. The message, ultimately, was that we are each the owners of our own experience.

GENDER FULL OR GENDER LESS?

Most people have an attachment to their gender expression, even if it is a sub-conscious one—we all participate in presenting ourselves in a certain way, even if that changes over the course of our lives. Some people are worried that by discussing society's gender restrictive norms, and any individual's relationship to them, it is actually a targeted effort to rid society of *all* gender expression. Is the goal to erase or discourage everyone's gender expression entirely to create a "gender-less" world? No, that is not the case. Even parents who wish to raise a child in a "gender-neutral" way will find it impossible to keep that child from experiencing society's gender influences as the child steps out into the world—whether playing at a park, walking through a store, attending daycare, and engag-ing with children at school, or spending time with extended family and family friends. Gender is everywhere. If gender influences are pervasive and inescap-able, should we consider that a bad thing? The answer is no. The goal is not to strive for a gender-less world, but rather one that is gender-full. The goal is to decrease the harm to children that is done in the name of gender and replace it with one that brings them safety, authentic self-expression, and joy.

GENDER IDENTITY

Children can recognize and discuss differences related to gender expres-sion. We've grown up with these conversations—in various iterations—during our own childhoods. So have our parents and grandparents and many genera-tions prior to that. Children can readily grasp the variability and inconsistencies within gender roles, stereotypes, and gender expectations. Encouraging children to have conversations about gender *expression* is perhaps the easier part for edu-cators. The challenge shows up as teachers consider how they might bring in the topic of gender *identity*. Teachers may feel tempted to stick close to the familiar terrain of gender expression, yet talking with children about gender identity is crucial.

Most people, whether they are five, fifteen, or eighty-five, if asked, would easily be able to articulate their internal sense of gender. At the same time, they might feel puzzled, even offended to be asked about their gender. "Am I a man? Of course, I am a man, open your eyes!" The majority of people experience a sense of congruence between their gender identity and the sex they were presumed to be at birth. This congruence, and the ability for others to perceive it, is the expected norm. If someone does not fully look the "part," the expectation of that person is that they work harder to project that congruence. Men must project enough masculinity, and women enough femininity, so that others can easily determine their gender. This responsibility—successfully projecting one's gender—and the collective agreement to adhere to this responsibility, means that most people find no reason to examine or name their gender identity.

If a child experiences feelings of gender congruence, end of story, right? A boy's gender identity is validated by the presence of a penis, a girl's by the presence of a vulva. We have assumed that identity and genitalia are one in the same. So, when a child expresses a different gender identity than expected, we are quick to assume the child is confused. We may feel a need to clarify that the child has a specific gender identity by pointing to the child's anatomical configuration. Indeed, we may even feel that it is our responsibility to clear up that child's "confusion."

In the 1960s and 1970s, there were some attempts to expand gender representations, including the ground-breaking children's record album, *Free to Be, You and Me*.[1] Produced in collaboration with the Ms. Foundation and author/ actor Marlo Thomas, it also featured Alan Alda, Rosey Grier, Cicely Tyson, Carol Channing, Roberta Flack, Shirley Jones, Jack Cassidy, and Diana Ross. One of the album's tracks, entitled "Boy Meets Girl," places the listener into a conversation between two newborns. The babies are working to sort out which of them is a boy and which is a girl. One says, "fireman" for future career choice while another says, "cocktail waitress," followed by the realization that both babies are bald. "Don't look!" says one, "A bald girl, yuck!" When the nurse comes to change diapers, both babies have the definitive "proof" of who they are as they see their genitalia. This skit allowed for greater latitude in how people might *express* their gender (career choice, hair style) but still relied on a synonymous relationship between identity and anatomy.

Today, we know that anatomy is *not* synonymous with identity. Our gender expression is just that, our way of expressing ourselves. Our identity is our own internal sense of gender, and all three components have a beautiful way of coming together to comprise the experience of each unique child.

Gender Identity Is Conceptually Simple, But How to Get Going?

Until more recently, educators, parents, and other adults have not engaged children in conversations about gender identity because no one thought to do so. This is the primary reason that so many are apprehensive about discussing it with children. It is unfamiliar. When equipped with simple, straightforward language, they can more confidently begin these discussions. Witnessing the straightforward simplicity with which children understand and embrace the concept of gender identity provides the relief and confidence needed to move forward. How, then, do we begin?

Consider the following example of a class with a trans student.

Third grade teacher: "Good morning class. I'd like you to circle up because we have something important to discuss. Many of you may be learning about this for the first time. This learning is new for me as well and I'm excited about what I am discovering.

But first, one of your classmates has something important to share with us. Many of you have known Caleb since kindergarten. What Caleb would like to share with us is that, in his heart and mind, he feels himself to be a girl. He wanted us to know this. And he would like us all to refer to him by the name Kaliyah. It can take a little time to get used to a new name, even for me, so I'm hoping you all will remind me if I forget to call *her* Kaliyah. Can you all help me with that?"

Heads nod and the conversation continues.

"Kaliyah was a little worried about this conversation today. She was concerned that some of you might tease her about this. I sure hope none of you will do that. As a matter of fact, how many of you have been teased about something? Raise your hand."

At that, all students raised their hands.

"Please keep your hands up and look around the room."

The students were surprised to see all hands raised. Some of their classmates, they knew, were the ones who had teased them, others, they understood, were ones that they themselves might have teased.

"When others teased you, how did that make you feel?"

The universal response throughout the class was that it made them feel either sad or mad or both. The teacher had created an environment where the students recognized a shared experience (teasing) and a common reaction (feeling sad/mad). He then gave the students the opportunity to share their stories. The students better understood the impact of teasing on everyone and had a greater sense of empathy for each other. When the teacher asked if there were any other questions about Kaliyah, only one student had one comment: "It makes sense, he's always been mostly a girl anyway."

The teacher wrapped up by reminding the children of Kaliyah's new name. He had matter-of-factly switched Kaliyah's pronouns in the very first part of the conversation and then consistently did so from then on. He then asked the students again to remind him if he himself made a slip (to which they heartily agreed) and finished by thanking them for their kindness to each other throughout the whole conversation.

This conversation can be modified in a classroom where there is no (known) trans or nonbinary child disclosing their gender. A teacher needs simply share that some people have a different gender on the inside than what we might expect based on what we see on the outside.

Components of Successful Conversations with Children

USE TERMS THAT CHILDREN THEMSELVES USE

In the above example, the first paragraph highlights the simplicity of language that can be used with children. Notice, too, the way the pronoun change occurred. The teacher used the original pronoun to launch the conversation. As soon as the gender identity of their classmate was mentioned, including the new name, the teacher switched to the pronoun "she." No explanation was given, nor was there any need to define what pronouns are. Children use pronouns from a very early age (at least, in languages that have gendered pronouns), well before they learn the terminology associated with different parts of speech. Some may have questions about nonbinary identities and/or the use of they/them pronouns. Children as young as preschool age can readily understand this too, if provided with straightforward explanations. Don't underestimate them. Children easily understand the concept of who we are internally as opposed to what others decide about us based on our external attributes. Trans children often describe their gender as existing in their "heart" and/or their "mind" and, just as other children do, *know* their innate gender. It is a universal human experience.

RED: A CRAYON'S STORY

While this book, *Red: A Crayon's Story* by Michael Hall, makes no mention of gender, it is an excellent, sweet story of who we are on the inside versus what others see on the outside. A book for all ages, it provides children with a simple, straightforward way to describe gender identity. "Funny, insightful, and colorful, *Red: A Crayon's Story* is about being true to your inner self and following your own path despite obstacles that may come your way."

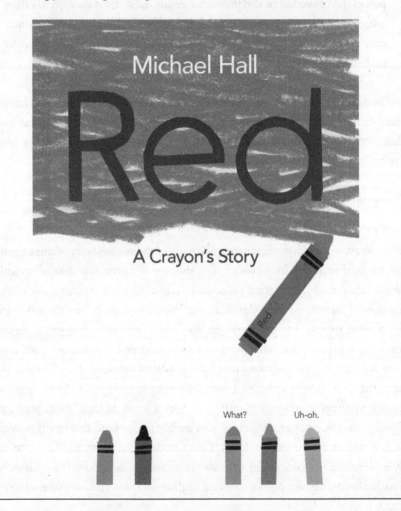

They have an inherent ability to understand who they are "on the inside" and moreover, they recognize that gender is only one aspect of who they know themselves to be and how that impacts their engagement with the outside world. In one fourth-grade classroom discussion, when asked to provide additional examples of who they are on the inside versus how others perceive them on the outside, one student somberly told her classmates this:

> My family has darker skin and when my mother moved here from East Africa, some people told her she was a bad person. They said she was ugly and didn't belong here. They don't know my mom! She's a very good and beautiful person.

FRAME THE CONVERSATION AS AN OPPORTUNITY FOR LEARNING AND DISCOVERY

The most important point is to simply *introduce* the concept of gender identity to children. Children can readily understand that we all have an internal sense of gender. If they do not understand that diverse gender identities are possible, then they are left with no context with which to understand the gender-diverse children they meet. Teachers can discuss the diversity of identities, experiences, and physicality that are represented within the student body and the world beyond. And, a teacher can discuss how those differences, including gender, provide depth and value to the school community and should be respected, celebrated, and a source of pride. The concept of gender identity can be introduced to students of any age as part of the educational framework that includes discovery and ongoing learning.

With the previous example, Kaliyah's teacher shared how he, too, was learning. He shared his excitement. He invited the students to remind him if he made a mistake when referring to her and that he would do the same for them. In doing this, he shows the children that learning can occur at any age and that there is always something new to discover. The teacher acknowledged that, with learning something new, anyone can make a mistake. Gentle correction can help everyone. This is the opportunity to introduce new terms (*transgender* and *nonbinary*, for example) to provide the more expansive realities of gender beyond girl and boy.

Many of the examples provided in this book focus on ways younger children engage and respond to conversations about gender diversity. This is deliberate. If adults are able to clearly and simply articulate the notion of a person's internal gender (gender identity) and then the ways in which anyone, regardless of age, might convey their gender (gender expression), then they can more confidently add any complexity they deem developmentally appropriate as conversations progress and children mature.

Adults, whether teachers, parents, or others, can inspire in children a sense of inquisitiveness and excitement about the process of learning. Learning about gender diversity should be no exception. Not every person will have definitive answers to all questions, as we know. Answering a question with another question like "I have my thoughts, what do you think?" allows for multiple perspectives and mutual learning.

RECOGNIZE THE POWERFUL OPPORTUNITY TO EXPAND THE DISCUSSION

Educators are often inclined to wait until they have a known trans child in their school before they consider any gender-expansive discussion with students. It is understandable as these conversations, even under the best of circumstances, can feel intimidating and awkward. There is no need to wait and plenty of reasons to begin early. There is also a tendency to believe that a conversation about gender identity needs to be an in-depth, lengthy discussion about the lives of transgender people. This is not so.

Any discussion held, with the purpose of disclosing an individual student's gender identity, can be broadened in a thematic way to include the rest of the students. Kaliyah's story is just such an example. The student discussion, guided by the teacher, was expanded to include all the students' experiences of being teased and how that made them feel. This allowed them the opportunity to share the ways in which all of them differed from each other, including physical differences like height, skin color, hair, and other attributes. The children did not limit their sharing solely to bodies but also spoke of their families, their language(s), food, and many other examples related to culture, ethnicity, experience, and circumstance. Because the discussion was expanded in a way that included these identity and experiential differences, a powerful environment of *empathy and compassion* had been created, one that allowed the students to see their shared experience of hardship with respect to teasing and bullying.

The Benefit to All Students

When students are given room to consider the diverse experiences and identities of their fellow students, they are able to discern how these differences improve the lives of some, while providing greater challenges for others. This lays the foundation for discussions about power, privilege, who has it, who doesn't, and under what circumstances. Studies have shown the positive effects on students of any age who are able to engage in this manner of learning.[2] Children have stronger, kinder relationships with their peers, bullying decreases, and they have a greater sense of confidence in the world. We also see how these benefits extend into adulthood. The result? Children who are better able to handle conflict, exhibit stronger leadership and workplace success, and have more satisfying relationships with coworkers and loved ones. What an amazing outcome. Who wouldn't want to foster this compassionate environment in the classroom?

The topic of gender diversity provides educators with a fantastic channel for engaging in these empathy-building conversations. Because students are learning, some may make comments about "normal boys," for example, with the implication being that trans boys are not normal. Most of the time, when a child makes a comment like that, there is no malice intended. While there is no need to chastise that student, gentle correction is needed.

A teacher might respond by saying:

All boys are normal, *and* all boys are different from each other, too. Some boys have more experiences in common with others and some less so. If you were in an all-English-speaking classroom, you might assume that speaking English is "normal" but if you were in a classroom with all kids speaking Spanish, those students would assume that Spanish language was normal. Who is right? Neither. It is actually a situation in which one language is more common depending on which situation. There is no "normal" way to be a boy either. Just some ways and circumstances that tend to be more common.

Exploring gender diversity within the broader context of human diversity achieves several valuable objectives beyond a classroom environment of empathy and compassion.

- Students are provided with a foundational base for early conversations about diversity, power, and privilege. This fosters a culture of inclusion and equity throughout their K-12 education.
- Critical thinking skills are cultivated as students learn to assess and reassess societal norms. As they do so, they will be able to better examine their own lives, and the lives of others, within the context of history, culture, and social justice.
- With social and emotional learning opportunities spanning a broad array of topics, including gender diversity, students understand that their inquisitiveness and perspectives are valued. Respectful engagement in the classroom strengthens the students' interpersonal communication skills—skills that will last them a lifetime.

During any educational discussion—whether exploring societies, language, politics, geography, the natural world, racial and ethnic diversity, history, biology, literature, and more—there are opportunities to discuss gender differences. Schools that take a proactive approach to introducing the concept of human gender diversity find that when a gender-diverse student enters a classroom, they are readily accepted and included by their peers. The students have already gained the needed conceptual understanding to be welcoming.

PRACTICAL SUGGESTIONS FOR STUDENT DISCUSSIONS

Invite Students to Engage in Discussion

Gender norms and stereotypes impact all students regardless of age. Many instances of these gender expectations occur on any given day and will go largely unnoticed or unacknowledged. A teacher can change this! Encourage students to notice and comment when they see examples throughout their day. Model this for them. A teacher may pause instruction for a moment to point out a gendered example. "Hey class, take a second and tell me what you notice about these two math problems":

Problem 1: Stephanie found three dresses on the sale rack which were originally priced at $135, $150, and $195 respectively. The first is discounted ten percent, the second is marked down by twenty percent, and the third is half-off. What is the total Stephanie will pay for the three dresses?

Problem 2: James and Miguel play on the basketball team and were looking at their end of season statistics. Miguel scored, on average, four out
of nine free throws per game while James made an average of three out
of five free throws each game. If each boy played in all ten games of the
season, what is the total average points that each boy scored?

Before entering into calculations, a teacher could ask the students for their observations about the stories—and any implicit messages—delivered within the
context of a story problem. The gender associations are readily apparent—girls
in dresses and boys in sports. But these two problems present an opportunity to
extend the conversation beyond gender.[3] For example, Problem 1 reinforces a
culture of consumerism and accompanying middle/upper-class status as a societal norm. Regardless of any discount offered, the purchase of one dress, much
less three, at those prices is going to be out of reach for many poor and working-
class families. Problem 2 places value on the student that scores the most which,
upon solving the problem, turns out to be the boy with the Western European
name inadvertently reinforcing a notion of racial superiority.

There is no need to derail any activity or lesson simply because an example
is noticed nor, of course, does this activity need to be limited to math. Have the
students notice words like fireman, caveman, mailman, and spaceman, instead of
gender-inclusive terms like firefighter, cave dweller, postal carrier, and astronaut.

A teacher could have a dedicated place to "parking lot" any number of gender presumptions, restrictions, or stereotypical examples that students notice
throughout any given day. These examples could be discussed on the spot or
during a weekly designated class time. Encouraging an observational approach
for students, regardless of subject, allows them a powerful opportunity to reflect
on the implicit biases within the educational system that reinforce many of the
societal "isms" such as consumerism, classism, racism, heterosexism, sexism,
and ethnocentrism. Children do not need to know these terms to feel the impact
on their daily lives. Teaching a student to recognize implicit bias will also provide them with tools to navigate situations where these biases touch their own
life and the lives of others.

Incorporate Rules of Engagement and Restorative Practices

There is no need to re-create the wheel. Applicable tools are at hand and can be
used when inviting children into gender diversity discussions. For example, a

teacher may draw from basic debate parameters for how to engage a classroom of students and honor multiple perspectives. This may especially apply to older students, but these rules can be used for students of any age. Task students with creating their own guidelines as well. They will likely generate some that are very similar to the following:

- Never offend, disrespect, or insult another student.
- Do not speak out of turn or interrupt another student.
- Present facts truthfully. Do not knowingly falsify or distort the facts. Avoid conjecture.
- Stay focused on the topic, theme, or question.
- While the conversation may become lively, do not allow it to become too heated. Avoid quarreling and bickering. Do not point fingers at anyone. Control your tone of voice.
- Focus on the topic, not another student. Personal attacks are off-limits. Do not discuss a person's physical attributes, experiences, or limitations.

While a teacher can work collaboratively with students to establish guidelines and hope for optimal conversations, the reality is that mistakes happen. Restorative practices—for adults and students—can help when these inevitable mistakes do occur. These practices provide a way for everyone to find their way—and be held accountable to each other. It gives the class a chance to course correct. And, importantly, an opportunity to forgive others *and themselves* when mistakes are made.

Students (and teachers) can assess an unfortunate situation by asking, "What happened?" and "What was your thinking at the time?" These questions accomplish a few things. It allows a person to be heard and to get out their whole story. It facilitates a personal reflection regarding their thoughts and emotions at the time, and a person has a chance to be the first to identify their own missteps. Then, an inquiry can occur into who or what has been harmed as a result. Sometimes that harm is directed to someone else, sometimes to ourselves.

Reparative practices make a powerful space for closure as well. How might one repair harm done? What steps might be done in the future to better honor each other and reduce harm? Students and teachers build trust in each other as they engage in reparative practices and decision-making. Empathy is strengthened. Full agreement is not needed but respect, compassion, and dignity are.

Wrap It Up on a High Note

I believe it is important to acknowledge that the prospect of stepping into newer, more expansive conversations about gender can feel unpredictable and even difficult. Teachers will be well-served if they prepare themselves to guide these topics with children from beginning to end. I keep emphasizing that these discussions are generally more intimidating for adults and less so for children. Because we are introducing a newer element—gender diversity—to existing conversations about diversity, the bottom line is that there is still a feeling of unpredictability about what might arise when first stepping in. So, model openness and take time to celebrate!

Educators can acknowledge the challenges that come with learning something new. Express gratitude to students for thoughtfully listening. Thank them for respectfully contributing to the dialogue. Applaud the courage that it takes to express a thought or opinion that is not shared by the majority. Celebrate the bravery of anyone, including the gender-diverse student, who shares their authentic selves with others when the outcome can be uncertain.

For any teacher who leads these conversations, congratulate yourself on embracing an important conversation during this historical time. In decades to come, this kind of heroism likely won't be needed. By then we'll have a deeper, more extensive understanding of gender diversity in children. For now, know that you will have inspired learning for your students that will not be easily forgotten and in which the students will be proud to have been active participants.

USING EXISTING TOOLS FOR DISCUSSIONS ADDRESSING INCLUSION, DIVERSITY, AND PRIVILEGE

Launching a discussion with students of any age can be a bit intimidating without an understanding of the concrete language needed. Once those initial steps are understood, the path for continued discussion is already charted. The most successful way to engage students is to utilize the educational tools that address the *importance of belonging*, the ways in which children have *shared experiences*, as well as the variables that make *each child's journey unique*.

Children of any age understand these concepts and are able to express their feelings about them. One of the earliest laments we hear from a youngster is,

"That's not fair!" Examining "fairness" is an important pathway to understanding gender diversity.

Everyone experiences the possession of or the lack of privilege. Some may experience both albeit in differing circumstances. Any person's ability to recognize privilege is unpredictable as well. This interplay affects us in a host of devasting ways many of which are not fully brought to light for examination. It can be deeply uncomfortable to acknowledge inequities. White people are rarely followed by security staff in a department store, an experience that people of color might experience regularly. This is an example of white privilege. Hearing people are able to access many more public events because they have no need for an ASL interpreter whereas a deaf person does—this is an example of ableism. Most gender-typical presenting people are able to access restrooms without being questioned, barred from entry, or in danger of violence—this is gender privilege. While examples of racial and hearing privilege may be readily understood by many, the ways in which a gender-typical person (cisgender) experiences gender privilege can be complex and nuanced, and likely something they've never thought about. The more we examine the many forms privilege can take, the more students will comprehend privilege, lack of privilege, and ultimately be able to recognize the harmful effects of power imbalances in their own lives and the lives of others.

It's Not a Competition

Provide children with tangible examples of intrinsic and extrinsic privilege that help students see their own privilege and that of others without engaging in a "who's got it worse" dialogue. In doing so, students are able to recognize that others may have more challenging lives in certain ways while not invalidating the experiences of others. Remember, this is about empathy building and relatability, not a hardship competition. Once the students grasp a basic understanding, they can then be encouraged to contribute examples that they themselves have experienced or examples that they recognize happen to others.

If It's Not Mentioned, It Doesn't Exist

Teachers can rely on existing tools that address privilege and provide guidance as to how to engage students in these classroom discussions. The most crucial aspect of this is to ensure that "gender diversity" is included in discussions of racial, socioeconomic, cultural, and other forms of diversity. If a resource includes gender only within a binary framework, be sure to expand the conversation to include nonbinary and other gender-diverse identities. Trans people, once invisible, are now an increasingly visible population. Let students know about this. Use books, images, videos, and films to facilitate conversations and encourage observations throughout a student's day-to-day activities. Include positive role models of individuals who have made a difference in social justice movements. Discuss action steps that a student can take—big or small—including ways to be an ally to oneself, to others, and to fellow members of society.

Addressing What Is New, Unknown, or Unfamiliar

If classroom conversations about diversity and privilege are new to you, that's okay. Don't be too intimidated. Instead, step in! Do not assume that young children cannot understand—they can and regularly do.[4] The content is relevant to all children of any age. Teachers can share that some conversations are new to them, too. What student wouldn't find that refreshing?! Incorporating difference—whether that involves different people, new knowledge, and/or changing communities—provides opportunity *and* upheaval.

Know that these unfamiliar topics can cause discomfort for both teachers and students. This may be especially true for older students who have begun to form opinions about the outside world and their own place within it. It is okay to acknowledge that discomfort. We can acknowledge any discomfort we might have while celebrating a new, unfolding chapter. Do not pass judgment on a student (or yourself) for these feelings. Instead, emphasize mutually respectful ways of engaging in discussions of difference, diversity, and privilege. If feelings of discomfort, even resistance or denial, can be acknowledged as an important part of learning, the likelihood of students staying engaged is much higher. Engaging the children in a collaborative learning endeavor that acknowledges that newness—one that asks everyone to step into a process of discovery— allows everyone to experience a dynamic, thought-provoking conversation that enhances critical thinking skills.

Of course, there is much more to say regarding classroom dialogues that address privilege and disparity than can be addressed in this book. There are many books, articles, films, and other resources that you (or the students) may wish to incorporate. These tools will serve you well as you seek to demonstrate universal themes to which all students can relate.

Building on a Foundation

As students mature past early childhood, the subjects they learn also gain depth and complexity. They delve further into subjects like biology, anatomy, psychology, communications, culture, geography, sociology, and politics. Our human experience is centered in these classroom studies. Students know there is no homogenous human experience, therefore gender is an important factor to incorporate. Embedded within these subjects will be opportunities in which to converse about diverse bodies, identities, and experiences.

For example, to whatever degree *anatomy and physiology* are discussed at each grade level, so too should diverse gender identifications be included. If youth already understand that there are different gender identities beyond male and female, it will not be confusing for them. They will clearly delineate between someone's gender and the body they inhabit. Just as the youngest children can understand a point like "most boys have penises, but some don't," older children recognize that the bodies of gender-diverse people may be different in certain ways, too.

If students are exploring *different cultures* across the world, gender roles and sexual orientation terms or labels will vary significantly. Many cultures acknowledge more than two genders. The global diversity of gender can be explored by examining terminology used in other cultures, gender roles and expectations within those communities, and the degrees of acceptance of relationships with gender-diverse people.

Within the study of *communications, physics, civil rights,* and *politics* there are aspects where gender and sexuality are critical factors that moved human rights forward. Students can examine stories from the women's suffragist movement in the early 1900s when many women advocated for the right to vote, while some, many of whom were white, privileged, and held power due to their social status, fought against it. They can explore the impetus for the 1968 Memphis sanitation department's strike calling for safer working conditions for the predominantly African American sanitation workers who fought to be acknowledged as *men*! Their protest signs stated, "I AM a MAN."[5]

Many may learn about astronaut Sally Ride, the first American woman in space, but they may not know that she was also the first LGBTQ+ person in space. Many students will be inspired to learn about Oprah Winfrey's rise as a media powerhouse and consider her life trajectory navigating the intersections of gender and race. Why not add the stories of other historical figures, like gay civil rights activist Bayard Rustin, lesbian poet Audre Lorde, and transgender pioneer Christine Jorgensen?

HOW DO WE TALK ABOUT BODIES?

Much of my work in schools involves working with adults—teachers, principals, and other parents—to emphasize the ease with which children comprehend the experience of their trans or nonbinary peers. When presented in a straightforward manner, and not one fraught with adult complexity, children will readily understand the experiences of their fellow students. Utilizing the AEIOU gender framework, with emphasis on "E" for expression and "I" for identity, the pathway forward for educators will feel manageable and relieving.

As an abbreviated refresher, here it is again:

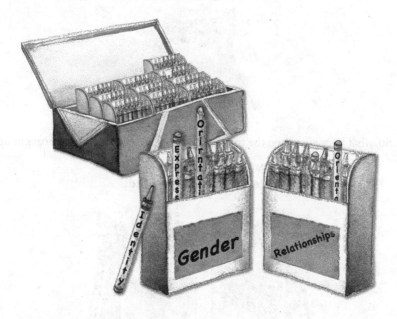

- A is for ANATOMY
- E is for (gender) EXPRESSION

- I is for (gender) IDENTITY
- O is for (sexual) ORIENTATION
- U is for UNIVERSAL.
  Each of the four terms listed above is relevant to *all* people. We are born with a certain body, a way of expressing our gender, an innate sense of our own gender identity, and, as we mature, a recognition of our physical and romantic attractions (or lack thereof as evidenced by terms like *asexual*) to others.
- Y is for YOU—All of us wish to be our full selves and to have that self-authenticity recognized and respected. We strive to teach this to our children at even the youngest ages. All children long to hear, "You are amazing, special, and beautiful for exactly who you are!"

It is always reasonable to begin gender discussions with children of any age by focusing on the "E" (gender expression) and the "I" (gender identity).

With younger children, focus here.

So, what happens when the topic of bodies ("A" for anatomy) is brought up?

**With older children,
more can be incorporated.**

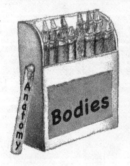 

Most schools address the topic of pubertal body changes with children at the age at which they experience these changes, beginning at the fourth, fifth, or sixth grade levels. Typically, this is the same age range in which students begin to learn about all bodies. This is the appropriate time to learn about the bodies of gender-diverse people too.

We can teach children that *most* bodies will mature in a certain way, but there is quite a bit of variation as to how and when that happens. For example, if we were to discuss height, one physical attribute that typically changes as we mature, we might read about "average heights" with a range from low to high. Do we accept that that range includes everyone's height? Hopefully not! Any categorization of height could vary country by country, ethnicity by ethnicity. There would be people shorter than the low end of the range and taller than the high end. The ranges provided would likely be separated by gender. It could be influenced by a host of additional variables such as one's genetics, climate, or nutrition. Why and how do these variables impact height? This is an important student opportunity to encourage critical thinking.

We can discuss anatomical/genitalia differences in a more accurate, expansive way. For example, a biology or health teacher might consider these statements:

- As we've been learning in class, there are different blood types like O+ , O-, A-, B+, AB+, and so on. Some are more common than others. Did you also know that while most people have XX or XY chromosomes, others have XXY or X or XO or XYY?
- As we learned last week, one's sense of being a man or a woman (gender identity) is independent of one's chromosomal designation. We also learned that reproduction requires certain gametes—a pairing of ova and sperm—but that that is not contingent on gender identity either. Yes, it is more common for a man to produce sperm, but some don't. Most women will have ova but not all.

The topic of gender diversity is opened in a matter-of-fact manner that is relevant to the subject at hand. It will not be difficult for inquisitive students to understand gender diversity in relation to human diversity. What are other human qualities that have been, or still are stigmatized? Why was that? Why did it change? What present-day changes are being debated? For example, most people are right-handed. Some are left-handed and others are ambidextrous. Historically, lefties were considered unlucky, unclean, possessing other undesirable qualities, or even experiencing demonic possession. Fortunately, these notions are less supported today.

Encourage inquisitiveness in students so that they might consider why stigma once was, or still is associated with physical differences that are less common. Do factors such as religion, race, and differing cultural norms play a role? Again, this expansive reflection will foster a better understanding of human diversity and critical thinking skills. What a powerful gift to give a child as they become a member of our global society.

Discussing Bodies with Younger Children

Some families readily discuss topics related to bodies, sexuality, safe/unsafe touch, and reproduction with their children at early ages. Others will save birds and bees conversations for later, or will allow a school's health/sex education curriculum to instruct their children. Some caregivers will never discuss it. Schools tend to introduce this curriculum when students are of a particular stage of physical and cognitive development, typically in late elementary or early middle school, and will also accommodate an individual family's desired level of participation or opt-out preferences.

What about classroom conversations with children in early elementary grades? What about kindergartners? Do they raise questions about bodies, genitalia, and making babies? Of course they do. This will not be news to any elementary school teacher. Children are curious and it is important to provide them with age-appropriate, correct information about bodies.

Developmentally appropriate discussions about bodies are important to have with children.[6] There are several reasons why:

- To reduce bodily shame and stigma,
- To increase positive body image and autonomy,
- To support healthy boundary setting,
- To decrease the risk of sexual abuse or molestation,
- To reinforce the importance of privacy—one's own and that of others, and
- To establish healthy communications and safe, trusting relationships.

These important factors do not change or go away because children have bodies that are different from each other. Nor will these positive outcomes change because we include all bodies, including the bodies of transgender and nonbinary-identified children. Parents can decide how, when and to what degree they will engage in these discussions. An important part of any teacher's training is to also determine the needs of their students and the parameters within which to address them.

This is about validating any child's identity as it relates to their body. Conversations about this can and should be simple and straightforward. Important conversational elements include:

1. Discuss and define gender identity. Children use language like "heart," "mind," and "on the inside."
    Example: "While we think we can know who someone is based on what we see on the outside, it's what is on the inside that matters. Someone we think is a girl based on what we see, may feel like a boy on the inside. A person's gender on the inside, or in their heart and mind, is called their gender identity."

2. If body parts—and specifically genitalia—are part of a classroom conversation, then a more accurate discussion of that should occur. It is not as simple as boys having penises and girls having vulvas.
    Example: "While most girls have vaginas, some girls have penises. Some boys have vaginas."

3. Respecting a child's right to bodily privacy applies to all students. While there might be curiosity about a trans child's body, the importance of privacy needs to be strongly emphasized.
    Example: "We do not have the right to ask about someone else's private parts. We call them "private" for an important reason. You would not want someone asking about your private parts either."

4. Our gender identity is what matters, not the body parts we've been given.
    Example: "You are not a girl because of your private parts, you are a girl who has certain private parts."

As challenging as conversations like this may initially feel, they are surprisingly matter-of-fact. The positive impact on a gender-diverse child's psyche is profound. It gives them language to confidently understand, describe, and accept themselves just as they are. Their peers are easily able to do the same.

Parents of gender-diverse children find that, when their child's gender identity is validated, the child is often much more at ease with their body as a whole. They have the freedom to exist, as they are, where none was present before.

Incorporating Sexuality as Students' Mature

Gender expression and gender identity are, respectively, observable and innate, and they are an inseparable part of any student's day-to-day school engagement. Therefore, all students should have a basic understanding of these two human qualities well before entering into conversations about bodies and sexuality. This ensures that student daily interactions are respectful and honor each other's experiences. One simple, yet important, example is that every child's name and pronoun are consistently used by all. If students are provided with this conceptual understanding early, they have an ideal foundation upon which to build. As children mature, so too will their conversations about gender identity, roles, stereotypes, and expression. These older students are experiencing pubertal changes, attraction, and stepping into romantic and/or physical relationships. It would naturally follow that a discussion about gender might include sexuality, bodies, relationships, and how all these intersect. Why? Because teens talk about these things anyway! Our educational systems have recognized this and have already built this learning into the curriculum.

Of course, many students may not yet have had a foundational introduction to the concepts of gender identity/expression. These concepts can be incorporated at any time, and in as many ways as possible. However, examining the context is key to determining how, when, or if to delve into a discussion of sexuality or genitalia. Is there any reason to discuss sexual experiences in geometry class? Probably not! Should gender identity/expression be discussed in a health education class? Absolutely! A sociology course? Certainly. Most students do not engage in conversations about gender identity in sexually explicit ways—ways that adults *fear* they will.

The following is an example of an eighth-grade classroom discussion where the concepts of identity and expression were introduced. After a bit, the discussion moved into the arena of attraction and dating:

> What if you were to have a trans student in your class, and that student expresses an interest in dating you?

There was a long pause. After a few moments, a student confidently shot her hand in the air:

What I want to know is this. Are they HOT? Because if they're hot, then that's good enough for me!

Heads nodded, and many were smiling. Everyone felt like she had gotten to the crux of the matter. It seemed to relieve the students of their apprehension of possibly being judged by each other. The conversation was respectful, light-hearted, and empathetic.

It is important to note that the presence of a gender-diverse student(s) does not mean it is a time to discuss that person's body, sexuality, or whether or not anyone would want to date them. Any student could contribute to the conversation in whatever way they feel comfortable doing so. In the above example, no openly trans or nonbinary student was present. In 2007, when this discussion occurred, there was no visible presence of any gender-diverse students throughout the entire school and very little discussion of trans youth in the national media. Students today have a deeper contextual understanding of their trans and nonbinary peers, so posing this particular question would likely not be needed.

A Note about "Coming Out"

Adolescence is a time when young people begin the process of individuation: the separation of self from parents and others. It is a normal part of a child's journey into independence. This individuation often includes making declarations about themselves to others. They may articulate their growing interests in certain areas of study, activities, friend choices, and of course, descriptors of sexuality. Many children won't feel the need to make such declarations about sexual orientation because, if they feel themselves to be heterosexual, the default assumption *is* heterosexuality. Kids with whom that does not resonate may feel a need to "come out." In making a declaration about their attractions, these youth communicate to others that society's heteronormative assumption about them is inaccurate. It is not uncommon for gender-diverse students to first disclose a descriptor for their sexual orientation, even as young as nine or ten.

Because society's acknowledgment of gender identity is so recent, many youth may have less familiarity with this concept. Additionally, trans and nonbinary people tend to be significantly less represented in society. It can be easier for gender-diverse youth, who are making initial forays into self-descriptive language, to first believe that they are gay, lesbian, or bisexual. This step at least differentiates them from their peers and/or from the expectations of conformity. Because we have greater societal visibility of LGBTQ+ people (media personalities, for example, many of whom present gender-diverse forms of self-expression), it is understandable that youth may lay claim to sexual orientation identifiers. They eventually may come into a later understanding of *who* they are (gender identity) rather than who they are *attracted to* (sexual orientation). While we might *expect* an earlier disclosure of gender identification for these youth, they may have only had exposure to language describing sexuality.

A FEW POINTS TO CONSIDER
Incorporate Diverse Family Composition

Discussions about puberty, sexual orientation, and gender identity are frequently and appropriately presented within a *social* context. Families are part of that context. It is important to present the wide range of family composition in the proper manner.

What we can and should discuss is the fact that what we consider to be the "traditional family" composition—one mother and one father in one household—is a decreasing reality for many children across the United States.[7] Any classroom of students will have some who belong to single-parent families, separate households due to separation or divorce, grandparent(s) who serve as primary caregiver, two mothers or two fathers, or have other adults who care for them in foster situations or blended families. Sometimes an older sibling or family friend is the primary caregiver. Many families are racially diverse. Some families have multiple generations in the household, while some families have experienced difficult changes due to the death or deportation of a parent(s).

Children in pre-K and kindergarten classrooms come from these families and they need their family/home lives validated to achieve a sense of classroom belonging. There is often hesitation to discuss the variety of families that are part of these children's lives. There is a stigma associated with being in foster care or a ward of the state. Children who have multiple generations under the same roof are less common compared to other cultures where that is the norm. If a child has two dads or moms, it may be difficult to have their family accepted as well.

Educators often express a hesitation to discuss diverse family composition when the parent's sexual orientation is a factor. Many feel that they need to discuss the sexuality of same-sex parents to acknowledge this type of family. If a child has two fathers, there is no reason to discuss the private, intimate aspects of the relationship shared by these two parents, *in the same way that the sexual practices of heterosexual parents are not discussed.*

In most schools throughout the United States, conversations about dating, pubertal changes, and sexual relationships do occur within the district-approved curriculum for older students. Yet, the conversation about families and caregivers is not the same. This is a simple, yet crucial distinction that does not often occur to many teachers, parents, and administrators. If we can embrace this distinction, we can easily move forward with age-appropriate conversations about family diversity with students of all ages.

Educators could discuss these, and other family compositions or living situations, with K–12 children every year. Teachers and students alike can point out inaccurate generalizations or assumptions that are made about families (in conversation, classroom exercises, videos, or readings) to remind students that our experiences are very diverse.

Do Not Rely on Gender-Diverse Students to be the Teachers

One of the most crucial aspects for an educator to understand is the distinction between a conceptual conversation about gender identity with students versus a probing inquiry into a trans child's personal experience. Discussing the concept of gender identity is different than directly asking a student about their gender history, or if they have plans to take hormones and pursue surgery! Students have a federally protected right to privacy and that includes personal information about their bodies.

We can better understand how to remember the distinction between conceptual learning and individual inquiry if we examine a parallel example as it relates to racial diversity. If there were only one or two students of color in a classroom, we know that we should not ask those students to be responsible for educating the white students on the topics of racism, inequity, and bias. Alternatively, if students are engaged in learning about neurodiversity or differing levels of physical ability, we do not turn to the student who is on the autism spectrum or the one who is deaf to provide the tutorial. Of course, this does not preclude a student with a personal affinity to a topic from contributing to a classroom conversation, engaging in a research paper, or even offering a presentation to their classmates, *if appropriate and if they choose to do so*. A teacher's lack of familiarity with a subject is not an excuse to turn to a child for the answers. Consider this second grader's experience:

> One family moved to a new town and their outgoing seven-year-old trans daughter was excited to start at her new school. The family was forthcoming about their child's gender history with the administration. The child was comfortable with others knowing her gender status as well. However, when another child in class loudly asked a question about what being transgender meant, the teacher was unprepared and said nothing. Seeing the teacher's hesitation, the seven-year-old stepped in to explain. The teacher allowed the young child to lead a conversation that sidelined their usual classroom activities for over thirty minutes. At no time did the teacher add or guide the conversation, and even asked questions to satisfy his own curiosity.

The situation might seem, on the surface, innocuous. Yet, because the child was sharing her own experience, that meant that continued questions and attention focused on her in the following weeks. It culminated when the child finally shared with her parents that one boy on the school bus kept insisting that she show him her genitals so he could take a picture and get "a lot of likes" on social media. She also shared that another student, an older fifth-grade boy, cornered her when no one else was around, pressuring her to be his "girlfriend" and to kiss him. Her teacher had not even taken the time to inform the parents of the initial classroom episode. The chagrined teacher apologized for not handling the classroom situation well. He admitted that he had let his own curiosity cloud his judgment and that he was anxious about sharing the situation afterward with the parents. He understood that his own apprehension and inaction had placed this young child in two different potentially harmful situations.

A Gender-Diverse Child Has a Right to Privacy

While a number of gender-diverse children feel comfortable and confident to share their gender status with their peers, many do not. Sharing their gender status, if they choose, does not mean others can inquire about their bodies and genitals. Under no circumstances, does someone have the right to inquire about a child's anatomical configuration. These children have a right to privacy. It is important to reemphasize for teachers, principals, and others that at no time, or under any circumstance, do others have a "right to know" a child's gender status or history especially if that child wishes to keep that information private.

Sometimes educators feel a sense of obligation to disclose a child's private gender history to the child's teacher, school nurse, the staff, or even the entire school parent community! Some have felt pressured by others to share which of their students are transgender. The situations vary but it is important to know that this desire to disclose personal information about a student should not be pursued without the consent of that student (and, especially in the case of younger students, the consent of the parent(s) or guardian). The motivation to disclose a student's personal gender information is often rooted in the inaccurate notion that keeping it private is akin to an act of deception. This is a recurring theme that is often perpetuated by a society that believes transgender people are being duplicitous in some manner and that their very presence could cause harm to others. This is simply not true.

Drive It Home: Children Are Diverse Humans Capable of Multifaceted Discussions

It is important to state again that children readily comprehend and embrace concepts addressing differences in experience and identity. They also understand how one's sense of self and one's experience can be diversely influenced by skin color, place, age, socioeconomic status, sense of spirituality, and other factors. We as adults sometimes add our own convictions regarding our personal relationships to sexuality, politics, and religion. We do not need to debate the superiority of one experience over another and we do not need to assert any one perspective on children.

We Need to Remember a Few Things

WITHIN THE CLASSROOM AND THROUGHOUT THE SCHOOL

- Express the values of inclusivity, equity, and diversity as the contextual framework.
- Realize that *not* addressing gender diversity is making a statement. The omission of gender as an aspect of human diversity falsely implies that it does not exist or is in some way inappropriate.

- Incorporate the concepts of gender identity and gender expression at all grade levels.
- The topics of sexuality and genitalia should be incorporated when it is deemed age-appropriate either by each individual family at home and/or at school as determined by the curriculum.
- Conversations about gender diversity should not focus solely on one student's experience. Rather, all children should learn about different gender identities.
- Approach student conversations with openness, curiosity, excitement, and gratitude.
- Expand discussions of gender differences into the broader context of human diversity. Do not engage in "othering" or "body-shaming" for any reason. Encourage/guide children to find the *shared* experiential and embodied themes of human diversity.
- Regularly discuss the ways to support and be an ally for each other.
- Include gender when discussing history, social justice, culture, and other classroom topics.
- Identify individual societal change-makers who are gender diverse (with respect to identity or expression). Gender diversity could be the focus of learning or could be tangential—the important part is acknowledging rather than ignoring it.
- Don't hesitate. Stepping into conversations, or interceding if misbehavior occurs, is crucial to confidently communicate classroom expectations to all students.
- Make room for differing perspectives while maintaining the expectations for a respectful environment and respectful engagement.
- Be prepared to facilitate restorative conversations when children or adults unintentionally say something that is awkward or even hurtful. Recognize that the conversation won't be perfect all the time, but *not* having it may be worse.
- Remember that discussions about gender—identity and expression— are appropriate at any grade level. Laying an early foundation allows for deeper discussion over time. Be proactive—an ounce of prevention is worth a pound of cure.

WITH RESPECT TO TRANS AND NONBINARY STUDENTS

- Any trans or nonbinary student has a right to privacy to whatever degree possible.
- A trans or nonbinary student should not be named/singled out in communications to staff, students, or parents unless that is desired by that student and/or family with express permission granted.
- Curiosity about a trans student's experience is understandable but not all gender-diverse students are open to questions. Even if they are, educators should not rely on a child to be the sole source of information and education for others. Teachers need to guide learning in a way that is inclusive of all.
- Do not fault the trans/nonbinary student for any misbehavior from other students, teachers, or parents. It is not the responsibility of the gender-diverse child to stop being who they are, make changes to appease others, or develop coping skills for bullying or other behaviors that should not be tolerated in the first place.
- If possible, keep the caregiver of the gender-diverse child informed of any gender-related conversations or experiences that occur at school so that they may best support the child at home. Be receptive to any information you receive as well.

MAKING CHANGE WITHIN OUR SCHOOLS— DANGEROUS FOREVER OR TEMPORARILY UNCOMFORTABLE?

When the national fight for access and inclusion of citizens of color occurred during the U.S. civil rights movement, much of the action—and resistance—centered on drinking fountains and bathrooms, seating in theaters, and busses, and inclusion in schools. When the disability rights movement occurred, conversations began focusing on access to books in Braille or audio, wheelchair seating on busses, wider doorways, rails in public bathrooms, and inclusion in K–12 schools. Theaters, grocery stores, workplaces, and many other areas of public accommodation were constructed or retrofitted to be more accessible. These efforts were made in an attempt to address social justice disparities.

While there are distinct differences among social justice movements, there are commonly held undercurrents of thought held by the purported majority. One such undercurrent is that some people's rights are more valued because they happen to be in the majority and that by supporting the rights of minority populations, the majority will be deprived of theirs. Another undercurrent is that the efforts needed to increase equity and inclusion are either too daunting, too costly, or both. The critique toward the disability and trans communities share this in common. Fear and stigma associated with minority populations contribute to an emotionally laden undercurrent as well. All these undercurrents are present in the efforts toward gender rights and inclusion.

If we recognize these common factors, then we can also visualize the path forward. Increased visibility results in the ability to make connections with others. These connections facilitate the sharing of knowledge and information. This is of incredible value to families of gender-diverse children as well as schools as they seek to create paths forward. Lastly, when understanding improves, fear and stigma diminish, making room for an open-hearted approach to gender inclusionary steps.

When provided an opportunity to deepen understanding, society can better recognize that what they initially perceive to be *dangerous*, is actually temporary discomfort with something *unfamiliar*. If we do not address the crucial distinction between our responses when encountering danger (fight or flight) and our feelings of discomfort for something that is temporarily unfamiliar, we disrupt the important dialogue needed for forward movement. It is all too easy for children, taking their cues from resistant or apprehensive adults, to adopt the same, unnecessary distress and bias.[8]

Today, we need to deepen our understanding of gender diversity. We as adults need to shift our thinking away from genitalia and sexuality when considering the gender experiences of trans children. Similar to other human rights advocacy efforts, we find ourselves bogged down in lengthy, polarizing debates about largely irrelevant issues. We focus on pronouns, locker rooms, and bathrooms when the actual issues at hand are inclusion, acceptance, and belonging. Children do not experience the same struggle to understand as adults do because they can accept their gender-diverse peers for who they say they are.

Schools are a place where children learn how to learn, acquire critical thinking skills, and learn how to navigate the world. Teachers can work with the youthful openness of their students to encourage a climate of compassion and understanding. We would be better served if we allowed children to guide us back to the simplicity of gender that we once understood ourselves. Who are we on the inside? How do people perceive us on the outside? Are those perspectives incongruent? Are we then presented with the notion that we are "less than" because of the perspectives of others? If so, how do we feel when this occurs?

In one school, where I had the opportunity to provide training to teachers, and parents and then classroom discussions with students. One teacher was surprised at the ease with which her seven-year-old students engaged in the conversation about gender identity. She said:

> I was really impressed by the presentation and happy to see that information that might seem controversial or surprising to us was taken at face value by the kids. When presented in a factual manner about gender identity, children are not confused by these subjects. As with any new subject, if you [teacher/ parent] do not know enough about gender variance to feel comfortable discussing it with your child, a fine response is, "This is something I don't know much about. I would be happy to learn more if it interests you." The main message of the presentation was one that our kids have gotten throughout their time at [our school] and which is deeply ingrained in them already— that they should be kind and accepting of other people, and a good friend and ally to people who might otherwise be teased for being different.[9]

Having a firm grasp on the concepts of gender expression and gender identity is foundational to fostering conversations with children, regardless of age. Because our adult society is keenly curious about the experiences of trans people—often with a fixation on sexuality and genitalia—educators need to feel confident and ready to make this important delineation to parents.

"Here is what we *are* talking about with your first grader—expression and identity—and here is what we *are not* discussing—anatomy and (sexual) orientation. Later, when we bring in the topics of bodies and relationships, you'll find that it is congruent with our established curriculum." A teacher needs to articulate this conceptually and be ready to provide concrete examples.

When educators and parents proactively work to deepen their own learning, then we are well on our way to clearly seeing the age-appropriate pathways for discussions with children. Acknowledging our own fears, concerns, and misconceptions allow us to see that children have not yet acquired the same baggage.

The conversational simplicity is evident and the brilliant way in which children engage is remarkable.

NOTES

1. *"Free to Be . . . You and Me,"* *Wikipedia* (May 6, 2022), https://en.wikipedia.org/wiki/Free_to_Be..._You_and_Me#Track_listing_(New_York_Cast_album).
2. "The Benefits of Inclusion and Diversity in the Classroom," *American University School of Education* (July 24, 2019), https://soeonline.american.edu/blog/benefits-of-inclusion-and-diversity-in-the-classroom/.
3. Anita Bright, "The Problem with Story Problems," *Rethinking Schools*, https://rethinking schools.org/articles/the-problem-with-story-problems/.
4. Caitlin L. Ryan, Jasmine M. Patraw, and Maree Bednar, "Discussing Princess Boys and Pregnant Men: Teaching about Gender Diversity and Transgender Experiences Within an Elementary School Curriculum," *Journal of LGBT Youth* 10, no. 1–2 (January 1, 2013): 83–105, https://doi.org/10.1080/19361653.2012.718540.
5. "Memphis Sanitation Workers' Strike," The Martin Luther King, Jr., Research and Education Institute (June 2, 2017), https://kinginstitute.stanford.edu/encyclopedia/memphis-sanitation-workers-strike.
6. Courtney Schmidt, "How and Why to Talk to Your Kids about Their Private Parts," *Arnold Palmer Hospital* (March 29, 2018), https://www.arnoldpalmerhospital.com/content-hub/how-and-why-to-talk-to-your-kids-about-their-private-parts.
7. U.S. Census Bureau, "Percentage and Number of Children Living with Two Parents Has Dropped Since 1968," *Census.gov*, https://www.census.gov/library/stories/2021/04/number-of-children-living-only-with-their-mothers-has-doubled-in-past-50-years.html.
8. Danielle R. Perszyk et al., "Bias at the Intersection of Race and Gender: Evidence from Preschool-Aged Children," *Developmental Science* 22, no. 3 (2019): e12788, https://doi.org/10.1111/desc.12788.
9. Susan Lee, "When It Counts: Talking about Transgender Identity and Gender Fluidity in Elementary School," *Trans-Parenting.com* (June 2014), www.trans-parenting.com/wp-content/uploads/2014/06/Teaching_About_Gender_Identity_and_Fluidity_in_Elementary_School.pdf.

9

How to Talk to Parents about Gender

Being ourselves means sometimes having to find the courage to stand alone, totally alone.

Brené Brown

CONVERSATIONS WITH PARENTS OF OTHER CHILDREN

Educators consistently bring up the fact that they don't know how to talk to children about gender. Through education and strategic training, they are ready to engage their students and often excited to do so. But this aspect—how to talk to children—is not what hinders them most. Often, they are hesitant to mention their biggest concern of all—the parents of other students. Their newfound confidence takes a nosedive when they consider the potential reactions from these parents, or even their community as a whole.

One teacher said, "I feel good about this! I'm ready to talk with my students but I'm definitely *not* ready to send them home at the end of the day!" While students of all ages are generally more able to discuss gender differences in a straightforward manner, their parents are another story. They are more likely to feel emotionally charged, apprehensive, and conflicted. Teachers have enough on their hands each day, and a conversation with a distressed parent(s) is understandably something that requires preparation.

How do educators discuss gender diversity when the audience shifts from inquisitive child to concerned adult? In this chapter, we will explore how to handle these conversations in a respectful and compassionate way. The content that follows will be helpful for engaging any adult, parent or otherwise.

ACKNOWLEDGE THE COMPLEXITY

At this time in the United States, the conversations regarding transgender people are mired in debate, volatility, and unease. Should trans people serve in the military? Should they have access to restrooms and locker rooms that correspond to their gender identity? How do we address the needs of trans students in schools? Should we allow trans athletes to engage in sports? Should doctors use gender-affirming medical interventions for children?

We know that decades of misinformation, misrepresentations, and stigmatization have negatively influenced society's view of trans people. Our historical lack of scientific research regarding the physiobiological nature of gender led us to unfairly connect being transgender with mental illness—or worse. The pathologizing of trans people often resulted in desperate actions and frightening outcomes. Trans people may be rejected by family and friends, face insurmountable employment obstacles, engage in sex work for survival, be forcibly institutionalized, experience homelessness, and are at a heightened risk for suicide and mental health challenges.[1]

These adverse experiences do nothing to improve society's overall opinion of trans people. Simply put, some will argue that trans people are deservedly judged for their "choice" to be trans and feel that family rejection is an inevitable outcome (i.e., they bring it on themselves). Others feel that trans people are ostracized because of their "choice" to engage in sex work rather than recognize that, for many, that may be the *only* available form of income for survival. Still others inaccurately conclude that being trans, in and of itself, *causes* mental health decline and suicide instead of realizing that it is societal rejection, not gender difference, that is the prevailing risk factor.

When we factor these variables together, it is easy to understand how parents would be troubled by "gender conversations." These conversations are fraught well before we get to the prospect of discussing the needs of trans children. Teachers may feel conflicted. On one hand, these parents (and teachers) know and love their students, including the gender-diverse children. The families of trans children are their friends, neighbors, coworkers, and church members. On the other hand, they are struggling to reconcile the harsh past portrayals of adult trans lives with the innocent nature of the gender-diverse children they see in their classrooms every day. This reconciliation can feel counterintuitive. If they are being asked to accept that a third-grader is transgender, are they also being asked to accept that this child is mentally ill, sexually deviant, or dangerous?

There is no need to place judgment on any particular teacher, parent, administrator, or other adults for the distress they may be feeling. It is better to acknowledge the distress, discuss its origins, and recognize that the cultivation of gender-inclusive school environments is new territory for everyone. The good news is that our early efforts toward gender inclusivity, while not free of controversy, *are* effective. There is a pathway to gender inclusion that can be traversed in a way that is respectful to those from all walks of life.

GENDER: WHAT EVERYONE NEEDS TO KNOW

A great book that examines the complexity of gender in a way that is easily accessible for any parent, teacher, or student is *Gender: What Everyone Needs to Know* by Laura Erickson-Schroth and Benjamin Davis

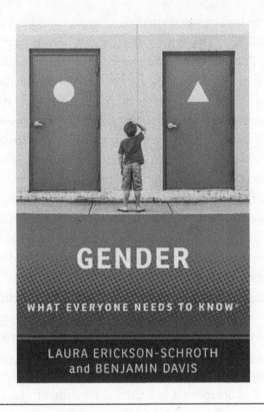

STEPPING IN

Before entering into conversations with other adults—whether they are parents, teachers, or community members—there are some helpful factors to consider. Not every situation will be identical, participants will vary, and the emotional landscape can widely diverge. Focus on the one person you can control—*you*. Approach each discussion in a centered manner. Use any method that works well for you in situations that require clarity and calmness.

When I am getting ready to lead an educational session for school district staff training, I consider a few things in preparation:

1. I review notes about any particulars that were shared with me ahead of time. This could include details about individual circumstances and broader scope considerations so that I step into the conversation as informed as possible.

2. To ensure my own sense of calm and clarity, I make sure to eliminate distractions. This could be as simple as ensuring I don't have back-to-back meetings. These conversations deserve our full attention.

3. As with any group discussion, some people are eager to step in while others are quieter. Therefore, I may need to direct audience engagement to optimize both participation and perspective. This could be as straightforward as saying, "I would love to hear your further thoughts in a second, but I noticed the person sitting behind you nodding (shaking their head, looking quizzical, etc.) so let me get back to you. Would you (person behind the first) like to add some thoughts on this?"

4. I feel it is important to engage with people in a respectful and honest way. Avoiding questions or topics is not the way to do that. I will introduce controversial topics that others may be hesitant to address so that the audience may acclimate.

I feel it is of deep value to treat people, regardless of perspective or opinion, respectfully and compassionately—as I hope that they would do for me. While it is not always easy, it is always worthwhile. If I regularly consider how I want to step in, and prepare myself to do so, it creates a positive environment where others will also feel welcomed. We can keep listening, keep engaging, and find our way to common ground even when at first it seems elusive.

START WITH YOU: GET EMPOWERED

Parents of trans children invariably struggle with how best to describe their child's experience to others because they are often still confused about it themselves. Teachers can also feel hesitant or anxious when introducing conversations about gender differences to children for similar reasons. Imagine, then, a teacher's apprehension when faced with an angry parent demanding answers. Even a principal or superintendent, having no greater understanding of gender-diverse children than anyone else, may find themselves tasked with leading the entire school community through a time of change—even upheaval—without any guidance on how to do so.[2]

If you—parent, teacher, principal—are the person tasked with answering questions while still very green on the topic yourself, you are not alone.

When it comes to inclusivity for trans and nonbinary children in schools, we are *all* on a learning curve. I believe we can all benefit from acknowledging this commonality.

What are the best ways to ready yourself for conversations with other adults?

1. Recognize that *knowledge is power.* Read all that you can find on the subject of gender-diverse children. Be inquisitive. Check your information sources for relevancy and authority. Understand that there is misinformation from outdated sources as well. Commit yourself to becoming informed because others will be looking to you for guidance.

2. If you are able, *reach out to others* who are more informed. Call on your peers, colleagues, mentors, or those in leadership who've had experience not only with the needs of trans children but with guiding others through times of contention or uncertainty.

3. *Get centered.* The more prepared you are for conversations with those who may be upset, the better. When faced with a person who is experiencing uncertainty, apprehension, or anger, you will have an ability to influence the outcome of that conversation, if you are calm and confident. Confidence does not mean you have all the answers, it means that you are confident that an optimal outcome can and will be found.

4. *Observe your own learning process.* Learning a new subject or skill can often be slow, awkward, and uncomfortable. It is also easy to forget what that felt like once you've moved past it. If you are able to revisit your own learning process, you will be able to better meet others where they are with compassion. Shared experience deepens the engagement with others. It can be relieving for others to hear a conversation that starts with, "I understand what you are saying. I've felt the same way."

5. *Be proactive.* Don't delay a needed conversation. For example, if you have received an email or call from another parent in the school who has expressed a need to have their concerns addressed, get back to them right away. That immediate communication, even if it is to only schedule a later time to talk, will help that person feel heard and respected. Additionally, an offhand comment from a teacher during a staff meeting—"Well, I don't know how *that* is going to work!"—is not something to brush off. It may not be appropriate to address the comment on the spot, but it should be attended to as soon as possible.

6. Acknowledge to yourself that *it takes courage* to have conversations where conflict or different opinions may be present. If you recognize that it takes courage to engage in these discussions, then you will be less likely to minimize a situation or, just as importantly, another person's experience. Understand that courageous leadership means modeling the engagement you would like to see from others.

PREPARATIONS FOR SUCCESSFUL CONVERSATIONS

Be Discerning

When we consider how to optimize adult discussions about gender diversity in children, incorporate inclusionary school practices, and consider the bearing on the rest of the school community. It is wise to take into consideration the diversity of people to whom you might be speaking. Situations will vary, some will be expected and some that are unanticipated. Some questions to consider in advance of a conversation could include:

o Will you be speaking one-on-one with someone or to a group of people?
o Do you have an existing relationship with the person(s)?
o Have you had prior engagement with them? Under what circumstance? What was the outcome?
o What do you know about them? For example, are they from specific communities of faith, race, ethnicity, political leanings, etc.? There may be certain culturally specific perspectives that are important to respectfully consider.
o If you have the ability to anticipate that the person's beliefs, cultural norms, political perspectives may be factors in your conversation, what might you do to better prepare?

Be Attentive

As mentioned earlier, being proactive is an important part of achieving successful interactions. Even if it doesn't feel urgent to you, it may be considerably different for that other person. Of course, using active listening skills can be of great benefit in many situations and addressing divergent perspectives about gender is no exception.

1. Give the person your full attention including offering good eye contact and removing any distractions (close computer, turn phone off, etc.).

2. Show you are listening by nodding, taking notes of important points, and paraphrasing to ensure that you have heard that person's concerns accurately.

3. Ensure that you have built-in enough time for the conversation. If need be, schedule another time and/or follow up by email to make sure nothing was overlooked.

Express Gratitude

If you are a principal, for example, and someone requests a meeting stating, "I hope *our* school is not going in *that* direction!", you know the implication for them is that "that direction" most likely means the *wrong direction*. While the inclusion of trans students in schools is not "wrong," it does not mean you cannot meet that person where they are. An inviting and appropriate response might be:

> Thank you, Mrs. Delgado, I am so glad you called. We've had questions from both staff and our parent community. I'm grateful that you took the time to reach out to me and that you are invested in our school community.

Validate

Feelings of uncertainty, fear, anger, resistance, and confusion are common when we encounter any unfamiliar situation. Transgender people's lives have gained greater, and more positive recognition in society, but this positive recognition has not permeated all of society. It is important to acknowledge that this is not only a time of discovery and learning but also a time of discomfort and volatility. I strongly recommend an approach of validation for any person's distress. No one likes to feel dismissed or invalidated when experiencing strong feelings. Going back to the previous example:

> Mrs. Delgado, I recognize that this is distressing for you, and certainly others as well. Yes, we do have some transgender students in our school this year and, since this is new terrain for most of us, we as a staff—and of course me, personally—are digging in to learn more. The questions you've brought up

have been mentioned by others, so know that you are not alone. I want to assure you that we strive to address the needs of all our students in accordance with our school's values. I know that those values are the one thing everyone can agree upon. I hope you can hang in there with our process and know that the questions and concerns of our parent community are absolutely part of that process.

The principal has acknowledged that they have heard this parent's thoughts and the urgency in accompaniment. It has been validated that, one, this is new terrain (trans students in school) and two, there are others with similar concerns and questions. The principal also validates Mrs. Delgado's voice as an important part of the full school community voice followed by an invitation to engage in the solution. The school's shared values are mentioned. This is an important element to bring into the conversation. It clarifies the distinction between *the school's responsibility* to all students *compared to a parent's responsibility* to their own child(ren).

Validating someone else's feelings and perspectives doesn't mean there is always agreement. I recommend to parents and caregivers of gender-diverse children that they consider this technique when first sharing their child's gender identity with extended family, friends, and others. It can be helpful for all to operate under the assumption that any hesitancy or resistance expressed by others is rooted in a place of care and concern for that child's well-being. For example, a parent may consider this kind of response should an initial conversation get off to a bumpy start:

> Dad, I know this is a lot to absorb and we may have different perspectives at the moment. However, what I do know to be true is that you love your grandchild with all your heart. We both want what is best for them. I am so grateful for that as this is such an important time in our family's life. Let's just know that we can come back to this conversation again.

Of course, there can be dissension. Rifts between family members or friends can and do occur. Conflict can occur between teachers at school. The goal of offering a *validating* approach at the outset is to keep the lines of communication open during those first tenuous conversations. It is valuable to acknowledge that these can be hard conversations. When you send a clear message that you care and value that friend/family/staff member in your life and that you want them on this journey with you, you are gently setting a level of expectation as well. Will they step up? Many, many people do—especially over time. Regardless of the outcome, you are telling them that—even in times of disagreement—they matter.

Honor Different Perspectives

I have had the opportunity to enter many school districts across the nation. Administrators consistently share with me that their school(s) are unique and that it "may not be what you are used to in your work." You know what? They are partly right—their schools *are* special! Mormon families may make up over fifty percent of one school community. Another district is rural, mostly Republican, and high in the mountains. One midwestern school district has a diverse, yet transient student population because the neighboring military base provides a constant turnover of families. Another school has students who are deaf, hard of hearing, and students whose primary mode of instruction is in sign language.

Yes, each school community is unique, yet there is a surprising consistency to what they *all need* when it comes to discussions about their gender-diverse students. What they all request is guidance on how to engage their unique school community in this collective learning process in a manner that is respectful and honors that very uniqueness.

Acknowledge That We're Addressing Something New

Many of us have grown up during times when gender expression stretched beyond the accepted norms of the prior generations. Each time, some lament while others celebrate. The Woodstock-era lyric from the song "Signs," "Long-haired freaky people need not apply," is one of many examples of how each generation strove to distinguish themselves (i.e., men with long hair) from their parents who were representative of the repressive "Establishment."

There are many examples throughout history of people pushing the existing boundaries of gender expression, but for many, especially Western cultures, we have not conceptually understood nor pushed on the boundaries of gender identity specifically.[3] Today, we are faced with a reconceptualization of the many truths of gender. We have begun and will continue to incorporate empirical evidence into our scientific understanding of gender as more diverse than we once understood. Meanwhile, our societal understanding of gender evolves more slowly. I believe it is important to acknowledge for ourselves and for each other—without judgment—that this progression of understanding is a bit turbulent for everyone!

CONSISTENT FACTORS THAT SHOW UP

There are a number of factors that people raise when considering the presence, inclusion, and acceptance of trans children: Here are a few ways they can play out:

- Faith: "I cannot support such a sinful choice. If I call that child by a new name and pronoun, I will be going against my faith."
- Politics: "The push for all-gender bathrooms is just an attempt by liberals to erase the line between the sexes, placing girls and women in harm's way."
- Age: "Discussing transgender topics with children is not appropriate at such young ages."
- Culture: "Men's and women's roles in my community/country are very traditional. We have no idea how to talk to our children about this and are deeply concerned."
- Geography: "That kind of thing may happen in California but not here in Tennessee."
- Science: "There are only two genders, male and female, and that is made clear by our chromosomes. We can't ignore the science."
- Norms and Traditions: "We have a tradition at our all-girls school to refer to our students as 'ladies.' Are we supposed to stop doing that?"

These examples make it clear that conversations about trans children are fraught with complexity and strike a deep chord for many. It is a wise person who prepares for these layered and often intersecting discussions. Yes, educating oneself and/or seeking support from an expert requires more time and work but, the age-old adage of *an ounce of prevention is worth a pound of cure* is truly appropriate here. It is important to honor and respect the much-needed learning process so that all may move forward with confidence and understanding.

Now, let's explore these examples in greater detail.

Faith

There is not much that runs deeper than a person's connection to that which gives purpose and meaning to their existence—their faith in a higher power. If a person's belief in God, and the tenets of their faith, are interpreted in such a way that takes gender identity differences out of the context of human neurobiological diversity and places them in the context of sin, deviancy, and moral degradation, then everyone is set up for failure before the conversation even starts:

> One supportive grandparent of a transgender boy made herself available via a call-in support line to dozens of other distressed parents who had recently learned that their child might be trans. Another parent, who identified herself as a Christian, shared with the grandparent that she felt it was morally wrong to be supportive of her child's gender identity difference, believing that her child was confused and "going down the wrong path." The grandparent shared some of her own journey to acceptance of her grandson's identity. She discussed the significant risks—including suicide attempts—that are so often prevalent among teens whose gender identity goes unsupported. She asked a very direct question of the caller, "Would you rather have a dead child who wasn't trans or a live transgender child?" The caller said, "Dead. I would rather know that I will see him in eternal life than know that he is lost to me forever."

If the person that typically has the closest relationship with a child—that of a parent—can be presented with the potential outcome of losing her kid in this earthly life in exchange for an eternal life with her child, then it is crucial that we understand that this conflict can run very deep for some. The person closest to this child was so conflicted about their child's gender journey that they risked losing them altogether.

If another parent, or even a teacher, is experiencing a similar divergence between their accountability to their faith and what feels to be conflicting practices at school (e.g., switching pronouns and names for a gender-diverse student), that person may feel placed in a terrible predicament—choosing between the school or God.

So, what can a principal do if they were to encounter a staff member or parent experiencing this type of dilemma?

- Use the conversation engagement suggestions listed above to create an optimal, respectful exchange (be attentive, express gratitude, validate, etc.).
- Honor the conflict experienced by the person. This can be accomplished without releasing anyone from their expected obligations to the school community.
- Share that these kinds of seeming contradictions are a regular part of the landscape for any school community with a diverse array of students. For example, a child whose family has converted to Islam may give their child a new name. A Christian teacher who uses that new name usually understands that the act of using that name does not mean they fully embrace with the faith of Islam.
- Encourage the parent to return for questions or concerns at any point in the future. Point them to additional support if needed so that they might sort through any remaining conflict they are experiencing.

Remind them that this is not about choosing sides or pursuing an agenda, it is about optimizing the school environment for all students of diverse backgrounds and experiences.

FAITH-BASED SCHOOLS

School administrators usually understand their leadership role when it comes to the "separation of church and state" and how that is implemented within any school community. Even in faith-based private schools, a head of school can articulate the importance of multi-faith/multi-denominational inclusivity even if a greater percentage of students might belong to one specific faith community. Nevertheless, when conversations about gender diversity occur, they may feel conflicted, citing their faith values as the source of their distress. Whether it is the head of the school themselves, one of their faculty or staff, or a parent within the community, do not engage in debate. It is ineffectual to do so and, whether intentional or not, challenging a person's beliefs could easily be interpreted as disrespectful or dismissive.

It's easy to assume that faith-based schools might have consistent questions or concerns, but that is simply not the case. Of course, some gender-related questions raised within faith-based schools are consistent with those of non-parochial schools. Are these children going through a phase? Will they change their mind? How do we address questions from children? And so on. But schools that center spiritual values within their curriculum will bring those values into the conversation in ways that are quite varied. I am including a few examples of these differences in a number of faith-based schools that I've worked with over the years:

School # 1: An interracial family with a long family history of military service, found themselves—like any other family—unprepared for the realization that they had a transgender daughter. Feeling overwhelmed with what to do, they found support for themselves and began conversations with their elementary-aged child's parish school. The school principal and teachers were understanding and supportive even though this was a new situation for them. They felt they could honor the child's new name, pronoun, and, among other things, allow her to wear the correct uniform. The family felt great relief at knowing their child would be supported. The principal sought confirmation for this decision from the church leadership. The bishop, however, balked, specifically on the switching of uniforms. It was confusing to the parents (and the principal) as to why certain gender affirmations for the child—name and pronoun—were okay while one of the most gender-associated identifiers, the school uniform, was excluded. There was no explanation offered and no opportunity to appeal that decision. Their daughter must wear the boys' uniform. Recognizing how confusing this might be for other students as well as how invalidating it would be for their own child, the family decided to pull their child from that school. It was hard on the family to realize that when they needed their faith community the most, the church could not show up for them.

School # 2: In contrast to the prior example, another Catholic high school staff and leadership team took a two-year journey into a dialogue exploring the needs of their transgender students. They were aware of several trans students who had graduated but had *not* revealed their gender identity while actively in school. These students had shared that they simply hadn't felt safe to disclose. The dean and faculty were genuinely shocked that the students felt that their school was unsafe. They viewed their school as a haven, and it was deeply challenging for them to hear otherwise.

My engagement with this school began with a dozen staffers from the leadership team. Our conversation was informative, impassioned, and frank. I was later invited to engage with the entire staff.

The room was packed. This was not a ho-hum professional development session for them—they were electrified. Some were excited, many apprehensive, and some, conflicted. The dean began the meeting by sharing a conversation he had had, one week prior, with a longtime friend of his. They had known each other through college, marriage, children, and grandchildren. When his old college roommate shared the news about his own past gender identity struggles, it truly came as a surprise. She (now) said she was no longer going to hide who she was and wanted him to be one of the first to know. The dean movingly relayed to his staff how grateful he was to have had our previous discussion. He said he would not have known how to respond to his friend from a place of love and compassion—values that were at the core of his work and spirituality. The vulnerability the dean displayed in sharing this story and my invitation to them to share openly and honestly resulted in a powerful, intimate conversation. Much of the discussion centered on the school's stated ideals that *God may be found in all things* and that *each person is sacred.* This created space for everyone to speak candidly while all agreed that inclusion and safety was their top priority for all students.

While it is often assumed that faith-centric schools will be averse to deepening their understanding of gender because of a historically dogmatic framing of it, I have not found that to be the case. If anything, I've seen a willingness to add more complexity to a dialogue that extends beyond any single child's gender identification and explores the intersecting layers upon which gender is built. Many educators have posed questions to both themselves and each other: *What are the core values we work to instill in our students? Are we willing to practice what we preach? What would Jesus do?* As they discuss the core principles of their faith, they find that these discussions far transcend the conversations they expected to have. Many are deeply moved by this process and feel as if they are truly engaged in powerful spiritual work. Is every question resolved? Of course not. But they have established an important foundation for a thoughtful, ongoing exploration of how faith values and gender inclusion can brilliantly coexist.

Politics

When I worked with one school district spanning a period of six months, the political differences within the community came up over and over. This was due, in part, to timing. In 2016, nineteen states across the United States considered "bathroom bills" within their state legislatures and this school district was in one of those states. These bills would restrict "access to multiuser restrooms, locker rooms, and other sex-segregated facilities on the basis of a definition of sex or gender consistent with sex assigned at birth or 'biological sex."[4] Much of the political organizing seeking to repeal the decade of existing rights and protections for transgender students was centered in this more conservative district. As a result, the residents found themselves to be at "ground zero" for this state's political debate. At our first exploratory meeting, the district's leadership team told me that they wanted to "move as many people in their community forward as was possible." They also told me that their community was one that "solved their problems together" despite their wide-ranging political perspectives. The administrators understood the importance of investing the time to address the concerns of many. They worked alongside me to respectfully engage their school community and their stated goals of forward motion were successful. After six months of community discussions, staff and counselor trainings, and parent input opportunities, the gender-inclusive policy was unanimously approved by the district's school board. Shortly thereafter, the state also defeated the efforts to repeal gender identity protections.

Age

Sometimes school leaders, rather than make room for needed conversations, take an optimistic, but ultimately short-sighted, "low-profile" approach. A principal who lacks confidence to take a proactive stance may try to avoid direct discussion or proactive communications citing concern over age appropriateness of the subject matter, thereby postponing discussions into an unknown future. For some, the pursuit of staff training may feel like "taking sides" rather than increasing understanding. The conflation of sexuality with gender identity differences—and the inability to adequately delineate between them—continues to be one of the largest barriers to forward motion.

Delaying or dodging the topic because of the age of the children does not make it go away. Here is one example:

> In a culturally diverse school district, an elementary school had a teacher who had recently disclosed their "nonbinary" gender identity. They let everyone know, including their first-grade students, that they would be using they/them pronouns moving forward. This was confusing for the children.

No one had ever discussed gender identity with them, and they had not yet learned what the word *pronoun* meant.

Many teachers were confused too. The principal did not offer guidance to teachers on how to best answer the questions of students, and the teachers had no way of addressing their own questions so as to better understand the experience of their nonbinary co-worker. No communications were sent out to the parent community, leaving concerned parents wondering how to answer the questions coming from their own children.

The principal's approach was to wait for it all to "blow over," essentially leaving teachers adrift on a rudderless ship. Without guidance for themselves and no clear communications going out to parents, teachers found themselves in the uncomfortable position of ignoring questions from students while feebly deflecting those from parents. Inaction and avoidance served to reinforce parents' notions that whatever was going on was not appropriate for elementary-age children and fed into their fears that whatever it was must be of a graphic sexual nature.

The teachers were left to navigate this time alone. Most of them awkwardly avoided gender-related questions while only a handful felt comfortable talking with their students. One insisted that everyone should dive into the gender discussion and discuss sexuality differences as well. Arguments increased among the staff. How could they defend their discussions as being strictly about gender when sexuality was being discussed by at least one teacher? Growing divisiveness developed among the teachers causing harm to the camaraderie that once existed.

Volatility was increasing among the parents, too. They demanded to know why discussions of sexuality, normally part of the older students' curriculum, were now being taught to their first and second graders without their permission and without notice.

The school's beleaguered principal was at the epicenter of the turmoil. He had hoped that by "riding things out" everything would eventually settle down. That approach only served to deepen the very conflict which he sought to avoid.

When he had finally sent communication regarding a "parent learning night" he was still desperate to avoid hot button issues. In his letter, he stated what *would not* be discussed (particularly any religious or political viewpoints), sending a clear message to the parent community that their concerns about their young children would *still* go unaddressed. The abysmally low turnout was indicative of the parents' frustration with not being provided a platform for concerns most pressing to them. The recovery and healing process within that school has been long and difficult.

Would this situation have been less explosive if the nonbinary teacher had fifth-grade students instead of first graders? Perhaps. Fifth grade is a time in which discussions of health, bodies, puberty, and sexuality typically begin. For those teachers and parents unable to delineate between gender identity and sexual orientation, they would have at least felt like it was more appropriate to talk *about any of it* with eleven-year-olds rather than six-year-olds.

Might this situation also have been less divisive if the principal had sought out gender diversity education for himself and the staff? Most certainly! Each teacher would have been better equipped to answer the questions of students and parents.[5] The students, regardless of age, would have met the information in the matter-of-fact ways that they do when learning anything new. The parents would have felt heard and respected while experiencing their own learning.

Lastly, it is important to understand that the one teacher who talked about "sexuality" actually discussed *family diversity* rather than graphic sexual practices. Some children come from families that have two dads, some have a mom and a dad, some have a mom or grandparent only, and so on. We are completely capable of talking about those families without talking about adult sexual practices. If the principal and staff had developed a foundational understanding, they could have easily relayed these distinctions to parents as well.

Culture

Sometimes there is a lengthier time of exploration, discussion, and hesitation that occurs before a school is ready to pursue training. There is no right or wrong way to step in unless the delay causes harm to specific students. As is often the case, school administrators may not be able to immediately articulate the areas of greatest concern. Considering how to engage with students may be what is the most perplexing. At other times, internal challenges among the staff are front and center.

The leadership staff at one large school, grades six to twelve, was very deliberate in their process. As early discussions unfolded, it finally came to light that the area of greatest concern was the upcoming engagement with the parent community. This school had a large immigrant population, and the head of school was feeling hesitant about the upcoming "parent night." Some of the parents of diverse cultural backgrounds had raised concerns about certain subjects within the student curriculum and the topic of "gender diversity" was one of them. The school's ethnically and racially diverse composition meant that many of them were the first generation within their family to grow up in the United States. Despite the enthusiasm expressed by faculty during their training, and the students' excitement for their interactive assembly, the principal was still concerned as to how this content would be received by parents, especially considering the wide range of language, culture, and faith differences.

After the two-hour presentation, a number of parents—the very ones of which the school leadership had expressed the most concern—stayed afterward to talk even further. Two particular parents, one from the Middle East and the other from China, shared their dilemmas:

> Our children talk to us about these things but, for us, there was never any discussion in our home countries. We don't even know how to begin. It's frustrating to not know what our children are learning. We want to talk with our children about these things but to do so we need to understand this more ourselves. This event was so helpful. I hope that our school offers this again. Thank you for being here tonight!

The school principal seemed certain that many would express deep concerns—perhaps even pushing back on any future discussions. She did not expect immediate interest from her parents to learn more. The urgency of the questions from some parents, prior to the event, were assumed by the principal to be a negative response to the topic. She also assumed that the anxiousness from the parents was the result of cultural *opposition* rather than indicative of having little to no cultural *context*.

Another head of school I worked with made sure that I understood the specific cultural blend within their rural, conservative community. This district not only had a large percentage of migrant farm-working Latino/a families but, the principal shared, over one-half of the students were of the Mormon faith. He wanted to prepare me for a potentially heated exchange. I assured him that the best way to ensure progress within the discussion would be to respectfully and compassionately welcome the exchange:

There was a good turnout for the parent education session. Everyone who attended was enthusiastic. But, the principal said there were a number of people he had expected who had not turned up. He said, "I expected twice as many people, but our school is in the middle of a basketball tournament. Our team is doing really well, and we were able to advance to the finals. Because of that, a game occurred tonight that was unanticipated. I think a number of families went to that instead." I said, "I think the families' decision to attend the game must be a good sign. If the parents who had opted for the basketball game had been deeply concerned about the school's efforts toward gender inclusivity, and any potential negative impact on their children, they would have prioritized this session that had been on the calendar for weeks over the sporting event."

I went on to suggest that if he had additional inquiries from the parents who had not attended, he could share with them how the learning opportunity went and that many parents had found it helpful and insightful. I encouraged him to make himself available for any further discussions on a one-on-one basis. He understood that he had responsibly addressed the parent community's needs by providing the evening's conversational platform and that his teachers and staff were more confident of their own abilities. He said he, too, felt a lot more confident about how to move forward.

We need to remember that simply because a discussion topic is unfamiliar— even controversial—does not mean it is dangerous. The danger comes from avoiding it. Even though initial conversations may feel uncomfortable, especially at first, actively engaging parents in respectful discussion reduces their discomfort, increases the relief they feel, and gives them a more accurate perspective on a topic of which we are all learning. This pursuit of further learning is a powerful opportunity for growth and trust for the entire school community.

Geography/Place

Of course, all communities are comprised of people who care about their children. Yet, the *geographic location* where a child lives can make for different circumstances, some more challenging than others. Location-related factors can either optimize or detrimentally influence any individual student's educational experience. A principal in a densely populated area will have considerations that one in a smaller district would not. Economically challenged communities may discourage poorer students from college aspirations knowing that this pursuit is likely out-of-reach for families with limited means. Racially and ethnically homogenous communities may have greater difficulty addressing the needs of students of color in contrast to larger, racially diverse urban environments. Students with special needs because of cognitive or physical challenges could have less access to specialized teachers and resources because their remote, rural community is unable to attract more qualified teachers. The needs of gender-diverse students—a small percentage of the student body within any school—then can be viewed as a resource and/or attention drain.

An Oklahoma school principal shared that his school was having its first experience with a few trans students. He knew that these students were struggling but that he and his staff had no roadmap for how to best support the students:

> My faculty are brilliant educators, and student-centered people by nature. I know they are empathetic, yet also uneasy in these new waters. We are Southerners. This is not easy for us. Several have commented on the vocal resistance they anticipate will come from our town, and they seriously question the wisdom of stepping in when the number of students impacted is so low. I want to help my students and my staff but, first, I need someone to help me!

In a midwestern town, a school district offered training for its administrators. The attendees were attentive but much quieter than what I had come to expect. At the lunch break, I checked in with the superintendent about it. She laughed and said, "Oh, they are fine! That's just how we are around here. We're a real polite bunch."

It is unproductive, and potentially harmful to trans students in today's schools, to assume that educators are unsupportive or "don't care" strictly because of where they are geographically located. I watched one school district scramble to schedule professional development training because their neighboring conservative district had beaten them to the punch. Why might a politically conservative district proactively address gender inclusion before their neighboring district? Because they take pride in the fact that they care about all their students—including the ones who are gender diverse.

It is also dangerous to assume that a school district located in a politically blue state will know how to meet the needs of trans and nonbinary students, especially without having had any previous education. One small district in a liberal town opted not to pursue training despite repeated requests from their students. The district felt it was unneeded. Educators in this largely white district would say things like, "We don't see race, we see children," and "We are fine with our trans kids, our school counselor is a lesbian" (implying that a lesbian would surely understand the experiences of a trans child). Just because the landscape might, at first glance, appear to be an inclusive environment, doesn't mean it "just happens." Sadly, a disproportionately high number of suicide attempts by gender-diverse students have occurred in this district.

Science

The increasing scientific understanding of the neurobiological factors that contribute to the formation of gender identity is an ongoing study.[6] Many find this information helpful, and even relieving. How can any adult explain something to children that they themselves do not fully understand? Just as scientists understand that eye and skin color, left-/right-handedness, and height are genetically influenced, so too do they understand that gender identification is encoded in the brain and can be distinct from the genital configuration. We know that the development of genitalia occurs during the first half of intrauterine development, while the brain experiences gender influences during the second half of pregnancy. This helps clarify how and why gender identity may develop in ways that are independent of genital development. As we better understand the physiological variations that exist within humans—chromosomal, hormonal, brain, and anatomical differences—we are better able to shift our thinking out of a moral, ethical, or otherwise subjective debate and place it squarely where it belongs: within a framework of human biodiversity. Do we need to delineate these factors to children? Yes, but only on a level at which they can understand. For example, "Most boys have penises but not all. Sometimes girls do, too." It really can be that simple.

Norms and Traditions

Traditions and norms in schools are a regular topic of discussion when considering how to successfully include gender-diverse students. Many traditions, even if inclusive of all students, often have distinct differences related to gender. School guidance counselors often enforce gender norms, as they will more often suggest certain vocational programs to boys while pointing girls to the arts, nursing, or office skills. Some traditions are clearly articulated while other norms occur as if by default—*that's just how it's always been*. Student activities like athletic and homecoming events, for example, incorporate well-established gender traditions.

Toward the end of a school staff training, one educator got a startled look on his face:

> "Wait, what are we going to do about graduation?!" When asked to elaborate, he said, "Our entire community turns out for this event. Our students wear red and white robes, red for boys and white for girls, and we alternate the colors. It's visually quite striking. We've had this tradition for decades! Now, what do we do?"

He imagined the prospect of explaining to the entire community that a decades-old tradition now needs to be tossed out because it is not inclusive of a handful of gender-diverse students. What explanation could he possibly provide everyone that would justify discarding this long-standing tradition?

Before traveling too far down the path and assuming any gendered tradition needs to be discarded, let's back up for a moment. Traditions exist for a reason. What are those reasons? Do we need a complete revamp or just an adjustment or two? Let's look more closely at this example.

ASSESS THE OBJECTIVE(S) OF ANY NORM OR TRADITION

The educator clearly stated that the annual graduation ceremony is one that the whole community values. This small town, with just one high school, is one where people are familiar with each other and where families are proud to raise their children. The school colors are red and white, the robes of the graduates, also red and white. Some time back, it was agreed to alternate the colors student by student—the female students wearing the white and the male students wearing the red. This also ensured that the students would pair up boy/girl, boy/girl throughout. The first goal (alternating red and white) is easy to identify—to have a visually striking event. Beyond that, the gender pairing of boy-girl serves to reinforce other implied norms. What kind of norms? Heterosexuality? An expectation of marriage? Both? Is white—symbolic of purity and virginity—the obvious robe color for girls? Red—symbolic of courage and power—the obvious choice for boys? But isn't white also the color of status for men—white-collar workers? And red a sign of sexual promiscuity in women?

What if students were sorted based on other features or attributes? We once sorted students based on skin color as part of a long-standing, shameful societal tradition that valued white dominance. That tradition no longer exists nor would we, today, consider alternating pairs of students, one white and one student of color, either.

We don't make efforts to match students based on height/weight differences nor by physical ability. Would we rank students based on academic performance with the best students marching at the end as a sort of grand finale? We once segregated students based on skin color as well as cognitive or physical abili-ties. Very few people will suggest we return to that segregation. Most will find it deeply problematic and for good reason. So, why would we consider sorting based on genitalia presumptions?

Striving for inclusion is a foundational value that most share. We do not need to have boy/girl pairings to reinforce a heterosexual norm. It already is the norm, based solely on the greater frequency of heterosexual relationships. That won't change by changing the pairing of students.

The teachers were thrilled to engage in this layered discussion and the solu-tion soon became obvious. No one in the room felt it was important to maintain any norm, implied or otherwise, beyond the first one mentioned. They liked the way the alternating colors looked.

CAN WE STILL ACCOMPLISH ANY GOALS THAT WE DETERMINE ARE BENEFICIAL?
The first goal of achieving a visually striking event—no problem. Can we retain the alternating red and white robes for students? Sure! It is an important visual element of the processional line-up, and the community appreciates this aspect of a celebratory event.

Find an easy solution. There are a number of ways to divide the distribu-tion of robes, and genitals should not be one of them. If students are awarded diplomas alphabetically by last name (the most common approach for schools), simply distribute the red robes to every other student after the alphabetical sort-ing has occurred. Simple! But it could be an option to reorder students who have had a lifetime of going last based on the alphabetizing of their last name. Why not switch that up while you are at it?! Or assign each student a specific number.

Odd numbers wear white while even numbers wear red. Done! With seating arranged by number or by alphabet, the alternating colors are easily achieved.

Is an explanation needed? That depends on whether or not anyone asks. If someone were to inquire, simple answers are the best. What is not needed is an explanation that lasers in on the bodies of trans students! The school might communicate the benefits of this switch from a logistical perspective: *Some years there are more boys and some years there are more girls and we want to ensure there is always an even distribution. We've found that we are able to save money and hassle by focusing only on the size of the gowns while ensuring an equal number of red and white gowns.*

Traditions and norms are an established part of any culture or community and do not need to be summarily dismissed *but* these norms can be examined with fresh eyes. What was the original purpose and is it still relevant? If it can still be accomplished through a few adjustments, great. It may take only *one adjustment* to a tradition to ensure its continuation, and that adjustment may have numerous benefits that would not otherwise be discovered without this reflective process.

BE ATTENTIVE TO POWER DYNAMICS AND STRONG PERSONALITIES

Respect the Emotions That May Show Up

For a school administrator who finds themselves leading gender diversity conversations with staff or parents, it can be helpful to consider any power dynamics, parent or staff cliques, or individuals with influential (or sometimes domineering) personalities as you prepare. So, too, prepare for the possibility that someone may make statements that are *forceful but not factual.* One example of this occurred during a community meeting offered by a district that was considering the adoption of gender-inclusive policy:

"I'm a biology major. It's XX and XY, end of story!" said a middle-aged white man in the midst of a heated discussion.

While not a factual statement, entering into a debate about the accuracy of his statement at that moment would likely have added fuel to the fire and pulled the conversation off track. Despite some high emotions in the room, the district administrators leading the conversation remained calm and respectful. They understood that it might not be wise to correct him in the heat of the moment. His standing in the community was known and respected. (Even school board members, when debriefed about this particular meeting, inquired specifically about this community member.)

As district leaders, these administrators recognized the need for composure. Their calmness ensured that the audience's concerns and questions could be heard *and then adequately addressed.* If the two administrators had used their positions of power to dismiss this man's statement, rather than "let it slide," the outcome could have resulted in a deeper polarization within the room. Conversely, if they had *not* recognized their power to both guide the conversation and model the expected manner of engagement, they would not have been as successful either.

They even extended the conversation an additional hour past the scheduled end time to bring people to a shared place of understanding. As a result, there was time to address the man's frustrated statement about chromosomes with greater accuracy, and with respect. As the meeting was concluding, the biology major said, "Okay, I can get on board with this." Another attendee wrapped up the meeting with this comment, "As a Christian woman, with a strong faith in God's teachings, I did not expect to experience a change of heart. But now I see how this policy can actually be helpful in addressing *my* concerns. I see a way through."

These hard conversations definitely benefit from a healthy application of sensitivity and respect!

If We Are All on the "Same Side," Why Is There Still Contention?

The following example highlights how one strong personality can inadvertently derail forward movement even when most people agree:

> An elementary school principal spoke about her school's staff and their commitment to diversity, equity, and inclusion. Each month, the school dedicated time and attention to all K–5 students to learn about historical events such as the civil rights movement, Women's History Month, and so on. At the end of the previous school year, they had turned their attention to the LGBTQ+ rights movement. Conversations with students included, among

other things, the fact that some families may include two moms or two dads. They learned about historical figures who belonged to the LGBTQ+ community. The students also learned about what it meant to be transgender. Some parents, upon learning of that month's focus pushed on the administration. *All this happened too fast! Why weren't we notified? We should have been able to give input or at least had the chance for our child to "opt out."* Some wished they had had a chance, at the very least, to hear about what would be discussed with the children and that that might have made them feel more confident.

Because of this pushback, the school formed an equity committee to reflect on and consider how to move forward the following school year. The committee discussed the parental concerns and what, if anything, to do about it. A couple of teachers suggested that they could "slow it down" to more gently ease parents into the idea. One teacher felt differently. "No way! We do not need to slow this down. Actually, we need to do more, and more often! Too bad for these parents! We don't need to let their bigotry dictate what we do!"

Tension was building among the staff. While supportive of the curriculum for students, some felt it was wrong to disregard parental concerns.

The principal reached out for help. Her primary concern was the growing divisiveness because of one teacher's hardline stance. As this work progressed, the perspectives of the committee members expanded. They better understood that their approach did not need to be one that was placed in an either/or and right/wrong context. *Either* we move forward with an LGBTQ+ curriculum at the parents' expense, *or* we pause/stop curriculum to assuage parents. The two issues were acknowledged as important components of what would ultimately drive a shared solution. If consensus for this approach was gained, then student discussions could move forward while simultaneously addressing legitimate parental concerns. How could a solution be reached?

Step 1: Consider the needs of the parent community. There was no need to dismiss the concerns of parents but rather understand that they needed and deserved to understand more about what their children were learning. The task at hand would then be to find clear, effective ways to actively address parental concerns. One point that bears repeating would be to clarify that talking about LGBTQ+ people does not mean that anyone is discussing their sexual practices!

Step 2: Continue the work with the students. What additional books might they use, which biographies to highlight, and so on? We discussed that available resources are somewhat limited, especially for younger children, and how they might use other books, films, and media from other social justice movements or stories of courageous individuals to highlight the parallels of the LGBTQ+ movement.

Finally, it was discussed that students, teachers, and parents may be at different stages of the learning journey, but the exciting part of that journey was doing it together. One person, through no ill intention, was single-handedly on his way to derailing this opportunity for everyone. Pulling back and reassessing goals and priorities allowed all to see their shared common ground.

Parental Influences

Of course, students are not the only influencers within a school. Parents can shift the dynamic in a room as well. When doing work with schools, I recommend that education begin first with the district leadership. This builds support and confidence for teachers and principals at every school as they step into learning. Then, I stress the importance of offering multiple "parent nights" to provide them a chance to learn more. This allows space for adult questions or concerns to be addressed in a respectful manner and results in greater confidence for all adults before stepping into discussions with students. Here is an example from a public school's educational opportunity presented to parents:

> The principal of a racially diverse elementary school was excited about the topic of gender diversity yet wanted to move forward in a different manner than suggested. "First," she said, "we'll start with teachers and students. The parents come last." She said she didn't want to give parents the impression that they had a choice in whether these discussions would happen with students. "It's important, and we're moving forward!"
>
> After the staff training and after conversations within each classroom, a parent meeting was finally scheduled. The principal assured me that there would be no issue from parents, especially because only a half dozen or so typically attended parent offerings. By the start time, it was standing room only! There were two parents, in particular, one who spoke at the beginning and one toward the end, that seemed to have the most impact on the

audience. The first parent said, "I picked up my second grader today like I do every day. I always ask how school went, she always shrugs, says 'fine,' and nothing else. Today, she was so excited and would not stop talking. Whatever you talked about to the kids today, just keep doing it!"

We continued the conversation, letting the parents know what was discussed with the children, providing specific examples coupled with responses of their children. One man sitting toward the front looked unhappy. He had had his arms crossed from the very beginning. Toward the end, he raised his hand. When acknowledged, he turned his body and addressed the principal who was sitting in the audience. "So, I understand that you were not interested in giving us, as parents, the ability to make a decision about whether or not our kids heard from these speakers. BUT, I also understand that you gave the *teachers* the choice of having Aidan speak to the class about gender differences or they could do it themselves. My youngest child did *not* get to hear this powerful message today because his teacher opted out. If the teachers are just beginning to learn about this subject, how are they going to do it justice? Why did you make that choice? I need my son to hear this!"

His statement was not what I had expected to hear, nor had the principal—now feeling a bit on the hot seat—expected it either. Other parents also pushed against the principal's decision, and she finally committed to bringing me back to talk to the remaining classrooms.

Tips and Tools to Use When Engaging with Parents

- Respect the parent community by proactively engaging them. They deserve an opportunity to learn.
- Use the AEIOU framework so that parents better understand the age-appropriate ways in which their children are being engaged.
- Be sure to delineate how this framework is simplified for the youngest of students as the emphasis is on the E-I-U concepts.
- A and O discussions are appropriate for older children as typically indicated in a district's health education curriculum.
- Stay away from jargon. When engaging in conversations with parents, there is no need to use unfamiliar language—especially if it causes confusion. Conversations and terms can and will evolve over time. You may hinder forward progression simply because many are not yet familiar with recent gender terminology.

- Share with parents the fact that, for many, many generations, students at every grade level have engaged in classroom discussions about changing gender expectations and roles. This is not new. Provide examples.
- When discussing the students' diversity of experience when it comes to family composition, remind parents that these classroom discussions do not delve into the sexual practices of *any* families.
- Let parents know that the values the school embraces are exactly why conversations about gender-diverse students can and should occur. Celebrating the diversity of student identities, experiences, and families is what provides those students with a powerful, respectful learning environment.

COMMIT TO ONGOING CONVERSATIONS

It takes courage to engage others in conversations about gender-diverse students. We did not see these conversations modeled for us when we were children because we didn't understand that trans and nonbinary children existed. We are now tasked with addressing this new understanding. The more volatile and divisive school experiences—and ones that often show up in the evening news—have been ones where a school delayed too long or tried to sidestep it altogether. Movement is the key to more successful outcomes.

Once these conversations start, then everyone wants to be part of it, regardless of their perspective. Even if tensions are present, those tensions represent possibilities. Those who take the time to ground the conversations at the outset will not regret it. Express the shared values of all concerned. Acknowledge the newness of the topic and the discomfort that can come with it. Expect respectful and civil engagement from all. Make the statement that safety and inclusion for all students is the top priority—and that this is a goal shared by all. Even questions or comments that feel combative are sometimes ones that undoubtedly took courage to share. It is easy for people to feel frustrated if they do not feel heard. Voices rise and listening stops. Do not hesitate to validate and express gratitude for the people who showed courage. When someone expresses vulnerability that, too, shows courage.

In one of my parent trainings, a nervous parent expressed how scared she was to talk about her concerns for fear of being called a bigot. Another parent, one who has a trans child, turned to her and gently said, "We both want the same thing for our children. We want them to feel safe and included and supported." Each of them nodded, recognizing their common ground.

As most school administrators know, this is not a "one and done" discussion. Students advance through the grades and move on, parents are actively engaged or minimally so, school staff comes and goes, and school board members change. As our societal understanding increases over time know that conversations about gender inclusivity will be ongoing. Commit to these conversations. Your own ability to lead them will improve and everyone's learning will deepen.

NOTES

1. "National Transgender Discrimination Survey: Full Report," National Center for Transgender Equality (January 21, 2015), https://transequality.org/issues/resources/national-transgender-discrimination-survey-full-report.
2. For a discussion of inviting difficult conversations, see Melinda M. Mangin, *Transgender Students in Elementary School: Creating an Affirming and Inclusive School Culture*, Youth Development and Education (Cambridge, MA: Harvard Education Press, 2020).
3. Laura Erickson-Schroth and Laura A. Jacobs, *"You're in the Wrong Bathroom!" And 20 Other Myths and Misconceptions about Transgender and Gender-Nonconforming People* (Boston: Beacon Press, 2017), 117–122.

4. "'Bathroom Bill' Legislative Tracking," https://www.ncsl.org/research/education/-bathroom-bill-legislative-tracking635951130.aspx.
5. Kathleen E. Rands, "Considering Transgender People in Education: A Gender-Complex Approach," *Journal of Teacher Education* 60, no. 4 (September 1, 2009): 419–431, https://doi.org/10.1177/0022487109341475.
6. C. E. Roselli, "Neurobiology of Gender Identity and Sexual Orientation," *Journal of Neuroendocrinology* 30, no. 7 (July 2018): 1–8, https://doi.org/10.1111/jne.12562.

10

Creating an Optimal School Environment

Educators

Knowledge emerges only through invention and re-invention, through the restless, impatient, continuing, hopeful inquiry human beings pursue in the world, with the world, and with each other.

Paulo Freire

After more than fifteen years of gender-inclusion work within schools—regardless of the school location, size of the community, or particular political leaning—always present is the element of love and care they show their students. Every school wants its students to succeed, and they want them to be safe. This may seem like an obvious statement, but these qualities are worth emphasizing. This shared sense of purpose is the key to open dialogue, thoughtful solutions, and forward movement. This shared understanding reminds us that there is no "us" versus "them," only a "we."

Efforts toward gender inclusion can feel weighty, so much so that some people question the wisdom of dedicating valuable time and resources when the benefit seems to extend to only a select few gender-diverse students. This misperception subsides as educators understand more clearly the benefits to all students. The recipe for successful inclusion starts with a few basic ingredients: a measure of proactivity, equal doses of resolve and respect, and a generous portion of openheartedness.

Imagine it's 1980. Someone hands you a smartphone and asks you to look up a restaurant's phone number. But you've only ever had experience with using a phone book's yellow pages. It's not that you are not capable. It's just that you've been handed a new tool with which you are unfamiliar. How are we to understand the best ways to include trans children within our schools when so few of us have a baseline understanding of the issues at hand much less seen them in action? We can certainly air our fears, but who is there to knowledgeably address them?[1] If a parent asks, "What happens if . . . ," our dearth of experience may inspire nothing but hands in the air or a shrug of the shoulders.

Establishing foundational elements such as district policies that address gender inclusion is a start. It can provide a spark for a district's forward motion. Yet, by itself, a policy does not propel motion on the ground. Considering how to implement the day-to-day application of that policy within schools suggests the old adage that *the devil is in the details.* If no one is able to adequately address the *what-if* scenarios that people express, it only heightens the sense of apprehension and hesitancy of those articulating them. That lack of confidence and understanding is what can move a school community *away* from the sense of trust they have placed in their educators, leadership, and the educational system at large. Suddenly, the safe and supportive learning environment, and the trust people place in it when they send their children to school, feel in jeopardy. School can feel unpredictable and dangerous.[2]

A COMMITMENT TO LEARNING

Educators understand that the acquisition of knowledge is an ongoing process—for themselves and for their students. What students learn in a high school physics class today, for example, differs from the content delivered by their teachers just a decade or two earlier. Today's students benefit from a current understanding of physics that would have been unimaginable to earlier generations. Nutritional wisdom provided in past versions of the "food pyramid" has shifted as we continue to learn more about disease, diet, and our bodies. Profound advances in computer technology are so rapid that it is quite challenging for anyone to keep up.

Our knowledge of physiology, neuroscience, and genetics expands in scope and complexity as well. Sex and gender are included in this widened view. Yet, despite scientific evidence to the contrary, we've desperately clung to a static notion of gender. As we begin to ponder gender expansiveness on a conceptual level, our societal conditioning hinders us from embracing this diverse complexity clearly evident in human beings all around us today.

How do we move forward? How do we address the shared hesitancy and apprehension?

We decide to step in. We can acknowledge where we are—largely unfamiliar territory—and make proactive steps to change that. The learning opportunity presented to us today is to imagine and then create that environment. The good news is that we do know considerably more than we did just a short decade or two ago. What we once could not imagine—transgender inclusion in schools—is already in motion. Trans and nonbinary children *are* in our schools and teachers *are* successfully addressing their needs. Parents are recognizing the importance of supporting their child's gender identity. Health professionals are better understanding of what constitutes affirming care. Children are learning to allow each other to be themselves rather than enforcing gender restrictions upon each other.[3]

THE UNFAMILIAR—AND FAMILIAR—LANDSCAPE

As today's schools step into greater gender inclusion, it can be helpful to look at *what is and what isn't new*. It's a lot easier, even relieving, to have a familiar foundation upon which to start. A few core fundamentals now understood and embraced by the majority of school communities include:

- Acceptance: We understand that children thrive when they feel accepted, valued, and included.

- Opportunity: We know that education is a critical component in creating more pathways to life possibilities.
- Resiliency: We encourage flexibility in the face of difficulties. We hope to foster a sense of personal confidence and a sense of value and belonging in society.
- Diversity: We value the diverse perspectives, identities, and experiences of every student.

If those core objectives serve as a launching place for gender inclusivity, then what is the *less familiar* terrain?

- Language: The rapidly growing lexicon of unfamiliar terms like *cisgender*, *nonbinary*, *agender*, and *intersex*, as well as expectations with respect to pronouns, names, and other gender-affirming changes for students.
- The current shift in our understanding of trans youth: A research-driven recognition by our health professions that supporting gender-diverse children provides them with better life outcomes.
- Societal acceptance: Addressing cognitive dissonance—and any associated discomfort—that we experience as a result of creating more gender-expansive environments in schools.
- Tools: Straightforward ways to speak to children about gender, ways to provide deeper learning for educators and parents, and gender-inclusive modifications to systems and practices.

The key to our successful inclusion of gender-diverse children is recognizing that there is a genuine, identifiable, and urgent need for it. The visible presence of trans children in today's schools is still a relatively new phenomenon. These children have always existed, yet their identities were largely ignored, dismissed, ridiculed, or punished. In the past, they learned to hide. That is changing. How might a school or district welcome them? Where do we start?[4]

We need to address the needs of those within the school environment—teachers, administrators, and so many other employees and volunteers—as well as the needs of students and parents. The former are the adults tasked with facilitating a student's schooling journey. These individuals need the foundational infrastructure and systemic support to be able to do so. This chapter will delve further into the needs of educators and the systemic elements within schools. In the next chapter, the focus will be on the needs of students and parents.

INCREASING A DISTRICT'S ABILITY TO SERVE ITS STUDENTS

When it comes to identifying the needed steps to create a gender-inclusive school environment, the first particulars that come to mind for many people include topics like pronouns, bathrooms, and locker rooms. These, however, are just details that point to a bigger picture. These particulars may start a conversation but, by themselves, are not sufficient to address the scope of change that is needed.

If, for example, someone was to say, "I'm thinking of having a baby. Tell me what I need to know to take care of a baby." Would you, as someone who raised three children, launch into a discussion about diaper changes, feeding, and sleep routines? Possibly. Would that prepare someone for the ongoing rigors of parenting? Probably not. You may want to better prepare someone for the reality of not only "having a baby," but raising a child to maturity. The guidance you might then want to offer could include mention of financial preparations, identifying a personal support network, having an accommodating work environment, and childcare. You might also recommend the importance of having advanced discussions with a co-parent regarding parenting styles, approach to discipline, faith values, grandparent involvement, how to support a child's interests/activities, and the family's financial priorities.

Many families have shared the experience of approaching their child's school principal to discuss the recent gender disclosure of their child and anticipated next steps, only to be expected to educate the principal as to how to proceed. Most of these caregivers have little or no idea how to respond. They are focused on getting through the early days of their own adjustment and learning. They might be able to discuss the pronoun, bathroom, and name changes, but not much beyond that. In the same way that changing and feeding a baby gets a parent started on their parenting journey, the name/pronoun/bathroom requests are only the start of the child's optimal schooling experience.

This chapter will cover some of the foundational elements needed to optimize school environments for the long term. Fortunately, the fundamentals set forth in this chapter are not the result of a "best-guess" approach. Rather, they are the articulation of successful steps already proven to facilitate gender-inclusive environments within schools across the country.

THE ROLE OF LEADERSHIP

While the impetus for discussing gender diversity may be the presence of a single trans student, it should instead be viewed as a timely opportunity to address the needs of the school or district as a whole. A proactive assessment will pay off in the long run.

Often those with direct student engagement—teachers or counselors—are the first to become aware of the presence of gender-diverse students. They will surely turn to those in leadership for support and guidance. A counselor who has recently had a student confide in them, or a teacher who has been asked to switch a student's name and pronoun, needs unequivocal support from leadership to do their job effectively. If those in leadership can confidently articulate how the support of *all* students, regardless of gender status, is an integral part of the core values of any school, they then provide teachers with the supportive foundation needed for them to get back to what they love most—teaching.

The role of school leadership is not just one of authority, it is one of courage and collaboration.[5] At this pivotal moment in history, courageous and collaborative leadership is needed to create gender-inclusive schools. To get started, there are three steps. Addressing these early steps is not a small task, but the long-term benefits will far outweigh the early effort:

1. Establish expectations.
2. Recognize your stakeholders.
3. Incorporate foundational elements.

There is more to this than might first come to mind. Let's get started.

Establish Expectations

OVERCOME THE INTIMIDATION FACTOR

It should not be surprising that many educators feel apprehensive about delving into discussions of gender identity differences. Much of this book is dedicated to addressing that apprehension. We are pioneering an expanded way of considering gender that acknowledges a child's gender identity as the focal aspect of self rather than defaulting to presumptions based on their genital configuration. This new perspective may be unsettling to many people.

After all, how many of us learned about trans lives during our own upbringing? How many principals would have, during their academic career, engaged in courses discussing gender identity differences in children? None. Such content is pretty scarce even today. Curriculum content is becoming more available, but educators need support and guidance now.

We have found our way through unsettling situations and societal shifts that inspire upheaval. Administrative leaders at schools have the intimidating job of leading their schools through these changing times. Yet we can take comfort in knowing that, while we as adults make our way through the complex conversations, children are very capable of embracing their transgender peers, really taking things in stride if we let them.

We can look to historical precedents for guidance. Comic strip author, Charles Schulz, for example, took a simple, yet significant step in 1968 toward increasing the media representation of people of color by introducing Franklin, an African American character, into his nationally syndicated comic strip, *Peanuts*. In the immediate years that followed, two popular children's television shows, *Sesame Street* and *Mister Rogers' Neighborhood*, incorporated broader diversity by introducing topics that also touched on racism as well as neurodiversity, physical ability, death, illness, family composition, incarceration, and other socially relevant issues.

While these were considered to be controversial moves during the volatility surrounding the US civil rights and disability rights movements, what children saw were simply media characters that better reflected themselves, and the real-life neighborhoods and schools in which they lived.[6] Today's students already attend schools with trans and nonbinary students. If given the opportunity, they will readily understand and accept the expansiveness of the human experience that surrounds them.

NAME WITHHELD

I am a superintendent in a rural school district in a politically conservative region of the country. I've worked in conservative school communities for much of my career, including nine years in one of the Bible belt states. I know that the educators I've worked with over the years care about their students—all of them, including the transgender ones. Yet, the political climate is different and, as a result, knowing how to provide the students the support they need can be more complicated. Aidan came to lead an all-staff training about supporting transgender students and, I'll admit, I was a little nervous about how the training would land. The content itself can inspire some contention so the delivery of that content would be hugely important. We had recently had a trainer, presenting on a different topic, who had come in from the city. Within the first few minutes of her presentation, I watched as her finger-wagging approach caused the entire audience to shut down. Her message, important as it was, was lost on them.

The thing I appreciated about Aidan was how he was able to navigate questions and concerns in a direct but non-threatening way. He was able to anticipate people's concerns and questions, and he didn't shut them down for not fully understanding what it meant for students to be transgender or for not knowing how to support them. I paid close attention to the reactions of the staff during the training and, wow, were they engaged! Afterward, many let me know how much they had learned and how much they appreciated the open, nonjudgmental delivery. Aidan did not make the training political, and for my staff, that made all the difference. He helped everyone see transgender children as children, not some abstract, distant political agenda, but children within our own community who are in need of our support. Of course, I believe all people in education understand and can relate to the concept of children in need of additional support at a broader level. Our conversation was grounded in this understanding, which resulted in a safe space for people to ask questions and express concerns, both of which are truly important elements for tougher conversations to succeed. I feel that our staff grew stronger because of Aidan's informative, non-partisan approach and our district, especially our students, are all the better for it.

Name withheld

I've found that, when adults choose to move forward, despite unease with this unfamiliar topic, they find that children can easily keep up, and even quickly surpass them. The children do it without experiencing the distress of their adult counterparts. One rewarding part of my work with schools is witnessing the delight *and* relief of teachers as they witness the *actual* responses of their students rather than the ones they *anticipated*.

DON'T ABDICATE POWER

Perhaps all of us can remember a student whose personality was deeply influential on the entire student body. Maybe that was a cheerleader, star athlete, or child of a high-profile community member. The response of any one of these influential students matters. What follows is the experience of one school that let it matter too much:

> A newly disclosed trans student had decided to begin her social transition over the approaching winter holiday break. The faculty and staff at this academically rigorous private school felt unprepared and brought me in to consult. Toward the end of our time together, a teacher raised her hand. "We have one BMOC [big man on campus] who has a lot of influence over the rest of the students. I'm really concerned about the trans student coming back to school as a girl in a few weeks. This guy is really homophobic and I'm just afraid the shit's gonna hit the fan!"
>
> The room of close to one hundred educators, staff, and leadership vigorously nodded their heads in agreement. I asked, "Okay, let's explore this. Tell me, in the past, when this student made homophobic comments, what did you say to him?" I was surprised at the collective silence. I gently repeated the question. Still, no response. I shifted the conversation to one where we could discuss the intimidating prospect of confronting a popular and/or dominant student's disrespectful behavior.

This was a perfect opportunity to help the faculty recognize two things. One, I wanted them to understand that any engagement with the student need not be *directly* couched in the context of homophobia and transphobia, especially if they did not yet feel confident to do so. A later conversation revealed that the administration felt intimidated to address the student's homophobic behavior because they worried it would be construed as taking a "pro-gay" stance. The reality is that they can, and should, immediately take a stance against *any* disrespectful and disparaging behavior toward anyone.

Secondly, I wanted these educators to recognize that, by their inaction, not only were they giving implicit approval to that student's homophobic comments, but they were giving up their own power as adults with authority. The impact of a single student's anticipated response had immobilized all of them. Their inaction would ensure that the damaging behavior would continue, and the climate of fear remain unchecked. If the educators felt afraid to intervene, imagine the fear of the students. Remaining silent also means that the teachers would continue to abdicate their responsibility to create a safe and inclusive environment for every student.

If we consider the following quote, we can also recognize the opportunity that educators have to infuse gender equilibrium into the school environment. With a figurative sweep of the arm, educators can exercise their authority to describe a world that *already* exists, one replete with gender-diverse children:

> When someone with the authority of a teacher describes the world and you are not in it, there is a moment of psychic disequilibrium, as if you looked into a mirror and saw nothing. (Adrienne Rich)

RESIST THE TEMPTATION TO LEAN ON A FAMILY FOR GUIDANCE
It bears repeating. A caregiver of a trans or nonbinary child can be helpful when it comes to the specific needs of their child but should not be relied upon to guide the school through their responsibilities. It should not fall on the shoulders of parents or children to educate other caregivers, students, or teachers. If leadership does not set the expectations, they are deferring or avoiding the responsibilities that would otherwise fall to them. At one school, the teachers pressed their formerly hesitant principal for further training. He hadn't felt it was necessary because he had asked the parents (and they had agreed) to talk with the parent community directly. The clincher came for him when one of his teachers said, "We wouldn't expect a family from another *culture or religion* to come in every year and educate everyone. Why are we doing it in this situation? And, what happens when this trans student graduates? Will we be ready for the next one?"

No single caregiver, or student, will be able to (nor be expected to) shoulder the responsibility for guiding a school through the areas in need of change. Of course, a student or parent may have relevant input. That can and should be considered. However, the expertise needed for, and the attention dedicated to, important systemic changes must come from within the school and/or district.

LEARN THE LANGUAGE
The vernacular in use today to describe gender differences is exploding. And no wonder. If we consider that every person may have a unique gender identity, then the number of newly created terms to describe each person's identity could

theoretically number in the billions! No, you don't need to dive in to learn the 50+ gender terms that were offered up by Facebook in 2014. At a minimum, understanding the terms *gender identity* and *gender expression* is a must.

Students of any age will expect parents and educators to understand *nonbinary*, *transgender*, and *cisgender* (or *cis*, for short). Students will absolutely expect everyone to have a working knowledge of what it means to be *misgendered* (erring on pronouns). Often, older students will embrace additional terms to describe their gender, including terms such as *agender*, *demigender*, and *bi-gender*.

Children of all ages understand the concept of gender identity, even if they are unfamiliar with the term itself. They understand that gender can exist in the "heart" or "mind" and that one's gender on the inside may be different than what others perceive on the outside.

Gender expression is also a concept readily understood by children. Younger children engage in conversations about gender expression when speaking about the toys and games they play, the clothing they wear, or the length or style of their hair. As they mature, elementary-aged children can incorporate the term "gender expression" into their vocabulary. Children of all ages understand that gender expression and gender identity are distinct from the bodies we inhabit. Therefore, teachers can feel confident discussing gender differences with children of all ages. Having that confidence in place is the key to success.

School staff who familiarize themselves with the vocabulary that their students embrace will likely build more trusting and respectful relationships with those students. Even if the staff are unfamiliar with terms, knowing how to respectfully engage with a student is essential. At the very least, the responsibility of any educator is one of simply listening to each person as they share who they are. This straightforward listening approach to a person's gender descriptors is not a dismissal of the beautiful complexity of gender, and the language used to describe it. This simplicity is presented as a place from which educators can launch. Keep in mind that the evolution of the gender lexicon is rich, varied, and constantly evolving. By all means, dig in!

NO NEED TO DIAGNOSE

It is important to understand that creating a supportive school environment for a trans or nonbinary student is *not engaging in a gender identity assessment.* As counselors, teachers, and others support students in their gender exploration, they are not in the position of diagnosing gender dysphoria. They are simply taking identity-affirming steps so that students can feel more confident, included, and respected. There is no need for school professionals to ascertain a student's gender identity; they need only create an affirming environment for that student's pursuit of learning.

PRONOUNS

It is no wonder that there is so much resistance to considering a pronoun change for a child. We've only just begun to grasp the concept of gender identity. Honoring a child's request for a different pronoun, for many adults, can feel as if they are aiding a child in an imaginary reality or, at worst, assisting in an act of deception. Neither is true.

For a child, however, the correct pronoun can be a simple and straightforward validation of who they innately are. For children who strongly identify as either male or female, the pronoun that corresponds with that gender identity is the obvious one to use. When a child's expressed gender identity is less definitive, it can be harder to know which pronoun to use. The best place to start is to simply ask the child what pronouns do you want us to use? The answer you get might be "neither," "both," I don't care," or even "I'm just me!" More and more youth are opting for the singular pronoun, *they*. Occasionally, a student desires no pronouns at all, perhaps asking that only their name be used in place of a pronoun.

Not many adults are adept at switching pronouns quickly. It takes practice for a new pronoun to roll off the tongue with ease. Sometimes a person may temporarily avoid any pronoun usage until they feel they will be more proficient with the requested pronoun. This is reasonable, but only as a short, interim step.

Be assured that honoring a child's requested pronoun, in and of itself, will not change a child's gender—it is simply being respectful of what that child requests of you. If there is some uncertainty regarding a child's gender identity, the usage of a different pronoun allows that child to gather more information. It simply creates a little more breathing room for that child to explore their gender in a less restrictive and binary way.

IN THE TEACHERS' LOUNGE

In the classroom, a teacher will need to be diligent with students, and themselves, when a student requests a name or pronoun change. While it has been suggested that it takes approximately four weeks to create a new habit, learning a new pronoun for someone will take just as long as it takes. If you are newer to this practice, know that attention and diligence is required.

The temptation to let this diligence slide may show up when teachers are in the faculty lounge or other space where students are not present. It can be too easy to give in and slide into the very name/pronoun habit a teacher is trying to break simply because the lounge is a space where a teacher can temporarily step away from the attentiveness required in the classroom. Some teachers have shared that they inadvertently slide back into using the student's prior name and pronoun because they are tired. I encourage them to not give in to that temptation! It only prolongs the process. Better yet, view the continuous diligence as the quickest pathway to get to the other side where consistent name/pronoun usage becomes easy and rote.

Rather than just tough it out alone, I encourage teachers to support each other. For example, an educator could ask their peers for assistance:

> Hey all, I am working hard to get into a solid groove with my student's new name and pronoun. I need your support. It will help me a lot if you let me know if I goof it up. Also, I'll do the same for any of you. That way all of you, *and especially me*, can get there a lot sooner.

Someone may say that they just don't want to do that. Be gentle but persistent. It's not a matter of wanting or agreeing, it just comes down to respect for that student. And it comes down to the responsibility of our schools to provide a learning environment that is safe and respectful for that student. Why delay the process?

SUPPORT EACH OTHER

Another way to support fellow teachers is to be observant of distress a person might be experiencing. Distress can come in many forms. A staff member could be angry or grumbling about the topic or a specific student. *I'm not calling him that! It's just pandering to him.* It may not be obvious that a coworker is challenged but you may hear words of anger, flippancy, ridicule, embarrassment, or other display of discomfort. Some are simply quiet if the subject comes up, making it difficult to know what they are experiencing. If you notice any of these reactions, you could find a time to speak to them one-on-one. Let them know you would like to check in with them to see if they need additional support. Keep in mind that not everyone will be interested in talking. Nor will every teacher be up for engaging in a potentially contentious conversation. There is no obligation to do so. That said, if a teacher refuses to refer to the student with the desired name and pronoun (rather than just experiencing an initial struggle), that could be a situation to elevate to an administrator. The goal is not to have that teacher or staffer experience any disciplinary action, rather it is to facilitate getting them the support they need to move through their own conflicting feelings.

COMPARE NOTES: CLASSROOM CONVERSATIONS
Any teacher will have more confidence discussing familiar topics with students than those which are unfamiliar. Delving into newer territory means teachers can expect the unexpected.

There is no need to step into early conversations alone. Get together with other colleagues beforehand and brainstorm possible conversation scenarios. Will the students have familiarity with gender diversity? Will it be the first time discussing transgender people? Some students may express nonchalance, *Yeah, I get it. My cousin is nonbinary.* Others may be animated. *My mom is transgender!* Someone else could feel distress. *No, this is just wrong!*

How teachers respond is crucial to a successful dialogue. Possible responses might include:

- *Yeah, I get it. My cousin is nonbinary.* Can you tell us a little more about this? Nonbinary means a lot of things for different people. Has your cousin talked with you being nonbinary and what it means to them? What pronouns does your cousin use? What might others in the class want to add?
- *My mom is transgender!* Thank you for sharing that with us. You sound really proud of her. What are some of the things about her that you think are most special?
- *No, this is just wrong!* Just as a reminder, how an individual or group views themselves cannot be "right" or "wrong." How they see and define themselves is their truth. How do you think someone would feel—or might you feel—if someone said that who you are, what you feel, and what you experience was wrong? Does anyone in the class want to share how they might feel in such a situation? Has anyone experienced this before?

Reconvene with your fellow teachers and share those experiences. What worked well? What didn't? What was surprising, inspiring, or disappointing? It's very possible that these classroom discussions will be different than imagined but in what ways? Each educator's expectations going in will have been different as well. Swap stories, make notes. Sharing individual efforts further propels everyone's learning. This engagement allows teachers to support each other, trouble-shoot any sticking points, and build a new set of tools to add to their collection.

Students can be matter-of-fact but inquisitive about gender identity and gender expression differences. Learn from them. Explore their questions and be sure to challenge assumptions.

Conflicting perspectives can be acknowledged while simultaneously insisting on respectful engagement. Ridiculing or judgmental comments should not be tolerated. Successful dialogue does not include personal attacks that reference a person's physical attributes or limitations, culture or ethnicity, or lived experience.

Engaging students in a respectful dialogue, regardless of topic, fosters critical thinking. Do so with a high regard for the dignity of each person in the room. The classroom, as a microcosm of our broader society, is an ideal environment in which students are introduced to diverse people and experiences.

A teacher's work environment is one that includes diverse opinions, beliefs, and experiences. The crucial factor to navigating both classroom and workplace successfully is to recognize and balance one's responsibilities to self and to the group. Identify the core values shared by all as a launching place. Let those shared values serve as the foundation for all discussions moving forward. Students, past and present day, will often say that the most impactful teachers are the ones who celebrate learning, encourage reflection, and are ready to explore the unknown. Stepping into conversations about gender diversity provides an ideal platform for teachers to model these qualities.

Compare More Notes: Parent Conversations

Not only are student conversations new territory, so are any discussions that educators have with parents. Sharing these experiences with colleagues—and compiling them for use over time—will help any existing or future staffer increase their knowledge base. One example of this is as follows. A politically conservative district requested training for staff and administrators. The half-day trainings spanned two days to cover four separate groups of educators. One principal attended on the first day and opted to repeat the session on the second day. As the second session began, she shared this with her colleagues:

> I imagine all of you, like me, have been a little nervous about this training. I attended yesterday as well. I am so glad I did! I took a call from an upset parent just this morning. She said, "I heard about the transgender trainings our schools are doing and had to call. I sure hope this is *not* the direction *our* district plans to go!" If I had received that call before the training, I would not have known what to say at all. But, I just followed Aidan's recommendations. I thanked her for calling and said I was grateful that she had taken the time to do it. I told her that I imagined it was a hard call to make. I let her know that the questions she had were questions shared by the staff and that we all were feeling a lot more confident about how to move forward as a result of what we were learning. We talked about a few more things and then wrapped up the conversation. She told me she felt a lot better and that she appreciated the time I had taken to hear her out. That call would have gone so much differently if it had occurred just twenty-four hours earlier!

Recognize Your Stakeholders

If we recognize that every adult in the district may have influence within the school environment, then we can also see the importance of providing support for everyone involved. Every staff position represents a human in need of information and support. Parents and students are obvious examples of people with a vested interest but what about the librarian, the school nurse, or the cafeteria staff? The most effective path toward systems-wide gender inclusion requires a thoughtful, methodical degree of attention with each of these stakeholders in mind.

CONSIDER THE ENTIRE SCHOOL STAFF
The school or district employees who could benefit from a better understanding of the needs of gender-diverse children is a broader group than one might first imagine. Principals and teachers come to mind, of course, because of their daily

role in the lives of students, but the need extends far beyond them. A binary understanding of gender is entrenched in every aspect of the school system. Some of these ways are obvious, some more subtle, and some imperceptible. Yet, each employee position is an interdependent part of the school system that directly or indirectly touches the lives of students.

SUPERINTENDENTS, PRINCIPALS, AND DIRECTORS
Those in positions of leadership need to feel confident and knowledgeable regarding gender inclusivity. As administrators, they are accountable for ensuring that systems and processes are updated to address the needs of gender-diverse students. That accountability extends to advising and supporting teachers and staff and, finally, considering the needs of their students.

SCHOOL BOARD
School board members have a powerful role in district policy changes or additions yet access to professional development opportunities may be hard to come by. Board members are also in the unenviable position, as elected leaders, of making difficult decisions when there is volatility within the school community. It is important for board members to actively pursue their own learning as well as engage with district leadership as they address gender policy and inclusionary needs for the district.

OFFICE AND ADMINISTRATIVE STAFF
Some school employees have more administerial responsibilities such as registrars, human resources, administrative assistants, and others. From admitting a new student, receiving a name or gender marker change request, and managing transcripts or tracking attendance, there can be any number of mistakes that might lead to inadvertent disclosure of a student's gender identity or that would otherwise cause distressing, damaging, or confusing situations.

These staff members will need education and guidance not only with respect to a gender-diverse child's needs, but a systems assessment to address potentially problematic areas including student rosters, student ID cards, computer logins, parent communications, etc. This assessment and modification need to prioritize the privacy, safety, and gender-affirming needs of the student, first and foremost.

Using your child's chosen name and pronouns is an accepting behavior that helps protect against health risks and promotes well-being. Find information and resources at FAP's family website at https://lgbtqfamilyacceptance.org/.

TEACHERS, PARAEDUCATORS, AND BEYOND

The teachers in classrooms with students day-in and day-out are those with the most influence on classroom culture. Consistency from paraeducators and any parent volunteer presence is also necessary to sustain an optimal environment. These adults will set the tone for students by modeling the necessary gender-affirming actions: correct name usage, pronoun consistency, and respectful behavior. Professional development opportunities are needed to help address the how, what, and why of gender equity and inclusivity in the classroom.

Counselors are there to support a student's successful pathway through school. Therefore, a counselor will focus on that student's individual needs. Their need for heightened awareness and insight into the experiences of gender-diverse children will be significant. They will have a critical role as they consider how to directly support the student emotionally, assist in developing a student support plan, assist with plan implementation, and help troubleshoot any problems that arise.[7] A counselor has a critical role in helping navigate potentially delicate situations or relationships with caregivers, other teachers, and student conflicts.

Substitute teachers are often at the top of the list of when it comes to inadvertent missteps regarding trans and nonbinary youth. The number one factor? A classroom roster used for taking attendance that does *not* list a student's correct name. If a student's gender history is known, it can cause embarrassment and distress. For students whose gender history is private or largely unknown to others, calling out a student's former name can place their privacy in jeopardy as neither student nor substitute teacher know how to address the situation. The inadvertent disclosure can irrevocably and negatively alter that student's experience in school from that time onward.

Special education teachers can also benefit from additional support. When co-occurring variables such as physical- or neurodiverse differences are present in a student's experience, it can cause a special education teacher to wonder whether an expression of gender identity is valid or a result of confusion or temporary special interest. As a result, a teacher may attempt to dismiss or deny rather than affirm that identity. A gender-diverse identity can co-occur with other diagnoses like autism, ADHD, and others, but one is not the cause of the other. Nor should a teacher focus on one diagnosis over another. A better approach, regardless of whether there is certainty that a child is expressing a bona fide gender identity difference or not, is to take an affirming approach rather than one of invalidation or denial.

School psychologists, a critical resource to school because of their expertise in learning and mental health, are tasked with assisting in children's success—academically, socially, behaviorally, and emotionally. School psychologists differ from counselors in that they are a critical resource to special education teachers as information sources for individualized education programs, or IEPs. Because one of their primary responsibilities is to complete evaluations that qualify students for this special education support, the necessity for psychologists to correctly assess student needs is crucial. Psychologists will be significantly hindered in these efforts if they are unaware, overlook, or minimize the importance of the student's gender experience. They can even be stymied in their efforts by their own assessment tools that may not consider any gender identity factors.

Athletic directors, coaches, and physical education teachers work in some of the most gender-segregated arenas of all—student athletics. Sports and athletic participation have a long tradition of being separated by gender to optimize participation and competition. Addressing the inclusion of gender-diverse K–12 students in athletics is an active and fervent discussion in the news today. As the presence of visible trans and gender-diverse youth increases, so too do issues of inclusion, fairness, and participation. If gender inclusion policy exists within a school district, these employees are tasked with policy implementation. They also are in the position of fielding inquiries of varying intensity from the community. If no policy or guidance exists, then each coach or PE teacher may be left to fend for themselves with respect to eligibility and participation determinations.

Drama and music teachers regularly consider gender when making student participation decisions. Often these decisions are arbitrary and reflective of an individual teacher's bias, as when a band teacher decides that girls should play flute, violin, or the clarinet while boys are steered away from those instruments and toward the saxophone, drums, or trombone. Other teachers allow the student's interest in an instrument to be the determining factor. The same is true for a drama teacher who casts certain roles only to boys, others for girls only. That teacher may default to casting based on sex assigned at birth for a trans or nonbinary student, potentially placing them in a role that causes them discomfort, or even enough distress that they quit altogether. Inquiring, and then centering, any student's primary interest as much as possible will optimize their experience. Gender-diverse students are no exception.

Librarians often consider what books to order, which ones might be highlighted in a display, or what to recommend to a particular student. If the librarian relies on a gender normative approach, it could limit a student's access to books they might enjoy and from which they would benefit. Librarians can choose from an ever-expanding number of books that delve into the topics of gender identity and gender expression and that feature gender-diverse characters.[8] They may be in the unenviable position of experiencing community backlash for children's books deemed by some to be controversial or worse.

HEALTH AND SEX EDUCATION TEACHERS

As we delve into the topic of changing bodies, puberty, and relationships as children mature, these teachers will need guidance on how to clearly engage with students in a more gender-inclusive way. The approach to the health education curriculum, traditionally delineated by anatomical sex, can and should be expanded to better address the needs of gender-diverse students and their peers. It is equally important to discuss with all students the expansive nature of gender identity and how it interrelates with differing bodies, romantic and sexual relationships, and overall health.

Nurses and other medical providers in the position of completing sports physicals and addressing illnesses, injuries, or other medical situations are certainly in need of understanding the experiences of gender-diverse children. A clear understanding of the distinctions between a student's gender identity and their body is critical. Just as with any other school employee, they need to engage respectfully and appropriately with any student under their care. A misstep in the nurse's office can be all the more unfortunate because students may be in a position of increased distress and vulnerability.

OTHER STAFFERS IN THE DAILY PATH OF STUDENTS

Career counselors could find it challenging, at first, to offer career guidance to trans and nonbinary students. While gender equality efforts have furthered the access of woman in male-dominated professions, we know that gender bias—explicit and implicit—can still influence the direction of a counselor's advice. It is therefore not difficult to imagine that a guidance counselor could feel at a loss with what options to recommend believing that *any path* that a gender-diverse student pursues may be fraught with barriers. A counselor may default to recommending areas of study that they deem most *achievable* rather than areas of student interest and aptitude. Career counselors can benefit from broadening their conception of trans people as valuable employees within all professions. And, while barriers to career success may be plentiful, the student would be best served by receiving strong support and encouragement to pursue their areas of interest.

Speech pathologists can play an important role for a transitioning student who is hoping to better align their voice with their gender. A student may need vocal coaching or guidance as to how to achieve their desired vocal range.

A youth who gains more confidence with their voice is one that will more confidently engage in academics and other activities.

Language teachers are often challenged when it comes to gender inclusivity because certain languages—Spanish, for example—has gender-infused terms and structures that reflect the accompanying culture of the people who speak the language. Teachers often feel challenged to successfully maintain the integrity of that language, culture, and history while simultaneously working to be gender inclusive as well. On the other hand, an increasing number of people, especially younger generations, are changing the language expectations, replacing the masculine "o" and feminine "a" noun ending for with an "e" as in *Latines* (instead of Latinas or Latinos), or adopting the pronoun "elle" as the singular form of "they." In Spanish, as with English, language evolves to incorporate present-day efforts at gender inclusivity. Language teachers can find themselves in a challenging position as a result. An important first step is to ensure that educators and students are engaging with each in ways that honor every individual's gender identity.

Bus drivers, cafeteria, security, playground, and custodial staff have daily interactions with students and often will remember students from year to year. If they are not given an opportunity to learn district expectations or provided tools for addressing any situation or circumstance, then each person is left to manage on their own. The result is inconsistent, or even distressing outcomes for students who are reliant on the adults around them to maintain safe and supportive environments.

Crossing guards, parent chaperones, and other volunteers who monitor and support students in a variety of contexts throughout the day can often be overlooked when gender education is provided for others. This can be detrimental to the experiences of trans and gender-diverse children in ways that are often not anticipated. Some of these adults will make inadvertent mistakes. Others sometimes willfully disregard these needs. Regardless of intent, the impact can be devastating. This violation of a student's right to privacy can have disastrous results and radically alter the student's educational experience and safety.

Yearbook advisors need to be extra attentive to names, photos, and pronouns wherever applicable. **Choir, band, and dance instructors** should honor the identity of a student and set aside preconceived notions based on their sex assigned at birth, including any uniform or role expectations. **Drama teachers** need to be sensitive to gendered expectations and consider trans student for roles based on their interest and ability.

While not pursued by all districts, addressing the needs or concerns of **community members** *external* to the school community can be productive. This may include alumni families, faith communities, and any others with a vested interest in the future of their community. Further educational offerings may include school-supported events which are open to the public. This could include screenings of relevant films, such as the thought-provoking documentary focusing on one school district's journey to gender inclusion, *The Most Dangerous Year.*[9] The film's accompanying educational discussion guide could provide the structure for a post-film conversation. Or the district could offer regular learning sessions, even partnering with other organizations, that are designed to respectfully address some of the most commonly asked questions that arise.

When it comes down to it, every person who engages with students—directly or indirectly—will need to give attention to the needs of gender-diverse students. This may seem like a big "ask" but it is a necessary one. Just as the adjustment to a pronoun change first requires diligent attention before becoming second nature, the attention provided to each position and area of engagement will lessen as any needed changes are incorporated. The examination of each employee's responsibilities—and how our individual and systemic gender bias permeate those responsibilities—will better optimize the experiences of all youth, including those who are gender diverse. The end results? An environment where all are better equipped to maintain a consistent and identity-honoring environment.

Foundational Elements upon Which to Anchor Gender Inclusivity Work

LOOK TO THE SCHOOL'S MISSION STATEMENT

A school's mission statement (or a district's universally stated values) can provide the core grounding needed to ensure that everyone is on the same page. One district approached it this way. Equity, they agreed, was one of the district's values that applied to every student and their family. How then did equity apply when considering the student's right to engage fully in the school and school community, to experience and practice compassion in every relationship, and ultimately benefit from the commitment to fairness that ensures a level playing field for all? When examining this shared value, it was not a question of should equity be valued for some students but not for others. It was a matter of how equity applied and what needed to be done to accomplish it.

I engaged in my first school staff training in 2007. While this progressive K–8 school prided itself on its approach to diversity and equity, the staff were intimidated to broach the topic of gender-diverse people, especially with the younger grade levels. They were unsure of their own ability to discuss the topic of being transgender with children. It felt a bit taboo to them. They were even more apprehensive of their ability to address the fears that they anticipated parents would have. Yet, they courageously moved forward, holding tightly to their own mission to acquire "deep understanding through inquiry and discovery-based teaching."

Contextualizing this new learning within their own framework of courage, inquiry, and commitment to discovery is something they communicated to both their student and parent communities. It allowed them to take ownership of the learning and to invite everyone else along with them. This proved to be a successful approach. For three consecutive years, we engaged on this learning journey together until they were confident to move on independently. Not only did they feel confident to incorporate gender-expansive discussions at all grade levels, but they also felt assured in sharing their own learning with new families and new staff members. Years later, the school's mission remains unchanged. What did change was that they were able to establish a successful pathway for gender inclusion where none had previously existed.

When beginning an educational engagement with a school, it is very helpful to review with them their own mission statement. Each time, I am able to point to how the gender-inclusive work is already in alignment with the core values upon which the school was founded. Consider this mission statement of a faith-based high school:

We embrace that God may be found in all things, that each person is sacred and that we are created to serve others in community. Our mission is to form discerning, transformational leaders who are intellectually competent, spiritually alive, open to growth, loving, and committed to justice.

During the staff training, these educators expressed varying perspectives—some were enthusiastic, some were reticent, and many occupied a range in between—but *all* of them looked to their mission statement for guidance. Everyone could unequivocally accept the shared truth that, at their school, they would . . . *embrace that God may be found in all things, that each person is sacred.* This seemed to buoy everyone's spirits and they felt an energized confidence to move forward.

ADOPT A GENDER-INCLUSIVE POLICY

School districts need a gender-inclusive policy. It isn't enough to say, "Don't discriminate." Most of us were raised in a society that has no awareness of the gender diversity that exists throughout the world. The creation and implementation of a gender-inclusive policy encourages us to open our eyes to the fact that discrimination toward trans and gender-diverse people does exist. It requires us to see a reality that has been previously hidden or suppressed.

I believe that a school district that adopts gender-inclusive policies is one that is motivated by a recognition of disparity, takes pride in its proactive leadership, and that is driven by their compassion and love for all children.

MODEL POLICY AND GUIDELINES

In 2014, I worked with the Washington Office of Superintendent of Public Instruction (OSPI) to draft a gender-inclusive policy for the state's schools. It has undergone revision as time has passed and as learning deepens.[10] Policy serves as the foundational statement to guide districts.

Washington Office of Superintendent of
PUBLIC INSTRUCTION

Gender-Inclusive Schools
Policy: 3211
Section: 3000 Students

The board believes in fostering an educational environment that is safe and free of discrimination for all students, regardless of gender expression, gender identity, or sex. To that end, the board recognizes the importance of an inclusive approach toward transgender and gender-expansive students with regard to key terms, communication and the use of names and pronouns, student records, confidential health and education information, communication, restroom and locker room use and accessibility, sports and physical education, dress codes, and other school activities, in order to provide these students with an equal opportunity for learning and achievement.

This policy is a component of the district's responsibility to create and maintain a safe, civil, respectful, and inclusive learning community and will be implemented in conjunction with comprehensive training of staff and volunteers. Specific training requirements are included in the accompanying procedure. The superintendent will appoint a primary contact to receive copies of all formal and informal complaints and ensure policy implementation. The name and contact information for the compliance officer will be communicated throughout the district. The district compliance officer will participate in at least one mandatory training opportunity offered by OSPI.

This policy and its procedure will support that effort by facilitating district compliance with local, state, and federal laws concerning harassment, intimidation, bullying, and discrimination.

While policy serves to outline expectations, the associated guidelines (or implementation procedures) help spell it out in greater detail. GLSEN, a national student advocacy organization, drafts guidance for schools which includes terminology, definitions, the scope to which the policy applies, and expanded discussions addressing topics related to privacy, student records, access to facilities, and more. Policies and procedures regularly undergo revision to more accurately address the evolving needs of today's students. As we continue to consider the growing, visible presence of trans and gender-diverse youth, our need to examine and re-examine policies and practices will surely remain an ongoing endeavor.

GENDER DIVERSITY: STUDENT SUPPORT PLAN

There are different facets to consider when addressing a gender-diverse student's needs. Some can be anticipated. Others you will discover as you encounter each student's unique circumstances. While a generalized approach to a student's needs can provide a foundational start, it is important to understand that one approach does not fit all possible experiences. Adjustments can and should be made along the way.

There are several focal points to consider: one is to address the specific needs of the student, the second is the degree to which the parent/caregiver of the student is involved, and lastly, the readiness of the school faculty, staff, and administration to successfully include all gender-diverse students within the school community. Working collaboratively with the student (and any adult advocating on behalf of the student) to move through their established plan will ensure the highest likelihood of success for the student.

Unlike the student and/or parent—who are likely crafting a support plan for the first time—schools will have the benefit of advance preparation and experience to confidently support any gender-diverse child that comes to their attention. This support plan document will assist in the advance preparation and the achievement of optimal outcomes for all.

The support plan has a three-part process: assessment, discovery, and plan development. The student (and caregiver, if applicable) will work with the designated school personnel to move through these steps. The support plan process serves to inform the student of their rights and glean the student's specific needs. The student may identify one or more point people to whom they may turn if needed. It is possible that the support plan document may evolve over time as the student moves forward (see Appendix B: Student Support Plan).

Student Handbook

The student handbook is an important vehicle for students to discover their rights and responsibilities during their schooling career. Handbooks typically outline many key policies, processes, and a wealth of information for student success. It is logical that students (or their caregivers) will look to a student handbook for information or guidance regarding their gender pathways. The handbook is a powerful opportunity to concisely communicate the school's position regarding discrimination—including harassment, intimidation, or bullying—based on a student's gender identity and gender expression. It can also direct a student to additional resources and staff members that will provide further assistance.

Schools in Transition: A Guide for Supporting Transgender Students in K–12 Schools

Schools in Transition (SIT) is a sixty-two-page guide that highlights best practices while offering strategies for building upon and aligning them with each school's culture. Two excerpts are provided which address student records and information systems as well as an overview of how individualized learning plans might be used for gender-diverse students. The SIT guide is a great resource available in electronic format.[11]

UNINTENDED CONSEQUENCES

A family assumed that their eleven-year-old trans student's time spent at school was mostly trouble free. Yet, as the school year was progressing, they realized something was amiss. Their child, whose gender status was not known to the other students, was encountering a daily stressor. When any student's computer login is established, a gender-specific avatar was selected as well. This child was assigned a female-appearing avatar based on their sex assigned at birth (on their birth certificate) rather than a male-appearing avatar matching his gender identity. At every login, he was deeply fearful that students sitting in close proximity would see this and potentially mock him and/or that his gender history would be disclosed. This situation was hindering his academic progress because he was frequently avoiding the work he needed to do.

Schools In Transition
A Guide for Supporting Transgender Students in K-12 Schools

Washington Office of Superintendent of
PUBLIC INSTRUCTION

STUDENT RECORDS & STUDENT INFORMATION SYSTEMS

SIT: Chapter 4, pg. 21

The school's student information system typically uses the student's name and gender as reflected on their birth certificate. As a result, when a student transitions at school, there are a great many ways in which a student's incorrect name or sex assigned at birth may inadvertently appear on documents generated by those systems.

Processes like enrollment, taking attendance, assigning grades, and communicating with parents and caregivers can all easily compromise the student's privacy and undermine an otherwise supportive school environment. For example, a substitute teacher simply calling out names from the attendance sheet, which typically lists each student's legal name, can inadvertently disclose the student's transgender identity to their peers. Other typical stumbling points include after-school programs, school photos, outside professionals providing a service on campus, yearbooks, ID cards, posted lists, library cards, lunch cards, distribution of texts or other school supplies and standardized tests. Even in the most supportive of school settings, simple bureaucratic oversights can cause real trauma for a transgender student.

Although a schools' recordkeeping and reporting requirements are often seen as a barrier to preventing those oversights, many school districts have found solutions that allow them comply with those requirements while meeting their obligations to safeguard a transgender student's privacy and right to learn in a safe and supportive school environment. The following are some examples of those solutions. This is by no means an exhaustive list and the viability of these solutions in any school depends on a variety of factors, including each state's legal requirements for recordkeeping and student information systems. Examples of solutions include:

o   Maintain a copy of the student's birth certificate or other identity document that reflects the student's name and sex as assigned at birth under lock and key in the principal's office, while the student information system has the name and gender marker that correspond to the student's gender identity.

o   Allow the student to re-enroll in the school using a passport with the correct name and gender marker, or change the name and gender marker in the student information system to be consistent with the passport. If a student is a U.S. citizen and their family can afford the passport application fees, obtaining a passport that reflects the student's gender identity is usually easier than changing that information on their birth certificate.

o Use the student's chosen name and gender in the student information system, but switch it to the student's legal name and gender just before uploading the information to the state department of education's database. Schools that choose this approach pull that student's testing booklet before it is distributed and correct the name and gender marker on the label to ensure that the student's privacy and identity are respected.

o Create a uniform and public procedure at the district level that connects all electronic student databases and allows a student or their parent to fill out one form indicating the name and pronoun the student wishes to use. Some school districts have established such procedures to streamline the process and reduce the common bureaucratic barriers.

o Work with the student information system provider to develop a field or screen that would allow the district to maintain the student's legal and chosen name, but that would use the chosen name to populate attendance sheets, report cards, and other school-related documents.It is important to note that transgender youth can experience many obstacles to correcting their identity documents. From the high cost of obtaining a court-ordered name change to states requiring transition-related surgery before correcting the gender marker on a birth certificate, barriers prevent students—particularly those in earlier grades—from obtaining identity documents that reflect their true selves. Consequently, school and district personnel must develop policies and protocols for inputting the correct information into the student information system regardless of the student's legal name or gender marker.*"A school's recordkeeping and reporting requirements do not exempt it from its obligations to safeguard student privacy and create a safe and supportive environment. Those obligations co-exist and schools must find a way to harmonize them."*

Using the Gender-Diverse Youth Sport Inclusivity Toolkit

As the presence of gender-diverse students increases on gender-segregated athletic teams, in physical education classes, and other activities nationwide, continued efforts to better understand and implement inclusive practices are vital in creating an equitable playing field. This toolkit seeks to further these efforts toward the inclusion of transgender and nonbinary students in K–12 schools, by providing guidance and resources to assist administrators, educators, and coaches in providing an inclusive environment where all students are equitably welcomed. Included in this toolkit you will find up-to-date language, the applicability of federal law, definitions, policy, FAQs, current best practices, communication tips and strategies to optimize gender inclusion, guidance in nuanced scenarios, and more.

Developing an Individualized Education Plan (IEP) or 504 Plan

Schools In Transition
A Guide for Supporting Transgender Students in K-12 Schools

Developing an IEP or 504 Plan for a Transgender Student
SIT: Chapter 5, pg. 35

Special education laws create a mechanism for accommodating the needs of students who are experiencing difficulty in school. That difficulty does not have to be solely academic; it can include social and emotional well-being and development. Given the psychological distress that some transgender youth experience, these laws provide a potential tool for families and schools to address a transgender student's unique needs and create an environment

---

where the student can succeed. It is important to note that while transgender students may be eligible for special education because of their gender dysphoria, many transgender students will qualify because of the anxiety, depression and other forms of psychological distress caused by not having their gender identities affirmed in all aspects of their lives.

The Individuals with Disabilities Education Act (IDEA) and Section 504 of the Rehabilitation Act (Section 504) are the two main special education laws. IDEA governs the creation and implementation of Individualized Education Plans (IEPs), and Section 504 establishes the rules for Section 504 Plans. Although these laws serve similar purposes, the level of supports, services and accommodations a school must provide to meet its legal obligations under IDEA tend to be higher, which translates into more legal protections for students than under Section 504. A student also must be experiencing more significant difficulties in school to qualify for an IEP.

Parents and schools often shy away from invoking special education laws because of misconceptions like the belief that a student with an IEP must be placed in separate, specialized classes. In fact, special education laws require that a student be placed in general education classes unless there is a compelling reason to place that student in a different educational setting. These laws are designed to counteract the effects of social, emotional, and academic difficulties that are hindering a student's progress. By providing supports, services and accommodations, special education laws expand transgender students' future opportunities and help them get back on the path to success.

Through a special education plan, schools can provide basic accommodations like use of the student's chosen name and access to the appropriate restrooms. The IEP or Section 504 Plan can also account for other needs like stress breaks throughout the school day to help reduce anxiety. Even when the school is fully supportive of a transgender student, having an IEP or Section 504 Plan in place will help ensure that the student receives a consistent level of support throughout any changes in school or district administration, even if the student moves to another school or district.

One potential drawback to creating an IEP or Section 504 Plan is that it creates another school record that could inadvertently disclose a student's transgender status, so as with any other educational records, parents and school officials must make sure it remains private. Another issue to consider is that some students feel stigmatized by the association with special education and by having a legally defined disability. Again, it is important to reiterate that although transgender students may be eligible under special education laws because of their gender dysphoria, they may also be eligible because of the anxiety, depression and other issues that may be caused by not having their gender identity affirmed. Whether the potential feeling of stigma outweighs the benefits of having the IEP or Section 504 Plan is a decision that the student, educators, parents, and caregivers should consider as a team, with the parents and student making the final decision.

"Special education laws are not a replacement for strong, explicit school policies that affirm transgender students, but provide the added services and supports some transgender students may need to learn and thrive."

Applying Federal Law

I've yet to find a school that has a mission statement that says, "We strive to do best by our students because the law makes us do so." Societies around the world embrace many shared values and manage to do so because we inherently understand the value of looking after each other toward our mutual benefit. Laws exist to address situations in which these values are disregarded. When working with schools, I discuss applicable state and federal law, but I am not interested in the law being the prime motivator for change, in essence forcing a grudging acceptance of gender-inclusionary practices. I much prefer seeing educators who are motivated to look after gender-diverse students because that is what first inspired them to enter into teaching—looking after students.

That said, the law matters. It provides us with greater clarity for a nascent and, at times, confusing landscape. How do legal protections against gender discrimination apply when we have to consider a more expansive understanding of the concept of gender? We can look to the US Supreme Court for an answer.

Federal Antidiscrimination Law

Does sex discrimination under Title IX apply to gender identity? The short answer is yes.

As discussed in a previous chapter, the US Supreme Court ruled, in 2020, on a landmark civil rights case, *Bostock v. Clayton*, in which the Court held that Title VII of the Civil Rights Act of 1964 protects employees against discrimination because they are transgender. The US Department of Justice: Civil Rights

Division then issued a clarifying memorandum in March 2021 regarding the application of Supreme Court case *Bostock v. Clayton County* to Title IX of the Education Amendments of 1972.

In part, it says that the "Administration's policy [is] that '[a]ll persons should receive equal treatment under the law, no matter their gender identity or sexual orientation.'" Citing the Supreme Court's holding in *Bostock* that the prohibition on discrimination "because of . . . sex" under Title VII of the Civil Rights Act of 1964, 42 U.S.C. § 2000e et seq. (Title VII), covers discrimination on the basis of gender identity and sexual orientation, the Executive Order explains that Bostock's reasoning applies with equal force to other laws that prohibit sex discrimination "so long as the laws do not contain sufficient indications to the contrary."

The Executive Order directs agencies to review other laws that prohibit sex discrimination, including Title IX, to determine whether they prohibit discrimination on the basis of gender identity and sexual orientation. We conclude that Title IX does: "After considering the text of Title IX, Supreme Court case law, and developing jurisprudence in this area, the Division has determined that the best reading of Title IX's prohibition on discrimination 'on the basis of sex' is that it includes discrimination on the basis of gender identity and sexual orientation."[12]

This memorandum is also consistent with the many federal courts, including the US Court of Appeals for the Ninth Circuit and US District Courts within that circuit, that have held Title IX and other federal laws prohibiting sex discrimination protect transgender people from discrimination. In several of those cases, federal courts safeguarded the right of transgender student-athletes to compete in sports consistent with their gender identity. Federal law would also prohibit other forms of discrimination including access to facilities, harassment, and use of correct names and pronouns.

Family Education Rights and Privacy Act

Another excellent resource is from Lambda Legal which discusses FERPA, or the Family Education Rights and Privacy Act. The federal law exists to protect the privacy of students' educational records and is valuable information for any parent or caregiver of a trans or gender-diverse child. Schools can benefit greatly by understanding the law's applicability to the experiences of their gender-diverse students.

A Transgender Advocate's Guide to Updating and Amending School Records

Reprinted from Lambda Legal, https://www.lambdalegal.org/know-your-rights/article/youth-ferpa-faq

The Family Educational Rights and Privacy Act (FERPA) (20 U.S.C. § 1232g; 34 C.F.R. §§ 99.00 et seq.) is a federal law that protects the privacy of student educational records. FERPA gives parents certain rights with respect to their children's educational records. These rights transfer to the student when he or she reaches the age of 18 or attends a school beyond the high school level. (34 C.F.R. § 99.4–5).

Under FERPA, students, current or former, have a right to seek to amend their school records if said records are "**inaccurate, misleading, or in violation of the student's rights of privacy.**" (34 C.F.R. § 99.7(a)(2)(ii)). Transgender students wishing to change their name and gender marker on their educational records can seek such an amendment under this federal law.

What are my rights under FERPA?

Under federal law, you (or your parents or guardians if you are under 18) have the right to request that your school change your name and gender marker on your records if you feel they are incorrect, misleading, or violate your privacy. (34 C.F.R. § 99.7(a)(2)(ii)).

FERPA states that no educational institution shall be granted funding if it does not provide parents and/or students a hearing process through which they can challenge the content of school records, insure that the records are not inaccurate, misleading or otherwise in violation of the privacy or other rights of students, and receive an opportunity for the correction or deletion of any such inaccurate, misleading, or otherwise inappropriate data contained therein. (34 C.F.R. §§ 99.7(a)(2)(ii), 99.21).

Can I request this change if I'm under 18?

If you are under 18, your parent or legal guardian must be the one to make the request. That right transfers to you once you turn 18, or if and when you enter a postsecondary educational institution (higher than high-school level). (34 C.F.R. § 99.4-5).

Can I request this change if I've already graduated?

Yes. Once you are over 18 or enrolled in a postsecondary educational institution, you have the right to request a change to your records. (34 C.F.R. § 99.7(2)(ii)). Many transgender students wish to amend their secondary educational records after graduation to ensure that anyone who requests those records (for example, college admissions offices or potential employers) see only the correct name and gender marker on their transcript.

How are my records inaccurate or misleading?

Federal policies and regulations make it possible to change your name and gender marker on federal identity documents such as U.S. passports, U.S. consular birth certificates, Veteran's Health Administration cards, and Social Security Administration records. Additionally, most states allow amendments or corrections to gender markers on driver's licenses, state IDs, and birth certificates. When a transgender person completes the legal requirements to change identity documents to reflect who they are on official state and federal government documents, it can be misleading for a school to maintain the former records.

How does refusing to change my records violate my privacy?

You have the right to keep your transgender status private. But by keeping your former name and gender marker on your educational records, your school is essentially outing you to anyone who looks at them. As the Court of Appeals for the Second Circuit has stated, it is "beyond a doubt" that transgender status is "excruciatingly private and intimate" for those who wish to keep it private. *Powell v. Schriver*, 175 F.3d 107, 111 (2d Cir. 1999).

Why should schools change a transgender student's records?

As stated above, the legislature's intent in passing FERPA was to protect students' privacy rights. The guarantee of FERPA is to give students an opportunity to amend educational records that contain information that is misleading, inaccurate, or violates those privacy rights. If an institution refuses to comply with FERPA's mandates, it runs the risk of having its education-related federal funding withheld or terminated. When a school refuses to amend transgender students' records, it risks having its federal funding withdrawn, because it is willfully leaving misleading, inaccurate, and privacy-violating information in those documents.

Beyond FERPA, there are practical and ethical reasons why schools should duly amend transgender students' records. By not correcting a student's gender marker on their school records, the school is essentially disclosing that student's transgender status to anyone who sees their records. This has the potential to place the student in harm's way; exposure of transgender status is directly linked to high rates of discrimination, harassment, and even violence. These risks are present in nearly every aspect of life as an out transgender or gender non-conforming person. Of the 6,450 transgender and gender-nonconforming respondents to the 2011 National Transgender Discrimination Survey (NTDS):

- 90% reported experiencing harassment, mistreatment or discrimination on the job or taking actions like hiding their transgender status to avoid it.
- 47% said they had experienced an adverse job outcome, such as being fired, not being hired, or being denied a promotion because of their status as transgender or gender non-conforming.
- 53% reported being verbally harassed or disrespected in a place of public accommodation.
- 19% reported having been refused a home or apartment, and 11% reported being evicted, because of their status as transgender or gender non-conforming.
- 22% of respondents who had interacted with police reported police harassment.
- 19% of respondents reported being refused medical care due to their transgender or gender non-conforming status.

Only a transgender person should be able to decide when, if at all, to disclose their transgender status.

The refusal to correct a transgender student's school records can also be emotionally harmful. When an organization or agency is unwilling to issue identification that reflects a person's gender identity, it is making a value judgment on the legitimacy of that gender identity. There is no reason for a transgender student to suffer such indignity.

What does FERPA require my school to do?

If you wish simply to review your educational records, FERPA requires that schools honor a request to review those records within 45 days of receiving the request. (34 C.F.R. § 99.10(b)). Some states have laws similar to FERPA that require schools to provide access within a shorter period of time. You should consult a local attorney to find out how long schools have to respond in your state.

FERPA requires that schools provide parents with an opportunity to inspect and review educational records, but not to receive copies, except in limited circumstances. (34 C.F.R. § 99.10(d)). FERPA also requires your school to give you a formal hearing regarding a requested amendment should you request such a hearing. (34 C.F.R. § 99.20(c)).

How do I exercise my rights under FERPA?

If you have a trusted faculty member or administrator, it may be best to approach them first with this request. You may want to bring some helpful materials, including publications from Lambda Legal's Transgender Rights Toolkit, in order to help your school understand how important it is to be able to update your educational records.

Some school districts have been very open to assisting transgender students in updating their records. Other schools may be less familiar with transgender issues, and may need extra support in updating policies and procedures to support transgender students and be in line with best practices. The Gay, Lesbian & Straight Education Network (GLSEN) has drafted a great model policy for school districts to follow, and both Connecticut and Massachusetts have issued excellent guidelines on how schools should comply with nondiscrimination laws. If an informal approach is unsuccessful, we recommend sending your school administrators a letter like this one, which outlines the legal and practical reasons why your school should amend your educational documents.

Unfortunately, school districts are not always immediately cooperative, even when presented with compelling arguments. Often, we hear a school district say "We can't do that" or, in the same vein, "Our lawyer says we can't do that." If this is your school district's response, remember: There are no laws preventing your school district from making this change. The school district may have an established policy of not making name or gender marker changes, but remember that FERPA requires a school district to allow students to seek to amend misleading or inaccurate information on their educational documents. A transgender student's former name and gender marker inaccurately reflect that student's gender, and could be misleading to anyone likely to see those records. Thus, any policy that prohibits a school from changing a student's name or gender marker would be in direct conflict with FERPA.

What is the procedure for a FERPA hearing?

After you request a formal hearing, a third party who does not have a direct interest in the outcome of the hearing must conduct the hearing within a reasonable time; you will be notified of the time, date, and place. (34 C.F.R. § 99.22(a-b)). At the hearing, you have the ability to present evidence to prove your records are incorrect or misleading. (34 C.F.R. § 99.22(d)). The decision must be based solely on the evidence presented, must be in writing, and must include a summary of the evidence and the reasons for the decision. (34 C.F.R. § 99.22(e)).

If your hearing is successful, the school district will amend your records accordingly and notify you that the change has taken place in writing. (34 C.F.R. § 99.21(b)(1)).

What happens if my hearing is unsuccessful?

If your hearing is unsuccessful, you have the right to place a statement in your records commenting on the contested information, which your school must add to your records and disclose alongside pertinent parts of your record to any interested parties. (34 C.F.R. § 99.21(b)(2), (c)).

What if my school district doesn't reply at all?

According to FERPA, your school district "shall decide whether to amend the records as requested within a reasonable time" after they receive the request. (34 C.F.R. § 99.20(b)). But sometimes institutions do not understand their obligations fully and ignore FERPA requests for amendments and hearings.

If you believe your school is violating FERPA by not responding to your request, or for any other reason, you can file a written complaint with the Family Policy Compliance Office at the following address: Family Policy Compliance Office, U.S. Department of Education, 400 Maryland Ave., S.W., Washington, D.C., 20202. (34 C.F.R. § 99.63). Your complaint must contain "specific allegations of fact giving reasonable cause to believe that a violation" of FERPA has occurred and must be submitted within 180 days of the alleged violation. (34 C.F.R. § 99.64(a, c)). The Office will then investigate to find out if a violation has occurred. (34 C.F.R. § 99.64(b)). The violation does not have to be a part of the school's written policy, but can be based on their actions. (34 C.F.R. § 99.64).

For more information, contact Lambda Legal at 212-809-8585, 120 Wall Street, Suite 1900, New York, NY 10005-3904.

The efforts we make to provide greater equity and inclusion for gender-diverse students are directly related to the efforts we already make for any student. These efforts need to be more than "lip service." We need to examine the interrelatedness between individuals, systems, and everything in between. The path forward is a sustained commitment to action, ongoing reflection, and the incorporation of new learning.

In short, the recipe for success has a few core ingredients. Schools need to first make a commitment to these efforts in both principle and practice. Schools then need strong leadership to establish the expectations for all community stakeholders. These leaders can then build on the existing foundation elements already proven to achieve greater equity thereby meeting their legal obligations to do so.

This success will be evident in the students themselves. Students who are valued and included gain increased life opportunities, and for our gender-diverse students, these efforts may be truly life-saving.[13]

NOTES

1. Elizabethe Payne and Melissa Smith, "The Big Freak Out: Educator Fear in Response to the Presence of Transgender Elementary School Students," *Journal of Homosexuality* 61, no. 3 (March 4, 2014): 399–418, https://doi.org/10.1080/00918369.2013.842430.

2. Jack K. Day, Amaya Perez-Brumer, and Stephen T. Russell, "Safe Schools? Transgender Youth's School Experiences and Perceptions of School Climate," *Journal of Youth and Adolescence* 47, no. 8 (August 1, 2018): 1731–1742, https://doi.org/10.1007/s10964-018-0866-x.

3. Sonya Xinyue Xiao et al., "Characteristics of Preschool Gender Enforcers and Peers Who Associate with Them," *Sex Roles* 81, no. 11–12 (December 2019): 671–685, http://dx.doi.org/10.1007/s11199-019-01026-y.

4. Educators can find inspiration in this text, which covers both the theoretical and pragmatic ways of becoming more trans-inclusive: sj Miller, *Teaching, Affirming, and Recognizing Trans* and Gender Creative Youth: A Queer Literacy Framework*, Queer Studies and Education (New York: Palgrave Macmillan, 2019).

5. Melinda M. Mangin, "Transgender Students in Elementary Schools: How Supportive Principals Lead," *Educational Administration Quarterly* 56, no. 2 (April 1, 2020): 255–288, https://doi.org/10.1177/0013161X19843579.

6. The impact of these early television shows for children has been well-documented and they continue to receive cross-disciplinary attention: Shalom M. Fisch, Rosemarie T. Truglio, and Charlotte F. Cole, "The Impact of Sesame Street on Preschool Children: A Review and Synthesis of 30 Years' Research," *Media Psychology* 1, no. 2 (June 1, 1999): 165–190, https://doi.org/10.1207/s1532785xmep0102_5.

7. Roberto L. Abreu et al., "Supporting Transgender Students: School Counselors' Preparedness, Training Efforts, and Necessary Support," *Journal of LGBT Youth* 17, no. 1 (January 2020): 107–122, https://doi.org/10.1080/19361653.2019.1662755.

8. See the extensive Resources section of Laura Erickson-Schroth and Laura A. Jacobs, *"You're in the Wrong Bathroom!": And 20 Other Myths and Misconceptions about Transgender and Gender-Nonconforming People* (Boston: Beacon Press, 2017), 143–148.

9. "The Most Dangerous Year," *The Most Dangerous Year*, https://www.themostdangerousyear.com.

10. "Gender-Inclusive Schools," *OSPI*, https://www.k12.wa.us/policy-funding/equity-and-civil-rights/information-families-civil-rights-washington-schools/gender-inclusive-schools.

11. "Schools in Transition," American Civil Liberties Union, https://www.aclu.org/report/schools-transition.

12. "Application of *Bostock v. Clayton County* to Title IX of the Education Amendments of 1972," March 26, 2021, U.S. Department of Justice: Memorandum.

13. For a discussion of how to raise the bar on ally-ship for gender-diverse students, see Cal Horton, "Thriving or Surviving? Raising Our Ambition for Trans Children in Primary and Secondary Schools," *Frontiers in Sociology* 5 (2020), https://www.frontiersin.org/article/10.3389/fsoc.2020.00067.

11

Creating an Optimal School Environment

Students and Parents

As we start to really get to know others, as we begin to listen to each other's stories, things begin to change. We begin the movement from exclusion to inclusion, from

fear to trust, from closedness to openness, from judgment and prejudice to forgiveness and understanding. It is a movement of the heart.

Jean Vanier

The key to our successful inclusion of gender-diverse children is recognizing that there is a genuine, identifiable, and urgent need for it. How might a school or district welcome them? In the previous chapter, we considered some of the foundational elements that schools can have in place, such as the Gender Diversity Student Support Plan (see Appendix B), and we addressed the importance of preparing teachers, staff, and administrators to best understand their responsibilities. These individuals need the foundational infrastructure and systemic support to be able to do so.

We need to consider the important "stakeholders" not mentioned in the previous chapter: the gender-diverse student, the rest of the student body, and the parent community.

In my work with school districts, I have found that, as they make foundational, systemic progress to address the needs of educators, school districts are then in a more secure place to support the students and families within their schools as they move forward.

That all sounds reasonable, but the reality is a little different. Yet, we must start somewhere, and the arrival of a trans or nonbinary student is most frequently the impetus. This presents the administrative leadership with, ultimately, three concurrent paths to consider:

1. The immediate need: the support and inclusion of the gender-diverse student.
2. The ongoing support: the foundational changes within the school and district.
3. The middle ground: the needs of the student/parent communities.

The previous chapter addressed the foundational changes needed within the school community, while this chapter will focus on the needs of the trans students, their peers, and the parent community. Let's start with the obvious—the gender-diverse child.

SUPPORT YOUR GENDER-DIVERSE STUDENTS

Each individual school employee has the powerful, immediate ability to make a positive difference in a trans student's life. Many people can remember an exceptional teacher, one that went out of their way to offer an encouraging word or an unexpected gesture of support.

The stakes can be much higher for trans children, and a supportive environment can make all the difference. Step one for any school should be offering support to any trans or nonbinary student.

Caregivers often resist offering support for their child's gender identity, especially at first. While more families are understanding the importance of a supportive home environment, it can hardly be considered the norm. The number of parents who reject their children is still far too high.[1] The receptivity of an educator becomes all the more important and can make a life-changing difference. The positive impact of just one supportive adult on a child's life can be seen in this principal's story:

> I knew next to nothing about transgender people when, halfway through the year, a new seventeen-year-old student came to my school. As the principal of an alternative school, I often see students with extra challenges and this kid was no exception. He was bordering on failing and seemed a little on edge when I first met with him. With insistence, he told me his name, that he was transgender, and that his pronouns were he and him. He was so earnest. While being very inexperienced on gender issues, I just could not see a reason to ignore or reject his request. So, I made sure to refer to him in that way. With his permission, I instructed my staff to do the same so that everyone could honor his request. It was his senior year. He managed to graduate and then went on with his life. I didn't hear anything after that.
>
> Then, ten years later, I received a letter from him. He wanted me to know how much of a difference I *made*. He had all but given up on life when he came to my school, he said, and it was huge for him that I had honored his identity. He had expected yet one more rejection. In his letter, he excitedly shared with me his successful career path and that he was in a wonderful relationship. If I hadn't done what I did, he said, he wasn't sure he would even be alive. As a career educator, it's this kind of experience that makes it all worth it!

Some students will have no parental support for their gender identity. Others may have families with good intentions but who are still struggling. A teacher is someone with whom a student has daily contact. That teacher's welcoming smile, offer of congratulations, consistent pronoun usage, and/or a regular check-in to see how things are going can have a powerful and life-changing impact on that student's life.

It may be that not every school employee understands what it means to be trans or would choose to be supportive. At the very least, the straightforward acknowledgment and consistent use of a new pronoun or name is a reasonable expectation of every staff member. It is *not* reasonable under any circumstance to be dismissive, contemptuous, or ridiculing of a gender-diverse student. There should be zero tolerance for these kinds of harmful behaviors.

Gender Diversity Student Support Plan

What about the specific needs of the gender-diverse student? There are a range of considerations that require an attentive eye to each student's unique journey. School districts that use an individualized support plan find that the collaborative process between the school and student better informs both about factors that may otherwise be overlooked.

Crafting a support plan is a collaborative effort between students and other preselected adults (such as a school counselor or caregiver) to create a comprehensive, individualized approach. In general, areas in need of attention include, but are not limited to, the following:

- Grade level of student;
- Family considerations, including the level of support, siblings, parenting plans, etc.;
- Level of student interest in disclosure to others;
- Timeline for any transition-related steps;
- Access to appropriate facilities;
- Desired level of privacy in relation to disclosure, engagement with parents, etc.;
- Additional support regarding social, emotional, and specific learning needs;
- Engagement in gender-segregated activities;

- Any additional supports such as IEP or 504 plans; and
- Modifications of school records, rosters, logins, etc.

It is important to remember that working with a student on a gender support plan is not a gender identity assessment. The support plan process is not a diagnostic tool. It is not the school's responsibility to assess or determine whether a student is transgender or not. The school's responsibility is to help optimize the student's learning environment, and part of that is creating the space where they can feel most confident, included, and respected. Gender-affirming steps are an important part of accomplishing this.

Parents of gender-diverse students may look to a school counselor or teacher for additional resources. Having resources like the student support plan available for the family can be helpful but the learning curve is steep for parents. Pointing a caregiver to a direct support organization like TransFamilies.org could make a world of difference for them.

Advocate and Help Troubleshoot for a Trans Student

Resist the temptation to assume that, just because a student is trans, they know how to make their way through systems that are designed in a way that excludes them. They are finding their way through social environments where the presence of trans and nonbinary students has been largely or entirely invisible. Educators are key advocates for gender-diverse students. A teacher or principal is far more familiar with a school's inner workings. They will be better able to anticipate stumbling blocks the trans student may encounter and identify solutions. If a solution is not immediately evident, the educator can enlist the help of others to troubleshoot solutions.

SUPPORT THE FULL STUDENT BODY

Classroom Climate

Just as a superintendent sets the tone for the district, the principal does the same for teachers, and teachers—no surprise—set the tone for their students. The classroom is the teacher's domain, making it all the more important to set immediate expectations. A teacher's matter-of-fact engagement with a trans or nonbinary student models the expected behavior for all students. Using a new name or pronoun requested by a student is a great first step. Setting the same expectation for the students is an obvious next step. Consistency, kindness, and respect are a must.

When establishing gender-inclusive classrooms, there is no need to wait for a trans student to show up and get things started. In actuality, things will go better for everyone if that work is done in advance. Easy steps teachers can take to get started:

1. Begin the school year with a practice of sharing your name, the pronouns you use, and something that is important and/or something fun about yourself that you would like your students to know about you. This could be a hobby, a favorite book, something about your family, where you were born, your favorite food, or what kind of superhero you might want to be.

2. Invite students to do the same. Explain why you shared the pronoun (e.g., we don't always know someone's gender simply by looking at them). Note: Students can be encouraged to share their pronouns but need not be *required* to do so. to. A teacher could say, "Please share what you would like others to know about you. And please share your pronouns, *if you feel comfortable* sharing that with us." With this kind of introduction, a gender-diverse child who is ready to use a new pronoun will feel able to do so, and a gender-diverse child who doesn't feel ready to disclose won't feel pressured.

3. Take the opportunity to discuss gender norms. Share with students how and why these norms have changed over time. Provide examples such as this 2014 article "The Surprisingly Recent Time Period When Boys Wore Pink, Girls Wore Blue, and Both Wore Dresses" which explains how the marketing of children's clothing changed children's attire for no other reason than to increase sales for the manufacturers.[2]

4. Challenge the students to address gender stereotypes in the classroom when they see them. A teacher could acknowledge that many people, including themselves, perpetuate gender assumptions out of habit. The students could be encouraged to respectfully comment when those situations occur. If applicable, a teacher might then invite the students to research any back story that may be behind any particular gendered assumption, norm, or stereotype.

The student body within any school is a diverse compilation of children with unique experiences, perspectives, and identities. Staff and parents will express concerns as to how a trans student's experience will impact other students. Therefore, the way in which teachers or staff engage with students greatly matters. If adults react negatively, children will feel apprehensive or fearful. Conversely, if adults are matter-of-fact and able to answer the children's straight-forward questions, kids are more likely to easily digest the information and take things in stride. Despite the passage of more than four decades, the same is true today. Confident, knowledgeable teachers and parents are of significant importance when considering the impact on students.

WHAT DO TEACHERS NEED TO LEAD STUDENT CONVERSATIONS?

- Tools to engage students in age-appropriate conversations about gender diversity, specifically addressing gender identity and expression.
- An understanding of how to place conversations about gender diversity into the broader framework of human diversity so that all students can find ways in which to relate.
- Proficiency in building conversations among students that are centered on empathy, cooperation, and respectful engagement.
- An ability to address gender stereotypes and binary notions of gender when they arise.
- An ability to contextualize gender diversity, and gender-diverse people, within multiple disciplines such as history, health, science, and culture.
- Confidence in distinguishing between a child's genuine inquisitive questions and situations of teasing or mocking, as well as capability to address either situation.
- Knowledge of how to respectfully—and privately, if needed—address the questions or concerns of any student.

Engage the Students

Many schools establish an advisory team of teachers and parents to address diversity, inclusion, equity, and other student wellness objectives. So, too, can a school enlist the help and support of students to positively influence the student body response as a whole. Consider this story involving a sixth-grade student:

A trans boy had opted to keep his gender history private for most of his time at elementary school. When he was twelve, he decided he wanted to share his gender story with his classmates. I met with the student, the principal, his teacher, and his parents to discuss the best way to proceed, aiming for the most optimal outcome possible.

We landed on a plan for the actual day of disclosure, but we also took an extra step. We opted to have a meeting with his closest friends first. The day before, he and I sat to talk with these friends about their special place in his life. I told them that he thought of them as his closest, trusted friends and that he wanted to share something important with them before talking to the rest of the students the next day. He shared his story. I mentioned the courage it took to share it and that I knew he was pretty nervous about how his friends might respond. He was worried that they might reject him. His friends were immediately reassuring and said they were grateful that he trusted them.

After a bit more conversation, we then said how they, as his friends and allies, could have a positive influence on the rest of the class the next day. If they felt able and ready, then they could make a significant difference for their anxious friend the next day. None were pressured to engage if, for any reason, they did not feel up to it. All of them agreed that they were on board to support him.

The next day, I spoke to the rest of the class about gender-diverse people and then their classmate stood at the front of the class and shared his personal experience. When he was done, he said he would like to open it up for questions. The students were amazing! They were empathetic, inquisitive, and respectful. I saw the relief on the face of the trans student and watched his self-confidence soar on the spot. With just a little advance preparation, the school ensured a phenomenal outcome. He's graduated high school and college since then but still retains those important friendships that were deepened as a result of their shared experience.

There are many ways that other students can be brought in to support a non-binary or trans student. The benefit is not to the trans student alone, as these students discovered. They all learned first-hand the beauty of working together to create a positive outcome and doing so with love, friendship, and courage at the center.

FOSTER STUDENT LEADERSHIP

While the above story involved that particular student's close friends, it is also possible to enlist the support of other students who do not have a close relationship with the trans child. The approach will vary slightly in that the request for their support is because they are identified leaders and influencers in the eyes of their peers. It can be very gratifying for any student to be asked for their help because of their integrity and leadership. It means that the principal and teachers view them as powerful change-makers. To receive a request from these adults, seeking *their* assistance regarding an important moment—one that will make a positive difference in the life of someone else—will be something that could empower them for the rest of their lives as well.

A ONE-ON-ONE APPROACH

Just as teachers will ask another student to show the ropes to a student who's just moved to the area, a similar approach can be used in certain situations as well. For example, when a trans or gender-diverse student is expected to begin use of a different bathroom, steps can be taken to better optimize that transition. Arranging a temporary "bathroom buddy" to accompany the trans student as they and all the other students adjust to the switch is a great proactive step to facilitate an optimal outcome. The student may wish to ask a friend themselves. It can be helpful for those students to prepare for any potential questions that may arise.

EXPAND THE CONVERSATION

A student with a gender identity difference will likely always be in the minority but it does not mean they should be invisible. Because the experiences of gender-diverse children are unfamiliar, and often confusing, to adults, they often assume that gender identity differences will be difficult for other children to comprehend. This is not the case. While many students may not have encountered a trans or nonbinary student before, the experience of being judged or marginalized for being different is one that is all too relatable.

Most students have little difficulty discussing the parallels within their own lives whether it is disparagement targeting one's body, family, circumstances, or culture. Whether occasional or persistent, it just feels demoralizing.

I strongly recommend that teachers, when discussing gender differences, consistently expand the conversation into one in which every student can engage and relate. Do not wait for a trans child to be the catalyst for these conversations. Introduce the concept of gender diversity in simple ways when engaging in conversations about differences of any kind. Discuss the ways in which we humans have a shared experience and how our differences are what make our paths worthy of exploration and celebration.

For example, the starting place for a discussion that is complex in nature could go like this:

How many of us get hungry or thirsty? Raise your hand.

This, of course, is an example of a very simplistic, yet shared human experience.

What kinds of things do you want to eat when you are hungry? What might you eat if those things are not available? What do you eat that others may not? What if you don't have running water where you live? What if there is no store nearby to purchase water? What if you have no money to buy water? What if the only water available is dangerous to drink?

These questions show how each person's experience can begin to diverge. This approach allows a teacher to discuss a core theme (experiencing hunger and thirst) while adding complex—yet easily understood—variables that uniquely influence these circumstances (geographical access, privilege, agriculture, ethnicity, environmental dangers, poverty, and climate differences) and their impact on the core human experience of being hungry or thirsty. Children will assume that their personal experience is one that is shared by everyone until they see or hear otherwise. This simple approach allows children to consider a wide array of intersecting factors. It will cultivate an ability for them to see beyond their insular experience and what they mistakenly assume is true for everyone.

Now we can consider a gender-related example.

How many of you know or have met a girl? How many of you are a girl? How many of you know or have met a boy? How many of you are a boy?

Again, this is a simple shared experience for everyone. Children will respond affirmatively even though some may think the questions are silly. To expand the discussion, a teacher then asks:

How many people have met someone who was both a boy and a girl? Or someone who said they were neither a girl nor a boy? How many of you know or have heard of someone who was once a boy but is now a girl? Someone who was once a girl but is now a boy?

Whether or not any students have direct experience with gender-diverse people is not the point. It introduces the notion that these people do exist. A teacher now has the opportunity to discuss the concept of gender identity, or one's internal sense of gender, and that gender identity is not the same for everybody. This introduction provides children with an expanded view of gender and how each person experiences it differently.

Each and every conversation can emphasize our commonalities—we all get thirsty and hungry, we all have a gender identity, and we all have encountered negative repercussions as a result of own diverse lives. We have all suffered feelings of embarrassment, frustration, anger, sadness, or shame when others (children *and* adults) ridiculed, taunted, or reprimanded us for those differences.

Engaging children of any age in these more expansive conversations will provide them with a greater comprehension of things they may already observe but for which they may not yet have language to describe. Invite them to share their thoughts. Ask them what they've learned and how they relate to what's been shared. Ask how they feel about it. Not only will this enhance their social and emotional learning, but they will develop a foundation where empathy is valued, care for others is understood, and the responsibilities we have to our global community are embraced.

ESTABLISH A GSA

Many schools have GSAs, sometimes referred to as a Gay–Straight Alliance or, more recently renamed as Gender and Sexualities Alliance. These primarily student-led clubs are a place where LGBTQ+ students can gather for support, social engagement, and/or to engage in leadership opportunities to better improve the school environment. GSAs typically have an adult advisor who is a teacher, counselor, or other staff member. Any advisor should be knowledgeable about the distinctions between gender identity, sexual orientation, and gender expression as both separate and intersectional concepts that inform a student's identity (and are not restricted by one's anatomy). Students may or may not be fully understanding of these conceptual delineations, which is why the advisor's understanding is all the more necessary. If the GSA members are predominantly gay or lesbian, they may exclude or ignore a gender-diverse student simply because they don't understand that student's experience.

SUSAN LACY, RIDGWAY, CO

I am the superintendent of schools in a small rural mountain community. A few years ago, we began seeing some transgender students in our schools and questions from my educators were starting to pop up. A year previously, I watched as one transgender student took it upon themselves to teach a group of teachers about what it means to be nonbinary. The student openly shared some of the daily challenges they faced in school. The teachers listened with open minds and open hearts as this student bravely shared. This was an important start to our district's early work, but I knew that we needed more. I invited Aidan Key to be part of our continued learning.

Aidan spent three jam-packed days educating community members, school parents, and school staff culminating with discussions with our middle and high school students. I knew it was crucial to building a trusting environment. Because the adults were far less knowledgeable about gender identity than the students, I felt it important to engage them first. The actions, words, and perspectives of adults have a huge impact on students. No matter how much we tell them to be accepting and inclusive, we as adults need to show them how to put it into action. If we don't, these contradictions create harmful and challenging situations for our students.

I also knew that how these opportunities were framed mattered. I sent a letter to the parents inviting, rather than telling, them to attend and to share their thoughts regarding safety and inclusion for every student. It was important to consider the needs of my support staff—the bus drivers, custodians, and cooks who engage with students daily—as they had not yet been provided any education on the subject. Most, if not all, of them had never met a trans person before. I asked Aidan to share some of his personal story to give them context for the subject. His frank, vulnerable delivery had a profound impact on the staff. That sat riveted for three hours because of Aidan's coura-geous opening and respectful delivery.

The most moving part for me was when Aidan spoke with the students. Despite an unfortunately chilly gym and sitting on hard bleachers, the middle school students excitedly listened and engaged for a much too short span of thirty-five minutes. Aidan's gift for reaching into their hearts, showing his own, and inviting them to do the same was powerful to witness. The students expressed their curiosities, their own struggles, and asked how they could be better allies to their fellow students. Afterward, about eight students circled Aidan wanting advice for how to talk to their own parents about their identi-ties. I had to make sure their next period teachers knew their absence was excused because I recognized that their need to be heard—and their personal journeys to understand themselves—was far more important than what they might have learned in class that day. It was a moving reminder to me that if a children cannot be themselves and accepted for who they are, they cannot successfully engage in the learning we strive to provide.

STUDENT OPPORTUNITIES

There are additional ways that schools can support their students' learning about gender diversity. Invite a guest speaker to an assembly or classroom. In some communities, there are student or young adult speaker bureaus that can provide a panel presentation for students. Some pre-screening is recommended to find speakers who are experienced with engaging elementary-age audiences. There may be some trans or nonbinary students within the school who are comfort-able sharing their knowledge or personal story with other students. Including and empowering student voices adds a powerful, relatable element. Keep in mind that gender-diverse students should never be *required* to educate others or be the sole source of learning for the school community.

Encourage students to consider projects or assignments that are of personal interest to them. Or suggest that students step into a completely unfamiliar area, perhaps an assignment about an affinity group to which they do *not* belong. A teacher can pre-select a diverse array of conversational topics relevant to the class subject—history, science, culture, health, biology, language, current events, or media—and consider the presence, experience, or absence of gender-diverse people as it relates to the topic at hand. By including a diverse array of life experiences, students gain a stronger ability to see the interrelatedness that all humans share.

SUPPORT FOR THE PARENT/ CAREGIVER COMMUNITY

The adults in a child's life make up the third part of the school triad—staff, students, and parents—that are deserving of the chance to learn. School employees are increasingly insisting on learning opportunities as well. They are face-to-face with an increasing number of gender-diverse students on a daily basis. It's not hard to imagine that these employees need some immediate guidance to have conversations with their students. While the attention to the parent community may come last, it should certainly not be avoided or delayed. Addressing the needs of these caregivers is a must to achieve a positive cultural shift within the school. The temptation to dodge a potentially contentious conversation is present for many administrators. My advice to administrators is to bravely and respectfully step into these important discussions with parents. What follows are my recommendations for engaging the parent community as a deserving, necessary partner.

Communications

If a school is embarking on a learning journey, let the parent community know. Educators regularly pursue professional development because the field of education evolves, as do the needs of students. Share the reasons for pursuing specific topics, including gender diversity. The way this is communicated matters. I discourage schools from identifying any specific trans or nonbinary child as the impetus or motivation for this learning. The privacy needs of gender-diverse students need to be protected. What should be communicated, and is actually more accurate, is that the school prioritizes its mission, values, and efforts to ensure every child feels valued and included. Because the school prioritizes the importance of ongoing learning, that learning must extend beyond the students to include everyone. Inviting parents to engage in this learning delivers a powerful message that they are an essential part of the school community.

Here are some important points an administrator can include when extending the invitation for a parent learning event:

- As a school/district, we have been on a learning journey to better understand the needs of our students, including those with diverse gender identities.
- This is a newer topic for many, and we understand the importance of being proactive in our search for understanding.
- As a result, we as a staff have engaged in professional development addressing this topic so that we can continue to live up to our school's mission and values and, of course, live up to the expectations of our students.
- We needed to better understand the needs of our gender-diverse students and consider the ways this might impact all our students.
- Because of our learning engagement, we were able to get our questions addressed. It provided us with greater clarity, confidence, and relief. Many of you may have similar questions which made it all the more important that you can have those addressed as well,
- We hope you will join us on this day ____ and time ____ for a parent learning opportunity. We invite you to travel this journey with us. We'll provide the childcare and snacks!

Educators and Parents

Supporting the parent community in their learning is obviously an important key to a school's successful forward movement. Parent conversations are layered and complex, perhaps even more so than for the school personnel. Therefore, leading a conversation with parents should not be tossed to one individual alone with a lot of well-wishes. I encourage not only the presence of school leadership but district administrators as well. Principals should encourage some teachers to attend (and pay them as well). A second-grade teacher could share examples of student conversations and a seventh-grade teacher might share how the students helped him quickly get pronouns right for every student. A district superintendent would be ready to address questions that are broader in scope. A coach can share the realities of how gender-diverse team members are welcomed and valued by their teammates. Having multiple representatives from the school or district communicates that the subject is important *and* that the presence of parents is valued.

Content of Parent Learning Event

The following bulleted list outlines areas to include. Enough available time to move through them? Well, that's another story. It could be beneficial to offer a two-part event to be held a week or two apart. The first segment focuses on content while the second session can cover additional content and interactive discussion.

- Articulate mission and values.
- Introduce school/district personnel.
- Lay the foundation using the AEIOU gender framework:
  o Age-appropriate conversations with students emphasize the "E" (gender expression) and the "I" (gender identity).
  o Make the delineation between the student areas of focus and the adult areas of concern: the "A" (anatomy) and "O" (sexual orientation).
  o Make clear that these distinctions are what provide shared understanding.
- Address past misconceptions and stigmatization of gender-diverse people.
- Discuss the reasons for the increased visibility of trans people and the resulting societal shift:
  o Today's better understanding of harmful child-rearing practices,
  o Increased recognition of harsh risks factors experienced by gender-diverse people,
  o Current research that documents the positive impact of supportive environments,
  o Health professional associations that recommend supportive practices for trans youth, and
  o Growing body of scientific knowledge regarding gender identity.
- Share how conversations with students emphasize respect, inclusion, shared experience, and diversity.
- Provide parents/caregivers with the 3 Family Acceptance Project's evidence-based posters outlining some common family accepting and

rejecting behaviors from FAP's research and the Poster Guidance (see Appendix C: FAP Poster Guidance and the additional posters included in Chapter 7).

Welcoming your child's LGBTQ+ friends to family activities and events is a family accepting behavior that helps protect against health risks and promotes well-being. Find information and resources at FAP's family website at https://lgbtqfamilyacceptance.org/.

- Articulate school's policy/guidelines, applicable state and/or federal law, and how the implementation of these is both time-tested and effective.
- Discuss the value of gender-inclusive practices and policy:
  - o Addresses safety and privacy needs for all students,
  - o Empowers school staff to confidently act when/if needed, and
  - o Clarifies how to best incorporate gender-diverse students.
- Share where to find information on the school/district website.
- Q&A time.

A parent session is an opportune time to share resources and information. Be sure to point attendees to where this information is located on the school or district website, within the student handbook, and identify the leaders to whom a parent can turn for additional questions or further inquiries. Include a display of library books that are available to students. It can be helpful to have a librarian or teacher familiar with the books available to talk about them.

When concluding a parent session, express gratitude to the parents who took time out of their busy lives to attend. Celebrate the fact that everyone engaged in a way that was genuine and open. The newness and the complexity of the subject will present all with the opportunity to learn, assess, reflect, adjust, and iterate.

SCOTT PEACOCK/SNOHOMISH

In 2016, one of the most historically pivotal years for transgender rights, our district—a medium-sized, district of ten thousand students and fifteen schools—undertook what at first seemed impossible in our conservative-leaning community of Snohomish, Washington: adopting a gender-inclusive policy. Our first school board meeting addressing the policy was crowded and volatile. I even found myself unexpectedly on the evening news to address the controversy. The school board members decided that evening to table the policy vote to a later time when we all had a better understanding of the topic and our community's needs.

I have to say, the subsequent work was the most difficult and especially the most gratifying work in my many years as a school administrator. Our six-month journey was focused first and foremost on bridging different perspectives within our adult community. Our task was not to change any minds, nor to judge or to fix. We simply sought connection and understanding.

We knew that at the end, we would be presenting a new transgender support policy to our school board for consideration. At the time, we did not know what it would look like. Whatever we presented then was to grow out of more than twenty community conversations and reflect the expression of three core values explored during those sessions—safety, privacy, and support for all students.

At each meeting, attendance ranging from twenty to sixty people, our partner—Aidan Key—shared an introduction that we came to call "Trans 101." We then discussed how to ensure that these three key values applied to ALL our students. We explored through interactive sessions the ways that these values can and must be protected for gender-diverse and cisgender students, staff, and parents in public schools. Frequently, gender-diverse students as well as their parents spoke out, providing testimony of their most human of journeys—becoming and being themselves in the face of tremendous barriers.

For all who engaged in our organizing efforts, it took patience, compassion, grace, and a willingness to be vulnerable. At the heart of this undertaking was our newly formed Human Rights and Equity Team, consisting of staff, parents, community members, faith-based leaders, and school administrators. The group was co-facilitated by our education association president—a vital partnership.

Our primary goal was to engage our community, regardless of perspective, in conversations where everyone felt heard and valued as we did this important work together. We spent half-a-year hosting public gatherings. Some got emotional, even heated. I personally met with many individuals as well to ensure every voice was heard. Throughout all these discussions, everyone responded positively to the safe spaces for inquiry that our Human Rights and Equity Team cultivated. The key was engaging the most diverse array of belief systems and worldviews possible with open hearts.

In the end, the school board approved our community-informed, transgender-inclusive policy. We knew that the board's unanimous approval was indicative of the powerful work we had just completed. I believe this work strengthened our sense of community while making a promise to our gender-diverse students that they could be who they needed to be in our classrooms and activities. We also knew that we would have still more work ahead to realize and sustain this promise. Above all, our most important learning was recognizing that the experiences of gender-diverse students amplifies the experiences of all students.

Scott M. Peacock

Superintendent, Lakewood School District

Former Deputy Superintendent, Snohomish School District

Make a Commitment to Ongoing Parent Sessions

It may be stating the obvious but offering a parent session is not a "one and done" kind of thing. As has been stated multiple times, the inclusion of gender-diverse children in schools—and the steps it takes to do so—is a newer endeavor. We are all learning. That learning will continue as our society gains greater familiarity, confidence, and experience in the process. Parents move in and out of school communities as their children progress through as well. As the awareness of gender diversity increases—within schools and society-at-large—the need to offer frequent educational sessions will likely decrease. For now, make a strong commitment to ongoing learning within the school and keep the parent community regularly abreast of the progress.

Beneficial to All

Occasionally, someone will ask, "Why should we do all this for just one or two students?" It may seem excessive to some. But is it too much? No, it isn't. As we give attention to the gender experience of a trans or nonbinary child, each and every person is then inspired to examine their own understanding of, and relationship to, gender. For every gender-diverse child who seeks understanding, acceptance, and belonging from those around them, many other children bear witness to it. What they are seeing is a historical moment of learning and discovery by *everyone* who chooses to step in. If all that feels a little lofty, it is. Yet this resonates powerfully with children. As one parent put it, "Whatever you were teaching the kids today at school, just keep it up! My child was so excited she couldn't stop talking about it."

If we get mired in debates about bathrooms and pronouns, our view of what children are actually experiencing gets obscured. These children are witnessing their gender-diverse peers on a courageous path toward authenticity—courage borne not out of choice but out of necessity. They are also witnessing how society struggles to honor these children on their courageous, necessary paths.

Educators know the value of sharing the experiences of people who have overcome significant challenges to be their authentic selves. Helen Keller, Martin Luther King Jr., Anne Frank, Ruby Bridges, and Stephen Hawking are some of the heroes our children learn about. Race, disability, childhood adversity, and social upheaval are integral parts of these stories. As the Danish theologian, Søren Kierkegaard once said, "The most common form of despair is not being who you are."[3] Children need to learn about these amazing heroes who were determined to be who they are *and* they need to celebrate the humans they see every day, including the one in the mirror.

NOTES

1. For a discussion of the importance of the parental support role, especially in collaboration with schools, see Danielle Johnson et al., "Parents of Youth Who Identify as Transgender: An Exploratory Study," *School Psychology Forum* 8, no. 1 (2014): 56–74.
2. "The Surprisingly Recent Time Period When Boys Wore Pink, Girls Wore Blue, and Both Wore Dresses," *Today I Found Out* (blog) (October 17, 2014), http://www.todayifoundout.com/index.php/2014/10/pink-used-common-color-boys-blue-girls/.
3. Kurt F. Reinhardt, *The Existentialist Revolt* (Milwaukee: Bruce Pub. Co., 1952).

12

Parental Advocacy for Gender-Diverse Children in School

There comes a moment when you realize that what you're advocating for is more than just accommodations. You're really advocating for someone's quality of life.

Unknown

WHERE TO TURN?

Most school environments are still in the position of being reactive—meaning that they don't recognize or address their own needs (much less the needs of your child) until they are face-to-face with their first gender-diverse students. Even if they are willing to step in, available avenues for professional development are challenging to find. Guidance may be difficult to find as colleagues and district leaders are often in no better position. Many of the resources that do exist are often limited in scope or not applicable to younger students (e.g., a website for LGBTQ+ young adults entering college).

Other resources may offer school personnel a few tangible guidelines—*what* steps to take regarding bathroom access, pronoun, and name changes, for example—but they offer little in the way of *how* to best support the gender-diverse student or the rest of the school community in the process. It is also unlikely that these limited resources will address *why* a school should even begin such an undertaking.

WHOSE JOB IS IT?

With nowhere to turn, schools tend to look to the parents of these children for help. While this is well-intentioned, it is a mistake to expect each caregiver to take on the responsibility. While a parent can provide some detail with respect to their child's needs, they will be unable to address the needs of any other gender-diverse child and certainly not the systemic change needed within the school and district. Districts need to take ownership of the long-range responsibilities within schools and support the individuals who are tasked with their implementation.

Most educators recognize that it is inappropriate to ask any single caregiver to address the school's responsibilities. It should go without saying that neither the school nor the parent should rely solely on the child to advise or be responsible for these significant school responsibilities. A child can and should have input relevant to their own experience. But it falls to a school to address circumstances in which a student has a specific need—differing physical and cognitive levels of ability, cultural differences, unstable housing or homelessness, dietary considerations, or medical concerns. Gender diversity in children is one of these circumstances.

Any overwhelmed caregiver needs as much bandwidth as possible to manage their own family responsibilities and should not be expected to accept or manage any systemic barriers that arise at school.

A parent has the responsibility of raising their child. Schools have the responsibility of creating an optimal learning environment for that child. Understanding that these responsibilities are distinct is crucial. Yes, there is a learning curve for both family and school—but together they can address the needs of that individual child and hopefully set the stage for any future gender-diverse child and the school community as a whole. It is painful to see a gender-diverse child that has support at home but not at school. Some students receive life-saving support at school because none exists at home. More painful still is when a child has the support of neither. The information in this book strives to change that.

HOW SHOULD A PARENT/CAREGIVER GET STARTED?

There are two parallel tracks to optimal gender inclusion: one is to address *the specific needs of the student*, and the second is to address *the needs of the school community*. A caregiver (and student) is partly responsible for the former. The school is fully responsible for both.

Sometimes, a parent is not yet ready to be in a support position. The gender-diverse student would then be in the challenging place of advocating for themselves. In that case, the student should have an available adult advocate(s)—counselor, principal, coach, etc.—on whom they can lean for support and guidance. As much as is possible, this adult advocate should engage proactively on behalf of the student.

Whether a caregiver, parent, or advocate, start by doing an assessment of a school's readiness. Begin by combing the school and/or district's websites. Look to the student handbook to see what gender-inclusive statements and guidelines exist. Be knowledgeable about state and federal anti-discrimination laws. Contact the state superintendent's office, department of education, and/or district office to be fully informed as to the rights of the child. Recognize that inconsistencies will likely arise. Seek clarification until any inconsistencies are cleared up. Don't hesitate to ask for additional sources to contact so that this assessment is as comprehensive as possible.

I advise parents to document their information-gathering journey. If a parent encounters misinformation or resistance they will have made note of the details: with whom they spoke, what was said, and when. Again, do not be surprised if inconsistencies or obstacles occur. A school, district, or state's efforts toward gender inclusion are likely to be dynamic and changing. It can be both difficult and rewarding to be part of this systemic change. Hopefully, there will be many allies to assist along the way.

QUESTIONS TO ASK YOUR SCHOOL ADMINISTRATOR: A LIST FOR PARENTS AND CAREGIVERS (SEE APPENDIX A: TOP QUESTIONS FOR SCHOOLS)

A child's disclosure of their gender identity is often sudden and unexpected. Any parent or caregiver could potentially have a lot to contend with regarding their trans or nonbinary child, especially at first. It can be an emotionally difficult time for both the child and the parent. While a caregiver is navigating this crucial time, they must also consider the place where their child spends the most time outside of the home—their school. Children do not tend to consider any advance preparations that their school might need to do, nor should they. This is not their responsibility, and they are often unaware of what could or should be done to optimize their school experience. A caregiver that takes time in advance to learn more about the school climate (for example, the presence of gender-inclusive policies and practices, any prior experience with gender-diverse students, staff completion of relevant professional development, etc.) will find themselves better prepared for these next steps with their child's school.

The list of questions below can serve as a starting point for a parent/administrator conversation. A parent may not know if their child will be well-received or whether their needs will be accommodated. If uncertain of the administrator's receptivity, some parents will choose to make an initial anonymous call to preserve their child's privacy. Or they may ask a friend or family member for assistance. If this is the first conversation of this nature for the school principal or superintendent, you can be sure they too will be searching for answers.

Whether by phone, video, or in-person it would be of benefit to parent and administrator to request adequate time and privacy to ensure that both parties are free from potential interruptions. Regardless of the principal's familiarity with the needs of gender-diverse students, a parent will certainly be able to gauge their receptivity to the topic.

- **Have you had transgender and/or nonbinary-identified students in your school?**
  If so, how did you address the needs of that particular student(s)? Did you work directly with the student's parent or caregiver? Do you have a process/plan to support the needs of that student? If so, would you describe that to me? Who is involved in that process?

- **If you've had experience with gender-diverse students, how did it go?**
  This is an open-ended question and deliberately vague. How an administrator answers this will provide a parent with a sense of the administrator's responsiveness, hesitancy, or dismissiveness. This open-ended question can be followed with an invitation to say more. (Keep in mind that an administrator is required to uphold the privacy rights of all students and therefore should not reveal any identifying information about trans, nonbinary, or any other students).

  Please share some of the strategies you used or steps that you took? What did you learn from those experiences? What did the staff learn? Were teachers and students consistent with names and pronouns? How did taking these steps affect the school community?

- **Does our district have a gender-inclusive policy? If so, where can I find it?**
  Including gender identity and gender expression when articulating the diversity and inclusion values/commitments of any school is necessary to help foster a shift within the school culture. A gender-inclusive policy is a key to communicating this commitment to the entire school community. It is foundationally important to have these statements clear and easily accessible to students, staff and teachers, and the parent/caregiver community. Policy, guidelines, mission, and values are commonly found in student handbooks, school and district websites, and within parent communications/resources.

- **If a policy does exist, how is this communicated to parents/teachers/students?**
  The school community cannot benefit from policy and guidelines if they can't find them. Are teachers aware of their responsibilities? How might gender-diverse students know where to turn?

- **Has there been training on gender diversity and if so, please tell me about that training?**
  If the response is, *Well, yes, we've had some guest speakers at the high school GSAs (Gay–Straight Alliance)*, that's not enough. Educators at every grade level need professional development opportunities to further their understanding—especially to make the crucial delineation between gender identity and sexual orientation. If gender differences are continually framed in the context of sexuality, and therefore "too mature" to discuss

or address with children, then the experiences of trans and nonbinary children will be ignored, dismissed, or ridiculed.

- **If the school has had training, was it offered to ALL staff—teachers, counselors, leadership, office staff, coaches, etc.?**
  Different employees have different needs and considerations. It is just as possible for janitors, cafeteria staff, bus drivers, and paraeducators to inadvertently or purposely disclose a trans child's status as it is for teachers or principals. Every school employee needs to understand the factors that impact a child's safety and right to privacy.

- **Have you offered learning opportunities for the parent community? If so, how did that go? If not, do you have that in the works? And . . .**

- **How would you respond to inquiries from other parents about the presence of gender-diverse children?**
  The concerns of the parents usually land at number one on a "top five fears list" for most administrators. How a principal responds to this question will be indicative of how they might respond when, or if, a parent of another student makes a complaint. The parent community can tip the scales for a school's successful journey toward inclusion. Offering regular learning opportunities for parents is the best way to respect and include them in the school's journey. An administrator's response to these questions will give the parent insight into their level of confidence when engaging with the parent community.

- **Are you familiar with student support plans for trans kids? Do any of the staff have experience developing one with a student?**
  The answer may be no. What a parent can assess with this question is whether their administrator has an interest in hearing more. Working with a student on a support plan is a thoughtful, comprehensive task. Knowing whether a principal is receptive or dismissive of student support plans could be an indicator of their willingness to appropriately intervene if or when any problems arise.

- **How do you ensure the privacy of a student that does not wish to have their gender history disclosed to students or faculty?**
  A counselor may feel that everyone should be "out and proud," or a principal may feel that it would be deceptive to others to *not* share that child's gender history, but the bottom line is that students do have a right to request privacy regarding their gender history. It is their right to

determine whether, when, and with whom to disclose this history. For example, a parent may wish for the school nurse to know their child's gender status in case of any medical emergency but that does not mean the school nurse has the right to share that information with others.

- **How do you manage the experience of a student for whom privacy regarding their gender history is NOT an option and/or is NOT desired?**

  Some children socially transition with peers who have known them for some time. This means that their gender history will be known. Other trans children may not feel a need to keep their gender history private for any number of reasons. There is no singular approach that will work for all students. The safety of visible trans and nonbinary students should be a primary concern and it is important that a school understands and can respond to each student's needs. Ask what safeguards are in place for these kinds of circumstances. How the matter of privacy/disclosure is managed by the school should be explicitly clear.

- **How do you address the questions or comments raised by other children? Do you feel that some or all your staff are prepared to respond compassionately and confidently?**

  If the administrator replies in the affirmative, ask for an example. If you sense a hesitant response, this is a sign that further education may be needed. If you encounter a more dismissive response, it may represent future inaction, even opposition, if situations do arise. Worse still, and more common than you might imagine, is the assigning of blame to the gender-diverse student for any adverse experiences they encounter. If only some of the teachers feel confident, this would be an important consideration for classroom placement.

- **To what extent does the district administration, including the superintendent, stand behind the administration and staff in the process of supporting gender-diverse students?**

  Just as teachers and staff need support from their principals, principals will benefit from the backing of the district administration. If the message from higher up is one that is not supportive, or even antagonistic to doing the required work, a principal may be afraid or intimidated and thus not fully able to address a parent's concerns. A direct question may help you better understand if this is a principal issue or a larger district leadership issue.

- **How do you respond to teachers and staff who are resistant or feel conflicted about supporting the needs of gender-diverse students? What is your expectation of these staffers? What is expected of me, as a parent, if my child encounters this?**

  This is still a very real scenario for many school administrators. Some teachers may feel conflicted because of their personal beliefs. It is necessary to understand how a principal or superintendent will approach complex situations like these. A parent needs to know if their administrator feels confident and capable to outline to their staff the expectations of a professional workplace versus any one individual's personal convictions.

- **Are students able to use the restroom that best aligns with their gender identity? How will you ensure the safety and privacy needs of my student?**

  Too often, the solution proposed is that of an alternative bathroom such as a staff or nurse's facility. In some cases, such a restroom is a great distance away from classrooms, and/or using such a facility draws unwanted attention to the child who is using it. While such an option can be desired by some, most students will either opt for the girls' or boys' restroom. You'll want to know that the facility that works best *for your child* is available to them. Ask your school administrator how they are going to safely support your child as they begin using different facilities.

- **How do you/would you respond to inquiries from parents or teachers who may express concern or distress about the presence of gender-diverse children in classrooms, bathrooms, and locker rooms?**

  At the least, you need to hear that the administrator feels confident to address any conflict. It's okay to ask for an example such as "What would you say to a parent or teacher who questions whether a child should be in that particular bathroom?"

- **When considering sports and other activities, what are your considerations for participation? Do you have an athletic policy in place for gender-diverse students?**

  Like restroom usage and access to other gender-segregated spaces, trans and nonbinary students should have the ability to participate in activities based on the best fit for them with respect to their gender identity. You can provide them with the Gender-Diverse Youth Sport

Inclusivity Toolkit: http://genderdiversity.org/best-practices-for-youth-sports/.

- **My child starts school in a week. What are you able to do to ensure that my child is off to the most optimal start of the school year?**
  It does not always work out for a school to immediately prepare for the inclusion of a gender-diverse child. However, there are some short-term steps that a school can take to get off on the right foot for the school year. This can include direct support or training for a child's teacher(s) while planning for more comprehensive staff training at a later date.
- **My family is early on this journey. I may need to revise my child's support plan as time goes on. How do I do that?**
  Children of any age need room to explore and discover. Having a supportive environment at home and at school is needed for that exploration. This provides a child with more information than they would otherwise get if they felt pressured to "choose". The way they describe their gender identity—and actions they want to take as a result—may change. A child may shift from a nonbinary description of their identity to a trans identity, or vice versa. Certain pronouns may be requested early on and then changed as time progresses. It is important to provide flexibility as the child finds their path. This is crucial too when considering the possible, albeit less frequent, notion that a child will step away from diverse gender identification. While society fearfully anticipates the chance, a child might "change their mind," all the more reason to allow for exploration, discovery, and movement—even if that movement eventually is toward a cisgender identification. Modifications to a support plan need to address all possibilities *and* provide thoughtful support every step of the way.

FAMILIARIZE YOURSELF WITH THE GENDER DIVERSITY: STUDENT SUPPORT PLAN (SEE APPENDIX B)

Support plan considerations are best explored *before* a parent engages with an administrator, if possible. Ideally, a school administrator will have done the same. Schools that postpone taking proactive measures often find themselves dealing with more anxiety, confusion, and stress from everyone—students, parents, and staff. The assessment questions within the support plan, at the very least, offer a more detailed view of the big picture. If time allows, it may be wise to plan on *two* or more conversations with the administrator or other involved point persons (a counselor, for example).

PROVIDE SOME RESOURCES

Even in larger or more "progressive" communities, truly helpful resources may be scarce. The ones that do exist may only be nominally helpful because we are still so early in our efforts toward gender inclusivity. Understanding the ongoing needs of gender-diverse children of all ages and experiences presents challenges for everyone. As society moves from an exclusionary approach to one of inclusion, there is no doubt that existing resources will increase and evolve over time. That said, we must start somewhere. Caregivers can provide resources to a school administrator if needed. These will also be helpful for the administrator to disseminate to other staff.

> *Trans Children in Today's Schools (TCTS)*
> Suggesting this book is, of course, a great starting place. *TCTS* is based on successful gender-inclusion work in schools across the United States since 2007.
>
> *Schools in Transition (SIT)*
> This comprehensive sixty-eight-page guide from 2015 offers basic guidance on the needs of trans students K–12.
>
> *Gender Diversity*
> Gender Diversity provides education and professional development for school districts across the United States and beyond. These include online training, customized offerings, in-person training, and one-on-one consultations. Parent learning options are regularly provided as well.
>
> *Gender-Diverse Youth Sport Inclusivity Toolkit*
> This is a resource guide for inclusive transgender and nonbinary youth sport best practices.

Trans Families

TransFamilies.org offers direct support to parents and other caregivers of gender-diverse children. This is an excellent resource for principals and counselors to provide to other families of trans and nonbinary children throughout the district.

Welcoming Schools Book List

The Welcoming Schools program has developed a list of suggested readings for children of all ages. These books address the topics of gender identity, gender expression, family diversity, and gender stereotypes.

GLSEN and National Center for Transgender Equality

These two organizations have drafted a sixteen-page document entitled *Model School District Policy on Transgender and Gender Nonconforming Students.*

UNDERSTAND THAT A POLICY AND GUIDELINES "CHECKLIST" IS NOT ENOUGH

There are an increasing number of school districts across the United States that are adopting policies and guidelines to better support the needs of trans and gender-diverse children. Policies are typically a short paragraph of text that establishes the district's expectations with respect to gender inclusion. Guidelines for implementing that policy are then articulated. These guidelines elaborate on the application of a policy with respect to the following:

- Pronoun and name usage,
- Bathrooms and locker rooms,
- Dress codes,
- Sports and activities participation,
- Privacy, and
- School records.

While policy and guidelines are crucial elements—a checklist of sorts— toward creating gender-inclusive environments, they are not the full picture.

These early stages of inclusion are important, to be sure, communicating *what* should be done. However, it doesn't provide the roadmap for *how* to do it or even *why* it should be done in the first place. Sometimes, a district will adopt policies but take no action to explain this important how and *why* to those who are most in need of understanding—the very staff expected to implement them:

> I went to support a family whose high school age child was beginning a new school. The parent was very nervous about meeting with the school principal and asked me to come along. When the parent outlined the needs of the child, the principal surprised both of us by immediately agreeing to all that was requested. Yes, the child could use the bathroom and locker room corresponding to his gender identity; yes, his name and pronoun would be honored; yes, he could expect that his privacy needs would be respected and so on. The parent left the meeting surprised but optimistic, while I left feeling puzzled. This was not how these meetings typically went. The principal showed no interest in pursuing training. She had no questions herself and had seemed in a big hurry to get the meeting over with. She showed obvious relief when the mother said her child wanted to keep his gender history private.
>
> What came to pass, however, was a pervasive trans- and homophobic climate within the school that was never resolved while this child was in attendance. Any students that were out as LGBTQ+ had horrible experiences. He attended the school for four years with a constant fear of inadvertent disclosure. There was no way he could share his gender story with anyone should he have desired to do so. Even though the "checklist" of policy expectations was "in place," the climate of fear remained.

In this situation, the principal chose to sidestep the critical work necessary to create the climate change so needed for students. This does occur for a number of reasons. Some administrators do not think it is necessary, some are intimidated, some hope to avoid any conflict, and certainly, some have personal biases that get in the way. Still others are unable to take any inclusive steps for fear of losing their job.

KNOW YOUR RIGHTS

In the United States, there are federal requirements that apply to all schools that receive federal funding. As a parent of a gender-diverse child, it is important that you know where you stand.

Title IX of the Education Amendments of 1972 is a law that prohibits dis-crimination on the basis of sex in any federally funded school (most K–12 public schools). There have been challenges to the law's applicability with respect to the rights of trans students. However, when legal challenges have occurred, the federal courts have thus far ruled that discrimination or harassment based on a student's gender identity and/or gender expression is indeed prohibited under Title IX.

Other federal protections for students include the First Amendment of the U.S. Constitution's right to freedom of speech and freedom of expression. This includes the student's gender identity-congruent clothing, hairstyles, and other ways of expressing their gender and their right to speak about their identity to others.

The Equal Access Act ensures the rights of students to form student-led clubs such as a Gender & Sexuality Alliance (GSA) and the Federal Rights and Privacy Act (FERPA) which protects personal information about students in school records including gender status and related medical history.

The rights of gender-diverse students throughout the United States vary state-by-state and within public or private institutions. It can be challenging for a student to know their full legal rights and, even so, it is sometimes difficult to have these legal rights enforced.

A FRIENDLY MEETING OR A DEFENSIVE MANEUVER

I advise parents to refrain from entering into compromises or agreements simply because they feel pressured or outnumbered. Occasionally, when an initial meeting is scheduled with a principal, the invitation list begins to grow. Additional attendees may include a district administrator, the vice principal, even the school district's attorney. If the phrase "strength in numbers" comes to mind, it should. It is common for those in leadership to feel uncertain or intimidated when entering into what they feel are unchartered waters. It is understandable that they might invite others to feel more confident.

While an administrator might feel better in having some "back up," the result may not be as optimal for the caregiver and student. The majority of attendees at this meeting will likely be most concerned with the reactions from the rest of the school community as well as any possible legal liability for the district. Of course, the parent will be concerned about the needs of *their child*. The parent may be pressured into decisions that ultimately benefit the district far more than they do the student. If parents find themselves in a situation like this, they could decline the meeting or ask for the meeting to remain one-on-one as prearranged. At the very least, a parent can clearly state that no agreements will be made during the meeting. It can be helpful for a caregiver to have more time to reflect on the meeting before decisions are made and/or consult with an attorney if additional advice is desired.

A caregiver could cautiously proceed but should not hesitate to cut the meeting short if the tone is confrontational, condescending, or uncollaborative. If an attorney is present and taking an active role that is having a chilling effect on the meeting, the parent should cancel it and find an advocate or legal counsel of their own.

WHAT TO DO WHEN ACCEPTANCE IS NOWHERE TO BE FOUND

While the number of trans and nonbinary students rises, the tide change toward acceptance is much slower. Much of the recommendations and strategies for navigating schools presume a degree of school receptivity or, at the very least, a tepid passivity. What can a parent do when the school environment or the community-at-large is openly hostile toward trans students?

The most important thing to do is to protect your child and your family. Even if the school environment gradually changes over time, it may be unlikely that change will occur soon enough to be of any benefit to the child. The potential for harm, however, is great. Hostility may *not* be expressed initially. Some caregivers have reported that, at first, things were going well. But, as is sometimes the case, those not directly connected to the family, or even connected to the school, will go on the offensive to wage a political battle or religious crusade against what is touted as a "gay agenda" that is tyrannical and evil. The feared dangers *never* play out yet the *belief* in the dangers overrides this reality. The divisiveness that can occur pervades the parent community, the staff, and the broader community. It can cause a frenzy that is well beyond the control of any single family and, of course, no caregiver wants their child caught in the middle.

It can be difficult to gauge whether early resistance is worth pushing through. Each caregiver should carefully consider all variables, especially their child's physical and psychological safety. The child may be doing well at school, with no conflict amongst their peers, while troubles simmer within the adult community. District and/or school leadership may be strong allies, or they could forsake the rights of the family in an effort to appease others. School board members may, or may not, focus their attention on the rights of the student but could instead, as *elected* members, be swayed by the ferocity of others. Parents should carefully pick their battles, as the one who is impacted most, their child, will likely experience that impact for life. On one hand, a child could have an experience like Gavin Grimm, a former high schooler who fought for his rights all the way to the Supreme Court—ultimately winning his precedent-setting case.[1] This is a pathway not available to the majority of students who experience discrimination, however.

Most children, unfortunately, may have to navigate discriminatory practices, bullying, or targeting alone. Their stories don't make the news and they don't have the support of a team of advocates. For example, one high schooler was initially well accepted by her peers until the debate about trans inclusion boiled over within the parent community. A group of five or six students, daughters of some of the most virulent parents, turned on their one-time friend and leveled vague, inconsistent accusations of sexual assault. The charges were proven to be unfounded but that was hardly a victory for her. She suffers from PTSD as a result.

These experiences of this student, and that of Gavin Grimm, represent two ends of the spectrum of what can occur when community volatility is directed their way. These experiences resulted in both children being attacked and vilified simply for being themselves.

Documentation of any engagement with schools is very important. Caregivers should do this regardless of whether they anticipate trouble or not. Approaching any advocacy efforts with optimism is fine, recommended even, but taking protective measures will not diminish that optimistic approach in any way. Tracking all in-person conversations and email/phone communications including the day, date, and time should be part of that documentation. Also track the gist of what was said, by whom, and what follow-up steps are promised.

If possible, build a support team around you. That may include other families, supportive school personnel, friends and family, and other community members. This team may also include legal support and guidance. There may be local attorneys to seek out or national advocacy entities like the American Civil Liberties Union and the National Center for Lesbian Rights who advocate for trans rights. Hiring legal help is an expensive prospect but local and national attorneys will, at times, take on pro bono cases.

VOLUNTEER AT YOUR CHILD'S SCHOOL

If a parent is able, it can help to volunteer at the school. There are a number of options including providing support for office staff, assistance with school activities, offering to chaperone field trips, and supervising at lunches or recess. Parent volunteers often assist in their child's classroom providing support where most needed, either with students or for the classroom teacher. Providing help when the school needs it can increase the chances that school personnel will be responsive and helpful in return. Strong relationships make a difference. This is not about monitoring your own child's experiences but establishing mutually respectful relationships with school staff and other parents.

LOOK AFTER YOUR CHILD

Center the needs of your child throughout this process. It can be very difficult to know how to negotiate situations of contention. Avoid getting into a "right" and "wrong" way of thinking as the complexities involved won't always provide a parent with a clear delineation of what might be right or wrong. There may be times when keeping a low profile is prudent and others when engaging the local media could be helpful. A parent may decide to remove a child from the school rather than send them to a hostile environment each day. Online or homeschooling have become the optimal schooling pathway for a number of families who live in communities that have a high likelihood of being hostile toward their child. Some families have relocated their whole family hundreds of miles away to provide their children with a supportive school environment.

Homeschooling or moving across the country may be impossible options for many families. For those with barriers to these options—lack of childcare, financially disadvantaged, specific needs of child or siblings, for example—the choices are even tougher. In some of the more dire situations, a number of families have chosen to affirm their child's gender identity at home only, not at school. This is not an unsupportive act; it is a protective act. Keeping the child safe is paramount. In these situations, parents should have frank conversations with their children about the harsh realities of the communities in which they live. The age of the child needs to be taken into consideration as younger children may struggle to understand the reasons why they are not accepted. (Do not forget the siblings during this time either.)

Younger children have a more difficult time comprehending why they need to keep their gender a secret from others. Inadvertent disclosure could occur. A best friend who learns a secret will not understand the potential harm that could occur. Older children may better understand the need to maintain a façade, but they will be at a much higher risk for anxiety and depression as a result. These are horrible situations that no child should have to navigate but, again, for some families, the choices are very few.

If a child needs to hide their gender identity for their own safety, the amount of support and encouragement they will likely need is high. Find online groups for youth where they could get regular support. If possible, consider a gender-competent therapist as well. Continue to seek long-term solutions that can place the child in more affirming environments. Parents can reach out to organizations like TransFamilies.org and others to learn what might be available virtually or if there are any in-person local resources.

Seek out youth groups and events, whether in-person or virtual, so your child can find others with whom they can relate and develop friendships. I often encourage families to watch inspiring documentaries or films that feature courageous people who experience challenges as they fight for their rights. Connect the dots for them if need be—your child is the hero!

Taking your child to LGBTQ+ events is a family accepting behavior that helps protect against health risks and promotes well-being. Find information and resources at FAP's family website at https://lgbtqfamilyacceptance.org/.

NOTE

1. For a thoughtful discussion of where this case fits in the larger political climate for schools today, see Jules Gill-Peterson, *Histories of the Transgender Child* (Minneapolis: University of Minnesota Press, 2018), 195–197.

13

Bathrooms and Locker Rooms

When they say, you can't use the bathroom because you are not man enough or woman enough, what they are really saying is that you are not human enough.

Aidan Key

The visible presence of gender-diverse students in schools has a relatively short history, a scant one to two decades. Having led schools through these early discussions, as early as 2007, the most commonly asked question throughout that brief history has been, "But, what about the bathroom?!" The apprehension and urgency with which this question is so often delivered speaks volumes. Yet, this provocative and often angst-ridden question is frequently put forth as a *statement* rather than a straightforward inquiry. In other words, when people hear about a trans child, the notion of offering support and validation for that child's gender identity often seems impossible because they can't get past the seemingly immutable gendered boundaries of bathrooms. The question, "What about the bathroom?" is often expressed as a helpless proclamation that ultimately points to a psychological block experienced by so many.

Because most people have learned, and currently ascribe to, a binary representation of gender inextricably linked to genitalia, it is no wonder that most educators are distressed about bathrooms. To find our way to a productive exploration of the topic, it is important to recognize the possibility of internal conflict for many and that there can be varying levels of intensity as well. While it may be difficult to clearly articulate the nature of these concerns, the conversation can nevertheless, in the most extreme cases, be peppered with inflammatory words like *danger, rape,* and *deviancy.*

While fears for the safety of students (who are not gender diverse) are often fodder for sensationalistic media headlines, the statistical reality is that bathrooms and locker rooms—especially those facilities within schools— are the sites where harassment and bullying against trans children come to a head.[1] These facilities are emblematic of our society's tightly held belief that there exists a single fixed line between genders in which all children are placed firmly on one side or the other and the belief that this foundational element is under attack. Only by moving beyond society's outdated assumptions about gender can we begin to understand the experiences of children who experience a degree of incongruity between their physiology, anatomy, and identity.[2]

WHICH BATHROOM OR LOCKER ROOM SHOULD A TRANS CHILD USE?

While the debate rages, the answer is relatively simple. All children—transgender or not—should use the facility that works best for them. This is most frequently the one that most closely aligns with their gender identity.[3] For trans boys, this is typically the boys' restroom or locker room and for trans girls, the girls' facilities. Some trans students will opt for an all-gender facility, sometimes for reasons of increased safety or privacy. Children who have a more gender-expansive or nonbinary identity should also have access to the restroom or changing area that provides them the greatest degree of comfort, privacy, and safety. This may be an all-gender option or a specifically gender-designated facility. The important caveat is that it is the *student* who makes this determination and that they are not denied the use of the facility that serves to optimize their health, safety, *and* gender congruity.

If *all students* use the restroom that best aligns with their gender identity, then trans students are not singled out as the exception solely based on actual or *presumed* genital configuration. After all, no one is doing genital checks, thank goodness. One bonus of this straightforward approach is that it provides children with a better understanding of the term *gender identity*, in themselves and in others. If they understand that a trans girl has the gender identity of a girl, then it will be quite logical to them that she would use the girls' facilities—anything else would seem contradictory. When a transgender child uses the restroom that works best for them—taking into consideration gender identity alignment, health needs, and safety, it serves to remove a degree of guesswork for educators as well. For gender-diverse students, having the ability to select the optimal restroom is a crucial indicator of the school's support and understanding of that student's basic needs. For the rest of the students, it is simply the solution that makes the most sense.

Adults, however, are often hesitant to allow trans children to use the bathroom that aligns with their gender. One reason for this hesitation is that they feel ill-equipped to address questions from students and parents within the school community. To successfully implement this change, school personnel will need a basic knowledge base and audience-specific language to explain gender identity to those unfamiliar with the topic.[4] When equipped with such tools, they can confidently dispel any concern, confusion, or fear that may arise.

ADDRESSING QUESTIONS FROM CHILDREN

While a student-centric approach to facility usage sounds good in theory, putting this approach into action feels to be anything but. Ranking at the top of expressed hesitations are two questions:

- Won't other children be confused or uncomfortable if a child switches to a different bathroom?
- Why can't the transgender child use a separate bathroom?

As with any new situation, children typically look to the adults in their lives as a response barometer. If an adult is uncomfortable, fearful, distressed, or angry, children will both perceive and be influenced by this. This can cause the children to be confused, distressed, and fearful without knowing the reasons why. If the school leadership approaches the "bathroom question" with a matter-of-fact, respectful approach, they provide an excellent example for children to emulate. Consider these commonly asked questions presented by children themselves:

1. Why is Nadia using the boys' bathroom? Why is Noa in the girls' bathroom?
2. Peter is wearing a dress. Why is he using the boys' bathroom?
3. Doesn't she have a penis? Why is she using the girls' bathroom?

It is normal and natural for children to be inquisitive. What better environment than a school to encourage and address this curiosity? It fosters learning and a greater understanding of our diverse world. Consider the potential impact of *not answering* any of the above questions. Children will surely notice if a teacher ignores a question, quickly changes the subject, silences a child with no explanation, or appears awkward or uncomfortable while offering a stilted response.

Why Is Nadia Using the Boys' Bathroom? Why Is Noa in the Girls' Bathroom?

Questions of this nature will occur most frequently during the early stages of a child's social gender transition. A social transition typically includes a name change, a switch in pronoun usage, sometimes changes in wardrobe, and often a bathroom change. If the social transition has been previously addressed in a straightforward manner with children, the above questions may come from a child who has either forgotten about the gender change or who is still seeking greater clarity.[5]

Possible responses include:

Don't you remember? Nadia is going by the name of Avery now, and he iden-tifies as a boy. So, most boys use the boys' restroom, right?

Noa has told us that she is a girl. In her heart and mind, she feels herself to be a girl. We respect people when they share with us something important about themselves. It's okay to have questions, so please let me know if you have more.

Both responses address instances involving trans children. What happens if the child is not identifying as a different gender but simply has a more expansive gender expression?

Peter Is Wearing a Dress. Why Is He Using the Boys' Bathroom?

Peter does not identify as a girl; he is simply a boy who likes wearing dresses. This is an example of gender expression rather than gender identity. Here is a potential response:

Peter is using the boys' bathroom because he is a boy. Girls wear pants, dresses, shorts, and skirts. All boys, like Peter, can wear those things as well. Clothes are just clothes. I think it takes a lot of courage to do something to be true to oneself even if others may not fully understand?

Children can readily understand concepts like gender identity and gender expression if adults present these concepts in a straightforward manner and with language appropriate for their age.

Doesn't She Have a Penis? Why Is She Using the Girls' Bathroom?

This example can inspire an even greater discomfort in adults simply because genitals are mentioned. Especially in relation to the younger grades, how many student discussions occur where genitals are mentioned? To be sure, these discussions are likely very few. Some children are familiar and/or comfortable using words like vagina and penis and some are not. However, that is not the point. Consider this response:

> She's a girl and, of course, will use the girls' bathroom. A person's private parts are just that—private. It is not okay to talk about another student's private parts. I know you care about your privacy, so I expect you to do the same for others.

Notice how the response didn't delve into a debate about the gender identity of the other student. The response emphasizes a child's right to bodily privacy. This should be the first and foremost response to questions like this. Even though the question may be put forth with no malice or disrespect, that does not mean it is at all reasonable to discuss another child's genitals.

These types of questions require thoughtful, brief responses that get to the heart of the matter. A teacher or parent should also take into consideration other variables like the presence of other children, context, timing, and place to ensure respect and privacy for all students.

An elementary teacher sent this email after the staff had received training to address a particular child's gender transition:

> "Why is Joey using the girls' bathroom, I thought he was a boy?" This question came from a student in my third-grade class. I was immediately nervous. While we as a staff had had training regarding transgender students, we weren't sure how the students would actually respond to their classmate's transition from a male identity to female. After a deep breath, I explained how we all had thought Joey was a boy at first but he had let us know that, in his heart and mind, she feels herself to be a girl and that we would support her by referring to her with her new name, Tahlia, and that she would be using the girls' restroom from now on. Then, I held my breath. The student paused for a moment and then said, "Well, he's always been mostly a girl anyway," and walked away. I had expected the students to be much more confused and that they would need far more in the way of explanation. But the student simply accepted the information at face value.

Another high school was reticent to allow a trans boy to use the boys' restroom at school, being fearful of the reaction of other students. They assumed the other students would experience discomfort. As the administration's resistance to this simple step increased, the situation ramped up to the point where the family was considering legal action. The other male students in the school, aware of the conflict, simply told the trans boy that they recognized that he was a boy and encouraged him to use the restroom. With their blessing, the trans boy started to use the boys' restroom and no student distress or conflict ever occurred. The school, realizing their fears were unfounded, relented. Everything went smoothly from that point onward.

ACT OF DECEPTION OR DESIRE FOR PRIVACY?

A common misperception is that one can "just tell" who a trans person is by looking at them. If a trans person is not visually identifiable, others may immediately feel entitled to "know" who the trans person is. This sense of entitlement directly correlates with the belief that, if a trans person is not identifiable via their physical presentation, then that person is being deliberately deceptive.[6] Regardless of whether someone is visually identifiable as trans or not, they do not have a responsibility to share their history with others. For those unfamiliar with a trans person's experience, it is easy to misinterpret this need for privacy.

Many transgender people want to maintain a level of privacy regarding their gender and may share this with only a select few people close to them. Others are more open. The same is true for gender-diverse children. Children, like their adult counterparts, can be aware of the over-inquisitiveness of many, the judgment from others, and how this can place them under an unfortunate spotlight in their day-to-day lives. Placing a spotlight on a child in this way is disruptive to their schooling experience regardless of the intent of the person(s) doing it:

> "We do not hide who we are at our school!" one principal said. "We should
> be proud of our differences. We make sure that everyone understands who
> our trans student is and that there is no problem with being transgender."

However, this principal did not consider the impact of this pointed disclosure on this shy ten-year-old's daily experience. Every parent in the school was told who the trans child was and some even felt comfortable asking this child questions about her body. The teachers did not feel confident addressing questions from the students either. While the intent was to celebrate difference, the result was a persistently stressful environment where the child was expected to shoulder any and every inquiry from adults and children alike.

Some people may project notions of deception, deviancy, and danger onto even the youngest of trans children. If no one is able to alleviate the fears of adult school community members (through parent educational opportunities for example), these fears can, in a sense, gain false validity. A student transitioning within this kind of environment also experiences the misfortune of being at the center of negative attention and debate. Consider the following situation:

> A small town's school board met to discuss and adopt state-required policy for the inclusion and protection of transgender students. During their meeting, the bewildered school board was tasked with hearing and responding to the concerned—even angry—members of the community who voiced their fears. Stated objections included a fear that boys might simply declare that they are transgender girls to "get access to girls' bathrooms" and that the change in policy would result in "increased rape" and a "war on the middle class." The school board was at a loss for how to respond. Voices were raised and tempers flared. Through her tears, one parent of a transgender elementary school child kept repeating, "We are talking about my child here!"

The school board knew they were obligated by law to implement inclusive policy but, due to their own lack of understanding of transgender students and the simple, respectful ways to implement this policy, were unable to address the apprehensions raised. The board ultimately tabled the decision until a later time. The impact on the student and his family is one that is devastating and long-lasting.

When those responsible for implementing change are prepared and educated about how to respectfully respond in such situations, a completely different scenario can arise. Consider another example, where a teacher presented a similar worry about "safety," and how the moment turned into an opportunity for education:

> During an elementary school staff training where a nine-year-old was soon to transition at school, one teacher mentioned that she was concerned about

the trans girl using the same bathroom as the other girls. When I asked her to offer an example of a problematic situation, she said, "Okay, suppose a transgender girl goes into a stall to relieve herself. Then three or four other girls come in and look over or under the stall and see her penis . . ." Her voice trailed a little as she continued, ". . . and then the girls are traumatized as a result?"

I responded, "I wonder if the person who might be most traumatized in that situation would be the young person who's trying to relieve herself in private." The teacher began nodding. "The issue that needs to be addressed in this situation is the misbehavior of the girls looking over or under the stall. The emphasis should be placed on everyone's right to privacy and that there are repercussions for disrespectful behavior." The teacher and the remaining staff were relieved to realize that any situation they might imagine would also have straightforward solutions that examined student behavior, not student genitals.

The importance of addressing hypothetical "dangerous" scenarios allows most people to find their way to obvious, practical solutions, if solutions are even needed. In the above example, the stated fear was that other girls would see a penis and then experience trauma as a result. The reality is that these girls know their classmate is trans and likely to have a penis. They will not be surprised to see what they are actively looking for as they peer under/over the stall. It will not be a source of trauma for them, but rather an opportunity to laugh at and ridicule another student. If that educator had not voiced this concerning scenario, however, she may not have been able to discover that her unease was unfounded.

The leadership at another school district in a rural, conservative community knew they had transgender students, but they, too, felt at a loss for how to respond to the common questions coming their way. These administrators had an initial template addressing the ways to be inclusive of gender-diverse students and felt that a good portion of these guidelines were manageable. They were interested in handling things in the best way possible but, like many other districts, they too got stuck on the "bathroom question" and requested training.

I mentioned that they were not alone—many people experience a level of uncertainty regarding inclusion in spaces like bathrooms and locker rooms. When we take time to examine potential worrisome scenarios—step by step—the solutions, in my experience, are easily found. One district administrator, who had been silent up to that point, immediately raised his hand:

"I have one for you!"
  I said, "Okay, let's hear your thoughts."
  "What if, there is a girl who identifies as a boy, then this transgender boy also identifies as *gay*. What happens if he wants to use the boys' restroom!?"

He felt this was a clear example of a time when a trans boy should *definitely not* use the restroom that aligned with his male identity. The additional factor of the student's sexual orientation seemed to solidify this for him. Before I could respond, another staff member jumped in:

"Wait a minute! Are you saying that we should insist that all the gay kids have a separate bathroom too? Post a sign that says, "No gays allowed?""

Others in the room quickly agreed that this would *not* be the approach to take and how immediately problematic and discriminatory it would be. The aim is not to disparage the person who raised the objection. In presenting this hypothetical scenario, he, at the very least, was able to articulate his own concerns and those concerns may have been shared by others in the room. Any concerning scenario should be raised and clearly addressed. Unstated, vague apprehensions only serve to perpetuate anxiousness and hesitancy. Walking through these hypothetical scenarios will build confidence, whether these examples are far-fetched, complicated, or otherwise. It provides educators with the recognition that they already have the tools they need to address instances of misbehavior of any type. This particular example made it clear to the others that any trans boy—regardless of sexual orientation—should simply use the boys' restroom.

WHO IS AT RISK?

The staff member who voiced this scenario seemed to have gained some insight. Perhaps the responses of his colleagues helped clarify the issue for him. Because he didn't press any further, I can only speculate as to his initial concerns. Was he worried that the presence of the trans boy would somehow encourage consensual sexual relations in the bathroom? Was he worried that the trans boy might sexually assault one of the other boys? Was he concerned for the safety of the trans boy?

The reality is that the person most at risk for verbal, physical, or sexual assault is the transgender student.[7] Students who stand out in any unique way are more often the target because their difference serves to isolate them, increasing their vulnerability. Creating a safe school environment for transgender students requires education and action, not passivity, exclusion, or resistance. Administrators like these, and the proactive steps they take to prepare themselves, are exactly the steps needed to create a safe learning environment for all children, including trans children.[8]

IS A SEPARATE BATHROOM A REASONABLE ALTERNATIVE?

To a school administrator, teacher, or parent chaperone, providing a transgender child with the use of an alternate restroom can often seem like a reasonable compromise. Surely, it will satisfy all parties—the trans child, their family, the teachers, and the students, as well as the parents of any other children, right? At first glance, offering the use of the nurse's or a staff bathroom does seem like a way to "meet in the middle." A principal may feel they are between a rock and a hard place as they try to accommodate the needs of one specific student versus the pushback—real or perceived—from others within the school community, sometimes even the community-at-large.

There are a number of reasons brought in to validate this approach. One, it *appears* to eliminate awkward or uncomfortable situations where a staff member feels unable to address questions, such as "Why is *she* using the boys' bathroom?" Secondly, an alternate bathroom can appear to offer greater protection to the transgender student by theoretically providing a greater degree of safety from potential bullying. Some would also argue that it "protects the other ninety-nine percent" of students who they expect will surely be uncomfortable with the presence of a transgender student. Finally, it allows both staff and administrators to sidestep questions from potentially angry parents.

Everyone is happy, right? Wrong. It is important to recognize that this proposed solution of the use of an alternate bathroom is generated primarily to allay *adult* fears, or concerns without examining the impact on any individual trans child. Additionally, it presumes a particular response from other children that is rarely present. The person who will theoretically benefit from this—the transgender child—does not benefit and is the one now faced with other unintended consequences.

Administrators at schools, camps, and other youth programs are usually not suggesting an alternate bathroom with any ill intent. They are just seeking a simple solution to what feels like an extremely complex situation. However, this compromising shortcut can have detrimental psychological and health repercussions for the gender-diverse student.

Implications of a Forced Alternate Restroom

NEGATIVE ATTENTION, TEASING, BULLYING

Whether a trans student's gender history is known or unknown to the other students, it will surely be noticed when that student steps out of the normal routine for bathroom breaks. Other children may ask, "Why are you using the nurse's bathroom?" or "What's wrong with you?" This places the student in the position of providing awkward or embarrassing partial explanations, creating a fabricated reason, or saying nothing at all. Regardless of the explanation offered, students can sense the discomfort and distress of the trans child, potentially paving the way for progressive teasing or bullying. It is not right to put a child in any of these situations because a school hopes to sidestep its responsibilities in the matter. Rather than alleviating potential bullying, it is very likely to increase it instead.

SENSE OF BELONGING AND AFFIRMATION

Teachers and school staff who work with transgender students need to create an environment that instills respect toward transgender students and that also recognizes and validates their gender identity. Trans students who are told that they cannot use the bathroom that aligns with their gender identity have shared that they experience this as a direct invalidation of their identity.[9] And indeed it is! It is an obvious contradiction to say, "Yes, we see you as a boy, but not enough for you to use the boy's bathroom." At one point in history, the US Supreme Court confirmed the notion that we could have racially "separate, but equal" accommodations for restrooms and other facilities. We have since come to understand that insisting on separation for those who are "different" is damaging, unfair, and anything but equal. We must no longer place a greater value or sense of worth on certain people over others:

One family immediately noticed how, once they supported him in his gender identity at age seven, their son went from being despondent to smiling all the time. This changed, however when he was prohibited from using either the boys' or girls' restrooms at school and was singled out to use the limited non-gendered restrooms instead. The unwanted attention this created caused him to become anxious and unhappy while his health and academic performance suffered. His family pursued legal intervention and the school finally allowed him to use the boys' facilities. His confidence shot up, as did his academic performance.

Yet, by the time he got to middle school, a new set of barriers awaited him. He was not allowed to change for gym in the boys' locker room and was instead forced to use the coach's office. He was again required to use a restroom in the front office and denied access to both the boys' and the girls' restrooms. By seventh grade, the school installed a "porta-potty" close to his classes and solely for his use. A year later, his classes were too far from the porta-potty, so he, like so many trans children in similar situations, began restricting his water intake to avoid the restroom altogether. This resulted in recurring kidney infections, which, for him, were made even more dangerous because he had only one functioning kidney.

By the time he reached high school, he was required to change in the media center for gym class, causing him to be frequently late for class. Still required to use single-user restrooms, insult was added to injury as these restrooms were consistently locked. Bullying ramped up. His focus at school declined to the point of almost failing and he refused to discuss college or any other future plans. His family filed a lawsuit and prevailed when the district settled. The victory, his parents said, as well as finally having access to the boys' facilities, resulted in his confidence going "through the roof." With that burden lifted, his grades improved, and he soon made the school's honor roll.

For anyone, including a trans child, using the bathroom or locker room that best aligns with their identity simply makes sense, causes them the least distress (assuming it is handled appropriately), and it allows that child the ability to move through their school experience like any other student.

CHILD DISTRESS

Most young children do not have the ability to articulate the reasons why they feel so distressed about using an alternate restroom because they do not yet have the cognitive development to understand the broader adult issues at play. They simply feel the results of a social stigma without understanding its complexity.[10] Also, trans kids may feel that they (or their gender) are a source of distress or tension for the adults around them and therefore won't talk about teasing or bullying with their parents. While anxious parents often *do* recognize the broader issues associated with this stigma, as well as the possibility of negative attention toward their child, when they ask their child how school is going and hear that everything is "fine," they are so relieved that they may not notice the reticence of their child. Many children simply suffer silently through harsh experiences of teasing, bullying, mental, and/or physical distress to not be a burden to others, including their parents.

One family whose daughter was required to use an alternate restroom, related this story:

> My child's school said my trans daughter could use the bathroom in the staff lounge. We agreed, thinking that was as far as we might get in our conservative town. What we didn't realize was that she had to walk a quarter of a mile to get to the bathroom! No one, including our daughter, had ever mentioned this. She had an urgent need one day, and we were not talking number one, so set off to the bathroom as quickly as she could. But she didn't make it! You can't tell me that she is not damaged by that experience! I know I am!

HEALTH REPERCUSSIONS

Not only may the use of an alternate restroom bring about increased negative attention from other students, but the daily distress experienced by a trans child cannot be underestimated. Many trans youth, whether young children or teens, will avoid using the restroom all day to avoid negative attention.

The resulting health implications are significant, including extreme physical discomfort, bladder and kidney infections, and dehydration. Even mild dehydration can negatively impact mood, ability to concentrate, and energy level, which can obviously hinder a child's ability to learn in school. The psychological strain continues because the child often will not disclose their bathroom avoidance to their parents or other adults who could help. Even very young transgender children—out of a sense of internalized guilt or even protectiveness for their parents—will not disclose this fact in an effort to decrease the distress of their parents. Many parents are shocked to discover this, often only becoming aware of this avoidance when their child becomes seriously ill.

Time and time again, not providing gender-diverse students with appropriate access to facilities can cause them significant and sometimes irreparable harm:

One elementary-aged trans boy was supported by his family but not so at school. The school would not recognize his gender identity despite having initially done so. He had been successfully using the boys' restroom, but the school eventually surrendered to external political pressure and reversed its decision. School administrators said he had to go back to using the girls' bathroom instead. But the students no longer saw him as a girl. Now he was seen as an "in-between" no longer welcomed in either restroom. This resulted in significant feelings of isolation and exclusion. He started to restrict his use of any facility and severely limited what he ate and drank during the school day to try to avoid using the restroom altogether. Over time, this ostracism caused him to develop a severe eating disorder. His cardiologist told his parents that he was only weeks away from permanent heart damage. During his initial recovery period, their son was so skinny and wasted that, as the nutritionists prescribed small increases in calories, it was necessary to restrict how many steps he could take each day.

Sadly, these kinds of experiences are all too common for gender-diverse children in schools that are deeply unprepared to address their needs. Some environments are not only unprepared but willfully hostile:

Living in what the mother described as an "ultra-conservative" town in Texas, one family had supported their trans daughter's gender identity since before kindergarten. It was not an easy journey. The mother, an ordained minister and registered nurse, had been born in Alabama and raised in Mississippi as an evangelical Christian. The parents had had to move through a monumental and deep soul-searching time to get to the place of support so desperately needed by their daughter.

When their daughter entered kindergarten, the school district refused to allow her to use the girls' restroom. She could use the gender-neutral restroom when she was in her classroom but was otherwise required to use the nurse's restroom.

The mother contested the policy and tried to educate school officials, but the situation deteriorated. By first grade, her daughter no longer had the option of using any restroom inside the classroom. The school revised its policy so that the child was no longer allowed to even use the nurse's restroom, leaving the staff restroom as her only option. Because of the stigma and isolation she felt, the child desperately tried to avoid using any restroom altogether. This exclusion had devastating and traumatic consequences. She once tried to use the girls' restroom in first grade but was physically removed by school staff in a humiliating and painful manner. She became the target of daily bullying and stopped using the restroom at all, painfully holding it until she got home. This caused long-term consequences for her bladder. Over five years later, her bladder is still not functioning normally, and she remains under the care of a urologist.

UNDUE FOCUS ON GENITALS

Relegating a student to a separate bathroom delivers an inadvertent message to the transgender student. The subtext of this implies: *Who you are and, more specifically, your genital configuration require that we isolate you from the rest of the students.*

If a transgender student, whose gender status is known to the other students, is expected to use a separate bathroom, the remaining students will draw the conclusion that the trans student's body is somehow abnormal, wrong, and one from which *they* need protection. A simple and daily act—using the restroom—in which all students should be able to expect a degree of privacy, is now one in which the trans student is essentially spotlighted. All students are aware that a different bathroom is being provided because of that student's genital configuration. The message is loud and clear that the body of the trans student—specifically their private parts—is somehow bad or wrong, to the point that they need to be kept separate from everyone else.

Consider the approach of the following school, which explored the option of staff education and then decided against it. Instead, I was invited to "observe" a classroom discussion led by school staff in which a fourth-grade transgender student was sharing her forthcoming gender transition and name change:

The school seemed proud of how they decided to address this student's transition with the students. In each classroom, the students were told, in a twenty-minute PowerPoint presentation focusing solely on the trans child, that they [the other students] would likely experience "feelings of discomfort" with her transition. This statement was immediately followed by a statement that the trans child would be using a teacher's bathroom from now on.

While the principal felt he was being both pragmatic and progressive, he was unable to see the unfortunate repercussions of this approach. The inadvertent message delivered to the students was that (1) their classmate had an odd difference [her genitals] that could be deemed upsetting and that (2) all the adults felt the other children needed to be protected from this student by segregating her away to a different facility—one not accessible to the rest of the students. The trans girl and her grandfather, her primary caregiver, were African American. As someone who was deeply familiar with segregated bathrooms in the South during his own upbringing, this grandfather felt anguish and helplessness seeing his granddaughter separated away from the other students in much the same way, and for similar reasons.

While no one intends to draw attention to the transgender child's genitals, the notion of a separate bathroom does just that. This focus on genitals—and the implication that some genitals are "normal" and others "abnormal"—will be internalized by the trans student as well as incorporated into the understanding of the rest of the students. This can cause the trans child to feel a great sense of internalized shame and to experience both isolation and anxiety. Additionally, it can open the door to increased instances of teasing. Obviously, this student's ability to learn, develop strong social connections and positive self-esteem, are of grave concern.

When to Consider Alternate Bathrooms

Occasionally, there are students who may be uncomfortable when sharing a bathroom or locker room with a gender-diverse student. This occurs far less frequently than adults might think. Educating children about gender identity in age-appropriate ways goes a long way to achieving the greatest degree of comfort for all. There may also be a time when a trans or gender-diverse student is not comfortable using either the boys' or the girls' bathroom. These situations can happen for a variety of reasons and may or may not be temporary.

For those students who do experience discomfort for any reason, it is important to have a solution available. Therefore, a school should be prepared to meet the needs of *any* student experiencing discomfort—trans or otherwise—and that includes the *choice* to use an alternative restroom. The important distinction to recognize is that this option is not being *forced* on the trans student and it is one that is available to *any* other student desiring the need for increased privacy for any reason.

NEW TERRAIN OR ALL TOO FAMILIAR PATHWAY?

Concerns about bathroom and locker room usage by gender-diverse students are at a historical high. National dialogue addressing trans inclusion in public facilities reached such a frenzied pitch in 2016, that The Human Rights Campaign, identified that year as the "The Most Dangerous Year for Transgender Americans."[11] Yet, just a few years later, hard as it is to imagine, the same advocacy organization declared 2021 to be even worse, naming it "The Deadliest Year on Record for Trans and Nonbinary People."[12] It is heartbreaking to understand that this escalation of violence and anti-trans legislation directly correlates with gender-diverse children's courageous efforts to be visible and included within their homes, communities, and especially schools.

In 2021–2022, hundreds of legislative bills were introduced into state legislatures across the nation. The bills target caregivers who are supportive of their child's gender identity and medical professionals who provide these children with life-saving medical care. Ironically, these bills would criminalize the very actions so consistently recommended by numerous professional associations— associations comprised of the top experts in their respective fields including pediatricians, physicians, psychologists, social workers, endocrinologists, and others.

Proponents of these legislative efforts stoke the fires of unfounded fears and worries that, unfortunately, resonate with many people, especially those less informed as to the actual life experiences of trans children, teens, and adults. Ground zero often occurs in areas of public accommodations—bathrooms and locker rooms.

TMDY VLADA KNOWLTON

The Most Dangerous Year (2019)

The documentary film, *The Most Dangerous Year*, began when, in late 2015, I had a conversation with Aidan Key. He spoke with me about the wave of discriminatory "bathroom bills" and other anti-trans legislation that was beginning to sweep across the United States. As a parent of a trans child I understood the dangers that trans Americans and their loved ones were facing. I began filming legislative events, interviews with families of trans children, and Aidan's supportive work in schools, and developed what turned into an unexpectedly successful independent documentary. Given the dearth of realistic depictions of trans people and their lived experiences in popular culture, the film's journey after its release has been truly inspiring and hope filled.

The Most Dangerous Year (TMDY) premiered at the Seattle International Film Festival in 2018 and won several awards across the country, including Best Social Issue Documentary Feature at Atlanta's DocuFest. It was positively reviewed by the *New York Times, Los Angeles Times*, along with other film critics, while Common Sense Media placed it on the top of its "Best LGBT Movies for Teens" list. *TMDY* had a special screening before some members of the U.S. Congress and won a Human and Civil Rights International Peace and Understanding Award from the Washington Education Association.

TMDY was picked up by both theatrical and educational distribution companies and is available for streaming on several platforms including Sundance Now and Amazon Prime.[13] As a result of its educational distribution, the film has been screened numerous times by universities, high schools, community centers, and public libraries across the country.

Some of the most gratifying moments for me came from the people I met at film screenings. One trans youth in Missouri approached me to express his gratitude for the film. He said, "It's such a relief to see someone else helping to explain this to people so I don't have to keep doing it on my own." I believe we all need to do whatever we can to stand up for young trans people and make sure they don't feel like they're fighting for their identities, lives, and futures on their own.

To learn more about the film and how to view it, visit www.themostda ngerousyear.com.

Vlada Knowlton—writer, director, and producer of The Most Dangerous Year

As we seek to address the civil rights of gender-diverse people, we do not have to look too far in the past to recognize that similar fears were used as emotionally charged weapons in the fight against equal access and protections for other disempowered minorities. During the civil rights movement, segregationists argued vociferously against racially integrated bathrooms, citing dangers to white women that included increased sexual assault (from black men) and acquiring sexually transmitted diseases (from black women) sharing toilet seats. While research in no way bears this out, modern public facilities are continually deemed to be epicenters for sexual assault, disease transmission, and other dangers—especially to white women and children.[14] Anti-trans legislation seeks to reengage a fearful public into codifying the same illogical denial of equity and access that has been and, sadly, continues to be part of our nation's history.[15]

CYRUS HABIB INTERVIEW

"I understand that there are people out there who are being told that allowing transgender individuals to use the correct bathroom will lead to danger for themselves, or even worse, for their children.

That can be a very powerful threat or a very powerful way to instill fear in people. But let's be clear. There's no documented evidence that people who are transgender are any more likely to be predators than the general population. There's no reason to believe that individuals using the bathroom that fits their gender identity leads to any of these sorts of acts.

So, I think it's an attempt to try to broaden the appeal of this socially conservative measure by getting people to see a boogeyman where there simply isn't one."

Cyrus Habib, WA State Lieutenant Governor—TMDY film interview, 2016[16]

ARE SCHOOL BATHROOMS AND LOCKER ROOMS SAFE FOR EVERYONE? ANYONE?

Ask any educator, administrator, physical education (PE) teacher, or janitor about facilities misadventures and misbehaviors and they will likely tell you tales that would rival some of the best dramas or horror movies ever made. These tales range from the standard fare that includes student bullying, smoking, drug use, and sexual activity to newer episodes including social-media-driven destruction of school property. A number of variables contribute to well-functioning facilities. A different set of variables can contribute to student behavioral problems within those same facilities. Regardless of the form the problematic behavior takes, the management of these situations is not new. Every educator knows that handling student misbehavior is just an unfortunate part of the job. So why is it that the presence of trans children within these facilities is lamented as unmanageable?

Until we, as a society, shift to a better understanding of the experiences of people in diverse circumstances, we may initially lack the ability to appropriately and swiftly respond. If a teacher has not, for example, learned how to address instances of racism or xenophobia within the classroom, then that teacher's sense of intimidation could keep them silent, dodging the important need for swift intervention. The teacher's avoidance can then segue into a possible response that includes assigning some responsibility, even blame, to the victim. *If only he wouldn't wear his hair like that. That wouldn't happen if she wasn't wearing those clothes. When his English is better, this probably won't happen.* Add to this equation, the queasy discomfort that many people feel because of false portrayals of trans people as deviant, mentally ill, and dangerous and you most certainly have an individual who is deeply unprepared to act in situations where action is a must. The solutions an educator needs to employ simply do not come to mind when in this state of paralysis. This hands-off approach leads to the abdication of much-needed supervision from the people normally responsible for it. The way is paved for unrestricted targeting of gender-diverse students and, unfortunately, the educator becomes complicit in the harm caused because of their inability to act.

SUPERVISION AND BEHAVIOR PROBLEMS

The good news is that school personnel can find their way back to feeling empowered and confident. If all of us have, for generations, experienced gender-separated facilities, we can get stumped when encountering situations in need of urgent attention. Behavioral problems do not always originate from students as evidenced in the following example:

I had two elementary school trainings in a rural school district where they had become aware of a couple of trans students. On the day of the second school training, I received a call from the district asking if I would be able to "stop by" the administrative offices beforehand. Seven district leaders were present and, after a little hemming and hawing, they brought up the subject of the high school girls' locker room:

"What if," one said, "an adult walks into the locker room but we don't know if that person is transgender or not?"

"Do adults have access to use the girls' locker room?" I responded. My question was met with a resounding "No!"

"Easy enough," I said, "Ask them to leave."

"Uh, okay, great thanks," the administrator continued, "but that's not it, really. So, what if it *is* a facility that adults *can* access and we don't know if that person is a trans woman or not?"

"If that person is using the facility in the manner for which it was designed—changing, washing up, etc.," I said, "then trust that this person knows what they are doing. If the person inadvertently walked into the wrong locker room or bathroom, the presence of another person will likely make them immediately aware of their own mistake."

"Well, okay, we get that. But, there's more . . . This is really helpful, Aidan, but . . . ," he hesitated, "the reality is that there is one member of our community—he's actually the grandfather of one of our students—and he is threatening to put on women's clothes to access the girls' facilities in order to *prove how unsafe these girls are.*"

"Call the police," I said. "Let him explain his actions to them."

It had taken these district staff leaders more than half an hour to place on the table the *actual situation* they feared could occur. They were bogged down in their search for a one-size-fits-all solution to determining whether someone is transgender or not. In reality, they all understood that the potential perpetrator of illegal activity (this grandfather) was not transgender himself but clearly wanted to cause trouble for people who are. Because they could not find a definitive way of knowing if someone was a bona fide trans person, they felt stuck. This prevented them from seeing an obvious solution to a person engaging in illegal activity.

Solutions to this and other *perceived* dilemmas do exist, yet our access to critical thinking skills is often thwarted by heightened emotions and fears of making errors. This is temporary. These school administrators needed a little more understanding to get over a psychological barrier. Yet, for so many, this guidance and information are either unavailable or slow to reach those most in need. As we walked through each scenario together—especially the most daunting one—it was as if someone had turned on the lights in a darkened room. They now clearly understood the problem and knew what to do.

While the threatened misbehavior from an adult man temporarily stumped district leaders, the following example involving the behavior of another child's parents played out to an ugly conclusion:

A young African American couple with a third-grade trans daughter worked with their child's elementary school so she could begin her social transition. All went reasonably well, especially considering how new it was for the staff. One day, the child and several other girls were goofing off in the bathroom, snapping each other's elastic underwear waistbands. One of the girls mentioned it in passing to her parents later that day at home. These parents escalated the situation rapidly with an angry call to the school. When the school tried to explain the innocent nature of their playfulness, the enraged parents refused to accept it. Their next call was to the police station to file sexual assault charges against the nine-year-old trans girl. None of the other girls were targeted, only the known trans child. The convergence of several factors—the bathroom location, snapping elastic on panties, and a transgender girl—equated to a crime scene, criminal action, and perpetrator for the other family. The underpinnings of race cannot be ignored as African American people are historically portrayed as dangerous individuals who sexually prey on others. The police were required to investigate this situation and assured the parents of the trans girl that they understood there was no merit to the allegations. Those assurances did not mean that the experience wasn't traumatizing—it was for the entire family.

SAFETY

One nine-year-old trans girl was the victim of constant bullying due to a complete lack of intervention and leadership at her school. The family was helpless to effect any change to the daily violence. The school administrator felt that the violence "just came with the territory" of being transgender. It was sad to hear the mother, trying to be positive, say, "Well, our kid is really resilient. She's had stitches in just about every part of her body imaginable." While it could be framed as resiliency, the reality is that this child was sent into a war zone and the educators tasked with ensuring the safety of their students refused to do so. The family finally withdrew the child from that school and enrolled her in a school that took the responsibility of protecting its students seriously.

Ensuring the safety of students is no small task. Many safety concerns in the twenty-first century would make prior generations of educators shudder to imagine. School shootings, for example, have necessitated preparations that everyone wishes were not needed. Nevertheless, we understand that we cannot discard these responsibilities. It does not mean we initially have a clear idea of what to do but we learn and develop more informed practices over time. What works? What is ineffectual? One central Illinois school provides an example of this learning curve. An unidentified student had posted a note threatening a school shooting on a stall door in the girls' restroom. What preventative measure was taken by the school to prevent other threats? Remove the stall doors in every girls' restroom throughout the school! If you don't have stall doors, no one will have a door on which to post any future threatening notes. Problem solved? Of course not. There are a million places on which to post future notes. Problems added? Absolutely. Now you have the privacy rights of students stripped from them, causing every student seeking to use the girls' facility daily physical and mental distress. And, unsurprisingly, opting to avoid the restroom altogether resulted in health challenges that trans students know all too well.

We can only hope logic prevailed for this midwestern school community. This example highlights how a perceived threat that is unfamiliar can cause common sense to fly out the window. I respond to numerous inquiries when speaking to educators and parents as they express deep worry about "what might happen."

One high school teacher surprised me with this question:

"Suppose there is a trans boy in the boys' locker room and he is changing for PE..."

So many people bring up the presence of trans girls in locker rooms. It is much less common for someone to bring up a trans boy. I'm all ears as she continues.

"... he is changing for P.E., takes his shirt off and *his breasts are showing*?"

Now, all I can think of are the vast number of trans boys who are too intimidated to engage in PE and often beg to get out of a PE requirement. I've never heard of a trans boy who would be so comfortable in a locker room that he would strip a shirt off and have his chest bared for all to see. I'm also a little impressed that she was consistent with the trans boy's pronouns even as she is referring to *his breasts*. As I am pondering a response, I realize that this teacher has not yet finished with her question.

"Then, eight or nine other boys in the locker room see his breasts and all their little flagpoles go up! Then, I just don't know what is going to happen!"

She has progressed this scenario to one that she imagines could end in gang rape. I addressed the more common realities of trans boys who are deeply hesitant to use a boys' locker room under any circumstances and would more likely wear multiple shirt layers to hide their chest than so readily rip off a shirt and expose a part of their body that typically causes them so much distress. Some trans boys will shower at home with the bathroom lights off because the site of their own non-masculine chest is a despairing reminder that their body has betrayed them.

Yet, with all of that said, I still haven't answered her question. The actual question she framed but didn't directly articulate is, "How do we prevent the gang rape of a trans boy?" She presented a wildly unlikely scenario that extended where she imagined that the behavior of students would extend to violent criminal acts.

Barring trans boys from entering a locker room to prevent gang rape and removing stall doors in girls' bathrooms to prevent school shootings are not protective courses of action and will do nothing to improve student safety. If the goal is to minimize the prospect of gang rape and school shootings there surely are safety measures that will better accomplish this.

"What steps do you currently take to ensure that gang rape does not occur on school premises under any circumstance?" I asked. Surprisingly, no one in the audience responded. Does this mean that none of them had thought about this before? What is more likely is that these educators already have systems in place to decrease the likelihood of crime—lockers in which to store valuables, security measures to detect the presence of unauthorized individuals, well-lit school environs, and perhaps most importantly, proper adult supervision of students on school grounds.

I imagine that this teacher's inquiry was not one designed to find a solution to this proposed dangerous scenario but rather one that could be put forth as a solid reason to bar any trans boy from using the locker room under any circumstances.

PRIVACY

It is interesting to consider that—even while privacy is cited as one of the top needs of gender-diverse students—there is a belief that the privacy needs of every other student will disappear solely because a trans student is present. There is a level of helpless exasperation expressed when discussions turn to facilities access. One teacher statement succinctly exemplified this when she said, "We love our trans student. I just can't get past the locker room question."

One reason that people collectively encounter this impasse is that it feels new and unfamiliar. They are unaware that they've been sharing facilities with trans people without realizing it. Therefore, it feels as though it has never happened. Also, many of us, especially older generations, rely on our own childhood experiences in locker rooms and view them as comparable to the experiences of today's youth. Older individuals are often in school leadership positions and may not realize the days of the hyper-observant gym teacher supervising naked students showering is largely an occurrence of the past. One district administrator's concern highlights this:

> "If we have a high school trans girl using the showers with the other girls, won't that cause huge discomfort for them?" he asked.
>
> I said, "Do the kids still shower together?
>
> Everyone in the room, besides this district administrator, vigorously shook their heads no. He was incredulous.
>
> "They don't?!"
>
> He went on to talk about the times of locker room embarrassment and humiliation that he and the other boys experienced several decades ago. Another educator piped in.
>
> "We use the showering area for storage."

Times have changed . . . significantly.

NEW YORK TIMES ARTICLE ON SHOWERS

A *New York Times* article, taking an in-depth look at the usage—really, non-usage—of showers by students encapsulated this fact with the article's title, "Students Still Sweat, They Just Don't Shower."[17] The article, published almost three decades ago, did not discuss gender-diverse students at all. The stories of trans students in schools had not yet found their way to mainstream media outlets. This article addressed students' desire and right to bodily privacy. A few salient points from this article expand on this point as author Dirk Johnson writes:

[A]mong most American high school students these days, one thing is considered way too strange: showering with classmates after gym period.

. . .

In a striking measure of changed sensibilities in school and society, showering after physical education class, once an almost military ritual, has become virtually extinct.

. . .

Students across the United States have abandoned school showers, and their attitudes seem to be much the same whether they live in inner-city high-rises, on suburban cul-de-sacs, or in far-flung little towns in cornfield country.

. . .

A generation ago, when most schools mandated showers, a teacher would typically monitor students and hand out towels, making sure that proper hygiene was observed. In schools with pools, students were sometimes required to swim naked, and teachers would conduct inspections for cleanliness that schools today would not dare allow, whether because of greater respect for children or greater fear of lawsuits.

. . .

Some people believe that children today simply grow up accustomed to more privacy. Years ago, when bigger families lived in smaller houses with fewer bathrooms and bedrooms, it was the rare child who could maintain a sense of modesty.

. . .

Students who dreaded showering at school got a lift two years ago [1994] after the American Civil Liberties Union threatened to file a lawsuit in Federal court over a mandatory shower policy in Hollidaysburg, Pa.

. . .

The school district dropped its policy. But in the meantime, [the ACLU attorney] was deluged with calls and letters of support from people who remembered their own feelings of shame and embarrassment in the public showers.

> "In 25 years of doing A.C.L.U. work—cases on prayer in the school, you name it—I had never had any response like this," he said. "People remembered their own humiliation. I myself remember moving from my little country school to the city school and being mortified about having to take showers. But in those days, you did what the schools said, you did what the teachers said."
>
> Mandatory showers and teachers on shower patrol are virtually a thing of the past now, and rinsing off after gym is the student's option. In fact, some schools are considering removing showers because they are not used.

It can be a bit mystifying why the locker room question is still so ubiquitous when the issue itself appears to be a specter from the past. Students, for decades now, have been clamoring for a greater degree of privacy, trans students included, and schools are providing it. When students are deprived of facilities for any reason, their health suffers. Children will avoid using restrooms when cleanliness is not maintained, soap and paper towel dispensers are removed, or there is not enough time between classes to relieve themselves. We understand the needs of gender-diverse children because we understand the needs of all children. One superintendent in a conservative district shared this with me:

> I'm really frustrated with how much others will criticize all of us in Tennessee because we are a southern red state. They think we don't care about our kids! Two trans students took me aside one day. When one of them shared with me that he did not feel like he could safely use either restroom and would hold his pee all day long, I was shocked. When the second student, concurred and said, "Yeah, I've started to wear "pee pads" just to get through the day," I was horrified. I went to every principal in my district and talked to them about the importance of bathroom access for our trans students. Every single one of them felt just as strongly as I did. We worked with every student to make sure they had access to a restroom that worked best for them.

Another administrator shared this anecdote:

The question that shows up over and over again is always about locker rooms. While it seems to consistently revolve around the fears of predatory behavior, however improbable, we did want to respond to our community in a way that was respectful and would allay their fears. So, we toured every facility in the district. Guess what? It turns out we weren't doing a good job of protecting the privacy of *any* student. There were very few available options for students who might want to change in private. Once we realized this, we worked with our facilities staff to make multiple private changing areas without having to undertake any costly remodels. Just a simple, fixed "pipe and drape" approach did the trick. This meant that any student who wanted privacy had it. This satisfied most of the concerns—but not all.

A few people had concerns about trans students who might be "activists" and want to "let it all hang out," specifically a trans girl who might opt to be fully undressed with her penis visible to all. No amount of assurances offered about the fact that trans students rarely feel comfortable disrobing, making this scenario extremely unlikely, seemed to reduce these fears. I was able to respond to this concern very easily as we had already addressed it! A few years ago, we had three exchange students from Chile attend one of our high schools. These young women [not trans] were at ease being naked in the locker room and were unaware that the other students were uncomfortable. Even the PE teacher had mentioned it to me saying, "One of these young women, came up to talk to me. I found myself squirming a little. I'm not in the habit of having conversations with naked girls!" We decided the best approach was to speak to these students about the cultural differences in the United States and that their fellow students were more comfortable with a greater degree of modesty shown in the locker room. We made sure that this would not land as body-shaming, that was important too.

We knew what we needed to communicate to our students. First, the locker room is a place to change into gym clothes, not a place to socialize. Get in, get changed, and get out on the court/field. That, coupled with an expectation of modesty while changing, meant that we could address any situation with ease. Sharing this example, and how our approach could easily address any situation with a trans student, was just what was needed. Everyone seemed relieved.

SINGLE-USER AND SINGLE-STALL FACILITIES

If we can navigate our way through our initial hesitancy and address any facilities-related concerns, we clear our minds for solutions that are implementable, affordable, and safe.

PRINCIPAL CRAIG MCCALLA

In my daily activities as a building principal, inclusivity and accessibility for all students were something I purposefully advocated for and monitored. Of course, everyone wants to be included. Inclusionary policies, practices, and curriculum are important but there are other ways as well. When our Dexter, Michigan, community passed a bond to build a new elementary school, the door was open to look at inclusion and access in a new light.

We considered the physical spaces within our buildings, especially the school community bathrooms. Historically, we had constructed gender-specific bathrooms in hallways and larger gathering spaces like the cafeteria. In reimagining the layout of these bathrooms, we were able to create two all-gender bathrooms each with three individual private stalls.

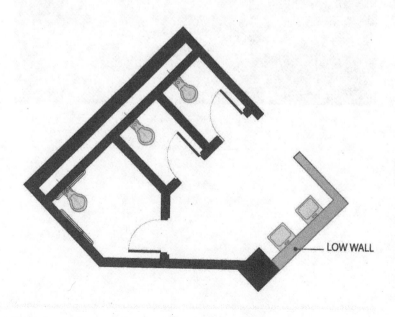

LOW WALL

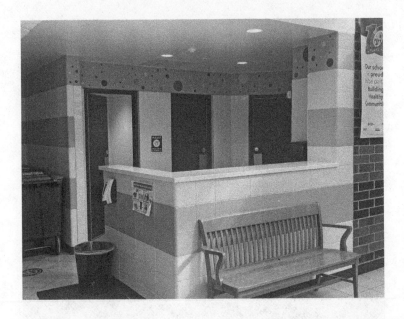

Within each bathroom, there is one ADA-accessible stall. One side of the bathroom was constructed with a half wall affording optimal visibility, and easy supervision, into the open hand-washing area while the floor-to-ceiling stall doors optimized privacy for anyone using them. Our staff can easily monitor the handwashing area and any needed assistance can be given without compromising the privacy of others using the bathroom. They don't need to even enter the restroom to do so!

We liked this layout so much that, when we had the opportunity for renovations of an older elementary school, we included this new design. It's been over three years and we have had nothing but positive reviews from staff (much easier supervision), the students (greater degree of privacy), and families (optimal safety for their children). Any student can use any bathroom.

Of course, there were initial concerns raised about the potential cost. When looking at the budget for our new elementary school we were able to make the needed adjustments for just $37,000, which was only a 0.14 percent increase to the budget. In the grand scheme of building a new school, this cost is negligible.

Across the country, discussions regarding transgender students often focus on safety and privacy within bathrooms. This model not only provides a private bathroom space for our transgender students but for everyone. What child is going to complain about having a private bathroom?!

Reimagining school space can be done in all schools. This bathroom design can be used at every level—elementary, middle, or high school—to create safer, inclusive environments for all. I would urge any and every school district to consider this design model for both new building construction and renovations to existing bathrooms. This design benefits ALL students, including those who are transgender. Behavioral problems are down, supervision is easier, and safety and privacy for all are set up. Who does not want that?

Single-user, all-gender restrooms are one of the easiest ways to address any issue or concern from all perspectives. It is a simple answer to what ought to be a simple question. Who wouldn't appreciate the greater sense of safety and privacy that comes with the use of a private restroom? A practical argument against single-user bathrooms is one of expense. We see from the previous approach in Dexter, Michigan, that expense is a manageable factor for both new construction and renovations to existing buildings. But some schools have found creative solutions that worked without spending a dime:

A Midwestern school came up with an idea that resulted in a simple, effective solution to their multi-stalled, but gender-separated facilities. Rather than have students descend upon the bathroom *en masse* during designated times like recess or lunch, students of any gender would simply request a pass whenever they needed to use the bathroom. This "pass" was a magnetized sign that was placed on the outer door of any multi-user bathroom indicating that it was occupied. If a second student came to use the bathroom, they understood that they were to wait until the first student was done, and could then follow suit with their own magnet. If a third or fourth student were to show up, they were required to find the next closest bathroom so as not to build a lengthy queue. The effectiveness of this approach was phenomenal. Behavior incidents of any sort were eliminated, adult concerns about "gender-mixing" became a moot point, and all students appreciated the increased privacy.

Addressing hot button issues like bathroom and locker rooms—including all underlying fears—allows us to much more easily identify solutions to not only these questions but any others that arise when we so easily—and so needlessly—bar gender-diverse children from the facilities that work most optimally for them. The "bathroom question" is no longer a show-stopper or even up for debate. Instead it is a question with obvious solutions.

It is our deeply ingrained societal norms that make us resistant to change and propel the belief that this change will lead to danger and chaos. Difficult situations can and do occur. This is evidenced by the harsh experiences of gender-diverse youth. Difficulties or dangers for other students, simply because a gender-diverse youth is present within these facilities, do not bear out.

If we step into the questions—what about the bathroom, what about the locker room—then we can step over the fears that bog us down. We find solutions that are creative, affordable, optimize safety, and *benefit all children.*

NOTES

1. See Arnold H. Grossman et al., "Lesbian, Gay, Bisexual and Transgender Youth Talk about Experiencing and Coping with School Violence: A Qualitative Study," *Journal of LGBT Youth* 6, no. 1 (January 2009): 24–46, https://doi.org/10.1080/19361650802379748; Lydia A. Sausa, "Translating Research into Practice: Trans Youth Recommendations for Improving School Systems," *Journal of Gay & Lesbian Issues In Education* 3, no. 1 (July 2005): 15–28, https://doi.org/10.1300/J367v03n01_04; "Harsh Realities: The Experiences of Trans Youth in Schools," *GLSEN*, https://www.glsen.org/research/harsh-realities-experiences-trans-youth-schools.

2. As a start, every educator and parent should have a copy of this book, which demystifies some of the basic misconceptions about gender and creates a new foundation for our understanding of transgender children: Laura Erickson-Schroth and Benjamin Davis, *Gender: What Everyone Needs to Know* (New York: Oxford University Press, 2021).

3. Aaron J. Curtis, "Conformity or Nonconformity? Designing Legal Remedies to Protect Transgender Students from Discrimination," *Harvard Journal on Legislation* 53, no. 2 (July 2016): 459–497.

4. Aidan Key, "Children," in *Trans Bodies, Trans Selves: A Resource for the Transgender Community*, ed. Laura Erickson-Schroth (Oxford; New York: Oxford University Press, 2014), 409–445.

5. For a discussion of different aspects of social transition, see Michele Angello and Alisa Bowman, *Raising the Transgender Child: A Complete Guide for Parents, Families & Caregivers* (Berkeley: Seal Press, A Hachette Book Group Company, 2016), 60–81.

6. Laura Erickson-Schroth and Laura A. Jacobs, *"You're in the Wrong Bathroom!": And 20 Other Myths and Misconceptions about Transgender and Gender-Nonconforming People* (Boston: Beacon Press, 2017), 63–68.

7. See Jenifer K. McGuire et al., "School Climate for Transgender Youth: A Mixed Method Investigation of Student Experiences and School Responses," *Journal of Youth and Adolescence* 39, no. 10 (October 2010): 1175–1188, http://dx.doi.org/10.1007/s10964-010-9540-7; Ann Travers, *The Trans Generation: How Trans Kids (and Their Parents) Are Creating a Gender Revolution* (New York: New York University Press, 2018), 48–51.

8. Wayne Martino, Jenny Kassen, and Kenan Omercajic, "Supporting Transgender Students in Schools: Beyond an Individualist Approach to Trans Inclusion in the Education System," *Educational Review* (October 19, 2020): 1–20, https://doi.org/10.1080/00131 911.2020.1829559.

9. Heath Mackenzie Reynolds and Zil Garner Goldstein, "Social Transition," in *Trans Bodies, Trans Selves: A Resource for the Transgender Community*, ed. Laura Erickson-Schroth (Oxford; New York: Oxford University Press, 2014).

10. Julie C. Luecke, "Working with Transgender Children and Their Classmates in Pre-Adolescence: Just Be Supportive," *Journal of LGBT Youth* 8, no. 2 (March 29, 2011): 116–156, https://doi.org/10.1080/19361653.2011.544941.

11. "Report: 2016 Is the Most Dangerous Year for Transgender Americans," *Advocate* (February 22, 2016), http://www.advocate.com/transgender/2016/2/22/report-2016-most-danger ous-year-transgender-americans.

12. "2021 Becomes Deadliest Year on Record for Transgender and Non-Binary People," Human Rights Campaign Press Release (November 9, 2021), https://www.hrc.org/press-releases/ 2021-becomes-deadliest-year-on-record-for-transgender-and-non-binary-people.

13. *The Most Dangerous Year* (2018), http://www.imdb.com/title/tt5532368/companycredits.

14. Scott J. South and Richard B. Felson, "The Racial Patterning of Rape," *Social Forces* 69, no. 1 (1990): 71–93, https://doi.org/10.2307/2579608.

15. Tynslei Spence-Mitchell, "Restroom Restrictions: How Race and Sexuality Have Affected Bathroom Legislation," *Gender, Work & Organization* 28 (January 2, 2021): 14–20, https:// doi.org/10.1111/gwao.12545.

16. *The Most Dangerous Year*, https://www.themostdangerousyear.com.

17. Dirk Johnson, "Students Still Sweat, They Just Don't Shower," *New York Times* (April 22, 1996), https://www.nytimes.com/1996/04/22/us/students-still-sweat-they-just-don-t-shower.html.

14

Other Areas of Gender Separation

Gender equality is more than a goal in itself. It is a precondition for meeting the challenge of reducing poverty, promoting sustainable development, and building good governance.

Kofi Annan

There are many instances over time in which children experience gender separation—for play activities, chores, and learning expectations, to name a few.

The feeling of some is that, to be inclusive of trans and nonbinary children, we must abandon those practices and traditions. It's easy to see how a tired, over-worked teacher might feel deflated at the prospect of what feels like additional considerations to make in their lesson planning. I do not feel we need to "throw the baby out with the bathwater" and eliminate all aspects of gender norms but we can certainly examine these situations with fresh eyes. Optimal gender inclu-sion does not mean erasing all gender-related practices but rather expanding our view of these practices so we can better discern what could be retained, what we might discard or add, and what would benefit from revision.

I encourage people to step into a reflective examination of existing gender separation practices and norms. Conversation starters include questions like the following:

- What are the goals meant to be achieved by this gender division?
- Does the division accomplish those goals? Fully? Partly? Mostly not? Why or why not?
- Can the identified goals be achieved without dividing by gender? In what ways?
- Do these factors exclude gender-diverse students? How can they be updated to be inclusive?
- Are there additional layers or intersections to consider (e.g., socioeco-nomic differences, cultural considerations, or racial disparities), and do they adversely affect some students more than others?

One school that I had worked with multiple times still felt it important to divide children by gender for math instruction. One teacher said, "Studies show that girls perform better in math if they are in a less competitive environment." If we look at the goal—optimizing the learning environment—yes, some girls will do better. But some boys would benefit as well. The separation *partly* accomplishes the goal. Can the identified goal be achieved without a gender division? Yes, because it is not the genital configuration that accomplishes the greater success. It is the additional *learning method* that is employed (students progress at their own pace). The educators would not need to make any changes to providing two options for the study of math—they would just change how students opt into either group.

It might feel that this reflection requires too much energy and would benefit too few. In my experience, however, engaging in these discussions proves to be more exciting than deflating. Solutions are easier to find than expected and benefit far more students than first thought.

BODIES, HEALTH, AND THE GENDER-DIVERSE STUDENT

All Sex Ed Curriculum Is Not Created Equal

School districts across the nation have vastly different areas of content emphasis within the health education curriculum they offer. Most will identify pregnancy prevention as a goal on which they can all agree; however, prevention pathways can range from complete sexual abstinence to instruction on the most effective forms of birth control and where to find them. Some schools allow a family to "opt out" of instruction while others expect families to "opt in" if they want their child to access this content. The age at which instruction begins is not consistent either. Some schools may start as early as fourth grade because some students often begin puberty this early while other schools opt for later instruction, even into the high school years. Regardless of a district's approach, the families within that district will have personal views, such as cultural or religious differences, that may or may not be in alignment with that district's offerings. The short story? It's complicated. None of these variables magically disappear when we add gender diversity to the mix. Some, such as conflicts of faith, are exacerbated. By now, most readers should not find this surprising. Until the lives of gender-diverse people are less politicized, feared, and stigmatized, the resulting clash will likely remain part of the equation.

Get the Conversation Started

Because curriculum parameters vary greatly, I am better able to answer questions from educators about trans and nonbinary student participation if I start with a question of my own.

Do you separate students by gender for these classes?

No: If the answer is no, I would like to know why not? What does an all-gender environment accomplish? *Learning about all bodies,* teachers say, *consent, reproduction, STIs, safety, safer sex practices, pregnancy, and more—and learning it all together—results in greater mutual respect, healthier relationships, decreased unwanted pregnancy, and better communication within relationships.* If by "all" genders they actually mean "both" genders, then we have the opportunity to consider what might be done to really get to all bodies and all relationships.

Yes: If the answer is yes, then I would also like to hear why. What do they hope to achieve? The most consistent response to this question is this: *The students feel more comfortable asking questions when not in front of the "opposite" sex.* Optimizing a student's comfort within what is often an uncomfortable conversation is of significant benefit.

What I enjoy about these conversations is that we are able to focus on what we have to *gain* regardless of whatever structure is in place. When we identify these objectives, we have something to work with. Who wouldn't want to decrease unwanted pregnancies, increase respectful relationships, and optimize the ability of students to engage in very important conversations? Of course, proponents of one approach will have their preference over another but nevertheless, the hoped-for goals of either approach are largely shared.

If classroom sexual health and anatomical discussions are divided by boys and girls, the division *does* reinforce a binary understanding of gender. We know that there are understood advantages to keeping students together regardless of gender and there are advantages to be gained by separating. Regardless, the question of how to include gender-diverse students remains (their bodies, identities, relationships, and experiences) and the binary notion of gender still goes unchallenged.[1]

Yet, what is important to acknowledge is that it is not always easy to switch from an established approach just because we decide it is the right thing to do. Educators will tell me that they feel their hands are tied because their school or district dictates the structure and content. Required textbooks and other curriculum offerings may be outdated as well. There are, however, ways to engage all students in easy, straightforward conversations that will result in a good step toward inclusivity of gender-diverse students.

The optimal way to begin is to present the AEIOU framework (see Chapter 3). This is true regardless of whether the class is all-gender or gender-separated. Make it clear, for example, that a person's genital configuration does not dictate their gender identity. This is a simple step that serves to shift gender-essentialist thinking. Students will readily grasp these conceptual differences. Don't make unilateral statements like *boys have penises, girls have vaginas,* or refer to reproductive systems as *female* or *male.* It could be as simple as saying, *people who have a uterus,* or *someone who has a penis.* Yes, it means breaking a habit. This habitual language can be changed with just a little attention given and helps us begin the journey toward more factual and inclusive information. I encourage educators to invite their students to help support this more inclusive way of speaking for everyone.

Another helpful action is to grant ourselves permission to step out of an "either/or" mindset. When we look at one of the earlier stated goals—creating gender-separated space to optimize safer, more frank conversation—we've encountered an opportunity. That opportunity is one where we can challenge ourselves to think beyond the "shortcut" of girl/boy gender separation. What if we actually took gender out of the equation? The question then is, "How do we create safer environments for more frank discussions among all students regardless of gender?"[2] The resulting brainstorming would surely generate additional thoughts. One teacher had this to say:

> I am really grateful for this conversation! Part of me wants to embrace an all-gender approach to sex ed, but I've seen firsthand how the students bring

up things that could be a lot harder in a bigger, mixed class. What if we split students into smaller groups for different learning activities? We could ask them to report on people's lives that are different than their own—like considerations or experiences for people with disabilities, differing gender identities, or those from other cultures or traditions? We could also set up an ongoing way for students to contribute questions anonymously. I've been teaching this for years, I know a lot of the more common questions. I could see a way that I could "prime the pump" at the beginning of the class with some of those questions just to get the conversation going. Then, no single student is on the hot seat for bringing up a question that may be interesting to all but they feel too embarrassed to ask.

Gender-Diverse Student Needs in Class

The question of which classroom to place a trans or nonbinary student during sex education takes center stage because the predominant approach within schools is to separate students by anatomical sex:

> Do we place the trans boy in with the girls? Even if he identifies as a boy, his body has female reproductive organs, right?
>
> Shouldn't a trans girl have to learn about her body, and therefore be in the section with the boys?
>
> We have a trans student but none of her classmates know that. Where does she go?
>
> We have a nonbinary kid who wants to be in with the boys. Their birth sex is female so that doesn't really make sense, does it? And won't they make the other boys uncomfortable?

While the desire to get concrete direction is understandable, providing single answers that apply across the board proves to be a bit challenging. That does not mean that solutions do not exist—they do. It takes very little imagination to recognize that sending a trans girl into an all-boys class could be a distressing experience for her. Any gender-diverse student could suffer if they are expected to engage in discussions where one's genitalia and reproductive systems are considered synonymous with one's gender identity. We need to assess, reflect, and think outside our existing gender box.

Determining Placement—Questions to Explore

- *Is there a student support plan established?* This is a good place to start. Does the student have a supportive caregiver in the picture? Will it be helpful to bring that person into the discussion? Does that caregiver have plans and resources to supplement the student's sexual health education?
- *Would the student be interested in a self-study or independent project option in lieu of the sex education class?* This approach could be tailored to better fit the student's physical and social experience as well as meet the established learning goals of the curriculum. Is there an optimal student/educator pairing that could team up to create and fulfill this course requirement?
- *Is the child's gender status known to the other students or is that private?* If the latter, insisting that a student participate based on their anatomical sex would then result in a direct violation of that student's right to privacy.
- *What is the student's placement preference?* This is an important consideration. It is not hard to imagine that a trans girl would very much prefer to be with the girls and that placing her with boys would be traumatizing. Their preference prioritizes the social environment rather than physical commonality. The same would be true for a nonbinary student—they would likely prefer to be placed with the students with whom they are most comfortable. Does the student have a supportive peer group (regardless of gender) that they could pair up with? If the core curriculum covers the same content regardless of body type, then the placement of the gender-diverse student can simply be a matter of social preference and not body-centric.

Gender-Diverse Students and Puberty Changes

An additional question to consider is this: What is the student's understanding of their own puberty progression?[3] Trans students may already be highly aware/informed of their current or impending pubertal changes. Or there could be some physiological factors that ought to be understood but are overlooked (by student or educator) simply because it doesn't occur to them. A trans boy, for example, may not believe he can get pregnant because he is a boy. This possibility may never come to mind for an educator who assumes the trans boy already understands his own reproductive system.

Gender-diverse students who do not experience gender-affirming pubertal intervention will experience pubertal progression according to their natal sex. This does not mean it is best for that student to be separated according to natal sex.

At this time, the sex education curriculum is unlikely to address the pubertal experiences of trans and nonbinary youth. Students who are not trans, we know, will experience puberty associated with their natal sex. Trans youth, on the other hand, may or may not have natal-congruent puberty. Some gender-diverse students will have earlier pubertal intervention in the form of GnRH analogues (puberty blockers) and/or gender identity congruent sex hormones (testosterone or estrogen). For these students, learning about either testes-based puberty or ovary-based puberty will not fully address the physical changes they will experience.

Room to Grow

All students should have an opportunity to learn about different bodies, respectful relationships, optimal health, and safety in the world. It is reasonable to believe that we can learn about these differences in body and experience without compromising the instruction that already exists—it is an expansion of knowledge, not a destruction of it as some fear. I operate under the belief that respectful and safer conversations can occur, and it would be of significant benefit to students in an all-gender environment if—and this is an important if—we prioritize these shared goals that we can all embrace.

CORY SILVERBERG

Cory Silverberg's books open a portal to a world where gender is exactly what we say it is rather than simply the sum of our "middle parts." Silverberg provides the template for all of us to see the simplicity with which we can step out of today's binary gender paradigm.[4]

What Makes a Baby (ages 2–8)

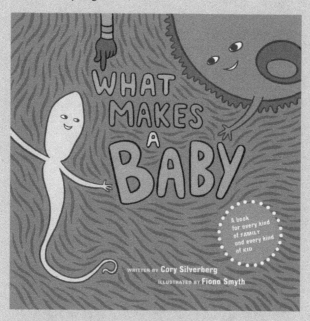

Sex Is a Funny Word (ages 8–10)

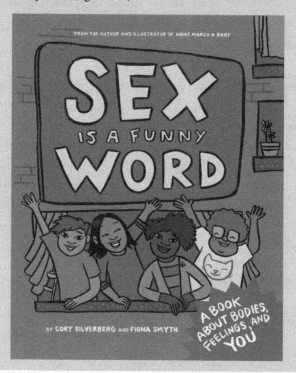

You Know, Sex (ages 10+)

These are twenty-first-century books for children, pre-teens, and teens that talk about where babies come from, and reflect the reality of our modern times by being inclusive of all kinds of kids, adults, and families, however they came to be. The publisher's summary of the book, *Sex Is a Funny Word*, states that "much more than the 'facts of life' or 'the birds and the bees,' Silverberg's books open up conversations between young people and their caregivers to convey their values and beliefs while providing information about boundaries, safety, and joy."

Voice and Speech Coaching

Gender-diverse students can experience multiple barriers that have an adverse impact on their educational participation and performance. One such example includes their confident ability to use their voice. A trans student may feel that their manner of speaking "gives them away" because they feel that their speech may sound too masculine or too feminine for their gender identity. This can prevent them from participating in class, seeking support or guidance from teachers or administrators, or engaging socially with their peers. An individualized education program (IEP) or 504 Plan are two vehicles that are sometimes used to facilitate a student accessing special education services for speech or language impairment.

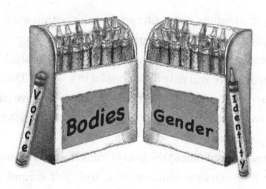

Speech Language Pathologists (SLPs), more commonly known as "speech therapists," can offer individualized or group instruction to gender-diverse young people, which may be of particular benefit to trans students experiencing voice changes due to pubertal development. Speech therapists working in pre-K and K–12 settings can have a positive impact on a trans student's ability to participate in school, especially if their gender status is not known to their peers.

There are important factors that a speech therapist should consider when working with gender-diverse children. The best first step is to deepen their own familiarity of gender diversity in children and to simultaneously consider the multiple communities in which they may belong.

One kindergartner, Ji-Yoo, was completely mute at school and selectively so at home. This resolved almost immediately when the family began to understand and support his identity as a boy. An SLP can benefit from knowing that gender identity could be a factor in situations like these and that they can play an important support role for trans and gender-diverse youth: "Without sensitivity to language, we run the risk of invalidating and misgendering the trans youth with whom we interact. . . . It is essential that clinicians see every client not simply through the lens of gender but globally through that of their culture and ethnicity."[5]

Offering supportive, accessible voice coaching will not be needed for every trans student but for those who do need it, it can mean the difference between active, successful school engagement or being isolated on the margins.

TRANS CHILDREN'S BODIES, IDENTITIES, AND THE NEED FOR DISCERNMENT

Creating boy/girl divisions is an entrenched habit within most schools and it is meant to accomplish any number of objectives based on perceived physical or social differences. What we discover upon closer examination is that, regardless of our objectives, we will only be successful to a degree. Does that mean we don't care about who it excludes? No, it simply means we have habits in need of reexamination and we need educators and parents who are better able to engage in a process of discernment.

As we continue to learn about the lives of trans children, we will gain a deeper perspective on their physical experiences as well. For example, I've known a number of trans children who have struggled with clothing sensitivities. Their clothing is too soft, not soft enough, the colors aren't right, they are too tight, too loose, and so on. Yet, when the child's gender identity was affirmed and social transition steps were taken, including wardrobe change, these sensitivities, for many, rapidly resolved. Sensory issues are typically associated with autism but have occurred often enough in trans children to warrant further attention.[6] We need providers, educators, and parents who can recognize that there are behaviors that could point to a gender identity difference and not just lean toward a particular diagnosis by default.

Our knowledge will increase over time. We need to incorporate our learning and exercise our ability to discern. A gender-diverse child is not just a child navigating life in a particular physical body but a child negotiating a social environment that is still largely unprepared for this child's experience.

Let's look at the experience of an elementary-aged trans girl who was pulled out of class to join the testing process for color blindness. Her mystified classmates immediately noticed as it was only boys who were selected for testing. Does that mean only boys experience color blindness? No, girls do too. Using gender as a shortcut measure for testing color blindness means that any girls who experience color blindness will be overlooked. If the expected outcome of testing students is to identify all the students who experience color blindness, then all students should be tested. It can be that simple. Because a gender transition has largely been viewed as synonymous with an adult who pursues genital surgery, many people will fixate on genitals regardless of a child's age and circumstance. Their decision to test her for color blindness was based on knowledge about her body (and getting stuck there) but did not take into consideration her personal experience of the event in relation to her peers. Here is another example of this kind of inadvertent fixation:

> A parent of two seventh-grade trans boys attended a meeting with multiple school staff including administrators, teachers, a counselor, and the school nurse to discuss the social transition steps the boys were undertaking. After an hour of discussing the questions from the staff and considering the ways to best support the boys, the meeting wrapped up. The school nurse immediately pulled the parent aside and said, "Do the boys have penises?" The shocked parent was given no explanation for such an abrupt, invasive question. The school nurse surely was not meaning to be intrusive and, if she had taken a moment to think about this question, she might have found a better way to get the information she felt was needed. Alternatively, had the nurse taken a day or so to reflect on the immediacy of her question, she may have concluded that she did *not* need to know the genital configuration of these children to provide care for them in any emergency or non-emergency situation.

And this unfortunate situation where common sense did not prevail:

> A first-grade trans girl had a clothing mishap when another classmate accidentally spilled some paint all over her pants. The teacher sent her on to the nurse's office to change because there was a box of spare clothing available for situations such as these. The clothing offered by the nurse was too small, but the child tried to make it work anyway. When the nurse came into the room, she demanded to know what was "stuffed" into the child's pants. When the child insisted that there was nothing there, the nurse forced the child to drop her pants exposing her genitalia. The child was deeply upset about this experience as were the child's parents. The nurse did not even notify the parents of the incident. The principal readily acknowledged that there was no legitimate reason for the nurse to ask a child to expose her genitalia. Neither the parents, nor especially the child, felt they could be trusting of the nurse's judgment in the future.

While the nurse may have been curious about why there was a bulge when she didn't expect one, it did not warrant her subjecting the child to a strip search. Even if the nurse suspected theft, this is not a sufficient justification for such an invasive search. The thoughtless act could have cost the nurse her job and subjected the school to a possible lawsuit.

While these situations are not commonplace, they occur more frequently than one would hope. What occurs far too often is that a provider's curiosity overrides their professional judgment.

It is truly important for school nurses to deepen their understanding of gender-diverse children. It is through a lack of awareness that a nurse may ask deeply inappropriate questions, seek to satisfy their own curiosity through actions violating a child's right to bodily privacy, or potentially find themselves unable to address a child's medical emergency because an unexpected variable causes them to freeze. It is not an exaggeration to say that a child's life could depend on it.

For now, we should prepare for the likelihood that unexpected situations will occur as we take continued steps toward trans student inclusion. Gender-diverse students should not have to bear the brunt of these unexpected situations where adult judgment flies out the window. Without a doubt, we need to end the collective fixation on genitalia that serves to interrupt rational thought.

The good news is that, of course, adults can and do find their way back to responsible decision-making even if they are initially uncertain about how to get there. What follows is just such an example. I received a call from a state activities director who wanted my feedback regarding his recent conversation with a wrestling coach. This was a situation where both the student's identity *and* body were important factors:

> The activities director fielded a call from a wrestling coach about a trans boy on the boys' wrestling team. The coach did *not* ask the typical question— *should he be on the boys' team or not*—his eligibility to wrestle had already been determined. Instead, the coach had a question about the parameters for safe weight loss in preparation for any upcoming meets. These parameters were different depending on a student's gender—one set of requirements for girls and another for boys. The coach felt that he needed to lean toward the boys' parameters because the child identified as a boy, yet he was still uncertain.
>
> The coach's hesitation is an excellent indicator of increased critical thinking, even if he hadn't quite pinned it down himself. The operative element

here is determining *safe* weight loss based on the athlete's *body*. These testing parameters consider things like body fat composition, age, and current weight. The coach knew that unsafe weight loss can decrease athletic performance despite any perceived advantage from competing in a lower weight class and possibly result in dangerous health consequences when taken to the extreme (dehydration from restricting fluids, using laxatives, excess exercising). He reached out for guidance because he was thinking, first and foremost, about this student's body and what would be safe for him.

In my conversation with the activities director, he and I agreed that the student's physical safety was the top priority. The safe weight loss parameters are guidelines for coaches to use. Most likely, these guidelines do not fit all situations for all boys. In the same way, a coach might work to refine specific parameters for any athlete, the same approach can be taken for the trans boy. The weight-loss guidelines need not be categorized under two gender labels. Instead, any difference based on body type could then be considered. Considering the body type differences for any wrestler in a composite way means that the safety and health of all students would then be more accurately assessed.

CLASSES, CLUBS, AND ACTIVITIES

Gender has been a factor for inclusion, and exclusion, in many student activities over time. And it changes. Cheerleading, for example, was once an all-male activity, until it became almost exclusively female. Today, there are cheer opportunities for all students, but the roles and uniforms of cheer can still be strongly delineated by gender. If both boys and girls are able to join the cheer squad, great. But we then balk because we don't know which cheer squad "role" to impose on the trans student and we don't grant the student the autonomy to let us know what works best for them.

The same could be said for instrument selection in the band, role-casting in drama, and uniform selection for dance. If a student joins a choir, the choir director can consider the voice range for placement—alto, soprano, tenor, or bass—but should not decide placement based on an assessment of a trans student's genital configuration. While it might sound crass to state that genitalia are employed as a criterion, in essence, it can influence a director's decision. For example, if the choir director is aware of a trans boy's gender status, the director may place that student with those who sing alto. If unaware of the boy's gender history, the director may place him with the tenors. Same voice, different outcome. There is such a pervasiveness to the social conditioning of gender norms that it may be difficult to believe its impact. Many individuals would deny this bias, yet it is challenging to escape. So much so, that in the 1970s, professional orchestras began employing a "blind" audition process in which the musician performs behind a screen, invisible to the selection committee to decrease gender and racial bias that some insisted did not exist. The results of the new practice showed that this bias did indeed exist, and it was remedied to a degree by this approach.

During a training for middle and high school teachers, one teacher raised his hand and shared his thoughts:

> You know, we are talking around a pretty important issue here. I teach shop and, yes, girls take shop too. But boys come into class and right away, they grab a hammer and start pounding nails into the table. Girls just sit there. They hesitate. I know no one else will say this, but let's face it—BOYS PENETRATE!

While his comment caused some of his colleagues to groan and others to bury their faces in their hands, it did inspire an excellent conversation where we could discuss a number of things in more detail. I asked the audience to suggest some reasons why the girls might hesitate and why the boys might dive right in on the first day. It didn't take long for those in the room to identify the discouragement that girls, at the earliest of ages, were more likely to receive *Put that hammer down, you don't want to get hurt*. Contrast that with the encouragement toward boys: *He sure has an interest in tools—he takes after his dad*. The examples were numerous, and it was easy to see how the experiences could accumulate to the point where a girl, despite her keen interest in woodworking, would be more cautious, even intimidated, by the time she actually had time to receive some instruction.

There are barriers to participation for many students, regardless of gender. School environments are the places where we work to overcome these barriers. Girls were at one time excluded from shop class and boys were excluded from home economics. That is no longer the case. We recognize that some students have greater opportunities presented to them that result in greater confidence. Other students may lack that opportunity. A hesitant student in shop class could be paired up with a more confident student for a joint project where their individual success is tied to their successful collaboration. And, if a trans student has a voice in the higher ranges of soprano or alto, he may have to accept that being in the lowest baritone range is out of reach. Yet, if the student desires, a choir director might work with him to reach the lower range of tenor.

There is an added bonus that comes from examining ways to be inclusive of gender-diverse students in environments and activities that are traditionally separated by gender. This examination allows everyone to more clearly see any disparities that exist for other students. All students can benefit.

Overnight Trips and Changing Areas

The subject of housing and sleeping arrangements on student trips is one that often comes up. Where does the trans or nonbinary student sleep? The solutions can be fairly straightforward . . . eventually. Just as is needed with so many other situations, we must first consider why we separate children by gender in the first place. This is a typical exchange with teachers:

ME: What is the goal you hope to accomplish when you separate the kids by gender?

THEM: *We don't want them messing around or making out.*

ME: Okay, so separating the arrangements by boys and girls will then eliminate that right?

THEM: *Well, mostly. I mean, they are teenagers after all. If they want to make out, they will sneak off and find a way.*

ME: Yes, but this makes it a little harder, doesn't it? So, then I guess it is okay for girls to make out with each other, is that right? Or for boys to do so? Because they do. They will.

THEM: *Well, . . . no. I guess I hadn't thought about that before.*

ME: All right, well there is something additional to consider. If your objective is to keep kids from making out with each other, I imagine having a chaperone in the room would be an effective mood killer. So that is one avenue you could take, if you don't already. But, let's carry this objective out a little further. Making out is one thing, sex is another. Surely, all can agree that what you really want to ensure is that no sexual relations occur, and that you especially do not want any student getting pregnant on your watch. Am I right?

THEM: Emphatic head nodding. *That's for sure!*

Whether the field trip has one overnight or many, the bottom line is that the teachers are responsible to these children to keep them safe while under their care. There are ways to increase the likelihood of achieving this objective. As was mentioned, having adult chaperones in the room is one. Also, if there is any known relationship among the students, adult supervisors can attempt to make sure that those students are not sharing sleeping arrangements, regardless of gender.

There are additional concerns that are mentioned that extend beyond the notion of physical affection. Teachers so often are in the position of addressing unfounded fears from the *parents* of students who may be housed together with a trans student. They fear that their child will not be "safe." This ties directly to the belief that trans people (even children) are dangerous and predatory. Of course, teachers may feel intimidated to engage with these parents. Yet, it is crucial that teachers confidently address these fears, as irrational as they may sound, by clearly articulating the ways that they ensure the safety of every student. It is not reasonable to separate the gender-diverse student away from others. That is not a workable solution and, indeed, it is one that is discriminatory.[7]

Sometimes, the gender-diverse student is the one who is nervous about sleeping arrangements. The primary reason has to do with students who may be unkind and disparaging because of the student's gender status. It is reasonable to find out if there are students with whom the trans student might be more comfortable rooming.

The question of where a trans student might change their clothes can come up as well:

> A second-grade class had a special Halloween event where, for part of the day, the kids could change into their costumes. A trans girl, whose gender history was not known to her classmates, had prearranged with her teacher to use the bathroom for changing. The rest of the students were expected to change in the classroom. One boy asked, "Why did Akira get to use the bathroom to change?" The teacher said, "She wanted some privacy while changing into her costume." The boy responded, "I'd like privacy so I can change too."

It was not necessary for the teacher to ignore the question, to share anything about Akira's body, or to be vague or dismissive. He only needed to address the interest in privacy. While this situation was in a classroom, the same can be considered for overnight trips. The chaperones/teachers can communicate to the students the option that they change into their bedclothes in the bathroom if they would like a greater degree of privacy.

Common sense responses and expectations like these are the kind of tools that educators need in their toolkit. As Akira's teacher learned, there are other students who want privacy. Not every inquiry about a trans child has to do with being trans! In fact, many are not. It is often the adult mindset that gets hung up on a gender loop. Getting unstuck is the key to confidently addressing any situation. This allows us to find ready solutions that are manageable to implement and are often of benefit to other students in a variety of situations.

We would be hard-pressed to find an environment where gender has *not* been a part of the story. For some, their gender meant having the right to vote, to own land, seek an education, to serve as a priest, but for others, it meant having to fight for those same rights. Gender divisions are used to retain (or take away) power and to preserve (or prevent the accumulation of) wealth. It is pervasive. Gender influences are present in every classroom, every subject, and every activity offered to students. There are textbooks and traditions that ensure that gender norms are continually woven throughout. Yet, these norms are ever-changing.

The level of rigidity or elasticity changes over time and circumstances. Any person can surely identify some of the changes that have occurred just within their own lifetime. We do not need the presence of transgender children for us to examine, and reexamine, this gender permeation—we've been doing it for generations. We do however need to keep at it. The presence of trans children today requires us to stay attentive to gender equity, but it also insists that we expand our understanding of gender and step out of the familiar gender debates of generations past. In a sense, we are required to let go of our gender complacency and shake it up a little.

NOTES

1. Samantha G. Haley et al., "Sex Education for Transgender and Non-Binary Youth: Previous Experiences and Recommended Content," *The Journal of Sexual Medicine* 16, no. 11 (November 1, 2019): 1834–1848, https://doi.org/10.1016/j.jsxm.2019.08.009.
2. L. Kris Gowen and Nichole Winges-Yanez, "Lesbian, Gay, Bisexual, Transgender, Queer, and Questioning Youths' Perspectives of Inclusive School-Based Sexuality Education," *The Journal of Sex Research* 51, no. 7 (2014): 788–800.
3. Dennis M. Styne, "Puberty," in *Pubertal Suppression in Transgender Youth*, 1st ed., ed. Courtney Finlayson, MD (New York: Elsevier, 2018).
4. Aidan Key, Review of *Sex Is a Funny Word* by Cory Silverberg, https://www.corysilverberg.com/sex-is-a-funny-word.
5. Sandy Hirsch, Jack Pickering, and Richard Adler, "Meeting the Needs of Trans and Gender Diverse Youth: The Varied, Ubiquitous Role of the Speech-Language Pathologist in Voice and Communication Therapy/Training," *Perspectives of the ASHA Special Interest Groups* 4, no. 1 (February 26, 2019): 111–117, https://doi.org/10.1044/2018_PERS-SIG3-2018-0016.
6. Varun Warrier et al., "Elevated Rates of Autism, Other Neurodevelopmental and Psychiatric Diagnoses, and Autistic Traits in Transgender and Gender-Diverse Individuals," *Nature Communications* 11, no. 1 (August 7, 2020): 3959, https://doi.org/10.1038/s41467-020-17794-1.
7. "Student v. Arcadia Unified School District," *National Center for Lesbian Rights* (blog), https://www.nclrights.org/our-work/cases/student-v-arcadia-unified-school-district/.

15

Sports

An Historical Perspective

No person in the United States shall, on the basis of sex, be excluded from partici-pation in, be denied the benefits of, or be subjected to discrimination under any education program or activity receiving federal financial assistance.

Title IX

As the presence of gender-diverse students on gender-segregated athletic teams within physical education classes and in other school activities increases, we need to better understand and implement inclusive practices vital to creating an equitable playing field for all students. Sounds good, right? The question is, "How?" If most teams are separated by gender, how do we go about including gender-diverse children in K–12 sports activities? Will their presence impact these teams and, if so, in what ways? Do we find the team that is the "closest fit" for a nonbinary child? If so, what criteria do we use? Will trans girls dominate the field, adversely affecting other girls? Will trans boys be at greater risk for injury, and perhaps be in increased danger, because they join boys' teams?

Whether you are a parent, administrator, coach, or just an interested reader, you can recognize that these questions represent many layers of consideration. To begin the conversation about trans athlete inclusion in sports, should we discard the binary gender foundation upon which it all rests and start over? One could argue that that would be a worthy, even ideal approach, although it's not likely anyone would agree to it.

We do not need to look back very far, historically speaking, to remind ourselves that the recent growth of girls' and women's sporting opportunities exists *because* there was a long, hard fight to create opportunities where few had previously existed. Full inclusion for gender-diverse athletes, or any athlete for that matter, is not accomplished solely by eliminating gender as a factor. It is only one part of an ongoing broader discourse in which to consider equity and inclusion—and the barriers to achieving this within K–12 activities.

Other factors include disparate school funding for access to skills-building workshops, mentoring/coaching staff, proper facilities, uniforms, and equipment. Even if a school is well-funded, it doesn't mean every student has an equitable path to participate. Socioeconomic status, racial inequities, unstable family environments, and housing are just a few additional barriers that hinder a child's eligibility and participation.

The effort to reduce barriers to any student in sports participation is an ongoing endeavor for educational institutions. As we consider historical efforts to decrease these obstacles, we can more readily address the disparities particular to gender-diverse students today. The conversations, and the solutions, will sound very familiar. However, there are unique aspects to these conversations. Just ask the parent of a trans child who joins a team or seeks to fulfill a physical education (PE) requirement. Some of their concerns include:

- Will my child be able to join the wrestling team? Will their teammates be accepting?
- Are there private changing areas in the locker room? What if the school says no?
- My child doesn't want to take PE but the school requires it. What do I do about that?
- The district expects me to produce documentation of my child's gender and has said they may have to do a physical exam—is that even legal?
- The coach has told me privately that they are supportive, but they feel resistance from the principal—is there anything that can be done?
- I'm worried that my child will be targeted by competing schools or that they will be the center of some media storm.

When I work with schools to address the question of trans students in sports, my first objective is to create an environment where everyone feels comfortable sharing their thoughts. If people feel unable to place their questions, hesitations, or feelings of resistance on the table, then we have no dialogue, only lecture with no analysis.

The initial apprehension that many may bring to the conversation can cause friction, and frustration, none of which are elements of productive conversations. Decades ago, Title IX was crafted and implemented to address gender inclusion in sports. This effort toward greater gender equity was also fraught with uncomfortable conversations and contrasting arguments. Yet, the tide had changed—girls and women were already engaged in sports in increasing numbers. Title IX paved the way for the next layer of considerations—not *if* girls and women should be afforded equitable opportunities in sports but rather *how*.

Gender-diverse students are engaging in sports. Coaches and PE teachers are addressing their needs today, not at some hypothetical point in the future. While the learning curve may be uncomfortable at times, it is necessary to engage in constructive conversations that address the realities of today's trans athletes.

TITLE IX

In the United States, K–12 athletics have historically operated under what is considered an immutable, binary understanding of gender—boys' sports and girls' sports—and, with that foundational understanding, we then considered how we might achieve equitable, optimal participation for those boys and girls and do so without discrimination. We can reference the U.S. Department of Education's Office for Civil Rights statute, Title IX of the Education Amendments of 1972—a landmark example of these efforts. This federal civil rights law states:

> No person in the United States shall, on the basis of sex, be excluded from participation in, be denied the benefits of, or be subjected to discrimination under any education program or activity receiving Federal financial assistance.[1]

Title IX was instrumental in increasing opportunities for girls and women to participate in competitive sports. Good news, and a good start. Few today would debate the benefits of Title IX, but just as women once fought for the right to vote, to pursue education, and for equal opportunities in the workforce, there was resistance along the way. In "A History of Women in Sport Prior to Title IX," Professor Richard C. Bell notes, "The critical element lacking after the passage of Title IX was the implementation legislation that would specify how it was to be applied and to whom."[2]

We are faced with a similar dilemma today in regard to the increased presence of trans youth in athletics. We need to consider how this law is applied and to whom. How does Title IX, or other sex-specific policies/practices, apply to athletes whose gender is not fixed within our binary understanding of who is a boy and who is a girl? How do we ensure that *trans* athletes are not excluded or discriminated against "on the basis of sex"?

To start, we must have—and indeed are actively engaged in an in-depth examination of what we mean when we use the word *sex*. As is so often the case, the conflation of the terms *gender* and *sex* is part of the problem. Incorporating our present-day understanding of gender identity is needed to gain clarity regarding trans athlete participation. Up until now, we haven't considered children with gender identity differences and how that translates into sports activity inclusion because we didn't know we needed to. Nor have we considered children with physiological differences related to sex.

We do not address the intersex differences present in K–12 children when we talk about children and athletics, perhaps out of convenience, more likely from denial. More likely, it is an unwillingness to subject children to the humiliation of genital, hormonal, and chromosomal exams that have been imposed on elite athletes, sometimes leading to coercive surgical procedures.[3] If an athlete refused, it could lead to the end of their athletic career. The World Medical Association and the United Nations Human Rights Council have condemned the private governing body, World Athletics, for these practices that are "unscientific, unethical, and violations of domestic and international human rights laws."[4] The notion of subjecting children to invasive genital exams and procedures in order to play would be something the vast majority of people would find abhorrent, outrageous, and discriminatory.

Does that Mean that Sex Discrimination under Title IX Applies to Gender Identity?

In recent years, federal courts, including the U.S. Supreme Court, have taken up the question of whether discrimination based on a person's gender identity constitutes discrimination on the basis of sex. The short answer is, yes, the courts have determined it does. The federal government offered the following explanation for a Supreme Court ruling that occurred in June 2020:

> The U.S Department of Justice: Civil Rights Division issued a clarifying memorandum in March of 2021 regarding the application of Supreme Court Ruling case Bostock v. Clayton County to Title IX of the Education Amendments of 1972. In part, it says, the Administration's policy [is] that "[a]ll persons should receive equal treatment under the law, no matter their gender identity or sexual orientation." Citing the Supreme Court's holding in Bostock that the prohibition on discrimination "because of . . . sex" under Title VII of the Civil Rights Act of 1964, 42 U.S.C. § 2000e et seq. (Title VII) covers discrimination on the basis of gender identity and sexual orientation, the Executive Order explains that Bostock's reasoning applies with equal force to other laws that prohibit sex discrimination "so long as the laws do not contain sufficient indications to the contrary." Because their statutory prohibitions against sex discrimination are similar, the Supreme Court and other federal courts consistently look to interpretations of Title VII to inform Title IX.[5]

While this, and other rulings from federal courts are helpful in understanding the applicability of Title IX as it relates to gender-diverse student participation, the hope of any young athlete and their school district is to engage in sports and other activities *without* the distressing experience of a legal challenge.

As we better understand the need to address the expansiveness of our gender- and sex-differentiated human experiences, the impact on a gender-segregated society, including student engagement in sports, needs reevaluation. If we don't reevaluate, we will find ourselves inadvertently perpetuating the very discriminatory practices we strive to remedy. The good news is that this work has already begun.

HOW DO WE GET STARTED?

What we need is practical guidance for everyone—athletic directors, teachers, coaches, students, and their families—as to the *realities* of transgender inclusion in sports rather than the apprehensive speculations of what *might* occur. This chapter seeks to further efforts toward the inclusion of gender-diverse students in K–12 schools, based on the successful inclusion that is already occurring in our nation's schools.

A coach may have recently had a trans athlete try out for their team, a PE teacher could feel uncertain about placing a newly identified trans athlete in a different locker room, or an athletic director wonders how to address questions from parents. School boards may be asked to address the school community but have no baseline knowledge themselves. It feels as if there is no road map. It's a tough spot to be in.

WHAT ABOUT THE INTERNATIONAL OLYMPIC COMMITTEE? DON'T THEY HAVE GENDER PARTICIPATION REQUIREMENTS WE COULD USE?

The International Olympic Committee (IOC), is one of a few entities that had made efforts to determine athletic participation parameters for trans athletes. Specifically, these parameters address the engagement of *adult* professional athletes. Anyone doing a cursory read of these eligibility requirements would see the problem—they are clearly not applicable to children. Waiting periods (sometimes up to four years), endocrine assessments, and even genital surgical documentation have been expected for these elite adult athletes. These require-ments for adults are not based on any substantive statistical analysis because the presence of transgender Olympic-level athletes has been almost non-existent. The Tokyo Games in 2021 were the first to have qualifying trans and nonbinary athletes (four in entirety) with none of them advancing to the level of medal competition.[6]

Some of the IOC requirements were modeled on the punitive steps imposed on athletes with "doping" (illegal performance-enhancing drugs) violations. Rather than considering the medical needs of transgender people, the punitive wait periods were based on the myth that gender-affirming endocrine treatment was akin to deceptive practices of athletes seeking out illegal substances to unfairly gain a physical advantage.

It is crucial to note that many trans people do not want genital surgery, and forcing them to do so in order to compete would be extreme and unethical. Even those who want genital surgery would still find multiple barriers that could inhibit/delay their ability to compete. Many would have little to no access to qualified surgeons and/or find such surgeries to be financially out of reach. Surgical intervention could take years to complete—quite possibly the same peak performance years of their career. For those trans athletes who *do not want surgery*, this discriminatory requirement would either exclude them entirely or force an athlete to make the terrible choice between pursuing unwanted genital surgery and their lifelong athletic aspirations. Surgical requirements or not, logic dictates that the presence/absence of certain genitalia, in and of itself, provides zero competitive advantage.

Again, because children do not undergo genital surgeries, these IOC parameters certainly do not apply. We need a policy that pertains specifically to children.

THE FIRST U.S. STATE ACTIVITIES ASSOCIATION TO ENACT GENDER-INCLUSIVE SPORTS POLICY

In 2007, I was invited to a roundtable discussion with the Washington Interscholastic Activities Association (WIAA), the service organization that administers policies, rules, and regulations to WA state schools. Up until that time, there was nothing in place to address the unique needs of gender-diverse K–12 students because these youth were scarcely visible within schools. The WIAA had initially considered adopting previously mentioned IOC guidelines for their student handbook but quickly understood the inapplicability to the lives of K–12 students.

The task that the roundtable set out to accomplish was to address the question of athletic participation for these gender-diverse children. Local and national representatives joined this think-tank, and all had diverse perspectives to contribute. Attorneys from the American Civil Liberties Union (ACLU), WIAA leadership, athletic directors from Washington and Colorado, and community leaders like myself were present. We considered questions from school administrators and coaches that many were beginning to encounter. Some of those questions included:

- How would we know if a child's gender identity was solid, for example, or just a phase?
- Would a doctor need to provide an affidavit affirming the student's gender identity?
- Would trans girls have an unfair physical advantage over other girls?
- Might a student pretend to be a different gender in order to play on a team on which they would otherwise be ineligible?
- Should we require participation based on the gender designation listed on an athlete's birth certificate?
- Would a male athlete join a girls' team with the hopes of increasing their chances of securing a college scholarship?
- What if other students did not feel safe around trans athletes? What about *their* concerns and right to privacy?

OUR PROCESS—SO MANY QUESTIONS

During the WIAA roundtable, we initially spent time contemplating how to address these questions in ways that we hoped would satisfy *the concerns of others*. Were these questions ones we *needed* to address or were they, like the IOC requirements, rooted in future apprehensions of violations or deceptive practices we feared *could* occur? How well would our guidelines help school personnel address any "what if" concerns expressed by others—parents, competing teams, or even an average person on the street?

Many of these concerns were familiar to me. I had heard them many times, in many situations, and from individuals who are close to a gender-diverse child and from those completely removed from a trans child's life. *What if a child is going through a phase, what if they change their mind, and aren't they too young to be making this kind of gender "decision"?* For the roundtable participants, these questions were part of the terrain even though they are not directly sports-related. How do we acknowledge that these questions added complexity to our process while simultaneously recognizing that establishing a policy was *not* a process for making gender identity assessments? If these questions are a constant part of the larger backdrop of unaddressed questions for everyone, how do we consider these concerns without being dismissive—as if the answers don't matter? I knew we needed to ask some deeper questions:

- Do we need to have these questions definitively answered before a student tries out for a team or steps into a locker room?
- Are we depending on the child to "prove" their gender identity to us? If the onus is not on the child, then who makes such a determination?
- How do we make gender determinations for *any* student-athlete? Do we have a practice of asking any of the above questions for children who are not transgender?
- If we established specific gender criteria for trans athletes only, would we then find ourselves in the position of instead instituting a different discriminatory process?
- How do we step into a newer context of what it means to be gender inclusive while building the confidence of those tasked with implementing a first-of-its-kind policy?

WHAT ABOUT BIRTH CERTIFICATES?

It could be argued that sports teams request birth certificates to make gender determinations but, the fact is, they don't. Schools and athletic teams do request birth certificates with the primary purpose of knowing a child's *age* but do not take direct action to match the gender designation with a child's genital configuration. In order to be non-discriminatory, all children, not just trans children, would need to be subject to genital checks. Thankfully, no one has suggested putting this into practice. If they did, the subsequent uproar for invading a child's right to bodily privacy and jeopardizing their safety from potential predators would surely make the evening's news in any community. A review of a child's birth certificate provides the school or team an opportunity to simply *continue* their gender assumptions solely based on how a child *looks* (gender expression). Keep in mind that many trans youth keep their gender status private and may not be known as trans to anyone within their school community. Would their right to this privacy be revoked? How would we know their gender history in the first place?

Should we expect a trans student to provide a birth certificate that names their gender identity rather than their sex designation at birth? It is important to recognize that there is no nationally uniform process for birth certificate amendments. The requirements to change one's gender designation vary widely state by state while some states refuse gender marker changes under any circumstances. Any child born in one of the latter states, if required to produce an amended birth certificate, would simply have no way to do so.

WHAT ABOUT REQUIRING A GENDER-CERTIFYING LETTER FROM A SURGEON OR PHYSICIAN?

For the sake of discussion, what if we *did* require an amended birth certificate? In some states, to change the gender designation on a birth certificate, a letter from a *surgeon* is required indicating the completion of gender-affirming surgery. If proof of surgical intervention is required, children are immediately excluded. The vast majority of trans youth do not pursue genital surgery before they reach adulthood. Some never will. Again, a condition like this would mean that gender-diverse students would never be able to meet eligibility requirements.

Some roundtable participants suggested that, in lieu of an amended birth certificate, we could instead require that an athlete provide a gender assessment from a health care provider validating their gender identity. There was an assumption that this would be a necessary step. After all, any adult pursuing a gender transition had been expected to have one, sometimes more, gender assessment letters from providers in order to proceed with medical intervention. This pathway too would present immediate barriers for most gender-diverse youth.

First, it presumes that every student-athlete has support from their parent or primary caregiver. This is a huge presumption considering the current level of rejection still experienced by today's trans youth. Secondly, even if familial support were present, this step would only be available to those occupying a high level of socioeconomic privilege. The availability of providers who might be knowledgeable enough to make a gender assessment for a child in the mid-2000s was minimal or nonexistent in most major cities, much less small cities, or suburban or rural areas. Would a family be expected to travel to another state to gain documentation? Often providers expect to see a patient for six months or more—would that family have to relocate in order to gain that assessment? It's immediately apparent how this would disproportionately affect marginalized students, those who have undocumented or temporary citizenship status, and those who live in politically and/or religiously conservative regions.

Requiring medical provider validation would be deeply challenging for most students, and impossible for many. Lastly, an expectation like this ignores an important distinction. The gender assessment process began with the presumption that it applied only to the pursuit of a surgical/medical transition for adults, not a *social transition* for children.

WHAT ABOUT REQUIRING A MEASUREMENT OF BODY MASS INDEX?

During our roundtable, the two attorneys from the ACLU were excited to share an approach that they felt might offer a solution. Implementing body mass index (BMI) parameters, they said, could serve as an effective participation determiner for trans athletes. An expectation of BMI (weight-to-height ratio) would be established for girls' and boys' teams—if a trans athlete's BMI fell within a certain range, that would determine the team on which they would participate.

Would this mean that we would need to test the BMI of *all* athletes? Many children whose body height to weight ratio falls outside of the set range would be disqualified from *any* team. How would that ratio be determined in the first place? BMI ranges vary around the world. How would these tests be implemented so as not to be discriminatory?

Every effort to establish specific criteria for trans athlete participation took us down a path that was more and more complicated and, we realized, ultimately discriminatory toward the trans athlete. It became increasingly clear throughout our discussions that imposing *any* of these requirements solely on trans athletes (or those suspected of being trans) is not the way to go. They would immediately be recognized as discriminatory in nature and certainly not the end goal for any entity whose commitment to all students is that they have the opportunity to participate in what the WIAA, according to its mission, deems "excellent, fair, safe, and accessible" activities. Establishing *any* prohibitive criteria exclusive to trans athletes is not a way to optimize that athlete's experience, but rather one designed to decrease everyone else's imagined future problems and fears.

NAVIGATING IMPLICIT BIAS—A ROUNDTABLE CHALLENGE AS WELL

Inaccurate representations of trans people and the themes associated with those representations influenced many roundtable participants, despite everyone's best intentions to remain unbiased. Whether we recognized them or not, these biases were affecting both our discussion and our search for solutions as to how gender-diverse youth might engage in sports.

For example, expecting a health provider to assess and diagnose a child's gender identity reinforces the notion of gender identity as a mental illness. This serves to cement the gender identification of trans youth as abnormal (rather than less common), unlike the gender identification of their cisgender peers.

The notion that trans people are looking to deceive others is evident when a trans child is expected to disclose their gender identity regardless of their own need for privacy. The theme of deception shows up again when we address the worries of some that a student will pretend to be trans in order to play on a team on which they would otherwise be ineligible.

The belief that trans people are dangerous to others is clearly evident when others bring up concerns about the safety of other students. The presumption is that a trans athlete is inherently dangerous simply because they are trans. These themes provide a harmful undercurrent even though the realities of trans youth engagement in sports do not support these imagined scenarios.

A DIFFERENT APPROACH—KEEP IT SIMPLE AND EQUITABLE

I suggested to the WIAA roundtable that we shift our approach from one that seeks to assuage the nebulous apprehensions of others to one that was centered on the student-athlete. The clearest, most equitable way to move forward is for the student to participate on a team that aligns with their stated gender identity. Period. We decided to move forward with that simple approach. It removed a great degree of the student's burden of having to "prove" their gender identity thereby removing the discriminatory elements outlined above. The most powerful part of this student-centered approach is that it entrusts the student with being the best person to make that determination.

We understood that we were crafting policies where none had previously existed. Some felt that we should put into place a review process *only* if a student's eligibility was legitimately placed into question (e.g., the fear that a student might lie about their gender to gain an advantage). This created a vehicle for addressing any problematic scenarios—imagined or otherwise—if a student's eligibility were to be challenged for any reason. It was felt that this approach could serve as a safety net. It would minimize participation barriers for trans students, and build the confidence of those tasked with policy implementation, and identify a pathway to address potential problems.

OUR POLICY'S FIRST DECADE

After more than a decade of implementation in over eight hundred WIAA member schools, we were excited to see the ongoing success of our approach. Since then, more than fifteen states have modeled their policies on this WA state policy and their results are similar. The primary lesson learned? It's working and working well. Since its creation and adoption, there was only *one* case where a student's eligibility was challenged by an opposing school. One case in over a decade!

This case was put before the WIAA's review committee. A trans girl had joined her high school's track team and a competing school filed an eligibility challenge. The challenge was likely based solely on the fact that she was trans. The review committee's responsibility was *not* to determine whether or not trans students should be allowed to compete. That determination had already been made over a decade prior at the inception of the policy.

Because the gender identification of any student is something that is self-determined, the question raised for the review committee was whether this student was deceptively stating she was female *in order to gain a perceived advantage*. It was determined that she was not. The student's track coach attended the meeting and shared with the review committee how much the team embraced her presence, celebrated her wins, commiserated with her losses, and unequivocally supported her inclusion on the team. Their statements were not needed as part of the evaluative process but they certainly provided a clear message—they valued their trans teammate and were fighting for her right to be an included, integral member of the team. Only one eligibility review in a span of fourteen years within the entire state of Washington? Even we had not anticipated such uncomplicated success.

EVENTUALLY: A NEED FOR POLICY REVISION

I was invited to step in again with the WIAA in 2019 to review our established gender identity participation philosophy and eligibility rules. While the approach we introduced to the nation was still strong and applicable, we understood societal changes warranted a review. Were there any changes that might require an update or reconsideration? Turns out the answer was yes. We updated a few areas needing reconsideration that are outlined below.

Language and Pronouns

The number of trans-identified athletes in K–12 schools continues to grow. The ways in which these youth describe their gender have also expanded. Our original WIAA policy referenced *transgender* youth but the gender identifier of *nonbinary* had not been mentioned. Why not? Because *nonbinary* as a gender identity descriptor was not yet a part of the common gender-diverse community vernacular in 2007. We updated our language beyond the sole use of the term *transgender* to the use of *transgender and other gender-diverse identities* to better encompass the array of terms used by students including terms like nonbinary, gender-expansive, and so on. As time progressed, gender-diverse students were more frequently adopting the pronouns *they/them* to describe themselves rather than *he/him* or *she/her*. As this became a more commonplace occurrence, usage of *they/them* to reference a singular person was embraced by editors of dictionaries like Merriam-Webster, making the argument of being "grammatically incorrect" a moot point. We made a simple update to use *they/them/theirs* for the dual purpose of including the gender-diverse students *and* referencing all students in a manner consistent with the language found elsewhere within the *WIAA Handbook*.

Eligibility Review Process

Even though, a dozen years after policy implementation, we had experienced only one eligibility challenge from a competing school, we recognized that our existing requirements for an eligibility review placed an undue burden on the student-athlete and were worthy of reexamination. The eligibility review process placed this particular young track athlete in the intimidating and fraught position of having to defend, to a group of adult strangers, her identity and her right to play.

We realized that in no other situation when an athlete's eligibility was in question (address of residence, status as a transfer student, academic performance, and so on) would a student be placed under such stressful circumstances. Fears that students might lie about their gender to gain an athletic advantage— reasons that some WIAA roundtable participants argued for establishing the review process in the first place—were unfounded. It just didn't pan out, statistically or anecdotally. It is important to note that actions for addressing deliberate dishonesty or misconduct already exist.

We also eliminated the full eligibility review process should a trans student's right to participate be challenged by an external entity or individual. Once a student is deemed eligible according to their school or district requirements, that eligibility could not be challenged by a competing school where the defense and burden of proof then fall on the shoulders of that student. This approach would then be consistent with any other eligibility requirements.

"Known" Gender Status Versus "Private" Gender Status

While the original gender inclusion policy addressed privacy considerations, our committee felt it necessary to more deeply address the importance of any student's privacy needs. When we first considered trans athlete inclusion, our conversation centered on our own assumption that the gender status of trans students would be known to all within their school community. At that time, the presence of any trans student within schools was rare. Today, as inclusive approaches are more available within schools, children are better able to live in congruence with their authentic gender regardless of whether their gender status is known or private. The notion that a child might transition at an early age and live in accordance with their gender identity throughout their full years of school attendance was something we had not considered during our early WIAA roundtable session, nor did we consider the reality that a student, who may have transitioned some time ago, might later enter a new school and opt to keep their gender history private.

MAKING MORE ROOM FOR GENDER IDENTITY PROCESS—IT DOESN'T GET DECIDED OVERNIGHT

It is important to recognize that each gender-diverse student has differing variables and experiences that inform their gender identity pathway. Socioeconomics, level of family support, role of coaches/teachers, and the presence of existing support systems are just a few of the factors that influence a child's experience.

In an effort to be both nondiscriminatory and honoring of any student's journey, it is imperative to recognize that a child shouldn't be *forced to declare a gender identity that doesn't fit* or one which they are not yet ready/able to embrace solely in order to participate. A nonbinary-identified youth, for example, could then participate on the team that they determine most closely aligns with their gender identity, or they might opt for a team based on factors that would be more likely to promote the greatest sense of camaraderie or to best match their skill level. If a child, regardless of sex assigned at birth, has the choice of engaging on the boys' team or the girls' team, that child could then consider which team was the best fit without having to lie or tell a story that only serves to satisfy the expectations of others.

CONCLUSION? SUCCESS!

The WIAA in 2007 had stepped into the daunting task of creating a brand-new policy—the first in the nation—and showed a lot of courage. It is intimidating to implement new, untested practices. I believe the student-centered approach is at the core of the policy's long-lasting success. The policy revision process a dozen years later has only furthered that success. As a result, athletic directors and coaches have acquired a higher degree of confidence and clarity. By the time the amendment for policy revisions was put before the state's entire WIAA member-ship for review and approval, not only did the fifty-three voting members pass the amendment, they did so unanimously!

The staff at the WIAA continue to make themselves available to help any member school seeking assistance. Every school with eligible trans or nonbinary athletes has successfully onboarded these students while some schools have yet to have gender-diverse athlete participation to date. Regardless, the WIAA and athletic directors statewide have a firmer foundation for building on this success. Because of this groundbreaking policy creation, many other communities will replicate the success of Washington State.

CREATING A GENDER-INCLUSIVE SPORTS TOOLKIT

Outside Washington State, I've had many one-on-one conversations with coaches, principals, and athletic directors where I'm able to share the success of the WA policy implementation. However, this one-on-one approach will not keep pace with the needs of today's student-athletes. After the policy revi-sion and unanimous approval by the full WIAA membership, I approached the WIAA team once again.

Knowing that the WIAA staff were also fielding numerous inquiries across WA state, I wanted to find a way in which we could collaboratively share our experience and success. I pitched the idea of creating a toolkit that we could disseminate nationally. WIAA excitedly agreed. The Seattle Sounders, the city's popular professional soccer team with whom I had begun gender diversity train-ing, was enthusiastic to get on board as well. Many of their youth league coaches had been contacting the Sounders leadership, unsure of how to be inclusive of the increasing numbers of gender-diverse athletes. This toolkit could help in multiple ways.

With its simple, straightforward approach, this toolkit had the support of the Sounders and *all* six of Seattle's professional sports teams (Mariners, Seahawks, Storm, Sounders, OL Reign, and Kraken) signed on as endorsers. Every pro team felt strongly that all student-athletes deserved a chance to play and were eager to add their name to the toolkit. At the beginning of June 2021, we announced the publication of the first version. You can find this toolkit at http://genderdivers ity.org/best-practices-for-youth-sports/.

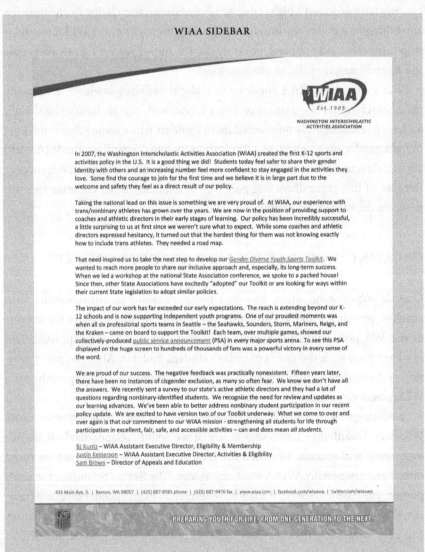

WIAA SIDEBAR

WASHINGTON INTERSCHOLASTIC ACTIVITIES ASSOCIATION

In 2007, the Washington Interscholastic Activities Association (WIAA) created the first K-12 sports and activities policy in the U.S. It is a good thing we did! Students today feel safer to share their gender identity with others and an increasing number feel more confident to stay engaged in the activities they love. Some find the courage to join for the first time and we believe it is in large part due to the welcome and safety they feel as a direct result of our policy.

Taking the national lead on this issue is something we are very proud of. At WIAA, our experience with trans/nonbinary athletes has grown over the years. We are now in the position of providing support to coaches and athletic directors in their early stages of learning. Our policy has been incredibly successful, a little surprising to us at first since we weren't sure what to expect. While some coaches and athletic directors expressed hesitancy, it turned out that the hardest thing for them was not knowing exactly how to include trans athletes. They needed a road map.

That need inspired us to take the next step to develop our *Gender Diverse Youth Sports Toolkit*. We wanted to reach more people to share our inclusive approach and, especially, its long-term success. When we led a workshop at the national State Association conference, we spoke to a packed house! Since then, other State Associations have excitedly "adopted" our Toolkit or are looking for ways within their current State legislation to adopt similar policies.

The impact of our work has far exceeded our early expectations. The reach is extending beyond our K-12 schools and is now supporting independent youth programs. One of our proudest moments was when all six professional sports teams in Seattle – the Seahawks, Sounders, Storm, Mariners, Reign, and the Kraken – came on board to support the Toolkit! Each team, over multiple games, showed our collectively-produced public service announcement (PSA) in every major sports arena. To see this PSA displayed on the huge screen to hundreds of thousands of fans was a powerful victory in every sense of the word.

We are proud of our success. The negative feedback was practically nonexistent. Fifteen years later, there have been no instances of cisgender exclusion, as many so often fear. We know we don't have all the answers. We recently sent a survey to our state's active athletic directors and they had a lot of questions regarding nonbinary-identified students. We recognize the need for review and updates as our learning advances. We've been able to better address nonbinary student participation in our recent policy update. We are excited to have version two of our Toolkit underway. What we come to over and over again is that our commitment to our WIAA mission - strengthening all students for life through participation in excellent, fair, safe, and accessible activities – can and does mean *all students*.

BJ Kuntz – WIAA Assistant Executive Director, Eligibility & Membership
Justin Kesterson – WIAA Assistant Executive Director, Activities & Eligibility
Sam Brown – Director of Appeals and Education

435 Main Ave. S. | Renton, WA 98057 | (425) 687-8585 phone | (425) 687-9476 fax | www.wiaa.com | facebook.com/wiaawa | twitter.com/wiaawa

PREPARING YOUTH FOR LIFE, FROM ONE GENERATION TO THE NEXT.

NOTES

1. Office for Civil Rights (OCR), "Title IX of the Education Amendments of 1972," HHS. gov (October 17, 2019), https://www.hhs.gov/civil-rights/for-individuals/sex-discriminat ion/title-ix-education-amendments/index.html.
2. Richard C. Bell, "A History of Women in Sport Prior to Title IX," *The Sport Journal* 10, no. 2 (2007).
3. Ruth Padawer, "The Humiliating Practice of Sex-Testing Female Athletes," *The New York Times* (June 28, 2016), https://www.nytimes.com/2016/07/03/magazine/the-humiliat ing-practice-of-sex-testing-female-athletes.html.
4. "'They're Chasing Us Away from Sport': Human Rights Violations in Sex Testing of Elite Women Athletes," *Human Rights Watch* (December 4, 2020), https://www.hrw.org/ report/2020/12/04/theyre-chasing-us-away-sport/human-rights-violations-sex-test ing-elite-women.
5. "Application of *Bostock v. Clayton County* to Title IX of the Education Amendments of 1972," U.S. Department of Justice: Memorandum (March 26, 2021).
6. "International Olympic Committee Issues New Guidelines on Transgender Athletes," *NBC News* (November 16, 2021), https://www.nbcnews.com/nbc-out/out-news/international-olympic-committee-issues-new-guidelines-transgender-athl-rcna5775.

16

Sports

Gender Inclusion in K–12 Athletics

Authenticity is about being true to who you are, even when everyone around you wants you to be someone else.

Michael Jordan

In my work with K–12 schools, the question of sports inclusion for gender-diverse youth is a common one. For educators, this conversation may be their first foray into a topic that is fraught with apprehension. They may have their first trans student wanting to join a team, a parent inquiring about physical education (PE) requirements for their child, a coach wondering how to field questions from others, or all of these at once. Regardless, they may recognize that they are on a steep learning curve, uneasy about that learning, and in need of support while they do so.

Debates surrounding whether trans students should be "allowed" to play, and if so, in what capacity, are focused on what *might* happen rather than the reality of what *is* happening.

Trans athletes in schools have been engaging successfully in K–12 sports for years. The first K–12 gender-inclusive policy in the nation, developed by myself and the Washington State Activities Association was implemented, without fanfare, *over 15 years ago*. The *Gender-Diverse Youth Sport Inclusivity Toolkit* I authored in 2021 was developed to highlight the state's successful policy implementation, address frequently asked questions, and make evident that all athletes have a right to play. Concerns have been raised that trans athletes will have an unfair physical advantage over other athletes. This does not reflect reality. Since the implementation of this policy, trans K–12 athletes have not dominated their sports—they win some and they lose some—just like their own teammates and their competitors.

What makes this effort challenging is the nascent awareness of trans student inclusion in schools, especially within gender-segregated arenas such as sports. Yes, Washington State has had a head start, but it is still actively engaged in learning and discovery. Elsewhere, the majority of schools are just beginning to take their first steps. Everyone can benefit from learning more—but where do we find the information? My hope is that the information in this book will move us from emotionally driven, yet factually deprived, scenarios to a perspective rooted in experience.

What we must gain is a greater sense of confidence among staff, parents, and students, and what we have to lose are feelings of uncertainty and apprehension. It's no longer a hypothetical approach but current practice from which we know others benefit.

LAYING THE FOUNDATION: BE ABLE
TO ARTICULATE WHAT'S BEING DONE AND WHY

While the inclusion of gender-diverse K–12 student-athletes on sports teams may feel unfamiliar, or even a bit intimidating, the practical steps to do so prove to be something quite achievable. In my experience working with schools, hesitancy turns into confidence, apprehension turns into excitement, and the positive outcomes come with a strong sense of accomplishment. It's a win-win situation for everyone.

As you consider best practices for moving forward, recognize that the foundation you need is already there! Here are some of the elements of that foundation:

1. When considering how to honor a student's accomplishments, we know that for an athlete to win a medal, break a school record, or take the team to the championship level, they must have the courage to try out for the team in the first place. Having that courage doesn't *just happen*. A child needs *encouragement* along the way. It's one of the reasons why we set up opportunities for them in the first place.

2. The importance of visible role models is recognized as influential on a young person's ability to cultivate self-esteem and persevere in sports and other activities. It's why we need to see stories of a man on the cheer squad, black women excelling in tennis, immigrants overcoming poverty to compete professionally, or a champion wrestler, missing a limb, who finishes the season undefeated. These athletes provide children from adverse circumstances *with visible role models who exemplify diverse bodies and experiences.*

3. Making sports inclusive by providing children with the opportunity—actually, the *right*—to participate is a powerful part of the history of sports. The fight for racial and gender access to opportunities, previously available only to those who are white and male, is part of that history. The fight for this access is about equity, and the reason we do so is that all children benefit from this sense of belonging. It provides a child with a sense of personal dignity, respect for others, a feeling of safety, and an understanding of their own worth as an important part of the whole.

Not many people would disagree with these basic principles—encouragement, visibility, and inclusion—but changing *systems of inequity* requires more than collective agreement, it requires a sustained commitment. However, recognizing that we have an existing foundation means we are better able to articulate the reasons for gender advocacy in the first place.

It also means there is no need to wait for the arrival of a trans or nonbinary athlete to launch from this foundation. A proactive effort will pay off. Foundational elements, like gender-inclusive policies, guidelines for implementation, and the pursuit of additional learning opportunities for staff take time to implement. Getting started now means a better chance of being ready when that trans or nonbinary athlete does show up.

In the same way that engaging school community stakeholders is essential to the successful inclusion of gender-diverse children in schools, the same is true for the inclusion of K–12 athletes in sports. Each stakeholder within the arena of athletics needs to be considered when implementing gender-inclusive practices. They include:

- The gender-diverse student-athlete;
- Coaches, athletic directors, and PE teachers;
- School and district leadership;
- The parent base and other community supporters; and
- Students/peers.

The acknowledgment of trans youth and efforts to create environments in which they might more fully participate is a relatively new initiative in many schools. As trans athletes move toward their authentic selves, they do so primarily within gender-divided activities. This requires a reexamination of gender-divided practices as a result. Each school community stakeholder will benefit from the clear communication of policies, practices, expectations, and responsibilities. Let's take a closer look at the pertinent issues for each of these stakeholders.

Gender-Diverse Student-Athletes

Supporting and including any individual trans or nonbinary student includes the consideration of variables that are part of their day-to-day lives. Schools can support any individual by working with that student to develop a support plan that addresses factors including sports participation, bathroom/locker room usage, names, pronouns, privacy considerations, and others. A support plan has two primary purposes: to optimize the experience for the student themselves and to provide clarity for everyone else. A student often works in tandem with a school counselor, principal, or other designated support person to best determine any steps and time considerations to optimize the transition pathway for that student.

Coaches, Athletic Directors, and PE Teachers

Often a coach or athletic director is sought out to provide clarity regarding the participation of gender-diverse athletes, especially on gender-divided teams. If that coach or athletic director does not have the language and/or understanding, there is potential for frustration. The successful implementation of inclusionary practices for trans athletes occurs when these athletic leaders are able to clearly and confidently communicate the ways in which these practices work to the benefit of all student-athletes, including the trans athlete. If we are able to understand the principles of inclusion and their day-to-day applicability in real-life life situations, we are well on our way to optimizing equitable student participation.

School and District Leadership

Like those individuals who are in direct engagement with student-athletes, any principal, superintendent, or person in a leadership role will benefit from having clarity on participation policy, practices, and obligations. If there are questions or concerns raised regarding student eligibility, all will benefit from the clarity provided. This is of particular importance when inclusionary practices are first implemented. Confident leadership serves to strengthen the confidence of coaches, teachers, parents, and students.

The Parent Base and Other School Community Supporters

While the educators, staff, and administrators are considering the needs of the student body as a whole, it is often a different story with any individual parent or caregiver. Understandably, that person will be focused on the needs of their student in particular. Educators and parents have a strong, collaborative role in ensuring the optimal experiences for these students even as their perspectives may vary. While coaches, teachers, staff, and principals will benefit from learning opportunities, so too should the parent/caregiver community be considered.

Whether that is engaging in direct communication with a single parent or offering educational sessions for the parent body as a whole, they too deserve to better understand and to have any concerns allayed.

Students

The peers of trans and nonbinary students are often the ones most knowledgeable about gender diversity and adaptable to the inclusion of their trans and nonbinary peers. The acceptance and embracing of their trans teammates are what typically provide the forward movement for their adult counterparts. That said, direct communication is what facilitates any adjustments with greater ease. Good sportsmanship practices—not just skill-building—is an integral part of why we provide athletic opportunities for youth. Graciously winning and losing, being a team player, and having a supportive and encouraging attitude toward yourself and others are all attributes that we would like to see among student-athletes. Communication of these expected practices is what builds the foundation for any unexpected situation, including the welcoming of a new trans teammate.

District Website and School Handbook

Gender-inclusive policy and implementation practices aren't very helpful if you can't find them! Consider where the information might be most visible—for students, staff, and parents. School and district websites are logical sources to display information as is any student handbook or other resource that addresses eligibility and access to participation. It is important to address gender diversity—including the terms *gender identity* and *gender expression*—where statements regarding inclusion, equity, and diversity exist. Students and their families will appreciate and expect to see this commitment articulated and visible.

BEST PRACTICES FOR GENDER INCLUSION

(Excerpted from *The Gender-Diverse Youth Sport Inclusivity Toolkit*)
Which restroom and locker room should a trans student use?
The short answer:
A student uses the facility that most closely aligns with their gender identity.

A little more explanation:

Transgender athletes, as a general rule, will opt for either the boys' room (for trans boys) or the girls' room (for trans girls). Nonbinary-identified and other gender-diverse youth are also in the position of selecting the specific gender-separated facility that works best for them. There are different considerations that may be present that will influence any student's choice. Safety and privacy need top the list. Some athletes may request an all-gender facility; some may use a particular gender-separated room but request a slightly different changing schedule to accommodate their desire for greater privacy. Some may seek a private changing area within a particular locker room. These requests can likely be readily accommodated.

Bonus:

Any student, regardless of their gender identity, may request similar accommodations to gain a greater degree of privacy and/or sense of safety. Schools and districts across the nation have seen the positive effect of a gender-inclusive approach for the entire student body.

Caveat:

No student should be forced to use an all-gender facility, such as a staff bathroom, simply because they are trans or gender diverse. Federal court rulings have determined this to be a discriminatory practice.

How do we address pronoun change requests?

The short answer:

Everyone should use the pronoun a student requests.

A little more explanation:

It used to be very rare for someone to request a different pronoun. Today it is more and more commonplace. Conceptually, it is a very easy switch to make. The most common pronouns in usage are *she/her*, *he/him*, and *they/them*. In practice, it can be challenging and awkward to change a pronoun for someone we've known or for whom we make an automatic pronoun assumption. Recognize that this awkwardness is temporary, and that practice makes perfect. It is a respectful act and a crucial affirmation of an individual's gender identity. Using the correct pronoun is a necessary and non-discriminatory practice. Ask for pronouns on any athlete information forms. This disarms any concern that a student-athlete might have in raising the subject of pronouns, a sometimes-daunting prospect for a newly disclosing student. It also sends a clear message that a team is a safe place for them.

Bonus:

Pronoun change requests are more and more commonplace. Younger generations especially are embracing gender-expansive language and even people who are not transgender are adopting pronouns like *they/them*. We once may have questioned the grammatical correctness of this, but Merriam-Webster and other dictionaries now say otherwise. Practice, practice, practice.

Caveat:

It is easy to make mistakes but recognize the importance of being consistent with the requested pronoun. If you make a mistake, quickly apologize and correct the pronoun so everyone can get back to the conversation at hand. Expect that of everyone else as well.

Should we be asking for proof of gender, like a birth certificate or doctor's statement?

The short answer:

No.

A little more explanation:

Enrollment in public school, sports, or other activities should use the student's requested name, pronoun, and gender designation. The gender identity and/or gender history of some students will be common knowledge while other students will want privacy.

Bonus:

This approach eliminates the arbitrary and discriminatory practice of imposing certain requirements on some students while not having the same requirements as others.

Caveat:

A student has the right to disclose their gender identity if they wish. They also have a protected right to privacy. The Family Educational Rights and Privacy Act (FERPA) (20 U.S.C. § 1232g; 34 CFR Part 99) is a federal law that protects the privacy of student education records. The law applies to all schools that receive funds under an applicable program of the U.S. Department of Education. Unless required by law (or with appropriate permissions granted), a student's gender status, legal name, or other private information should not be shared.[1]

How do we successfully onboard trans/nonbinary athletes?

The short answer:
A little preparation goes a long way to ensuring optimal outcomes for the athlete, their coach and teammates, their fan base, and competitors.

A little more explanation:
The visible presence and inclusion of gender-diverse athletes within our schools and on our sports teams present new challenges for coaches and educators. With any new situation, being attentive to communications, learning processes, and outlining expectations will pay off for the entire team. The following are some steps that a coach might take when a trans/nonbinary athlete joins a team:

1. Work with the student-athlete to gain their input as to what steps might be of most benefit to them. For example, one gender-diverse athlete may want to share their story with their teammates while another may wish to have their privacy respected by not doing so.

2. Enlist the assistance of your team captain or other student leaders to welcome the new teammate and to help them acclimate. There is more to sports than just playing the game—the sense of belonging and camaraderie is high on the list for any student.

3. With any new situation, there may be questions. Make space for those questions and make yourself available if any student has questions that they wish to discuss in private.

Acknowledge that new situations may have a period of adjustment and that is to be expected.

With the launch of any sports season, a coach or PE teacher will often use this time to articulate the values embraced by, and the expectations of all teammates. Welcoming any new student-athlete—including the gender-diverse athlete—provides another opportunity to review team values, goals, and expectations including some of those listed here:

Values: humility in winning, grace in defeat, discipline, courage, empowerment

Goals: resilience, self-confidence, collaborative relationships, sense of belonging, self-growth

Expectations: teamwork, celebrating accomplishments, setting goals, accomplishing goals, sportsmanship

Bonus:

There is no need to wait for the arrival of a trans athlete to begin conversations with team members about the value of inclusion. Any team would benefit from the articulation of, and expectations surrounding good sportsmanship values.

Caveat:

Even with advance preparations concerning students, questions about locker room privacy, for example, do occasionally come up. Let all students know that their need and/or request for privacy is important. Any student who desires a greater degree of privacy for changing in and out of uniform should be provided with options to do so. Additionally, do not put the trans/nonbinary athlete in the position of educating everyone. Just as we would not task a student of color to educate their teammates about racial equity, nor should we expect a trans athlete to educate others on gender equity.

Common Questions from Coaches and PE Teachers

Q: A student is currently expressing themself as nonbinary and would like to participate in athletics. How do we determine on which sports team they might participate?

A: Because of the existence of male/female gender divisions on most teams, this creates a need for nonbinary students to determine which gendered team they feel most closely aligns with their gender identity. Alternatively, they may select the gendered team on which they feel most comfortable participating. Factors that the nonbinary athlete may take into consideration include established camaraderie with fellow athletes, personal safety, and/or privacy concerns.

Once this determination is made, the student will be eligible to participate in sports offered for the selected gender. If a student wishes to change the selected gender during any remaining years of athletic eligibility, they will be allowed to do so if this change is a result of a deeper understanding of their gender identity (e.g., a nonbinary student wrestler may determine, after time, that their identity more closely aligns with male and are then ready to participate on the boy's team) and may need to attend an eligibility hearing to gain varsity eligibility. A student may have other reasons for changing their gender identity and those can be considered with an emphasis on optimizing the athlete's confidence, safety, and privacy.

Q: A nonbinary student would like to participate in girls' volleyball in the fall and then boys' tennis in the spring. Because they are nonbinary, is this allowed?

A: Situations such as these may be reviewed on a case-by-case basis. The previous example could be one such case. Over time, a student who has gained a deeper understanding of their gender as a male could then move forward to participate on the boys' teams. What is important to recognize is that a student's understanding of their gender identity may take some time to fully discern. They may understand the gender that they are not, but still need to discover the gender that they are. It is both an internal journey and an external experience.

Q: A transgender boy is participating in high school swimming and would like to have a waiver of the uniform requirement to wear a swimsuit that is more appropriate for his body.

A: Uniform waivers are allowed.

Q: What if a boy decides to falsely identify as a girl to participate in girls' teams or gain access to the girls' locker room?

A: This question is often raised as one of the primary reasons why trans and nonbinary athletes should not be allowed to participate on teams that are in congruence with their gender identity. The deceptive behavior of one student should never be identified as a reason to discriminate against gender-diverse students. Gender-diverse students are not typically offered immediate access to a locker room or team based on a single statement because optimizing the experience for that student often requires some level of preparation. The creation of a support plan/process is recommended for any student—this could include the involvement of a parent, principal, counselor, fellow students, and so on. Some schools pursue additional training to deepen their own understanding of what may be a first-time experience. Proactive measures to optimize any student's experience are often welcomed by the gender-diverse student while these measures simultaneously provide a vehicle for addressing the possibility of deception, pulling a prank, or any other unacceptable motives.

Q: Don't transgender girls have an unfair physical advantage over their teammates?

A: The presence of trans female athletes on teams throughout the nation has not been shown to diminish opportunities for others. The athleticism of any female athlete, as we know, can vary widely from that of other peers. Height, musculature, build, and weight are a few variables that impact performance. Additional factors that contribute to a potential advantage include access to skills-building opportunities at earlier ages, access to facilities and coaching, greater funding for programs and teams in certain privileged communities, chronological age, birth order, and more. For these, and other reasons, some athletes have advantages and opportunities over others. Many of these known variables are ones we strive to remedy. Others are variables we work to counter in different ways—team defense strategies, weight class divisions for certain sports, addressing Title IX violations, and so on. The belief that trans female athletes will dominate any team on which they participate is not a given, as some fear it will be.

One high-profile example is as follows:

Several Connecticut high school cisgender female track athletes took legal action in federal court against the Connecticut Association of Schools stating that there was no way they could compete against any transgender female competitors and hope to prevail, potentially denying them championships, and athletic scholarships, and other opportunities. Just days after filing suit, one of the plaintiffs in the lawsuit upped her game to beat her trans competitor and win the state championship.

Athletes and coaches all recognize the value of competition and the subsequent positive impact on the individual performances of any single athlete. Many of the top professional female athletes across the nation, rather than fearing an unfair advantage, have stated their support of trans athlete participation. As we celebrate the exceptional athleticism of any female athlete as they dominate and add to their sport, so too can we embrace the talents that any trans female athlete might bring. The cultivation and celebration of the athleticism of all athletes, including trans athletes, is a valuable part of any team's culture.

Teams who have welcomed the inclusion of their trans and nonbinary teammates see their presence as a crucial element in strengthening the entire team—ultimately serving to optimize participation for all students as they engage in excellent, fair, safe, and accessible activities.

Q: Does sex discrimination under Title IX apply to gender identity?

A: Yes. The U.S. Department of Justice: Civil Rights Division issued a clarifying memorandum in March 2021 regarding the application of the Supreme Court Ruling case *Bostock v. Clayton County* to Title IX of the Education Amendments of 1972. In part, it says, "... the Administration's policy [is] that "[a]ll persons should receive equal treatment under the law, no matter their gender identity or sexual orientation." Citing the Supreme Court's holding in *Bostock* that the prohibition on discrimination "because of ... sex" under Title VII of the Civil Rights Act of 1964, 42 U.S.C. § 2000e et seq. (Title VII), covers discrimination on the basis of gender identity and sexual orientation, the Executive Order explains that *Bostock*'s reasoning applies with equal force to other laws that prohibit sex discrimination "so long as the laws do not contain sufficient indications to the contrary." The Executive Order directs agencies to review other laws that prohibit sex discrimination, including Title IX, to determine whether they prohibit discrimination on the basis of gender identity and sexual orientation. We conclude that Title IX does ... After considering the text of Title IX, Supreme Court case law, and developing jurisprudence in this area, the Division has determined that the best reading of Title IX's prohibition on discrimination "on the basis of sex" is that it includes discrimination on the basis of gender identity and sexual orientation.

This memorandum is also consistent with the many federal courts, including the U.S. Court of Appeals for the Ninth Circuit and U.S. District Courts within that circuit, that have held Title IX and other federal laws prohibiting sex discrimination protect transgender people from discrimination. In several of those cases, federal courts safeguarded the right of transgender student-athletes to compete in sports consistent with their gender identity. Federal law would also prohibit other forms of discrimination including access to facilities, harassment, and use of correct names and pronouns.

ONGOING LEARNING AND EVALUATION

Today we are at a crossroads regarding the participation of trans and gender-diverse youth in athletics. While the debate rages, those for and those against the inclusion of trans student-athletes (especially young trans women) in sports are arm-wrestling over the ownership of Title IX protections and how they apply. Yet, the federal courts are weighing in on the subject and have repeatedly ruled that Title IX protects *all* female athletes, including trans girl and women athletes. Even the U.S. Supreme Court, as stated in a previous chapter, weighed in with a 6–3 decision in the case of *Bostock v. Clayton County* to Title IX of the Education Amendments of 1972. Regarding the application of Title IX, the Department of Justice said, "all persons should receive equal treatment under the law, no matter their gender identity."

Yes, this is a newer frontier. The efforts to provide greater equity for girls and women in schools through Title IX was itself once a new frontier, met with fierce resistance. Decades ago, many fought against the racial integration of our nation's schools. The common thread is that the imagined fears of what *could happen* were not the realities of what did happen. So, too, do people today fear what they do not understand and anticipate destruction (i.e., athletic scholarships will only go to trans athletes, performance records of girls/women will be decimated by trans athletes, etc.) that will not occur. We've learned over and over that the solution is not to deny the rights of inclusion and participation. The solution is to deepen our understanding.

As of the writing of this book, there have been multiple legislative efforts across the United States to exclude or restrict the athletic involvement of trans girls and young women in K–12 sports. Some have passed, and many have not. Even politically conservative politicians have balked at passing such discriminating and pointless legislation.

Utah Governor Spencer J. Cox, a man of the Mormon faith, vetoed such a bill with his stated reasons delivered in a letter to the Speaker of the House and the President of the Senate. In part, he says:

I believe in fairness and protecting the integrity of women's sports. I know both of you are committed to these same ideals and that we have worked very hard together to resolve the many issues surrounding transgender student participation in sports. Unfortunately, HB11 has several fundamental flaws and should be reconsidered.

. . .

They are great kids who face enormous struggles. Here are the numbers that have most impacted my decision: 75,000, 4, 1, 86, and 56.

- 75,000 high school kids participating in high school sports in Utah.
- 4 transgender kids playing high school sports in Utah.
- 1 transgender student playing girls' sports.
- 86% of trans youth report suicidality.
- 56% of trans youth have attempted suicide.

Four kids and only one of them playing girls' sports. That's what all of this is about. Four kids who aren't dominating or winning trophies or taking scholarships. Four kids who are just trying to find some friends and feel like they are a part of something. Four kids trying to get through each day. Rarely has so much fear and anger been directed at so few. I don't understand what they are going through or why they feel the way they do. But I want them to live.

And all the research shows that even a little acceptance and connection can reduce suicidality significantly. For that reason, as much as any other, I have taken this action in the hope that we can continue to work together and find a better way. If a veto override occurs, I hope we can work to find ways to show these four kids that we love them and they have a place in our state. I recognize the political realities of my decision. Politically, it would be much easier and better for me to simply sign the bill. I have always tried to do what I feel is the right thing regardless of the consequences. Sometimes I don't get it right, and I do not fault those who disagree with me.

But even if you disagree with me, I hope this letter helps you understand the reasons for my decision."[2]

Governor Cox's veto was ultimately overridden. The outcome of costly litigation for the Utah High School Athletic Association (UHSAA) and local Utah school districts will inevitably face costly lawsuits asserting the bill's discriminatory nature, the outcomes of which remain to be seen.

It is not appropriate to be legislatively addressing problems that do not exist. If there are areas of concern that develop over time, those can and should be addressed at that time. A commitment to improving equity is something that schools across the nation embrace. To do so, we look at *existing* inequities.

The letter from the Utah governor outlines some pretty low numbers when addressing the perceived threat of dominance by trans girls engaging in K–12 sports—one trans athlete, to be exact. Her participation hardly constitutes a threat to the tens of thousands of other girls participating in athletics. With at least double the number of K–12 student-athletes as Utah, Washington State's efforts at inclusion certainly add clarity to the overall picture. In fifteen years' time, and with multiple trans athletes engaging in sports and other activities, there has been only one situation that resulted from an eligibility review:

> A competing school challenged a high school girl's eligibility to compete in track. She came to the eligibility review meeting feeling intimidated and frightened, uncertain how things would turn out. The young women on her team wrote a collective letter in support of their teammate and her coach showed up to the review meeting to advocate for her as well. He shared how she was a valued and loved member of the team. The Washington Interscholastic Activities Association (WIAA) team reviewed the case and unanimously determined that she indeed was eligible. When this young trans woman spoke about her inclusion on the team, she noted that she did pretty well and was ranked 37th in the state—37th! That is hardly a decimation of her competitors.

The reality is that the feared impact of trans inclusion—taking away opportunities from other K–12 female athletes and dominating athletic competitions—has not come to fruition. This experience-driven reality has served to counter the fear-driven imaginings offered up as reasons for exclusion. The most important step at this point is ensuring that the day-to-day realities of successful inclusion are not obscured by the specters of doomsday predictions.

Do Trans Athletes Have an Unfair Physical Advantage?

Today's most pressing sports-related question is whether or not trans athletes have *an unfair physical advantage.* Let's be clear. This question is really about trans women. The presence of trans men in sports is rarely addressed in the larger-scale debate. The presumed athletic inferiority of trans boys/men relegates them to a conversational footnote, if they are mentioned at all. If they are mentioned at all, the risk of injury from cisgender male athletes is cited as the primary issue. This paternalistic concern is then incorporated as yet one more reason to exclude trans athletes from participating anywhere.

Do trans women have an unfair physical advantage? Because this is the predominant question, let's consider this question head on. When we frame this as a "yes" or "no" question, it sets us up for a polarizing debate by requiring us to essentially pick a side. To select an answer, we are required to set aside the complex layers of the topic and to completely ignore factors that would otherwise cause us to answer the question differently. Nevertheless, we can examine this question further.

UNFAIR ADVANTAGE? WHAT'S AT PLAY IF WE SAY "YES"?
For the sake of discussion, let's consider a "yes" to the question of trans female athlete advantage.

First, the question presumes that all trans girl athletes are of a certain post-pubertal age and have gone through (or are going through) testosterone-driven puberty. That is not the case for many. An increasing number of trans and nonbinary children are receiving puberty delay intervention to arrest unwanted pubertal development. With respect to them, the question of gained advantages from testosterone is a moot point. For those who have had some pubertal development, some may have gained a height and/or weight advantage over some of their peers but certainly not all. In some sports, a height/weight advantage can be of benefit (basketball, for example) and in other sports (gymnastics) it is a detriment. Cisgender girls experience these realities, too, and yet we do not label these biological differences as unfair. These physical *gifts* are not regulated but are instead celebrated by the team who feels fortunate to have a star athlete on their team.

A "yes" answer must address the age distinctions at play. All arguments against sports inclusion for trans athletes focus on the exceptional—and rare—adult trans women athletes at the college and professional levels. Collegiate and professional parameters for participation are understandably different simply because most of these athletes have experienced a greater number of years of pubertal development in addition to *greater time engaged in elite athletic competition*. That said, the high-profile example of collegiate swimmer Lia Thomas, a young trans woman attending the University of Pennsylvania, caused quite a stir when she competed in the NCAA Division I national championships. While her win in the 500-yard freestyle event made international headlines, no attention was given to the fact that she placed a more distant fifth in the women's 200-yard event the next day. First place winner, the Canadian Taylor Ruck, when asked about Lia Thomas said, "Competition is competition. I was excited to race against someone who goes so fast."[3]

The collegiate and professional sports governing bodies are tasked with setting their own eligibility requirements for involvement. These entities engage in ongoing review and incorporate any needed revisions to these requirements over time. The NCAA, for example, recently revised its trans athlete participation policies in a way that more broadly disperses the responsibility for determining regulations to the national governing bodies of each respective sport. This means the specifics may not be a one-size-fits-all approach. Rules regarding swimming may be quite different from endurance events, like long-distance running, or skills-based competitions, like Olympic sharp-shooting.

As mentioned in the previous chapter, the WIAA immediately understood that the International Olympic Committee (IOC) rules for adult elite athletes, regardless of sport, could not be applied to *children*. There are differences between a nine-year-old, a nineteen-year-old, or a twenty-nine-year-old athlete that must be considered.

The present-day argument has been focused almost exclusively on collegiate, Olympic, and professional athletes to then draw erroneous conclusions about K–12 sports. Just as WIAA realized many years ago, the participation parameters for adult athletes do not apply to these children. Recognizing this important fact allowed them to focus on the needs of children and now the WIAA has a long, successful track record of saying yes to all K–12 trans athletes. A track record that shows trans girls are not hurting their cisgender peers in any way, and a record that shows trans boys are not being hurt by their cisgender teammates either.

UNFAIR ADVANTAGE? AN EXPLORATION OF WHAT'S AT PLAY IF WE SAY "NO"?
If a person answers "no, they do not have an advantage," they could be perceived as trying to circumvent the fact that testosterone can supply an athletic edge.

Taking exogenous testosterone for performance enhancement is already banned in athletics for this very reason. If this biological reality is ignored or denied, the person arguing this position risks painting themselves into a corner. The only rebuttal left may be to declare that transphobia is at play: *You don't want trans students to participate because you hate trans people!*

Certainly, transphobia is the predominant driving force for the most vehement objectors. The harsh prejudice specifically targeting trans women (or nonbinary people assigned-male-at-birth) is undebatable. However, if transphobia was the only driving force, those raising objections would be equally up-in-arms about trans boys participating on boys' teams, regardless of whether they had any physical advantage or not.

What is more likely the primary source of resistance for the majority of people is that the question itself is designed to inflame emotions and shut down dialogue. The majority of people have not personally encountered trans children, have not considered how they might engage in athletics, and have no tangible understanding of the factual realities of successful trans youth participation.

No doubt there is a sizeable dose of transphobia saturated throughout some of the debates, especially within the political realm. But to assume that transphobia is the sole driving force behind any and all hesitation or critique will ensure that this important dialogue never gets off the ground in the first place. As emotions get heated and the arguments get louder, the ability to listen can become elusive. Efforts to deepen learning on either side of the debate may be perceived as treasonous because the yes or no framing has provided us with no other choice but to entrench.

UNFAIR ADVANTAGE? IT'S THE WRONG QUESTION

The question of whether trans female athletes have an unfair advantage only serves to divert us. The question itself is misleading because it presumes that a level of fairness exists in the first place. It also presumes that trans girls and young women, by sheer nature of being trans, are uniformly better than cisgender girls. This simply is not true. The framing of this question distracts us from important considerations. The better question to ask is how do we best include trans and nonbinary student-athletes in sports? Not whether or not we should.

In the world of youth sports, there is already acknowledgment and consideration of the vast range of athletic excellence that exists among athletes of all genders and abilities. We celebrate the athleticism of these exceptional female athletes and generally do not legislate against them. Exceptions occur when we consider how the intersections of race *and* exceptional athleticism result in rule changes, such as what occurred when African American gymnast Simone Biles was underscored by judges because the difficulty of *her* moves posed a potential risk to *other* gymnasts. Olympic runner Caster Semenya of South Africa also fell victim to rule changes that many believe were made to specifically exclude her from competition because of being born with an intersex condition. Semenya is a national hero in South Africa and many there feel that the targeting she experienced was a result of racism.[4] Of course, it is not just female athletes that come under fire when considering the intersections of superior athleticism and racial discrimination. Basketball legend Kareem Abdul-Jabbar's excellence instigated a rule change in the NCAA where the basketball dunk was banned for ten years in an effort to reign him in. These examples highlight the fact that the sporting world has always had exceptional athletes where those who are white and male are celebrated heroes while women of color experience challenges to their femininity and/or status as women. The attacks on these athletes are egregious, racist, and unnecessary.

Addressing Accommodations Without Resorting to Exclusion

Not all adjustments to accommodate exceptional athleticism are egregious, however. There can be creative solutions that strive to achieve two goals— participation by all and efforts toward competitive fairness. One extracurricular sports director shared the story of a nine-year-old volleyball player playing in the league. Already over six feet tall in the third grade, this cisgender girl was bumped up to the level normally reserved for high school students where her physical advantages were not as overpowering to the other players her age. The only additional consideration, successfully addressed by the coach, was ensuring that the older girls *remember* that she was only nine when conversing and socializing with her.

There is a plethora of creative examples—singular adjustments such as with this young volleyball player or broader adjustments where schools compete in separate divisions based on the number of students or team performance—of steps already taken to achieve greater equity in school sports.

It bears repeating. *Fair or not* is not the right question. It presumes that all trans female athletes are superior to all cisgender female athletes—this is simply not true. Interestingly, what is often not part of the debate—what is implied, but never stated—is a false belief that women are unequivocally inferior athletes. In the book *Playing with the Boys: Why Separate Is Not Equal in Sports*, authors Eileen McDonagh and Laura Pappano make a very compelling case that the presumption of female inferiority in athletics is not true. In example after example, the authors show how girls and women have prevailed against male athletes only to have the governing bodies for those sports change the rules to exclude them.[5] Even the differing regulations or parameters within female sports versus male sports (court size, game duration, eligibility, and other differences) ensure that statistical comparison is not possible.

Just as there are many women who would jump at the chance to compete against male athletes, there are a lot of cisgender female athletes that would love the chance to compete with, and prevail against, their trans competitors. They are already doing it. Even the Connecticut track athlete previously mentioned in this chapter, who stated in her lawsuit that it was impossible for her to win, proved herself wrong just a few short days later.

A COMMITMENT TO INCLUSION

The inclusion of trans athletes has not yet, nor will it, result in the doomsday predictions that are so feared today. School districts across the nation have and will continue to assess and, if necessary, adjust participation parameters over time. This will, as it already is today, be based on the examination of real-life athletic engagement over years and decades of trans student inclusion in sports. We can't assess the realities of trans student inclusion in the future if we don't let them play now, in the present.

Gender-diverse youth in athletics are little kids who just want to play, and they are also serious competitive athletes out for victories. They win some, they lose some. Along with their teammates, these young people take delight in the benefits that are gained from playing. And there are so many benefits—healthier stronger bodies, being a valued teammate, deeper relationships, self-confidence, personal achievement, improved mental health, and a better sense of self. The importance of these is all the more imperative for gender-diverse children who often face barriers to inclusion at every turn.

NOTES

1. "Family Educational Rights and Privacy Act (FERPA)," Guides (U.S. Department of Education [ED], August 25, 2021), https://www2.ed.gov/policy/gen/guid/fpco/ferpa/index.html.
2. "Gov. Cox: Why I'm Vetoing HB11," Governor Spencer J. Cox, https://governor.utah.gov/2022/03/24/gov-cox-why-im-vetoing-hb11/.
3. Dawn Ennis, "Lia Thomas Just Proved Transgender Athletes Don't Always Win," *Forbes* (March 18, 2022), https://www.forbes.com/sites/dawnstaceyennis/2022/03/18/lia-thomas-just-proved-transgender-athletes-dont-always-win/.

4. Cheryl Cooky and Shari L. Dworkin, "Policing the Boundaries of Sex: A Critical Examination of Gender Verification and the Caster Semenya Controversy," *Journal of Sex Research* 50, no. 2 (2013): 103–111, https://doi.org/10.1080/00224499.2012.725488.

5. Eileen L. McDonagh and Laura Pappano, *Playing with the Boys: Why Separate Is Not Equal in Sports* (Oxford; New York: Oxford University Press, 2008).

Epilogue

Looking Ahead

As often happens in science, when a theoretical paradigm comes under the pressure of contrary evidence, the paradigm totters for a period of time as researchers attempt to prop it up with various amendments and adjustments, and then, often quite suddenly and swiftly, it collapses as a new paradigm rises to take its place.

Michael Pollen

When I first started this book, it was with the full understanding that being inclusive of gender-diverse students in schools is a process of discovery for everyone. We are all on a journey of learning. What is important to my own learning is understanding that it is a journey, not an end destination. As cliché as that may sound, I know it is crucial. Even after twenty-five years as a gender educator, I am continually humbled by this. This is one of the reasons I felt it important to include the word *today* in the title of this book, *Trans Children in Today's Schools*. As a global society, we are at the beginning stages of that journey.

Secondly, I was also deliberate about including the word *children* in the title. As is discussed in this book, the ways in which we as adults experience and view gender-diverse people is different from the clarity and simplicity with which children do. I wanted to remind the reader of this over and over again. Students go through huge developmental changes as they move from pre-K to twelfth grade. Yet, whether students are aged seven or seventeen, they are still children. We need to remind ourselves of this as society takes on the adult responsibilities that come with upheaval during times of change.

In this book, I've included a number of photos of gender-diverse children, their siblings, and families, including a picture of myself and my sister at age eight. Just as Brenda always knew her gender identity, so did I. However, unlike her, I was not provided language or a pathway to articulate my gender. Society was less ready for me and my gender then than it is for the eight-year-olds of today. Yet, even in the 1960s and 1970s, my peers recognized my gender differences. They, too, were at a loss for ways to respectfully describe and engage with me and other gender-diverse children. I wrote this book for those children of the past, as well as those of the future.

Some wonder whether the visible presence of trans and other gender-diverse children is a temporary phenomenon. I'm hard-pressed to see their expression of gender expansiveness as a societal fad. Just as my peers and I were taught to view gender as rigid and binary, today's children are informed by an understanding of gender that allows for more breathing room. In my experience, today's children, if provided the opportunity, are untroubled by creating more room for their own identities and those of their peers. They view it as the respectful thing to do and, increasingly, have the language and context to do so. I view gender expansiveness as part of a generations-long path to greater gender equality. As we face our trepidation during these unprecedented times, our pathways forward become clearer.

Recently, I was invited to speak to coaches in a rural, politically conservative school district. I was a bit disappointed to see that it was scheduled late in the afternoon and in a high school auditorium. The coaches were tired and hungry. The spacious auditorium was cold, attendees were spread out sporadically in the seats, and I was placed at a podium on the stage. The tech manager, over the PA system, reminded the coaches multiple times that food and beverages were strictly prohibited. This was hardly conducive to the interactive discussions that are so necessary. Libraries, classrooms, and other smaller venues work much better. I did my best to engage them, but their energy for it was low. About halfway through, one coach finally raised her hand and said, "It seems as if you are dismissing all of our concerns."

Until that moment, no one had raised a single concern aloud. A little startled, I responded by welcoming her comment and thanking her for bringing it up. I said, "I don't know what your specific concerns are. I'm mentioning some of the concerns that others have brought up in the past and am sharing these with you. But I would really prefer to hear from you. What are your concerns?"

She explained she was concerned about the safety of the other students who may be in a locker room with a trans student. She also spoke of the discomfort they would experience and asked why they should be expected to experience that because of one or two trans students. As is often mentioned, she worried about perceived competitive advantages that trans athletes may have over others. These concerns were indeed what I had been addressing but until that moment, largely due to the venue set up, we had only had a one-way conversation—me providing them a lecture. Finally, over halfway through, we found our way to the interactive discussion that I believe is so necessary for progress.

The coach shared that she was Mormon and Republican and knew that even some of her colleagues might judge her for her reticence. From my perspective, her courage to raise her voice and speak frankly was admirable, and was what we all needed for genuine, true engagement. She said she did care about all her students, including those who are transgender, and understood some of the challenges they face. By speaking up, she provided me the path I needed to overcome the facilities barriers and it opened a door through which others then dove into the conversation. We could acknowledge the apprehension, and discuss potential situations where her concerns, however unlikely, might be founded, and what could then be done about it.

I shared with her that, in my experience of more than fifteen years of work with schools, the concerns that she and others have raised are not coming to fruition but, *should* they arise, we must discuss how they could be managed. I do not have a window into the future, I said, and my learning continues day-by-day. I was able to share the letter regarding trans student inclusion in sports written by the governor of Utah (mentioned in the previous chapter), who was, like her, Mormon and Republican. It is reasonable, I added, to consider worst-case scenarios, even if they are highly unlikely, and prepare for them, but do we unilaterally withhold support and inclusion for at-risk students at the same time? Could we make a commitment to move forward on good faith and assess as we proceed?

I was delighted to hear her embrace this approach and see that she felt heard and respected in the process. Our session was concluding, yet she and I remained for another hour-and-a-half sharing further thoughts. She had many questions about gender identity, gender expression, intersex differences (she had an extended family member that had an intersex difference), faith, acceptance, and love. At the end of our conversation, she said that she hadn't expected to experience such movement and understanding. She said she was so grateful for the time spent together. At this point, it was three-and-a-half hours after we had begun and we were all tired and hungry, yet she said, "Now, I need to go home and talk to my husband about this. He needs to understand this better as well."

I share this particular story now because people will often ask where "all of this" is going. My experience has been that the people I encounter, irrespective of political or faith views, if given the chance, show up as compassionate, loving people. This is the central factor to successful inclusion. Of course, that includes those considered conservative in their views. Their love for their students, and their desire to live in a more harmonious world, are strong motivators. Even educators who pride themselves on liberally progressive views struggle. One school was on the verge of *expelling* a trans child in kindergarten who was struggling to adjust after her recent social transition. The school staff didn't believe her behavioral issues were gender-related because, after all, the child's gender status was undisclosed to the other students. So, where was the problem? After multiple conversations, we gained greater insight, made adjustments, and a disastrous outcome was averted.

Whether an educational institution—or the communities in which it resides—is considered liberal or conservative, religious or not, it is comprised of individuals and families that most always come from a place of compassion and a desire to keep children feeling safe, supported, and happy. Whatever their background, they will experience some obstacles or challenges in their understanding simply because we are addressing new terrain. My hope for the future, indeed my prediction, is that society will progress in its understanding of how to be gender inclusive. Gender-diverse children inspire this progression and those that have a deep love for children will join them in paving the way.

> *When you are born into a world where you don't fit in, it's because you were born to help create a new one.*
>
> —*Anonymous*

Top Questions for Schools

Gender Diversity

Top Questions for Schools
The following questions serve as a starting point
for parent/administrator conversations.

A child's disclosure of their gender identity is often sudden and unexpected. Any parent or caregiver could potentially have a lot to contend with regarding their trans or nonbinary child, especially at first. It can be an emotionally difficult time for both the child and the parent. While a caregiver is navigating this crucial time, they must also consider the place where their child spends the most time outside of the home – their school. Children do not tend to consider any advance preparations that their school might need to do, nor should they. This is not their responsibility and they are often unaware of what could or should be done in order to optimize their school experience. A caregiver that takes time in advance to learn more about the school climate (for example, the presence of gender-inclusive policies and practices, any prior experience with gender-diverse students, staff completion of relevant professional development, etc.) will find themselves better prepared for these next steps with their child's school.

The list of questions below can serve as a starting point for a parent/administrator conversation. A parent may not know if their child will be well-received or whether their needs will be accommodated. If uncertain of the administrator's receptivity, some parents will choose to make an initial anonymous call to preserve their child's privacy. Or they may ask a friend or family member for assistance. If this is the first conversation of this nature for the school principal or superintendent, you can be sure they too will be searching for answers.

Whether by phone, video, or in-person it would be of benefit to parent and administrator to request adequate time and privacy to ensure that both parties are free from potential interruptions. Regardless of the principal's familiarity with the needs of gender-diverse students, a parent will certainly be able to gauge their receptivity to the topic.

Have you had transgender and/or nonbinary-identified students in your school?

If so, how did you address the needs of that particular student(s)? Did you work directly with the student's parent or caregiver? Do you have a process/plan to support the needs of that student? If so, would you describe that to me? Who is involved in that process?

If there were/are gender-diverse students, how did that go?

This is an open-ended question and deliberately vague. How an administrator answers this will provide a parent with a sense of the administrator's responsiveness, hesitancy, or dismissiveness. This open-ended question can be followed with an invitation to say more. (Keep in mind that an administrator is required to uphold the privacy rights of all students and therefore should not reveal any identifying information about trans, nonbinary, or any other students).

Please share some of the strategies you used or steps that you took. What did you learn from those experiences? What did the staff learn? Were teachers and students consistent with names and pronouns? How did taking these steps affect the school community?

Does our district have a gender-inclusive policy? If so, where can I find it?

Including gender identity and gender expression when articulating the diversity and inclusion values/commitments of any school is necessary to help foster a shift within the school culture. A gender-inclusive policy is a key to communicating this commitment to the entire school community. It is foundationally important to have these statements clear and easily accessible to students, staff and teachers, and the parent/caregiver community. Policy, guidelines, mission, and values are commonly found in student handbooks, school and district websites, and within parent communications/resources.

A gender-inclusive policy is a key to communicating this commitment to the school community.

2

If policy does exist, how is this communicated to parents/ teachers/students?

The school community cannot benefit from policy and guidelines if they can't find them. Are teachers aware of their responsibilities? How might gender-diverse students know where to turn?

Has there been training on this topic and if so, please tell me about that training?

If the response is, *Well, yes, we've had some guest speakers at the high school GSA (Gay/Straight Alliance)*, that's not enough. Educators at every grade level need professional development opportunities to further their understanding – especially to make the crucial delineation between gender identity and sexual orientation. If gender differences are continually framed in the context of sexuality, and therefore "too mature" to discuss or address with children, then the experiences of trans and nonbinary children will be ignored, dismissed, or ridiculed.

If the school has had training, was it offered to ALL staff— teachers, counselors, leadership, office staff, coaches, etc.?

Different employees have different needs and considerations. It is just as possible for janitors, cafeteria staff, bus drivers, and paraeducators to inadvertently or purposely disclose a trans child's status as it is for teachers or principals. Every school employee needs to understand the factors that impact a child's safety and right to privacy.

Educators at every grade level need professional development opportunities to further their understanding.

3

Have you offered learning opportunities for the parent community? If so, how did that go? If not, do you have that in the works? And...

How would you respond to inquiries from other parents about the presence of gender-diverse children?

The concerns of the school community parents usually land at number one on a "top five fears list" for most administrators. How a principal responds to this question will be indicative of how they might respond when, or if, a parent of another student makes a complaint. The parent community can tip the scales for a school's successful journey towards inclusion. Offering regular learning opportunities for parents is the best way to respect and include them in the school's journey. An administrator's response to these questions will give the parent insight into their level of confidence when engaging with the parent community.

Are you familiar with student support plans for trans students? Do any of the staff have experience developing one with a student?

The answer may be no. What a parent can assess with this question is whether their administrator has an interest in hearing more. Working with a student on a support plan is a thoughtful, comprehensive task. Knowing whether a principal is receptive or dismissive of student support plans could be an indicator of their willingness to appropriately intervene if or when any problems arise.

4

How do you ensure the privacy of a student that does not wish to have their gender history disclosed to students or faculty?

A counselor may feel that everyone should be "out and proud" or a principal may feel that it would be deceptive to others to not share that child's gender history but the bottom line is that students do have a right to request privacy regarding their gender history. It is their right to determine whether, when, and with whom to disclose this history. For example, a parent may wish for the school nurse to know their child's gender status in case of any medical emergency but that does not mean the school nurse has the right to share that information with others.

How do you manage the experience of a student for whom privacy regarding their gender history is NOT an option and/or is NOT desired?

Some children socially transition with peers who have known them for some time. This means that their gender history will be known. Other trans children may not feel a need to keep their gender history private for any number of reasons. There is no singular approach that will work for all students. The safety of visible trans and nonbinary students should be a primary concern and it is important that a school understands and can respond to each student's needs. Ask what safeguards are in place for these kinds of circumstances. How the matter of privacy/disclosure is managed by the school should be explicitly clear.

How do you address the questions or comments raised by other children? Do you feel that some or all of your staff are prepared to positively, confidently respond?

If the administrator replies in the affirmative, ask for an example. If you sense a hesitant response, this is a sign that further education may be needed. If you encounter a more dismissive response, it may represent future inaction, even opposition, if situations do arise. Worse still, and more common than you might imagine, is the assigning of blame to the gender diverse student for any adverse experiences they encounter. If only some of the teachers feel confident, this would be an important consideration for classroom placement.

Students have a right to request privacy regarding their gender history.

5

How do you respond to teachers and staff who are resistant or feel conflicted about supporting the needs of gender-diverse students? What are your expectation of these staffers? What is expected of me as a parent, if my child encounters this?

This is still a very real scenario for many school administrators. Some teachers may feel conflicted because of their personal beliefs. It is necessary to understand how a principal or superintendent will approach complex situations like these. A parent needs to know if their administrator feels confident and capable to outline to their staff the expectations of a professional workplace versus any one individual's personal convictions.

Are students able to use the restroom that best aligns with their gender identity? How will you ensure the safety and privacy needs of my student?

Too often, the solution proposed is that of an alternative bathroom such as a staff or nurse's facility. In some cases, such a restroom is a great distance away from classrooms, and/or using such a facility draws unwanted attention to the child who is using it. While such an option can be desired by some, most students will either opt for the girls' or boys' restroom. You'll want to know that the facility that works best for your child is available to them. Ask your school administrator how they are going to safely support your child as they begin using different facilities.

Caregivers need to know that the facilities that work best for their child will be made available to them.

6

How do you/would you respond to inquiries from parents or teachers who may express concern or distress about the presence of gender-diverse children in classrooms, bathrooms, and locker rooms?

At the least, you need to hear that the administrator feels confident to address any conflict. It's okay to ask for an example such as "What would you say to a parent or teacher who questions whether a child should be in that particular bathroom?"

When considering sports and other activities, what are your considerations for participation? Do you have an athletic policy in place for gender-diverse students?

Like restroom usage and access to other gender-segregated spaces, trans and nonbinary students should have the ability to participate in activities based on the best fit for them with respect to their gender identity. You can provide them with the Gender Diverse Youth Sport Inclusivity Toolkit: http://genderdiversity.org/best-practices-for-youth-sports/

My child starts school in a week. What are you able to do to ensure that my child is off to the most optimal start of the school year?

It does not always work out for a school to immediately prepare for the inclusion of a gender-diverse child. However, there are some short-term steps that a school can take to get off on the right foot for the school year. This can include direct support or training for a child's teacher(s) while planning for more comprehensive staff training at a later date.

7

My family is early on this journey. I may need to revise my child's support plan as time goes on. How do I do that?

Children of any age need room to explore and discover. Having a supportive environment at home and at school is needed for that exploration. This provides a child with more information than they would otherwise get if they felt pressured to "choose". The way they describe their gender identity – and actions they want to take as a result – may change. A child may shift from a nonbinary description of their identity to a trans identity, or vice versa. Certain pronouns may be requested early on and then changed as time progresses. It is important to provide flexibility as the child finds their path. This is crucial too when considering the possible, albeit less frequent, notion that a child will step away from diverse gender identification. While society fearfully anticipates the chance that a child might "change their mind", all the more reason to allow for exploration, discovery, and movement – even if that movement eventually is towards a cisgender identification. Modifications to a support plan need to address all possibilities and provide thoughtful support every step of the way.

It is important to provide a child flexibility as they find their path.

8

APPENDIX A

Of course, these are a lot of questions.

A caregiver may not be able to ask all of them. Be selective and prioritize the ones you consider most important to you and your child. Some questions may not be relevant to your circumstances. If you need to, schedule a second meeting to continue the discussion. The primary goal of this inquiry is to get a sense of your administrator's knowledge, experience, and receptivity. You will learn a lot! Take notes during and after the conversation. It is okay to ask the administrator to pause, or repeat something, as needed so you can properly document what was said. If follow up items are mentioned, document those too including what, with whom, and by when.

The Gender Diversity Support Plan and other resources will be an important part of everyone's journey. Every educator can benefit from having a copy of the book, Trans Children in Today's Schools (Oxford University Press, 2023). Be sure to mention or provide these resources to your school administrator to optimize the path forward.

Resources
Parent Support: TransFamilies.org
School Training: GenderDiversity.org
Book: Trans Children in Today's Schools
Best Practices for Supporting Gender Diverse Children: Family Acceptance Project
Sports: Gender Diverse Youth Sports Inclusivity Toolkit

9

APPENDIX B

Student Support Plan

Gender Diversity

SECTION ONE: Systemic Readiness

Considerations for both schools and for students are best addressed before you have a request for student support. Schools that postpone taking proactive measures often find themselves managing more anxiousness, confusion, and stress in the long run. Waiting for a gender-diverse student to request support before having a plan in place does a disservice to all. A prepared staff and leadership team is a relief for all students and families. In much the same way that advance preparation occurs for students with IEPs/504 plans, or students who are multilingual learners, we must also be proactive in our preparations for gender-diverse learners.

There are different facets to consider when addressing a gender-diverse student's needs. Some can be anticipated. Others you will discover as you encounter each student's unique circumstances. While a generalized approach to a student's needs can provide a foundation, it is important to understand that one approach does not fit all. Adjustments can and should be made along the way.

There are several focal points to consider: one is to address the specific needs of the student, the second is the degree to which the parent/caregiver of the student is involved, and lastly, the readiness of the school faculty, staff and administration to successfully include all gender diverse students within the school community. Working collaboratively with the student (and any student-designated adult(s)) to move through their established plan will ensure the highest likelihood of success for the student.

Unlike the student and/or parent—who are likely crafting a support plan for the first time—schools will have the benefit of advance preparation and experience to confidently support any gender-diverse child that comes to their attention. This support plan document will assist in that preparation and the achievement of optimal outcomes for all.

1

APPENDIX B

Gender-Inclusive Schools Policy and Procedures

Having a district policy for schools is an important component of the successful inclusion of trans and other gender diverse students. If a gender inclusion policy is not yet in place, work to create one. There are many time-tested and successfully implemented policies and procedures across the U.S. to emulate. Regardless of whether a gender-specific district policy currently exists, the foundational elements are already established within school districts across the U.S. Public schools have an obligation to address instances of bias and discrimination in any district educational program or activity offered, and are required to comply with federal laws concerning harassment, intimidation, bullying and other forms of discrimination based on sex.

Increased clarity for everyone is needed to achieve successful gender inclusion in school environments and to keep students safe and free from discrimination. Clear articulation of gender-inclusive policy, procedures, and related expectations are the key elements necessary to accomplish this.

Addressing the needs of gender-diverse students should include but is not limited to the following:

- Consistent use of names and pronouns
- Updates to student records, class rosters, diplomas, school pictures, computer logins, yearbooks, etc. to include student's name and gender
- Maintaining a student's right to privacy regarding confidential health and education information
- Restroom and locker room accessibility
- Equitable participation in sports, dress codes, and other gender-separated activities that are most closely aligned with the student's stated gender identity

"To me, gender inclusion means that everybody will be accepted and respected no matter how they identify. It means that all people will be treated as equal as any other person."

~Bobby

2

496

Advance Preparation: Checklist for School Administrators

o   Do you have a gender-inclusive policy and an outline of procedures which articulate the expectations and applicability of that policy?

o   Do you have an identified administrator(s) who will be available to support, educate or guide teachers, staff, or parents should questions arise regarding policy, procedures, and implementation?

Students

o   Are student rights with respect to name, gender marker, and others changes readily accessible to students in online and written formats?

o   Do students know where to gain further information about gender support plans? How is this communicated? (For ex. website, school counselors, student handbook, etc.)

o   Do faculty and staff know where to readily access this information and how to guide students to this information as well?

Faculty and Staff

o   Do faculty and staff know where to gain further information about gender support plans and how to implement them? How is this communicated to them? (Ex. Are P.E. teachers and coaches in possession of resources like the "Gender Diverse Youth Sport Inclusivity Toolkit" and/or other resources)?

o   Are they aware of their responsibility in ensuring student safety when developing any support plan and timeline?

o   Do faculty and staff understand their responsibilities regarding, and how to address, any instances of misgendering, disparaging comments, and misbehavior?

o   Have any professional development opportunities been provided for all staff on the topic of gender-diverse students? How do they gain any needed ongoing support?

o   Is there a dedicated person or team who can develop a school-wide assessment of all areas in need of updates (ex. procedures related to attendance records, standardized tests, athletics, student records, class rosters, ID cards, dress codes, facilities usage, overnight trips guidelines, etc.)? Gather input from administrative staff, the IT team, athletic directors/coaches, counselors, teachers, parents, and students. What are the subsequent recommendations and anticipated timelines needed for evaluation? Use that assessment to adjust any school-wide practices that are exclusionary for gender diverse students.

3

APPENDIX B

Facilities

o Do locker rooms and other facilities have designated private changing options available for those students desiring greater privacy for changing into or out of uniforms, P.E. clothes, costumes, etc.?

o How does the school regularly communicate (student/parent orientations, website, email, etc.) these facilities options to all students and their families?

o What practices are in place to ensure that students are able to utilize private changing areas in a timely and efficient manner?

Parent Community

o How will parents be made aware of gender-inclusive practices within the school (ex. school handbook, parent orientations, etc.)?

o Have you been able to provide educational opportunities for the school's parent community so that they may deepen their learning and have questions addressed?

o Do you have a dedicated person or persons identified to address any parent/caregiver questions or concerns?

"Our district is committed to a safe, caring, and mutually respectful environment within our schools so that all students, families and staff feel seen, included, valued and supported."

~ Michelle Reid, Ed.D., Superintendent
American Association of School Administrators
2021 National Superintendent of the Year

4

SECTION TWO: Getting Started

Student Considerations

o   What is the ideal timeline for the student's implementation of the support plan and what factors need consideration? If needed, negotiate a timeline with the student to provide the most optimal outcome for the student. Student's health, safety, and experience are paramount. (ex. would the student benefit by waiting for two weeks in order to better prepare staff, is the student in distress and needs immediate action, are there timing considerations due to holidays, home life, etc.).

o   Would disclosure to a parent or caregiver place a student in a place of emotional or physical danger? If so, how can the school ensure that there is no inadvertent disclosure?

o   Who is the person or persons tasked with drafting the support plan in collaboration with the student (ex. counselor, parent, principal, etc.)?

o   If parent/caregiver involvement is part of the support plan, does the caregiver understand that they have an open invitation to further discuss questions to allay any outstanding concerns to better optimize the outcomes for their child? Do they know who their school point of contact is regarding any questions/concerns or needs for further collaboration?

"Our child's school was ready to be supportive of her but lacked the necessary tools and guidance to do so. This student support plan was deeply instrumental in their ability to get on track with ease. Everyone is happy, most importantly, our daughter."

~Parent of trans child

5

APPENDIX B

*"When first considering how to support
a gender diverse student, it felt a bit
like feeling one's way in the dark.
With a student support plan, I much better
understood my role, the school's responsibility,
and the unique needs of each child."*

~Middle school counselor

Faculty and Staff Preparations

o   Do teachers and other staff feel adequately prepared for students' gender disclosure? If not, what are steps that can be taken to improve this?

o   Do teachers feel confident to address questions and inquiries from other students including the gender-diverse student?

o   Do teachers know how to respond and/or intervene appropriately if any inappropriate behavior occurs (ex. teasing, deliberate misgendering, etc.)?

o   Do teachers and staff understand their responsibility to correctly refer to, and engage with, a gender diverse student in a respectful, timely manner (ex. name, pronoun, etc.)?

o   Do they understand their responsibility to intervene and address instances of student misuse of name and/or pronouns?

o   Is there a debrief/check-in scheduled for teachers to share successes, strategies, and challenges with each other?

o   Do the faculty or staff understand that they may seek additional support if needed. (ex. a teacher who has a trans student in their classroom may initially need more support than one who doesn't).

o   Do they understand the need to respect the student's right to privacy, to the degree that is applicable, by not disclosing personal identifying information or other details that may jeopardize that right?

o   Do they also recognize that a student's right to privacy is federally protected and that others do not have a "right to know" a student's gender status if that student does not wish to have it disclosed?

o   Do faculty and staff understand that they do not have the right or obligation to disclose the student's gender identity to a parent or caregiver?

o   Do teachers/staff know their point of contact should they have additional questions or need to deepen their understanding with a more knowledgeable staff member?

6

SECTION THREE: Creating the Support Plan

Generating a Gender Diversity Support Plan is a process designed to be student-centric. The questions and considerations are reasonably comprehensive but may not cover every student's needs or circumstances. Nor is the plan a static one. A caregiver may not be involved at first but may be more ready to engage once they deepen their own understanding or find additional support. Initially, a child may not wish to disclose anything about their gender identity to anyone other than the educator helping to create the plan. Some children may need adult guidance on how or when information—like a name and pronoun change—is disclosed to peers or teachers. It is crucial to understand that a student will likely not be aware of all the areas in need of attention so the support plan process is meant to increase their understanding of their rights including how to access ongoing support. Lastly, a student should not be held responsible or expected to compromise their needs, because of unpreparedness on the part of the school.

1.   Assessment

Gathering Basic Information

o   Is the student requesting a new name?
o   Is the student requesting a new pronoun?
o   Is this a new, incoming student?
o   Grade level of the student?
o   Does the student understand that they can request a new student ID card, computer login, etc. to address any name/photo/pronoun changes?

2.   Discovery

Parent/Caregiver

o   Are the parent(s)/caregivers aware of the student's gender identity/expression requests?
o   If aware, are the parent(s)/caregivers supportive? Distressed? Oppositional? Ambivalent? Other? What additional supports can be provided to the caregiver?
o   Would disclosure to a parent or caregiver place a student in a place of emotional or physical danger? If so, how can the school ensure that there is no inadvertent disclosure?
o   What are the support steps being taken at home? Are there any areas of alignment from home to school that could help with the transition?

7

Parent/Caregiver continued

o   What resources can the school provide families? Are these resources readily available for families seeking additional help? (Ex. family support programs like www.transfamilies.org)

o   Foster care/ward of the state? (Ex. Is the caregiver supportive and will the caregiver be involved?)

o   Language barriers? (Ex. Will a translator be needed? Does the caregiver rely on the child for translation?)

o   Cultural considerations? (Ex. Are there culturally-specific wardrobe expectations?)

Family and Community

o   Siblings? If so, what support steps need to be in place for the sibling?

o   Divorced/separated/blended families? To what degree will additional caregivers be involved?

o   Is the family involved with any organizations or groups that could be beneficial for the school to know about? Does the caregiver expect additional support from these entities? (Ex. Church community, support group, child's playgroup, adoption group, etc.?)

Social Transition

o   Has the student already begun social transition? (names, pronouns, clothing, etc.)

o   Does the student have a preferred timeline for social transition steps?

o   Is the student's gender status known to fellow students?

o   Is the student's gender status known to teachers and staff?

o   To what degree does the student want their status known to peers? Teachers and others? This can vary from person to person, or situationally.

o   Is the student open & conversational about their gender history?

o   Is the student engaged in sports, P.E., or other gender-segregated activities?

o   What restroom and locker room is the student currently using?

Children have one shot at a schooling experience. I went into education to do my part in making that the best experience possible—for all my students! Setting up a plan for trans and nonbinary students is a powerful way to accomplish that.

~Principal

8

3. Plan Development

a. Informing Students of Their Rights

- o Is the student aware of their federally-protected right to privacy, including nondisclosure to a parent/caregiver if needed?
- o Does the student understand that they have a right to privacy with respect to any school-to-home communications, parent-teacher meetings, or other engagements with parent(s) or caregivers?
- o Is the student aware of their right to determine transition-related steps and subsequent timelines?
- o Does the student understand that they have the right to have access to the facility that best aligns with their gender identity?
- o Is the student aware of how, and with whom, to address when their rights have been dismissed, ignored, delayed, or overlooked, inadvertently or otherwise? Does the student know that they can discuss this with the designated support plan person (ex. sharing if a particular teacher were to deny their rights or take steps that were contrary to the support plan)?

b. Optimizing the Student's Pathway

- o Does the student understand that others do not have a "right to know" that student's gender status if that student does not wish to have it disclosed or discussed?
- o Has the student identified initial steps and associated timelines? How does the student describe their own level of readiness for each step?
- o Does the student understand that they can modify/adjust their transition plan as needed? Are they aware of the staff member(s) who will facilitate those changes?
- o Does the student know how to request any/all administrative updates?
- o Does the student understand that any gender-specific dress code requirements are based on gender identity, not anatomy?
- o If a student's gender identity is nonbinary (or another gender-expansive term), does the student understand that dress code parameters will apply to them based on requirements, not gender specificity? (ex. expected skirt length, shirt logo/image restrictions, etc.)
- o Does the student understand that they have the right to have access to the facility that best aligns with their gender identity?
- o Has the student identified a teacher or other adult point people to whom they can have immediate access for support or to address any unexpected situation that may arise?

9

Optimizing the Student's Pathway continued

o   Does the student want direct involvement with teachers regarding the communication of transition-related steps? With students? To what extent does the student wish to be involved? Does the student want any caregiver involvement in these communications?

o   Does the student have an existing level of peer/friend support?

o   Can these students be engaged as part of the support plan? In what ways?

o   Would the student like any additional support from peers, teachers, principal?

o   Is the transition timeline realistic and agreed upon by both student and all involved parties?

c.   Considerations for Support Plan

   I.   Facilities

   1.   What are the student's needs for optimal access to the bathroom?

   2.   Is the student aware that, if desired, an alternative restroom (ex. staff restroom) is available to them but not required?

   3.   What are the student's needs/requests for the locker room?

   4.   Does the student need any accommodation for facility usage (ex. alternate P.E. changing schedule and/or location, all-gender restroom access, etc.)?

   5.   Has the student expressed a preference for specific facilities (ex. restrooms, locker room, etc.)? Is their preference a temporary transition step (ex. using an all-gender restroom for an interim period)?

   II.   Activities/Classes

   o   What are the student's participation needs/requests for PE and athletics?

   o   What are students' needs with respect to gender-specific activities such as drama, dance, choir, and other activities?

   o   Are there alternative options available to satisfy P.E. requirements if the student desires a waiver?

   o   If an alternate path for a P.E. requirement is requested, is the student aware of self-driven or independent study options? (ex. athletic club membership, martial arts program, walking/running weekly benchmarks, extracurricular programs, etc.)

10

Activities/Classes continued

o   What are the student's needs regarding participation in the health/sex education curriculum that will optimize students' safety, privacy, comfort, and engagement?

o   What are the student's preferences when considering any school trips that include overnight accommodations (ex. pre-selection of friends/students to share room, private areas changing clothes, using facilities, etc.)?

o   Is the student interested in, or will the student benefit from working with a speech therapist?

d.   Adult Caregivers - Collaborative Involvement

1.   Does the student have any siblings attending the school? If so, what support steps need to be in place for the sibling?

2.   Does the student come from a divorced/separated/blended family and, if so, what relevant factors need to be addressed?

3.   Are there cultural considerations that need to be addressed? (Interpreter needed, wardrobe/uniform considerations, etc.).

4.   Are there aspects related to faith that need to be addressed? (ex. referral to a faith leader if caregiver is in need of support).

5.   Are the student's caregivers supportive of the plan and the student's transition? What are the support steps being taken at home? Are there any areas of alignment from home to school that could help with the transition?

6.   Is the family involved with any organizations or groups that could be beneficial for the school to know about?

7.   What resources can the school provide families? Are these resources readily available for families seeking additional help?

e.   Additional Considerations

·   Does the student understand that the implementation of a support plan does not mean that people will immediately "forget" a former name or pronoun, or that they won't temporarily misstep or have questions? (Ex: often a younger child who is socially transitioning and whose classmates are aware of the child's gender history).

11

APPENDIX B

additional considerations continued

- Students should understand that some discussion does need to occur when seeking name and pronoun changes. Students should have input on how, to what degree, and when this discussion occurs and whether they want to be present for it or not (ex. excused from class for that period or day).
- Discussion should occur if a student deems their parent to be "unsupportive" and to what degree. Some interventions could be helpful and additional resources provided to parents. (ex. potential for being kicked out of home versus a parent who occasionally slips with a name or pronoun).
- If a high degree of privacy is needed with the parent/caregiver, the student should be informed of how to best achieve this and understand that inadvertent disclosure could happen (ex. when a caregiver accesses the student management software system for grades). Student and counselor/staffer should collaboratively consider how this might change support plan decisions, timing, etc.
- Gender support plans, like other student support plans, should be updated periodically and with a timeline that is transparent (i.e. every six months, once a year, or as needed/requested). Plan factors and timelines can and should evolve to meet the needs of any particular gender-diverse student's needs and circumstances.

Supporting the journey of gender-diverse youth may feel daunting, which is understandable. The factors in need of consideration for a 10th-grade student, for example, will likely be different than those of a 2nd-grade child. The plan for a student with a gender supportive caregiver in their life may look quite different than for a student whose safety needs are much higher. As greater familiarity with plan considerations and successful implementation occurs, educators will gain greater confidence to manage the intricacies that each student may bring.

Resources

Parent Support: TransFamilies.org
School Training: Gender Diversity
Book: Trans Children in Today's Schools
Best Practices for Supporting Gender Diverse Children: Family Acceptance Project
Sports: Gender Diverse Youth Sports Inclusivity Toolkit

12

APPENDIX C

Family Acceptance Project Poster Guidance

FAMILY ACCEPTANCE PROJECT® POSTERS TO BUILD HEALTHY FUTURES
FOR LGBTQ & GENDER DIVERSE CHILDREN & YOUTH

https://familyproject.sfsu.edu/

The **Family Acceptance Project®** (FAP) has published new research-based posters to educate family members, providers, religious leaders, lesbian, gay, bisexual, transgender and queer-identified (LGBTQ) youth and others about the critical role of family support for LGBTQ children and youth to prevent suicide and other serious health outcomes and to build healthy futures. This overview provides information about the posters and gives suggestions for how to use them.

The posters are designed to be used in all settings:

• To educate the public, families, caregivers, providers, religious leaders and LGBTQ young people – about the critical link between specific family rejecting and accepting behaviors with risk and well-being for LGBTQ children and youth, especially suicide.

• To serve as an education and intervention resource to he lp families to decrease rejection to prevent risk and to increase acceptance and support to promote well-being for LGBTQ children & youth.

Research-Based Education Resource – The posters share information from FAP's peer-reviewed studies and family support work with ethnically, racially and religiously diverse families and their LGBTQ children. FAP's research has identifi ed *more than 100 specifi c accepting and rejecting behaviors* that parents, families and caregivers use to respond to LGBTQ and gender diverse youth. FAP researchers measured these behaviors to show how family rejecting behaviors contribute to serious health risks like suicidal behavior, depression, substance use, and sexually transmitted infections, including HIV. FAP's research also shows how family accepting behaviors help protect against risk and promote well-being. These new posters build on FAP's other evidence-based prevention and intervention resources including multilingual family education booklets and videos designated as Best Practice resources for suicide prevention for LGBTQ young people.

Different Versions – FAP has published 3 *versions* of the posters in 10 languages. These include: 1) a general family acceptance version; 2) a family rejection version; and 3) a family acceptance version for use in conservative settings that does not include family behaviors related to dating that might prevent the posters from being used in some settings.

A key finding from FAP's research is that a little change makes a difference. So, parents and caregivers that are struggling can start by decreasing some of the rejecting behaviors they use to try to change, deny or minimize their child's sexual orientation, gender identity and gender expression to reduce their child's risk for suicide and other serious health concerns and to increase their child's self-esteem and hope for the future. Parents that are struggling can start to adopt some of the family accepting behaviors that FAP has identified and measured to show their LGBTQ children that they love them, they want to support them and to help decrease their health risks.

Evaluation – FAP is evaluating how the posters are used and their impact on youth, families and others who use them. When someone downloads the posters, FAP asks for an email address to send them a short online survey with a request to participate in an optional phone interview to share feedback and stories about how the posters impact children, youth and families.

Where to Get the Posters – Anyone can download camera-ready versions of the posters from FAP's website with printing information to print the posters locally, including this guidance that describes the posters and gives suggestions for using them.

The Family Acceptance Project has developed a Poster Guidance that provides background information about FAP's posters, explains that they are evidence-based, and provides suggestions for using them at home and in schools, agencies, clinics, community settings, and congregations. As with the posters, each Poster Guidance is available in eleven languages and cultural versions, and the artwork is available for download from FAP's website next to each language's version (https://familyproject.sfsu.edu/posters).

APPENDIX C

Languages – The posters are available in English, Spanish, 8 Asian languages and a version for American Indian communities.

Poster Sizes – FAP's basic poster size is 24" x 36" to be easily seen in a waiting room, hallway, clinical exam room, library or training space. Other print sizes include: 18" x 24," 11" x 17," and 8.5" x 11" to use as a handout, for families to hang on a refrigerator, for home use and at activities and events.

Using the Posters – The posters are meant to be used everywhere. This includes: Clinics; schools; family service agencies; primary care & behavioral health services; prevention programs; child abuse programs; suicide prevention services; early childhood programs; child welfare, juvenile justice, homeless, residential and other out-of-home programs; college counseling centers; community centers; recreation centers; libraries and congregations.

- **Schools** – school provider services (counselors, parent advocates, psychologists, nurses, social workers); school health clinics; back to school nights and health fairs on a parent table with LGBTQ resources; for use in hallways; locker rooms; to share in diversity clubs and GSAs

- **Clinical Services** – exam and treatment rooms; waiting rooms; for use in assessment, counseling and psychoeducation with LGBTQ young people and families; home visits; family therapy; to teach children and youth about what acceptance and rejection look and feel like; for use in assessment to identify family reactions and the impact these behaviors have on LGBTQ and gender diverse children and youth; in school-based services and college counseling centers

- **Personal & Home Use** – give them to youth and families to use at home; hang in family spaces to review and routinely assess family growth and change and talk about how these behaviors affect communication, connectedness and relationships; give to extended family members and cultural leaders

- **Congregations & Faith-Based Groups** – use in educational spaces and events; share with religious leaders, pastoral care providers and congregation members

- **Community Events** – use as handouts at events and conferences and share in public spaces

- **Training** – use in trainings for agency staff, families, caregivers and providers in all settings, including professional training and student trainees, in continuing education and with parent and youth advocates

Information & Follow Up – If you have received the poster from someone else, and want to participate in our evaluation to help us learn how the posters are used and the impact they have with LGBTQ and gender diverse children, youth and families – or for more information – please contact us at: fap@sfsu.edu

FAMILY ACCEPTANCE PROJECT®

The **Family Acceptance Project**® is a research, education, intervention and policy project at San Francisco State University that helps diverse families learn to support their LGBTQ and gender diverse children in the context of their families, cultures and faith communities. FAP was launched nearly 20 years ago to conduct the first comprehensive research on LGBTQ youth and families and to develop the first evidence-based family support model to be integrated into systems of care and across practice domains. This includes behavioral health, primary care, school-based services, out-of-home and residential care, youth and family services and pastoral care to reduce risk and to support positive development for LGBTQ children and youth.

FAP's family support model is being integrated into behavioral health, family preservation and foster care, faith-based mental health and other services. FAP's intervention framework is also being applied in Trauma-Focused Cognitive Behavioral Therapy (TF-CBT).

FAP provides training on family-based care for LGBTQ children, youth and young adults and helps agencies to integrate FAP's intervention framework into their programs.

Caitlin Ryan, PhD, ACSW
Director, Family Acceptance Project®
fap@sfsu.edu

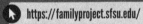 https://familyproject.sfsu.edu/

INDEX

For the benefit of digital users, indexed terms that span two pages (e.g., 52–53) may, on occasion, appear on only one of those pages.

Notes and boxes are indicated by "n" and "b" following the page number.

INDEX

documentation
of engagement with schools, 374
gender transitions and, 128
of misinformation, 361
documents
educational records (see Family
Education Rights and Privacy Act)
legal records and ID documents, 162–63, 323–
24, 444, 462
drama teachers, 314, 316–17, 430
drug use by transgender children, 99–100
DSD (Differences of Sex Development), 51. See also
intersex differences

Education Amendments (1972). See
Title IX of Education Amendments
educational records. See
Family Education Rights and
Privacy Act
Ehrensaft, Diane, 46
emotional turmoil of parents and caregivers, 79–81,
84–92
empathy. See compassion and empathy
empowerment
of teachers, 267–69
of transgender children, 121, 154, 349
Equal Access Act (1984), 371
equity, 259, 289, 317–18, 457
Erickson-Schroth, Laura, 10, 18, 265–66
estrogen therapy. See hormone interventions

faculty lounges, 306–7
faith. See religious beliefs
Family Acceptance Project (FAP)
Family Acceptance Poster for Conservative
Settings, 201
Family Rejection Poster, 199
General Family Acceptance Poster, 97
General Family Acceptance Poster for American
Indians, 180
parents, resources for, 98–108
poster guidance, 507
on pronouns, 312
research studies by, 35–36
ridicule/name calling poster, 202
silence and secrecy poster, 213
taking your child to LGBTQ+ events
poster, 376
welcoming your child's LGBTQ+ friends
poster, 353
family composition, classroom conversations
on, 252–58
Family Education Rights and Privacy Act
(FERPA, 1974), 328–33, 371, 462

family members and friends. See also parents and
caregivers
advocacy and, 359–76 (see also parental advocacy)
conflict, outcome for transgender children
and, 197–98
grandparents, responses of, 76–77, 95
loss of, 83–84, 128–29
questions of, 109–39 (see also parents,
questions of)
responses from, 107–8
strained relationships with, 106–7, 197
support from, 128–29
family time, 106–7
fear
bathroom use and, 396–97, 398–400
of bullying, 20–21, 196–97
cognitive dissonance and, 78–79
cultural dissonance and, 77
emotional turmoil of parents and caregivers, 79–
81, 86, 90–92
gender conformity encouraged, 16–17, 20–21
gender expectations based on, 196–97
gender transitions and, 118–19, 164
overnight trips and, 432–33
political and religious beliefs, 372–73
resistance to transgender individuals and, 31, 43,
101, 123–24
social justice movements and, 259
field trips, 416, 432–33
First Amendment rights, 371
first impressions, 31–32
504 plans, 325–27, 326b, 424–25
foster care, 137
Free to Be, You and Me (album), 231
Freire, Paulo, 295
frequency illusion, 8–9
friends. See family members and friends

Gay, Lesbian & Straight Education Network
(GLSEN), 332b, 369
Gay–Straight Alliance (GSA), 347–49
gender, defined, 50
gender, proving, 189–90, 204–5, 444–45, 462
gender, teaching
AEIOU framework for, 49–73 (see also AEIOU
framework for teaching gender)
to children, 221–61 (see also children, talking
about gender to)
to parents, 263–93 (see also parents, talking about
gender to)
Gender and Sexualities Alliance (GSA), 347–49
gender binary
bathroom use and, 378
cultural norms and, 143

512

imposing on children, 225
intersex differences and, 39
nature-based gender theory and, 38–39
nonbinary identity and (*see* nonbinary identity)
rigidity of, 73
societal insistence on, 30, 203–4
sports and, 437–40
gender cognition, 19, 78, 115–16, 124
gender conformity. *See also* gender norms
abuse resulting from lack of, 14
binary gender framework and, 30
emulating gender and, 190–92
to gain acceptance, 41, 57, 188
gender corrective therapy for, 17, 19, 36, 42–43
religious beliefs and, 203–4
self-expression vs., 16–17
young children and, 147
gender confusion, 18, 114, 116–18, 189, 231
gender corrective therapy, 17, 19, 36, 42–43
Gender Diverse Youth Sport Inclusivity Toolkit (Key),
325, 366–67, 368, 451–52, 456, 460–68
gender diversity
binary view of gender vs., 73
children, talking about gender to, 242–43
language to describe, 32–33
in natural world, 30
Gender Diversity: Student Support Plan, 320–34,
340–41, 364, 367–68, 458–59, 495
gender diversity training, 127, 135
gender dysphoria, 173, 178–84, 194–95, 305–6,
325–26b
gender exploration
children changing their minds, 118–19, 145, 367
nonbinary identity and, 89–90
as phase of development, 111–15, 129–30
support causing transgender identity, 122–25,
146, 205
gender expression
in AEIOU framework for teaching gender, 54–
61, 66
bullying and, 69, 70
changes in, 58, 191–92, 272–73
children, talking about gender to, 57–59,
226, 227–29
cultural norms and, 223
efforts to change, 20–21
gender identity and, 40, 41–42, 83, 179
gender norms and, 55–57, 231
gender transitions and, 159–62
language and terminology for, 304–5
nonbinary identity and, 161
observations of, 54–55
phases of, 111–13
sexual orientation and, 40, 41–42, 68–70

gender history. *See also* disclosure of gender identity
attendance taking and, 313
gender transition requirements and, 15
parental advocacy and, 364–65
sports participation and, 444
student information systems and, 323–24b
unintentional disclosure of, 322
gender identity
in AEIOU framework for teaching gender, 61–
63, 66–67
assessment of, 39–42, 115–16, 122–24, 179–80,
443, 445
awareness of, 18–19, 115–16, 131
bathroom and locker room use and, 379
biological influences on, 18, 38–39, 43–44,
53, 124
children, talking about gender to, 62–63,
226, 230–38
defined, 61
disclosure of (*see* disclosure of gender identity)
discrimination protections (*see*
Title IX of Education Amendments)
efforts to change, 20–21 (*see also* gender
corrective therapy)
gender expression and, 40, 41–42, 83, 179
historical diversity of, 62–63
inquiring about, 61
language and terminology for, 304–5
nature vs. nurture and, 38–39
overview, 18–20, 61–63
parenting styles and, 38
parents' questions on, 115–16, 122–24
as phase of development, 111–15, 129–30
proving, 189–90, 204–5, 444–45, 462
puberty and, 170
scientific study of, 273, 284
sexual orientation and, 64–65, 110–11, 278
teaching concept of, 62–63
Title IX protection for, 327–28, 439–40, 467–68
gender malleability, 16, 38–39, 40–41, 99, 188.
See also gender corrective therapy
gender norms. *See also* gender conformity
career guidance and, 284–85, 315
changes in, 41, 195, 227, 430
childhood interests outside of, 111–12
children learning about, 55–57, 223, 342
double standard of, 159
drama and music teachers and, 314, 430
gender assessment based on, 39–42, 179–80
gender confusion and, 118
gender expectations and, 196–201
gender expression and, 55–57, 231
gender presentation and, 159–61
gender rights and, 116–17

teachers supporting other teachers and, 307–9
unfamiliar terrain of gender inclusion and, 297–98
school environments supporting parents and
students, 337–57
classroom climates and, 341–43
Gender Diversity: Student Support Plan, 340–41,
364, 367–68
parent communications and, 350–51
parent learning events and, 350–57
questions for parent and administrator
conversations, 485–93
student engagement and, 343–50
student support plans, 320–34, 340–41, 364, 367,
421, 458–59, 495
support for full student body, 341–50
support for gender-diverse students and, 339–41
support for parents and caregivers, 350–57
school psychologists, 313–14
school websites and student handbooks, 321, 354,
361, 460
Schools in Transition (SIT) guide, 321–24, 325–
27, 368
Schulz, Charles, 301
scientific study of gender identity, 273, 284
security staff, 316
self-advocacy, 361
sensory issues, 426
sex education curriculum, 63–64, 250–51, 417–24
Sex Is a Funny Word (Silverberg), 423
sexual assault, 14, 384, 401–2
sexual orientation. See also LGBTQ+ people
adolescents and, 72
in AEIOU framework for teaching gender, 63–
65, 67
bathroom use and, 386
bullying and, 40
classroom discussions on, 63–64, 250–51
coming out and, 251–52
defined, 63–64
family composition and, 252–58
gender expression and, 40, 41–42, 68–70
gender identity vs., 64–65, 110–11, 278
gender transition requirements and, 14–15
LGBTQ acronym and, 64–65, 71–73
teachers' assumptions of, 68–70
shame
family turmoil and, 197
intersex differences and, 53
of parents, 85–86
rejection and, 31
shop classes, 430–31
siblings
of parents, responses of, 107–8
responses to transgender children, 105

Silverberg, Cory, 422–24
SIT (Schools in Transition) guide, 321–24, 325–
27, 368
social media
access to information on transgender people
from, 149
peer influence and, 120, 121
support groups through, 125
visibility of transgender people and, 12
social transitions
bathroom use, children's questions on, 380–81
name changes and, 22, 153–55, 158, 204, 215
overview, 150–55
pronoun changes (see pronouns)
reversibility of, 145, 150
special education
IEPs, 325–27
teachers, 313
speech language pathologists, 315–16, 424–26
sports
accommodations vs. exclusion, 474–75
best practices for, 460–68
birth certificates and, 444
body mass index measurements and, 445–46
coaches and athletic directors, 314, 481–82
eligibility review process of, 449, 470
equity and, 447
foundation for gender inclusion, 457–60
gender certifying letters and, 444–45
Gender Diverse Youth Sport Inclusivity Toolkit,
325, 451–52
gender inclusion, 455–76
implicit bias and, 446–47
International Olympic Committee and, 164, 440–41
National Collegiate Athletic Association and, 472
ongoing learning and evaluation, 468–75
parental advocacy and, 366–67
participation policies, 435–52
practical applications for participation policies,
446–47, 451
revisions to participation policies, 448–50
Title IX and, 437–40
unfair physical advantages and, 466–67, 468–74
Washington Interscholastic Activities Association
and, 442
wrestling and weight loss parameters, 428–29
spousal relationship strain, 85, 94, 103–5, 126.
See also divorced parents
stereotypes and myths. See also misinformation
gender norms and, 57, 342
impact of, 35–36
informing understanding of transgender
people, 82–83
in popular culture, 33–35